GYÖRGY LIGETI

György Ligeti
Music of the Imagination

RICHARD STEINITZ

faber and faber

First published in 2003
by Faber and Faber Limited
3 Queen Square London WC1N 3AU

Typeset by Faber and Faber Ltd
Printed in England by Clays Ltd, St Ives plc

Caricatures © by John Minnion, pp. 1, 215, 364

PLATE SECTION CREDITS
1, 2, 3, 5: György Ligeti Collection, Paul Sacher Foundation, Basle;
4: Internationales Musikinstitut, Darmstadt; 6: F. A. Z. – Magazin/Jürgen Röhrscheid;
8: Royal Opera, Stockholm; 10: Schott-Archiv/Peter Andersen;
11, 13, 14, 15: Huddersfield Contemporary Music Festival/Selwyn Green;
12: Ines Gellrich; 16: Marie-Noelle Robert; 17: Inamori Foundation, Japan

MUSIC EXAMPLE CREDITS
11, 12: Edition Peters Nos 5983 and 5935 © 1967 by Henry Litolff's Verlag,
Frankfurt, reproduced by kind permission of Peters Edition Limited, London;
4, 16, 23, 25, 31, 32: reproduced by kind permission
of Schott Musik International, Mainz

A CIP record for this book
is available from the British Library

ISBN 0-571-17631-3

For Emily, Adam and Ben

And as imagination bodies forth
The forms of things unknown, the poet's pen
Turns them to shapes, and gives to airy nothing
A local habitation and a name.

Shakespeare, *A Midsummer Night's Dream*, Act 5 Scene 1

Contents

List of Illustrations

Acknowledgements

It is eight years since I had the idea of writing a book about György Ligeti. For most of this time it has had to compete with the demands of directing a large-scale international new music festival and my responsibilities as Professor of Music in the University of Huddersfield. The book would scarcely have advanced at all, had the University not granted me two six-month sabbaticals. In addition to the support of colleagues, I am especially grateful to two former students of the Music Department: Maria Fisher created all the computer-set music examples, and Philip Clarke read the whole of my final text, making many perceptive comments and suggestions.

This book is fifty per cent bigger than the one Faber and Faber commissioned in 1996. During the intervening years much has changed, not least the economics of publishing. The Music Editor to whom I proposed the idea was soon succeeded by Belinda Matthews, whose enthusiasm and patience has been a constant support. Only temporarily disconcerted when, after spending three days with Ligeti, I told her that I would rewrite the eleven chapters she had just approved, her unflinching encouragement as the book expanded beyond its brief I have much appreciated. In the final production stages, Kate Ward as desk editor has been a tower of strength. Grateful thanks also to my copyeditor Michael Downes, to Ilsa Yardley who read the proofs, Ron Costley who advised over layout and photographs, and Diana LeCore who compiled the index.

I first met Ligeti at Glasgow's 'Musica Nova' in 1973, and came to know him better when he was our guest at Huddersfield Contemporary Music Festival twenty years later and we engaged in two public discussions. Nevertheless, in 1994 as I was contemplating writing this book, I was surprised when Ligeti said that he would like me to undertake it. The extent of his involvement I describe in the introduction. Here I want to thank him for giving so much time to our conversations and to checking the accuracy of my text. To Dr Louise Duchesneau,

xiii

Ligeti's personal assistant, I am greatly indebted for facilitating our contacts and for much assistance in between, and also to the composer's wife, Dr Vera Ligeti, for her comments and encouragement.

Not until the autumn of 2001 did I visit the Paul Sacher Foundation in Basle where most of Ligeti's manuscripts are housed. The Swedish musicologist, Ove Nordwall's collection was transferred to Basle in the late 1980s, but Ligeti's own much larger stock arrived only at the end of 2000. I am fortunate to have been able to consult this important archive in the Foundation's congenial building overlooking the Rhine, where its staff, notably Robert Piencikowski, Johanna Blask and Evelyne Diendorf, were unfailingly helpful. Photographs and manuscripts from the archive are reproduced by permission of the Paul Sacher Foundation. This is also the place to express my debt to Friedemann Sallis's pioneering work on Ligeti's early sketch books and the music he composed in Hungary, and to the authors of other previous books and articles on the composer, including Robert Richart's bio-bibliography published in 1990. Assistance with the translation of texts was generously provided by Rachel Beckles Willson, Bela Simon and Alison Slade.

David Whelton, Managing Director of the Philharmonia Orchestra, kindly sent me the schedules for the orchestra's extended Ligeti concert and recording project. He was shrewdly objective about what had gone wrong, as was Esa-Pekka Salonen in a long conversation. The most relevant week of this schedule I have described in detail. That British orchestras endure tough working conditions is well known; nevertheless, it may surprise some readers to discover how gruelling they can be. In recounting this unhappy saga – at little of which I was present – I have tried to be even-handed and accurate, but the judgments are my own.

Warm thanks also to the staff of Ligeti's principal publishers Schott Musik International, especially to Sally Groves in London and Rainer Schochow in Mainz for the provision of materials and access to their records. The archive so efficiently maintained in Mainz was a valuable resource. Finally my thanks to John Minnion. Having encountered his caricature of Ligeti printed in the The Times in 1996, I was pleased to receive another which he had given privately to the composer, and delighted when he agreed we should reproduce them, and that he would make a third specifically to illustrate this book.

Introduction

Everyone rewrites their history. We want to rationalise our actions, to recall pleasure and success, and to exorcise pain. Memory is interpretative. Nevertheless, when writing about a living person, the recollections of its subject are a primary source. In this account of György Ligeti, I have drawn extensively on the many published and recorded interviews with him, on documentary information, and on our private conversations recorded both in London and during three days in Hamburg.

Despite Ligeti's earlier encouragement, it was it was with some trepidation that I sent him a draft of my first eleven chapters in January 2000. A fortnight later he telephoned and told me they were full of errors. I feared the worst. But, in explaining that I had failed to understand the complexities of growing up in a multi-ethnic and politically turbulent society, he also warmly endorsed the musical and aesthetic exposition which forms the bulk of the book. Reassured, I felt honoured to be invited to Hamburg to go deeper into the background. Ligeti was keen to correct inaccuracies and misconceptions already in print, especially about his early life. Some events he amplified at length, some he related for the first time. Elsewhere, he unstitched stories which others had embroidered. Our discussions of technical and stylistic matters, and about the wide range of extra-musical ideas that have stimulated composition, were fascinating. My musical analyses he approved without any substantial disagreement, and with helpful suggestions regarding terminology. Returning with thirteen cassette tapes of our conversations, I resumed my task. Later Ligeti read again a large proportion of the revised text, particularly on personal and historical matters, and sent me his unpublished autobiographical essay written to deliver in Japan on the occasion of receiving the Kyoto Prize in November 2001.

Is this a biography? It was not intended to be, but it has become one. My original intention was, and remains, to write a stylistic and analytical study of a wonderful body of music. But I wanted to explore its context: the political and artistic background, the climate of ideas, the relation to other disciplines, the childish fantasies that burgeoned into an overflowing imaginative vision, the questing technical renewal and self-imposed rigour that have made Ligeti take up to eight years to complete a new work. Gradually I realised that his personal life was in itself an extraordinary story, and that his bizarre experiences in Romania and Hungary had deeply affected his personality and attitudes.

After Ligeti fled to the West at the age of thirty-three, following the Hungarian Revolution of 1956, he was so excited by his belated encounter with the European avant-garde that he scornfully brushed the past aside. Recently, though, he has wanted the Kafkaesque ambiguities of growing up in a mixture of Hungarian, Romanian and German societies – and under two brutally repressive regimes, Nazi and Communist – to be better understood. The fact that he originally intended to be a natural scientist, but was denied the possibility because he was a Jew, has fed his curiosity as a composer and helps to explain why every work is a fresh area of enquiry demanding new solutions.

Ligeti's career in the West was equally formative. His contact with Darmstadt and Cologne, his work alongside Stockhausen and Koenig in the first electronic music studio, the liberating impact of visiting America, his debt to the visual arts and literature, his dialogue with scientists and mathematicians, his role as a teacher, the 'pirating' of his music by Stanley Kubrick, the cavalier treatment of his opera by a succession of stage directors, the aborted Sony recording project, the uncompromising standards that can result in frosty relations with conductors and performers – but also their highest admiration – all these are part of the picture. I have touched on Ligeti's personal life in so far as it throws light on the composer: his relationship with his mother, his continued distress concerning the murder of his father and brother, the circumstances of his three marriages to only two people, his generous advocacy of little known composers, personal warmth and professional scepticism. Out of this, I hope, emerges something of a rich and charismatic personality and a vivacious and penetrating mind.

Ligeti is a dreamer who is a meticulous technician, a creator of mechanisms who believes in intuition, an insatiable explorer who is mercilessly self-critical, a hater of ideologies, a profound intellectual who is sensitive, witty, self-deprecating and devoid of pomposity. He is also, in the minds of some, a modernist guilty of defection. I realise that my counterpoint of contextual, analytical and biographical themes attempts a precarious balance, but hope that readers will find that each strand interestingly illuminates the others.

I have tried to make the musical discussions as clear and literate as possible. Many of the music's stylistic and structural characteristics are not unique to Ligeti, nor peculiar to music. So, following his example, I use analogy and metaphor. Key technical terms are defined in a glossary at the back of the book. Where detailed reference is made to pitch, rhythm, harmony etc., I try to ensure that these do not impede readers unfamiliar with musical notation. The musical analyses are most substantial in Chapter Thirteen, where they deal individually with all of Ligeti's (so far) eighteen piano études. But they are as much commentary as analyses, since these intriguing pieces involve ideas as colourful and varied as chaos theory, Baroque laments, African polyphony, pianolas, spindles, spirals, an abstract sculpture and an El Niño storm. Seminal ideas are introduced in advance, and those who find the quantity of piano studies daunting can move on, knowing they can return.

In 1996 Sony Classics launched its 'Ligeti Edition', for which it planned to record the composer's entire catalogue. Two years later the project came to grief with only eight CDs complete, and without any of the large-scale works being issued except the opera, leaving many of the participants acutely frustrated – including Ligeti, although it was he who vetoed its continuation. The explanation of why this ambitious plan imploded is a personal analysis, but I believe objective. There seemed no hope of any revival until, in 2001, the remaining and most demanding recordings were bravely undertaken by Teldec. Publication of this book coincides with the completion of Teldec's Newline 'Ligeti Project'. Triumphantly achieved, at the age of eighty Ligeti becomes the only major living composer whose entire output (including early work) has been recorded under his supervision for a definitive CD edition. It is evidence of Ligeti's exceptional stature, and of the widespread interest his music evokes.

Richard Steinitz
January 2003

Note on pitch designations

On the few occasions where I refer to pitch in a specific octave, C^4–B^4 denotes the octave from middle C to B above, C^3–B^3 the octave below that, C^5–B^5 the octave above the middle octave, and so on.

PART ONE

From East to West

I

The Making of the Man

Anything that happens in the world affects me – politics, literature, people. I reflect on these things in my own way, and these
reflections seek an outlet in music. This is also the reason why
so many of my compositions are hard to understand.
  Robert Schumann[1]

There is no doubt that the stance of the artist, his whole
approach to his art, his means of expression, are all greatly
influenced by experiences he has accumulated in the course of
day-to-day living.
  György Ligeti[2]

A Hungarian in Romania

György Sándor Ligeti was born on 28 May 1923. His parents were
cultured Hungarian Jews from Budapest, then living in the small
country town of Dicsőszentmárton, one of many Hungarian enclaves
remaining in what had recently become Romanian Transylvania.
Like other Hungarian Jews, their ancestors had spoken German in the
previous century and had German surnames, the name of 'Ligeti'
being an approximate Hungarian equivalent of 'Auer' (meaning from
the pasture or meadow), adopted to suit the changing times.[3] The family had already shown itself to be artistic. Ligeti's paternal grandfather
Soma Auer was a decorative painter of public murals, some of them in
Christian churches, despite his being a Jew, and others in railway stations – although most of these were destroyed in the bombing of the
Second World War. Tragically, whilst working on one of his murals,
Soma Auer had fallen to his death. One of Ligeti's great-uncles was a
well-known musician, the eminent violinist Leopold Auer,[4] a pupil of
Joachim, who left Hungary to spend most of his life as court musician
to the Tsar in St Petersburg, and for whom many Russians, including
Tchaikovsky, composed works. In 1910, the nine-year-old Jascha

Heifetz became the youngest member of his class at the Imperial Conservatory. When the 1917 Revolution occurred, Leopold Auer left Russia to settle in New York where he continued as a highly esteemed teacher. He returned to Europe and died in Dresden in 1930, but between Leopold and Ligeti's branch of the family there had been no contact. Although their lives overlapped by seven years, the international violinist and the great-nephew who would become a world-famous composer never met.

Ligeti's father Alexander (Sándor) had a scientific bent. He was born in 1890 in Kaposvár in south-west Hungary, near to Lake Balaton where the family had its roots. Ligeti remembers him as highly intelligent and cultivated, with a wide knowledge of the natural and human sciences. Although extremely hard-working, he was 'unpragmatic, without talent for money, a typically chaotic, smoking intellectual'. Sándor's thwarted ambition had been to study chemistry and medicine, but he was also interested in literature and music and had learnt the violin in his youth, although he soon abandoned it. Indeed, he was determined that his son – Gyuri, as he was called at home – should not waste time learning an instrument, wanting him to pursue the scientific career that he had been denied. Even at a young age, this was what Gyuri wished as well.

The sudden death of grandfather Auer deprived the family of income, and it was essential for Sándor and his brothers to earn money as best they could. Since Sándor was gifted at mathematics, after leaving high school he was enrolled as a clerk with the Anglo-Hungarian Bank in Budapest. Fortunately the bank recognised his intellectual ability and paid for him to attend the University of Budapest – not however to study science, but economics followed by law. In both subjects he gained doctorates, later writing several books on economics and ethics, as well as a utopian novel. He fought in the First World War, was decorated and promoted to lieutenant, but was also seriously wounded. Whilst in hospital he met his future wife, Ilona Somogyi (b.1893), a qualified doctor and ophthalmologist. Ligeti's mother was a women of considerable beauty, but to her children she seemed distant and reserved. 'She was extremely correct. She could be very nice in a formal way, but she had no warm heart,' Ligeti says. She did not believe in touching, let alone cuddling her children, nor did she want to breastfeed his younger brother Gábor. An avoidance of physical contact between parents and children was characteristic of the times.

But the lack of demonstrative motherly love probably contributed to Ligeti's own reticence concerning personal relationships, to his admitted inability to 'establish a continuous family'. Meanwhile, it was to an aunt and the family cook that he looked for affection.

After their marriage, Sándor returned to banking and the couple settled in Dicsőszentmárton, where Sándor had been appointed manager of the local branch. But the political upheavals following the defeat of the Austro-Hungarian empire in the First World War were to destroy his career. The victors wished to reward the countries on Hungary's borders for supporting the Franco-British alliance. President Wilson argued that Transylvania, a region larger than Switzerland and similarly having three communities and languages (Hungarian, Romanian and German), should become a separate state. But Clemenceau, the French prime minister, insisted that Romania should be well rewarded for changing sides. By the Treaty of Trianon in 1920, Hungary was required to pay reparations, and to cede the whole of Transylvania to Romania and large tracts of land to Slovakia and Yugoslavia.[5]

The settlement, which cost Hungary two thirds of its territory and a third of its population, set in train vast migrations. By 1924, some two hundred thousand Hungarians had left Transylvania. All the staff of the bank in Dicsőszentmárton returned to Budapest except for Ligeti's father, who stayed to work for its new Romanian owners. He spoke no Romanian, but believed that by remaining his family would be safer. Post-war unrest in Budapest had delivered Hungary into the grip of a Communist dictatorship – although for less than a year. Amid the ensuing chaos, Romanian forces marched on Budapest and ransacked the city. Pressurised by Clemenceau, the Romanians withdrew, and there ensued the 'White Terror' of Admiral Horthy's right-wing government, when Communist leaders were killed and leftist writers and politicians fled into exile. In September 1920 the *Numerus Clausus* was passed, the first anti-Semitic law of the century, which restricted the number of Jews who could enter Hungarian universities. In 1929, six years after Ligeti was born, the family moved from Dicsőszentmárton to Cluj, the principal city in Transylvania, where Sándor had been appointed manager of a small private bank. But only a few months later came the worldwide financial collapse, and all private banks in Romania were abolished. He remained to supervise the same office, but now selling lottery tickets at half his former salary. It was a humiliation which he hated.

For hundreds of years the Transylvanian Romanians had been ruled by Hungary, so it was a shock for the remaining Hungarians who now had to submit to Romania. To a large extent the communities remained separate. Romanian Cluj had been Hungarian Kolozsvár (called Klausenburg by the Germans, although few of them lived there) and retained its large Hungarian majority. Dicsőszentmárton, Ligeti's birthplace, was almost entirely Hungarian-speaking apart from its Romanian police. As a small child, Ligeti had no idea that other languages even existed, and was astonished when he heard the police shouting in an alien tongue. Nearly forty years later he would recall the experience in his two mini-operas *Aventures* and *Nouvelles aventures*, which use a nonsensical, hysterical artificial language based only on phonetics. It was also in Dicsőszentmárton where, one winter when Ligeti was three or four, he witnessed a shamanistic ceremony performed by itinerant Romanians from the surrounding villages. Some wild musicians playing violin and bagpipe forced their way into the Ligetis' courtyard, one of them wearing a goatskin cape and a diabolical mask with beak and horns. Pre-Christian in origin, the music he recalls as 'extremely interesting'; but at the time, the young Gyuri had no idea that inside the costumes there were actors, and he was gripped by fear.

Dicsőszentmárton had only five thousand inhabitants and Ligeti's other early musical experiences were necessarily limited. At home there was as yet no radio, but he got to know some short orchestral pieces on 78 rpm recordings, if of tantalisingly poor sound quality. There was little live music, except for the gypsy bands who also played popular nineteenth-century tunes. But, even as a small child, Gyuri imagined music in his head. To his daily routines he attached different musical ceremonies, a tune to brush his teeth to, a march for going to bed. The town had no electricity, only natural gas, and the family home, owned by the bank, lacked even running water. Then the bank decided to make improvements, including the installation of a bathroom. Whilst these works were carried out, at the age of three Gyuri was sent to stay with an aunt and uncle – his father's elder brother, a structural engineer – who lived at Csikszereda (now Miercurea Ciuc) in the east Carpathian mountains. This township was also Hungarian-speaking, but the herdsmen in the surrounding mountains were Romanian. To one of them Ligeti owes another enduring experience, for, as in Switzerland, the Carpathian herdsmen play alphorns.

Around three meters long and made of wooden staves bound together with bark, to sound correctly the instrument must be wet. Gyuri was fascinated to witness a player dip the end of his instrument in a stream, begin to blow, bubbling through the water, then lift the bell clear to sound an extraordinary series of natural harmonics. Their untempered strangeness stuck in his memory. Indeed, the rustic ancestry of the orchestral horn endows it with a special magic, which is briefly evoked in *Melodien*, more often in the Horn Trio, and frequently in the *Hamburg Concerto*, composed over seventy years after the composer's childhood experience, for solo horn and chamber orchestra, to which he adds four natural horns playing only untempered harmonics.

From Csikszereda Ligeti retained less happy memories. His aunt, a primary school teacher, was sadistically insistent that small children should be taught to master their aversions. Noting that Gyuri was afraid of spiders, she made him collect cobwebs with his bare hands, a task which terrified and disgusted him. Years later, in an analytical introduction to the first movement of his first major orchestral piece, *Apparitions*, Ligeti traced its structural basis to a horrific childhood dream triggered by his arachnophobia:

As a small child I once had a dream that I could not get to my cot, to my safe haven, because the whole room was filled with a dense confused tangle of fine filaments. It looked like the web I had seen silkworms fill their box with as they change into pupas. I was caught up in this immense web together with both living things and objects of various kinds – huge moths, a variety of beetles – which tried to get to the flickering flame of the candle in the room; enormous dirty pillows were suspended in this substance, their rotten stuffing hanging out through the slits in torn covers. There were blobs of fresh mucus, balls of dry mucus, remnants of food all gone cold and other such revolting rubbish. Every time a beetle or a moth moved, the entire web started shaking so that the big, heavy pillows were swinging about, which, in turn, made the web rock harder. Sometimes the different kinds of movement reinforced one another and the shaking became so hard that the web tore in places and a few insects suddenly found themselves free. But their freedom was short-lived, they were soon caught up again in the rocking tangle of filaments, and their buzzing, loud at first, grew weaker and weaker. The succession of these sudden unexpected events gradually brought about a change in the internal structure, in the texture of the web. In places knots formed, thickening into an almost solid mass, caverns opened up where shreds of the original web were floating about like gossamer. All these changes seemed like an irreversible process, never returning to earlier states again. An indescribable sadness hung

7

over these shifting forms and structure, the hopelessness of passing time and the melancholy of unalterable past events.[6]

With Jungian hindsight, Ligeti probably elaborated this nightmare, but it remains a potent metaphor for certain qualities in his music. As a bastion against such fears he retreated into an invented world which dominated his daily life. 'During my first years at school I hardly noticed the real world. I transformed clouds into mountains, giving them all names. Going to school I always imagined that I was flying in an aeroplane over my imaginary kingdom; stones along the kerb were the skyscrapers seen from above.'[7] He drew maps of imaginary lands, was susceptible to the fantasies of others and, above all, loved reading.

The first book Ligeti recalls in detail was a children's edition of *The Thousand and One Nights* given to him as a third birthday present, in which the stories of Sinbad the Sailor particularly appealed to him. Then, one summer when Ligeti was around five, somebody mistaken-ly gave him a collection of short stories by Gyula Krúdy (1878–1933), in whose work an introverted, dreaming Sinbad also appears. But it was a book quite unsuitable for children. 'I remember being overcome by a strange melancholy, perhaps because of the heat, or was it my reading these Krúdy stories all alone in the loft?'[8] Writing in an ornate style with a flow of ideas like that of Proust and Joyce, Krúdy develops a highly literate vein of nostalgia. Some of the stories involve a widow whose husband, 'either a botanist or a meteorologist', had been dead for years, leaving her alone through the winter in an isolated house on the Hungarian plain, full of clocks, barometers and hygrometers. 'Nobody comes, maybe for a hundred years. Nothing happens. So there is a combination of movement, which is machine-like, and absolutely nothing . . . a timelessness . . . no beginning and no end.'[9] Krúdy's ironic fantasies of an older Hungary, destroyed by its First World War defeat, Ligeti understood better as he grew older; but the whirring, ticking mechanisms were already feeding his musical ideas.

Because of its natural gas supply – an important resource before the widespread use of electricity – Dicsőszentmárton, although only a small town, was surrounded by industry. There was a printing works in which another of Ligeti's uncles worked as a typesetter; his wife, Sándor Ligeti's younger sister, was the aunt who supplied the warmth Ligeti lacked from his mother. He was able to visit his uncle at work, watch and listen, enthralled by the clattering presses. Here, as much as in

Krúdy, was Ligeti's 'basic image for the metronome piece', his Fluxus-inspired *Poème symphonique* of 1962, as well as for *Continuum* and the third movement of his String Quartet no. 2. Elsewhere there was glass-blowing, the paper mills and brick factories (three of them); and, at the railway station, the huge wheels, pistons and connecting rods of the steam engines. Even at home there was the incessant chatter of his father's typewriter as he toiled over his books. Far from being a sleepy rural town, to a child Dicsőszentmárton must have seemed like a symphony of machines, mysterious and magical, unwitting progenitors of the '*meccanico*' textures in his mature compositions.

Ligeti cannot remember where or when, but it was probably after the family moved to Cluj that, in somebody's house, he witnessed professional mourners intoning beside a coffin. The traditional Romanian funeral lament – the *bocet* – with its chromatically descending phrases, exists similarly in other Latin cultures including flamenco, probably spread by the gypsies. Of all archetypes leaving their imprint in his musical psyche, this was the most significant, since it would gradually resurface in the many manifestations of the '*lamento* motif' found in his music of the 1980s and 1990s. For the moment, these folklore impressions were overshadowed by the glamorous artistic culture of a city boasting not only its own symphony orchestra but also both Hungarian operetta and a Romanian opera company. Once the family had moved there, Ligeti's musical development benefited from many more opportunities. The aunt and uncle from Csikszereda had also resettled in Cluj. Ligeti didn't care for the aunt who had forced him to collect cobwebs; but he had grown fond of their daughter Kato (Kate) who was about ten years older than György and by now a student. In Cluj, Kato took her seven-year old cousin to the opera, first and most memorably to *Boris Godunov*, soon after to *La Traviata* and other productions. These early theatrical experiences made a vivid impact: the splendour of the sets and costumes, the ambience of the auditorium, even the sweets they shared. He was overwhelmed by the totality of the illusion, watching and listening in a dreamlike trance. The coronation scene in *Boris Godunov* and the dramatic styles of Verdi and Mozart remained fundamental models when he wrote his own *Le Grand Macabre*. Meanwhile, the medium of radio had advanced and, by the time Ligeti was in his teens, he could listen at home to symphony concerts broadcast from Budapest and Bucharest, including the comparatively modern symphonic poems of Richard Strauss.

9

When Ligeti was eight, he fell off some cliffs he was climbing and injured his knee so badly that he had to stay in bed for over nine months. He was delighted to miss school and spent much of the time reading, notably books on the geography and ethnography of Africa. He was not to know how deeply the music of sub-Saharan Africa would influence his own compositions fifty years later. Although Ligeti's elementary education was conducted in Hungarian, once they had moved to Cluj his parents decided to send him to a Romanian-speaking secondary school so that he would grow up bilingual. He arrived not knowing a word of Romanian, but learnt fast and was equally quick to fend off taunts. Romanian and Hungarian culture were as unlike as their languages, and between the two there was an undercurrent of hostility. Surface relationships – until the advent of Hitler – were reasonably courteous. Nevertheless, as a young man Ligeti sensed a twofold discrimination, being regarded by Romanians as Hungarian, and by Hungarians as a Jew.

Apart from his continuing interest in geography, Gyuri succumbed to new hobbies almost every year. Home-made chemical experiments absorbed him around the age of twelve and thirteen. He obtained a university textbook on inorganic chemistry and, in a drawer originally reserved for toys, set up a tiny 'laboratory'. On one occasion he managed to produce a small but spectacular explosion which prompted his grandmother, who happened to be in the next room, to move out.[10] By now the fictitious country of his imagination had acquired a name, 'Kylwiria', and he devised for its cities his own vision of utopia:

I wrote descriptions of the geological constitution of the mountains, deserts and rivers, also studies about the social system, and invented a thoroughly 'logical' language, even working out the grammar. The legal system and social structure were completely liberal and perfectly just. I didn't bother with illness and death. The cities had neither doctors nor hospitals, and no cemeteries. It was a kind of 'land of milk and honey' with no government, no money and no criminals. But it was not a fairy-tale land, rather a seemingly rational, high-tech world with a perfectly functioning everyday life. There were no problems to solve, no mistakes. There were schools, but no boring homework, and the whole population was dedicated to the sciences and the arts. Nobody had to work since machines produced and regulated everything. The engines needed no repair, the homes no cleaning.[11]

Another love was the cinema. It is hard to imagine the excitement it aroused in the early years of the technological age. Even Dicsőszent-márton had a small cinema with its own electric generator, which he was allowed to visit as a small boy. Here, and then in Cluj, he saw Chaplin, Keaton and Laurel and Hardy, cowboy and pirate movies, Mickey Mouse and other cartoons. Cartoons he liked the best.

Sándor Ligeti was a convinced socialist and atheist. Consequently his sons grew up largely ignorant of Jewish religion. Nevertheless, disregarding his father's displeasure, at the age of thirteen Gyuri was drawn into the left-wing Zionist youth movement Habonim. But he found that he could not subscribe to its collectivist ideals and, whilst reproaching himself for deserting their cause, three years later he left. Emotionally and intellectually he remained close to his father, 'a good-hearted and broad person'; although, like other teenagers, he began to reject his parents' views. Given Marx's *Das Kapital* to read at the age of fifteen or sixteen, he concluded that it might contain 'some nice formulas' but was otherwise 'silly . . . mere scientific socialism', a brusque dismissal which provoked heated argument at home. Earlier, at the age of twelve, Ligeti had discovered a more congenial model that would become a lifelong delight: Lewis Carroll's *Alice's Adventures in Wonderland* translated by the great Hungarian writer and humorist Frigyes Karinthy (1887–1938), its ironic wit and iconoclasm an antidote to all fanaticism. The art books possessed by his father were another joy, particularly 'a wonderful big book on the history of art' with reproductions in colour. Sándor wanted his sons to be familiar with painting and architecture – English cathedrals, for example – but liked nothing later than Cézanne. As for music, 'his taste stopped with Schubert.'

Music or science?

In 1936 Ligeti's younger brother Gábor began to learn the violin, his father's opposition overcome by the advocacy of a family friend who had noticed that Gábor possessed absolute pitch. Gyuri protested that he too should be allowed to take up an instrument; and so, in 1937, at the age of fourteen Gyuri began piano lessons. He practised zealously for several hours a day and made rapid progress. But he was already too old to have any chance of acquiring an advanced piano technique. At first there was no piano at home, so Gyuri went after school to the apartment of his teacher, who had a second piano in a back room, and, when she moved, to a friend of his mother's. Soon he began to compose, his first effort a waltz 'in the style of Grieg' and predictably in A minor.

Because as a practising ophthalmologist his mother needed a better address, around this time the family changed apartments. Previously they had lived in a quiet area away from the centre of Cluj, where his father had a separate study surrounded by his three thousand or more books, and could work in peace on his own writing. The new apartment looked luxurious and was close to the city's main square and its huge Gothic church. In reality it was much too small. His father had no study and his books were now stored in the cellar. Gyuri and Gábor shared a room with separate beds, but did their schoolwork at the same table, constantly disturbing each other. After Sándor decided to rent the piano belonging to their mother's friend, it too was housed in the boys' bedroom in which they could now scarcely move. But to be able to play at home was a joy, even though the instrument was badly out of tune. Gyuri practised in the bedroom whilst Gábor played his violin in the drawing room, and their father had to forgo his after-lunch cigar and nap. Although the boys greatly annoyed each other they shared, says Ligeti, 'a very intense friendship. I continuously fell in love with different girls (always in secret, being overly shy), but no girl could ever become more important to me than my beloved brother.'[12]

At school, besides being taught in Romanian, Ligeti learnt German and French, the latter supplemented by private lessons in French literature, which was favoured by Hungarian left-wing intellectuals as an expression of their anti-Germanic feeling. His aptitude for languages and love of literature proved their value. After learning Swedish in the 1960s, English in the 1970s, and with a working knowledge of Italian, Ligeti is more or less fluent in seven languages. In school he excelled in mathematics and continued to specialise in the natural sciences, firm in his intention of becoming a scientist. But events were to compel a different course. For millions of people they would be catastrophic.

Hitler's seizure of power in Germany in 1933 encouraged extreme right-wing factions elsewhere, and, during the late 1930s, anti-Semitism in Hungary increased. In 1940 Hitler forced Romania to return the northern half of Transylvania to Hungary. The boundaries were again redrawn and Cluj became Hungarian Kolozsvár once more. In the administrative and cultural upheaval all the main institutions changed hands. The Romanian 'liceu' became the Hungarian 'gymnasium' – although still in the same building – and Ligeti suddenly found himself

Ex. 1 Opening page of Ligeti's first sketchbook,
written at the age of sixteen

having to take his final school examinations in Hungarian instead of
Romanian. The Romanian staff of the University and Conservatory
were replaced with Hungarians, and the policy of the orchestra, now
infiltrated with musicians from Budapest, became notably national-
istic. With two classmates, Ligeti had been receiving private maths
lessons from an elderly Communist, Professor Antal, who had been
forced to leave Budapest but had a reputation as a 'maverick genius
. . . able to explain the whole architecture of mathematics'. After
Germany and Russia jointly invaded Poland, Antal proffered excuses
which neither Ligeti nor his father could stomach, despite their own
commitment to the left. Ligeti stopped his lessons and was angrily
'excommunicated'. Anxiously his father spent his evenings and into
the night glued to the radio, regarding the BBC World Service as the
only source of truth. In 1941 Hungary entered the war as an ally of
Germany, and Budapest became a target for bombs. But, for a couple
of years, life in Kolozsvár continued without undue disruption and
Ligeti was able to compose energetically.

Two years earlier, aged sixteen, he had bought a musical sketch-book, the first of forty-eight sketchbooks filled between 1939 and 1952 which are now deposited with the majority of Ligeti's surviving manuscripts in the Paul Sacher Foundation in Basle. Measuring twelve by sixteen centimetres and containing fifty pages each printed with eight staves, it could easily fit in a pocket. On the first page we see what is probably Ligeti's earliest surviving composition (see p.13). But it is not the string quartet it appears to be. Turn the page, and the mellifluous E minor opening broadens into an orchestral piece scored for double woodwind, two horns and strings, despite there being only eight staves to fit them on. The music breaks off after a few more bars. When Ligeti entered the Kolozsvár Conservatory in 1941, he used some of these books for his harmony and counterpoint exercises; but most are full of such beginnings, lists, notes, aide-memoires, sometimes complete compositions, entered in profusion. Their pre-cocity reminds one of the Brontë children's notebooks, although happily less minuscule. Ligeti still planned to be a scientist, but the sketchbooks suggest that he was thinking music for a large part of every day.

Perhaps the orchestral fragment was continued on larger paper. Inspired by hearing broadcasts of Wagner as well as Strauss, Ligeti began a four-movement symphony – his first and last – completing its opening movement in 1939 and an Andante in 1940. During two summers spent with relations in the peaceful country town of Târgu-Mureş, he worked alternately on planimetric constructions for his school geography and on the symphony, spreading the pages on gravestones in the local cemetery. None of them survives, but there still exists a Sonatina for string quartet, a relatively substantial com-position, complete except for its final pages. Also in E minor, the smudged and frayed fair copy bears two annotations – 'composed 1938–1939' and 'Ligeti Gheorge, 30 March 1940' written in another hand – suggesting that Ligeti may have revised it to present as evi-dence of what he could do. Competent but unremarkable, its ideas succeed each other rapidly and there are frequent changes of tempo – a common fault of student pieces, although arguably a positive characteristic of Ligeti's later music. Ove Nordwall, the Swedish musicologist, goes so far as to assert that the Sonatina 'shows an amazing similarity to the "real" String Quartet no. 1, *Métamorphoses nocturnes*'.[13]

Ex. 2 Final section of *Little Piano Pieces* (1939–41)

Whilst still at school, Ligeti composed a set of six *Little Piano Pieces* (*Kis zongorádarabok*) of more evident individuality. In 'Modern Prelude' he attempts some bold modulations. 'Christmas Carol' has charming melodies. In 'Hora' (Dance) he experiments with two simultaneous key signatures. 'Grotesque' contains sudden contrasts, beginning with a softly repeated cluster of six semitones spread over two octaves. 'Elmélyülés' (Meditation) is tonally adventurous in a different way. Its last thirteen bars have real beauty, their confident use of enharmonic modulation revealing an affection for early nineteenth-century style that has remained significant. Romantic sensibility also belongs to a projected orchestral treatment of Goethe's *Wanderers Nachtlied* that appears in two of the sketchbooks, the first dated 29 December 1941. The fragment begins like Weber or Bruckner, with an atmospheric string tremolando played muted and *sul ponticello* on an open fifth, against which a solo trumpet sports an arresting motif in sequential tritones.

At the age of seventeen, standing in for a member of an amateur orchestra who had left for the war, Ligeti began to play the timpani.

Ex. 3 *Kineret* (1941), Ligeti's first published composition

Around this time he heard the music of Bartók and Kodály in concert performances, and Stravinsky on the radio – but only *Petrouchka*. In 1941 he had a short composition published, a song for mezzo-soprano with piano accompaniment called *Kineret (Galilee)*, which had won first prize in a competition arranged by a Jewish organisation in Budapest. It was printed alongside pieces by six other Jewish composers in a collection called *The Ararat Songs* – an example of the cultural segregation now imposed upon the Jews. Editor of the set was Bence Szabolcsi who, after the war, became Professor of Music History at the Franz Liszt Academy in Budapest. Ligeti's contribution has a studied seriousness. The words are set in *parlando* manner above tonally disjunct consonant chords: dignified, but rather slavishly in root position (only one chord in the whole song is not). Despite this public success, it still had not occurred to Ligeti to pursue a career as a composer.

After taking his final school examinations in 1941, Ligeti sat the entrance examinations in physics and mathematics at the University of Kolozsvár. But passing them did not gain him admission. Due to the restrictions, only one Jew could be admitted in natural sciences, and another candidate had been selected. Like his father, but now for different reasons, Ligeti was unable to pursue the career he wanted. Considering whether to go to a music conservatory instead, he assembled some of his compositions and posted them to the distinguished Antal Molnár (1890–1983), Professor of Music Theory in Budapest. Lean and improperly tall, Molnár was a magnificent teacher and writer of the most informative books in Hungarian about modern music. In reply to Ligeti's request for advice, he was kindly and considerate. He warned Ligeti of the difficulty of earning a living by composition but added that 'if you really want to be a composer, I cannot prevent you'. After deliberations at home, it was agreed that Gyuri should apply for entrance – not, however, to the Music Academy in Budapest, since this famous institution had also virtually closed its doors to Jews. The Kolozsvár Conservatory was subject to the same regulations, but its director, Viktor Vaszy, chose not to apply them. Much to his surprise, Ligeti was accepted into the composition and theory classes. His formal knowledge was minimal, and he was admitted on the strength of the aural examination and because he had already composed so much. His portfolio included a *Little Piano Trio* in two movements for violin, cello and piano, which was included in a concert soon after he joined the Conservatory, played by Ligeti himself and two students – his first composition to be performed in public. The survival of a viola part replacing the cello suggests that it was played on a further occasion with Gábor on the viola, to which he had recently transferred hoping to get a place in a string quartet. The piano part cannot have taxed Ligeti's technique but the music reveals his nascent contrapuntal bent, the opening Andante boasting a four-voice canon in which the parts enter on successive beats.

The vitality of the Kolozsvár Conservatory was admirable. Here, between 1941 and 1943, Ligeti studied with Ferenc Farkas (1905–2000), a pupil of Respighi and an excellent if conservative teacher whose models were Mozart's sonata and rondo forms and Bach chorales.

From Respighi Farkas had acquired his practical knowledge of instrumentation. Farkas was a strict harmony teacher who emphasised correct voice-leading and covered Ligeti's exercises with red pencil: he had to rework them until there were no more corrections. He soon became adept at imitating Mozart, Bach and Couperin. But perhaps it was detrimental to his development that he lacked rivals amongst his peers, 'emulation being the main trigger for professional quality'.[14] On his own initiative he began to investigate Stravinsky and Hindemith. During a visit to Budapest, he purchased Hindemith's treatise, *The Craft of Musical Composition*,[15] and worked through all its exercises. At the Conservatory he sang in numerous choirs and extended his knowledge of Bartók through hearing works like the *Divertimento* and Second Violin Concerto. These were performed by the Kolozsvár Symphony Orchestra under Viktor Vaszy, who, although director of the Conservatory was also, in Ligeti's view, Hungary's best conductor. The playing of Bartók's String Quartet no. 2 by the Waldbauer Quartet was an even greater revelation.

To advance as a composer, Ligeti thought that he needed more practical experience. So, alongside the piano, he began to study the organ – practising hard and getting as far as Bach's Trio Sonata no. 1 before war intervened – and the cello, aware of the value of learning from the inside how to write for strings. He borrowed a cello from a school friend and for half a year received formal lessons. Meanwhile, he was taking parallel courses in mathematics and physics at a private academy whose teachers contributed their services free of charge for those who had been prevented from entering the university. He worked so relentlessly that, to keep going on only four or five hours' sleep, he resorted to performance-enhancing drugs. But the incessant expenditure of energy, with its nervous as well as physical stress, caused a breakdown. His parents misunderstood its causes and at their behest, during 1942 and 1943, Ligeti travelled occasionally to Budapest to receive psychiatric treatment. Characteristically, he put these visits to advantage by arranging additional private composition lessons from Pál Kadosa. Apart from his international status as a composer, Kadosa was a pianist noted for his Bartók performances. His discerning analyses, although applied to classical models, sharpened the insights Ligeti would apply to his own analyses of Boulez and the Western avant-garde. Years later, when Ligeti had settled into his seventeen years of teaching at the

Hochschule für Musik in Hamburg, he too focused predominantly on the classical repertoire.

Love and survival

In 1943 Ligeti met the girl who, after the war, would become his first wife. Brigitte Löw was the daughter of a German businessman living in Kolozsvár. Gyuri began to visit their house where, gathered around the piano with a few friends, they would sing through accompanied and unaccompanied choruses, including compositions of his own as well as classics of the choral repertory like the Mozart Requiem and Bach Passions. Inspired by such examples, and stimulated by the company, he was composing avidly. Early in 1944, he began a cantata for mezzo-soprano, double chorus and chamber orchestra, to an unwittingly symbolic Latin text, *Tenebrae factae sunt* (*Darkness descended*), the fifth of the Tenebrae Responses for Good Friday. He had composed only one movement for unaccompanied chorus, adding the date 19–20 January, when he had to put the score aside.

By now, the impact of the war had escalated alarmingly. The majority of young men had been called up to fight the Soviet army on the Ukrainian front, most of them never to return. Just after 20 January Ligeti received a mobilisation telegram ordering him to report in less than twenty-four hours to a Jewish labour battalion in Szeged, a handsome historic city significant for being the largest agrarian centre in the plains south-east of Budapest. It was a turning point in his life. Immediately he was put to work in the army grain silos. He and his fellow Jews wore no uniforms and were identified only by yellow armbands. A few weeks later German intelligence discovered the Hungarian government to have been in secret negotiation with the Allies. On 19 March German troops invaded the country, the government was replaced by pro-Nazis, and there began a systematic campaign to eliminate the Jews. Thousands were deported daily, mostly to Auschwitz where, in forty-six days during the summer of 1944, between 250,000 and 300,000 Hungarian Jews were exterminated.[16] The Jewish labourers at Szeged were sent to the copper mines in Serbia where, after months of arduous work, they were mercilessly shot by the SS.

Ligeti himself was exceptionally lucky, as he realised only after the war. Before the end of March he and a handful of comrades were detached from the rest of the company and transferred to the fortress city of Nagyvárad, east of Budapest. Billeted in the ghetto, he witnessed the brutal eviction of Jewish families. At the end of May came the awful news that his own family had been taken from Kolozsvár. Their fate he learnt after the war, when the Swiss Red Cross published lists of victims. His father, mother and younger brother were deported to Auschwitz. From there his father was taken to Buchenwald, then to Bergen-Belsen where he died from typhus fever. Gábor was removed to Mauthausen concentration camp and killed there by the Nazis in 1945 at the age of seventeen by an injection in his heart. The aunt and uncle from Dicsőszentmárton of whom Ligeti had been especially fond were also murdered in Auschwitz. Only his mother survived the Holocaust, because she had been useful as a doctor.

The attack on the Jews was accompanied by a vicious imposition of censorship. In the summer of 1944 half a million books were destroyed as libraries were 'cleansed' of undesirable books, including the works of Heine, Proust, Zola and Hungarian Jewish writers. But, despite its terrible impact, the Nazi occupation was comparatively short-lived. During a spectacularly successful Russian offensive in the summer of 1944, Romania capitulated and by September, the Russians had advanced their front line close to Nagyvárad. Ligeti was now involved in unloading munitions trains some distance from the city, a hazardous operation since they were regularly bombarded. But there was an atmosphere of surrealistic fatalism. 'The real danger, the Soviet air raids on the munitions trains, we thought not at all alarming. We weren't living in reality. Since the abduction of our families, life and death had become much the same. If you died, you died; if by chance you lived, then you lived.'[17] On 10 October, in the chaos following a German counter-attack, he and some companions found themselves unguarded. Treated as slave labour by the Germans, they were unlikely to fare better under the Soviets. Four times during the next ten days Ligeti was taken prisoner by Russian troops, each time regaining his freedom in the general confusion. On one occasion a German and Russian fighter pilot simultaneously shot each other down, both planes exploding in the air above. As his captors took cover in one direction, Ligeti ran off in the other. His final escape was bizarrely Chaplinesque. He and other prisoners were being marched under guard back to Nagyvárad, now under Soviet control. At a crossroads, the motley column was unexpectedly split in two as a convoy of Russian tanks thundered past at right angles. At the front of the column,

Ligeti and his group continued to march forward until they could disappear into the surrounding streets. Chance had again saved him. Had he remained a Soviet prisoner, he would almost certainly have been sent to Siberia.

Instead, he spent the next fortnight walking back to Kolozsvár, now also occupied by the Russians. The city was in a mess and his parents' apartment occupied by strangers. All his family had disappeared. His only remaining close friend was Brigitte, who was now studying as a medical student. Their relationship deepened and they began to talk of marriage. But Brigitte's father was opposed. Although German, he was emphatically anti-Nazi; but he was also a practical businessman who no more wanted his daughter to wed an impecunious musician than could Friedrich Wieck approve his daughter's marriage to Robert Schumann. Ligeti returned to composition, adding to his unfinished cantata two movements for voices and instruments, completing the work on 20 January 1945, almost a year to the day after he had started it. Having finished the cantata, he wrote a short unaccompanied piece for chorus, *Dereng már a hajnal* (*Early come the summer*) which gained the distinction of being published in Kolozsvár, then in Budapest, and (in 1947, with an English translation) by the Workers' Music Association in London. In mid-March he composed a second Latin cantata, on the text *Venit angelus Domini, descendit de caelo*, adding next to its completion date the words 'A hazatéröké' (For the returned). Brigitte was the dedicatee of several of these pieces, including a Bartókian *Little Serenade* for string orchestra in four movements, completed in December 1945 and reworked two years later for string quartet. Its opening pitches of B flat and C spell 'Bici', a diminutive form of Brigitte.

Meeting Kurtág

Being now allied to Russia, Romania regained Transylvania and Kolozsvár again became Cluj. Little over a year after Ligeti had been drafted by the Hungarian military, the Romanian army called him up to fight on the opposite side against Hungary and Germany. Mercifully he succumbed to a tubercular infection, spending three months in hospital, and by the time he was discharged, the war was over. His mother returned and took up work in a clinic in the city. But for Ligeti himself, there was at last the possibility of entering the

Franz Liszt Academy in Budapest as a full-time music student. Also sitting the entrance examination for Sándor Veress's composition class in September 1945 was György Kurtág. Born in 1926, Kurtág came from Lugoj, a small town near the Romanian–Yugoslav border, and had been educated in nearby Timisoara, the main city of another former Hungarian territory ceded to Romania in 1920. Ligeti and Kurtág were both from Jewish-Hungarian families with left-wing but non-Communist views; although because of the boundary changes they were now regarded as Romanians. Forty years later, Ligeti recalled how an immediate and spontaneous friendship arose between the two young composers:

... during the half-hour in which we waited with palpitating hearts to be called from the art-nouveau corridors of the Academy into the examination room. I felt that I had found in him a musical brother and companion with whom I could set out in search of a new musical style. I liked Kurtág's shyness, his rather introverted character and his absolute lack of arrogance and vanity: he was simple, intelligent and honest. He later told me that, for his part, he had taken me for a Protestant Ministry student, which made us both laugh: I think he interpreted my provincial shyness as religious zeal and strictness, indeed very different from my real self. [18]

Ligeti and Kurtág had a common bond in that each had illegally crossed the border in order to reach Budapest. They were typical young intellectuals, opposed to the Hungarian right and enthused by post-war socialist idealism. Besides the attraction of its fine conservatory – probably the best in south-eastern Europe – whose rich tradition stretched back to Liszt, there was the added allure of the imminent return to Budapest of Béla Bartók, who was due to arrive from New York in the autumn of 1945 to reoccupy his professorship. Neither of them had met Bartók in the pre-war years, but their admiration bordered on devotion. Alas, their eagerness was to be disappointed:

We could hardly wait for the day when we would see and hear him in person. Imagine our despair when, on the day of the entrance examination, we saw the black flag flying over the Music Academy: on that day, the message of Bartók's death in New York at the age of sixty-four had been received. The great joy of being admitted to the composition class at the Academy was overshadowed by the bitterness we felt at the irretrievable loss of our spiritual father.[19]

Sándor Veress (1907–92), however, was one of the most distinguished composers of the generation following Bartók and Kodály
and an inspiring teacher, if less for his attention to technical detail
than for his aesthetic and moral leadership. He was, says Ligeti, 'full
of *noblesse*, a wonderful person'. But he was frequently away, lecturing at conferences abroad (making the most of possessing a
passport), and left Hungary for good at the end of 1948 to settle in
Berne, where he became the teacher of Heinz Holliger and Jürg
Wyttenbach. Following Veress's departure, Ligeti completed his studies with Pál Járdányi and again with Ferenc Farkas, after Farkas was
appointed to the Budapest Academy as Professor of Composition. In
the idealistic aftermath of the war, Ligeti was urged to join the
Communist party both by Veress and by Endre Svervanszky, an older
composer much admired by the young. But he distrusted herd
behaviour and resolutely declined.

Post-war Budapest

When Ligeti entered the Academy at the age of twenty-two, only a few
months after the war had ended, three quarters of the city was in ruins.
Its inhabitants had suffered most terrible hardships. Many were dead.
The thin post-war newspapers printed long columns of small ads,
mostly from members of families looking for each other. It was almost
impossible to find a room or even a bed in which to sleep. Scarcely a
single unbroken glass window remained in the city and, as there was
virtually no fuel for heating, the bitter cold of winter penetrated everywhere. There was also a serious shortage of food. Ligeti managed to
find accommodation in a suburban apartment that had not been totally destroyed. His home was a mattress, without blanket or quilt,
occupying two square metres in the kitchen. He had no piano, but it
was unusual to have any sort of room to oneself. György and Márta
Kurtág, newly married, shared one small bedsit in which they also
crammed an upright piano. In the apartment where Ligeti lived,
Russian soldiers were also billeted, whose left-over scraps supplemented his meagre diet. Since there was no soap, he went unwashed
for weeks. Nor, at first, was there any public transport. But, having
walked to the Academy, students benefited from a daily free meal of
pulses provided by the American and Scandinavian aid organisations.
One could also take food from the University and warm it up in the

evening, except that the distance between Academy and University made it impractical.

The cultural life of Budapest had suffered from the agonising loss of around two thirds of its Jewish inhabitants, exterminated by the Nazis and by the Hungarian 'arrow cross' mobs. Despite these horrors and the many hardships, artistic activity bubbled up again with a tremendous fervour. Leo Weiner ran his celebrated course in chamber music. Erich Kleiber and Leonard Bernstein conducted symphony concerts. Even before the final liberation of Hungary, the Budapest Opera had reopened. An early production was of Benjamin Britten's *Peter Grimes* just a year after its premiere, and around the same time Ligeti heard a broadcast of the *Spring Symphony*. In 1947 Klemperer became conductor of the Opera, augmenting the Budapest company with fine Italian singers from La Scala, Milan. For a short period Ligeti could hear live the music of Stravinsky: *The Firebird* in concert, *Petrouchka* staged. *The Rite of Spring* he heard only on the radio and only in part, before all Stravinsky performances were forbidden by the Communists. Up to 1947 there was no censorship, except that it was forbidden to publish anything about Soviet army atrocities during the last months of the war, including its abduction of young men (who might have included Ligeti) for hard labour in the Soviet Union. The only evidence of occupation was the presence of the victorious army which had liberated the city. There was no overt repression, instead an intoxicating resurgence of intellectual energy.

The end of the war, and with it of the Nazi dictatorship, released an unprecedented pent-up energy and vigour, which found expression in a suddenly flourishing artistic and intellectual life. In those days we were totally unaware that the new dictatorship, the communist Stalinist police and military regime, was not any better than that of the Nazis, and would soon put an end to the freedom of art and culture . . . Both Kurtág and I were very much attracted to and subsequently influenced by this intense artistic life. Despite the terrible experience of the Nazi era, we were both filled with youthful optimism and hope for the future. We both felt strongly drawn to Bartók's style and saw our musical future in the development of a modern, chromatic-modal idiom, which would be international and yet reflect our Hungarian roots.[20]

During this short period of artistic freedom nearly all Bartók's major works were performed. In December 1945 *The Miraculous Mandarin* received its first Hungarian staging at the Opera, twenty-six years after

Bartók had completed it.[21] The Sándor Végh Quartet presented all six of Bartók's quartets in a series spread over two winters. But, although Ligeti knew the quartets from their scores and particularly admired the fourth, he missed most of the performances. Due to the shortage of fuel, the Conservatory, like other buildings, lacked adequate heat. During the winter living conditions in Budapest were spartan and Ligeti travelled to and from Romania as often as he could, crossing the border illegally on foot. In Cluj lived his mother, and Brigitte whom he had promised to marry. There he could earn money giving mathematics lessons, as he had done before the war. Back in Budapest, he secluded himself in the library of the Academy, where it was sometimes warm, both to compose and work on assignments. He didn't read the newspapers. It was enough to have survived the Nazi dictatorship. Communism might create a better system, although there was little direct evidence to judge it by. From 1945 to 1948 Hungary was governed by a democratic coalition of four parties including the Communists. From the outset, however, the Communists controlled the Ministry of the Interior and therefore the police. Behind the scenes they were secretly manoeuvring and political victimisation had begun. What seemed to be left-wing idealism was turning into fascism. Elated by their post-war hopes most people did not notice. They would soon find out.

Living under Communism

Ligeti spent part of 1947 attempting to regain his Hungarian citizenship. Because he was now officially a Romanian, his residence in Budapest was illegal. Grappling with the tangled bureaucracy, he eventually received his citizenship but no passport. Soon it was impossible to cross the border except on official business. The Romanian guards used trained dogs and shot without warning. Throughout 1948 Stalinism tightened its grip, and the Soviets began to establish a dictatorship. Non-Communist deputies in the Hungarian National Assembly were forced either to unite with the Communists or be imprisoned. Basic freedoms disappeared again, communications with the West were obstructed and cultural activities emasculated. In denying modern art, the Communist officials removed from the Budapest Museum of Art not only Picasso (despite the painter's membership of the French Communist party) but also the fine collection of French and Hungarian Impressionists. Books vanished; foreign-language classics, like *Don Quixote* and that subversive political activist *Winnie-the-Pooh*, were taken from the libraries and bookshops and pulped.[22] The music of Debussy, Ravel, Britten, Schoenberg and Stravinsky – who, for Ligeti, most embodied his idea of modernism – was now completely banned. Even the Bartók string quartets were forbidden; only his most straightforward works – the *Concerto for Orchestra*, Third Piano Concerto and folk-song transcriptions – could be performed. These repressive measures emanated from the All Union Congress of Composers held in Moscow in January 1948, at which Stalin's spokesman Andrei Zhdanov announced a policy designed to rid music and culture of all degenerate and Western influences. This was the fateful occasion when Khachaturian, Prokofiev, Shostakovich and other Russian composers were publicly reprimanded for their 'formalism', Prokofiev's entire output being condemned as 'alien to the Soviet people'. The endorsement of the Zhdanov principles in a manifesto prepared by the East German composer Hanns Eisler, and presented to the Second International Congress of Composers held in Prague in May 1948, ensured their rapid spread throughout the Eastern bloc.

In February 1948 Ligeti handed his teacher Sándor Veress the newspaper reporting the Zhdanov resolution and its application in Hungary. Veress said nothing, but two weeks later he had gone. That summer, before the onset of the restrictions, Ligeti and another student, Erzsébet Szönyi, a protégé of Kodály, were offered stipends to enable them to spend, in succession, their final year of study at the Paris Conservatory. Ligeti's former teacher Ferenc Farkas, from whom he felt he still had things to learn, had just joined the Academy, so Ligeti proposed that Erzsébet should go first. Soon after it became clear that the possibility of following her existed no more. It had never occurred to him that the borders would be closed and there would be no way out. 'I was stupid. I should have gone to Paris and not come back.'

Had Ligeti with his left-wing leanings succumbed to the massive propaganda, his first major composition, *Cantata for a Youth Festival*, might have set in chain a series of ideological pieces. He started it innocently enough in the middle of 1948, intending it to be his final graduation piece from the Academy. When an International Youth Festival was announced to take place in the summer of 1949, Ligeti was encouraged to have the cantata premiered at the festival. He was by now a relatively prominent twenty-five-year-old student soon to be appointed president of the Academy's student association. Péter Kuczka, a successful young poet fêted by the Communists and a friend of Ligeti, provided a text containing routine pro-Soviet platitudes but also extolling peace and freedom. Ligeti warmed to the task, writing a substantial three-movement work boasting a joyful Handelian fugue.

In the autumn of 1948 the political situation seriously worsened. Cardinal Mindszenty, head of the Roman Catholic church in Hungary, was arrested and accused of hiding American dollars (planted by the secret police in his apartment), it being illegal to possess foreign money. In January the Cardinal was tried and sentenced to life imprisonment. A few weeks later, as Budapest's Catholics came under attack, Ligeti was summoned and told to identify active Catholic students in the Academy. He was to return in a week and provide nine names. To refuse on the spot would have been fatal, but he did not go back, with or without nine names, and decided immediately to resign his post as student president. The forthcoming performance of the cantata, about whose text and style he now felt thoroughly uncomfortable, filled him with apprehension. But he was already lucky to have escaped punishment, and was warned that he could not withdraw it.

Despite the relative glamour of the cantata's premiere in Budapest's State Opera House, Ligeti was determined to distance himself from the universally imposed Socialist Realism. It was a time of extreme anxiety. During the summer of 1949 thousands of 'true Communists' were accused of absurd crimes and found guilty in show trials. Many were killed or disappeared in prisons and in camps, among them some of Ligeti's close friends. Encouraged by Farkas, he still continued his efforts to write a simpler, fundamentally popular music, neither dissonant nor chromatic, not realising the futility of compromise. By turning to classical Hungarian authors and drawing on traditional folklore, he hoped to avoid setting propagandist texts. Almost immediately, however, Ligeti was instructed to compose a new cantata praising the Hungarian dictator, Mátyás Rákosi. Refusal would have been disastrous; but the directive coincided with the offer of a scholarship to study folk music in Romania. It was a lifeline proffered at an opportune moment. Ligeti left Budapest, and when he returned nearly a year later, the Rákosi proposal had been forgotten.

27

Retreat into folklore

Like all students at the Academy, Ligeti had followed an obligatory foundation course in Hungarian folk music, as laid down by Kodály. The award of a scholarship meant that he could continue this research at the Folklore Institute in Bucharest, and then at a similar institute in Cluj and in the countryside nearby. The Hungarian ambassador in Bucharest, Jenő Széll,[23] happened to be a good friend and arranged a visa and passport valid for Romania. In October 1949 Ligeti travelled legally from Budapest to Cluj for the first time since the war. There he saw his mother, and Brigitte and he were married. The next day he boarded the train for Bucharest. Misunderstanding his financial resources, the embassy booked him into an expensive hotel for Western visitors. Half his scholarship money spent in a single night, the following day 'the nice people at the embassy made a bed for me in the ambassador's bathtub'. Although safely removed from the Hungarian capital during one of the bleakest periods of political and cultural oppression, in Romania things were worse and there was precious little to eat. Nevertheless, for some ten weeks during the autumn of 1949, Ligeti immersed himself in the Bucharest Institute, exploring its collection both notated and recorded, and learning to transcribe from cylinders under the guidance of an excellent folklorist Emilia Comişel. His account of this experience, published in the Hungarian journal *Új Zenei Szemle* (*New Music Review*),[24] shows how readily Ligeti succumbed to its charm:

The Bucharest Institute is, for a musician, an unbelievable paradise. One part is situated in a two-storey villa. On the ground floor we find a small vestibule. From here, open: the library, and the collection of phonograph rolls (which occupies two rooms – in the one, transcribers are at work, in the other, graduates undertake scientific tasks), the record library (this is a large hall with a powerful radio-phonograph and chairs for the audience) and the laboratory, where recordings are prepared (with electronic record-cutting equipment) – in the same place there is also a workshop for repairing phonographs. The office, one part of the library and the director's flat as well as that of his deputy are on the first floor. A couple of houses down, in a separate building, the folk orchestra of the Institute holds its rehearsals, near enough for them to stay in contact with the main building, but far enough away so that the music coming through does not disturb the work of the transcriber.

Their collection is immense. The Institute has twelve thousand phonograph rolls with more than thirty-five thousand tunes. They have realised the collecting method desired by Bartók: musician, linguist, dancer, sociologist, even the film-maker participates in collection gathering. Folk music is not collected separately from other manifestations of folk life, but is studied together with the customs pertaining to it.[25]

In January 1950 when Ligeti wrote this, he little realised that the Institute had been founded and much of the archive collected and organised by Constantin Brăiloiu (1893–1958), one of the most important of the ethnomusicologists who had worked closely with Bartók. Like Veress, Brăiloiu had fled to Switzerland in 1948, before settling in France, and his name had been deleted from the records. Emilia Comişel would eventually write and publish Brăiloiu's biography, but not for another thirty-five years.

At the end of December 1949, Ligeti joined a group of ethnomusicologists led by Mircea Chiriac on a two-week expedition to Covásint, near the city of Ared, where they listened to village string players performing elaborate heterophony. The researchers lacked recording apparatus, an impediment to notating such music, but Ligeti was fascinated by its polyphonic and harmonic characteristics, which he analysed in a second article, written first in Romanian and later published in Hungarian in the *Kodály Festschrift Musicological Studies I.*[26] In it he observes how the harmonic clashes arising out of heterophonic divergence (that is, from simultaneous variants of a single melody), as well as from chords changing out of step with their melodies, 'explain some characteristics in Bartók's use of dissonance'. Following the fortnight in Covásint, in January 1950 he moved to the Folklore Institute in Cluj, working under the guidance of János Jagamas. With a few colleagues, they would occasionally take the train for two or three days of 'field research' in different villages. Lacking wax cylinders and there being as yet no tape recorders, they had to transcribe by ear.

For nearly eight months Ligeti and Brigitte could live together, albeit in a tiny room shared with 'hundreds of bugs'. But the time was all too short. In August 1950 when the scholarship expired, Ligeti returned to Budapest. Although now his wife, Brigitte had also become a Romanian national and could not accompany him. Had he considered her more important than his studies, he might have stayed in Cluj. But he was 'egotistical and preferred to go to Budapest'. It took Brigitte a year to obtain papers allowing her to join him.

In Budapest the propagandist cantata had been forgotten, but a task was awaiting which Ligeti did not want. Kodály, who knew Ligeti and was aware of his recent folklore studies, conceived the idea that Ligeti should join the Academy of Sciences to help edit the ongoing publication of the large folk-music collection of Bartók, Kodály and others. Although retired from teaching, Kodály was still supervising this huge project, and invited Ligeti to his house to offer him a paid position. Ligeti was aghast and tried every ploy to extricate himself. 'He was not the right person for the work of transcription, had insufficient patience, was no solfège genius, no "insect-collector". He wanted to compose – and to subsist he needed a post teaching music theory.'[27] Kodály argued that without such meticulous work one could never be a composer, but Ligeti was adamant. In fact, transcription was an onerous responsibility since, after five to eight playings, the wax cylinders became unusable. Working voluntarily at the Museum of Ethnography, Ligeti had already destroyed some recordings and felt, with justification, that he did not have the right temperament. Kodály was displeased but, to his credit, harboured no resentment. Instead he helped Ligeti secure the position as teacher of theory, harmony and counterpoint at the Franz Liszt Academy which he assumed a month later, in September 1950.

The folk music of Romania and Hungary, together with the music of Bartók and what he knew of Stravinsky, provided a natural foundation for Ligeti's own compositions; but both Bartók and Stravinsky were now suspect influences. Fortunately, an entirely different music beckoned, the uncensored domain of Renaissance polyphony, whose central position in the Academy's theory courses was due to Kodály. Kodály was friendly with the Danish musicologist Knud Jeppesen, whose widely admired book on sixteenth-century counterpoint was a required text.[28] Thus the contrapuntal glories of Palestrina and other Renaissance masters, which Ligeti studied and then taught to his own students, became a profound and lasting influence. Later, Ockeghem's mensuration canons provided a model for his own polyrhythmic polyphony, particularly Ockeghem's ability to generate new contrapuntal lines at the moment when others reached their climax.

Although to some extent a 'wonderful island', the Academy was affected by the insecurity and tensions experienced throughout Hungary. It was the worst period of the dictatorship with some ten thousand people in jail and hundreds executed by hanging. Everyone was branded friend or foe. Following his appointment, Ligeti was regarded with deep suspicion by Antal Molnár, who had now become Dean. An implacable anti-Nazi and anti-Communist, Molnár was convinced that so young a tutor, who hadn't even taken his diploma, must be a stooge of the secret police, unaware that Ligeti owed his job to Kodály. At the forthcoming examinations which Molnár attended as Dean, he decided to put Ligeti's competence to the test. Whilst his students played harmony exercises at the keyboard, their teacher's ability to hear remote modulations and correct faulty inner voice-leading (i.e. consecutive fifths, falling leading notes, augmented seconds) was monitored by a panel headed by Molnár. Fortunately, Ligeti's sharp ear enabled him to make correct judgements, and Molnár quickly changed his attitude, becoming a close friend and mentor. His insight into the work of composers engaged in the dissolution of tonality – giants like Schoenberg, Milhaud and Varèse – was unrivalled in Hungary. The following year, after taking exams in Hungarian music history, orchestration and score-reading, Ligeti was awarded his diploma. But it was qualified. He could score-read at the piano but was abysmal at transposition. With his students he was instantly popular, his clarity and wit compensating for a ready application of red pencil to their counterpoint exercises.

As a young tutor, Ligeti admired another older colleague, the conductor and musicologist Lajos Bárdos (1899–1986). Bárdos was a conservative Christian whose circle represented for Ligeti a safe haven. He was a superb theoretician of functional harmony, whose Bach analyses were particularly probing. Ligeti took the unusual step of attending his colleague's lectures, and later acknowledged Bárdos's help and advice in the prefaces to his own two harmony textbooks. From Ferenc Farkas he learnt something different. Frequently in the early 1950s he assisted his composition teacher in the film studios, where Farkas exercised his technical skill with great efficiency. Ligeti timed the sequences, for which Farkas would compose music on the spot, his pupil helping to check and correct the material for the waiting musicians to record at sight. It was a revealing initiation, which convinced Ligeti never to get involved himself as a composer in what, even then, he regarded as artistic 'prostitution'.

An acute dilemma

Meanwhile there were developments in Ligeti's personal affairs. Towards the end of 1951 Brigitte arrived in Budapest to join him, but during the previous twelve months of further separation their love had cooled. The following spring they agreed to divorce. In Budapest Ligeti had established a different life and made new friends. The closest was a young psychologist, Veronika (Vera) Spitz, whose father had been killed in Buchenwald and whose mother worked as a book-keeper for a state company in Budapest.

Although Vera had entered the University of Budapest in 1948 to study psychology, she was obliged to transfer to Hungarian language and literature after the course in psychology was abolished. In Soviet minds psychology 'did not exist', having been replaced by Marxist pedagogy. Vera was fortunate even to be able to complete her degree. In 1951 the Communists formulated a policy of social categorisation which threatened anyone who in person, or whose family, had played a significant role in Hungarian affairs during the pre-war Nationalist dictatorship. State employers, managers and entrepreneurs under the previous regime were now suspect. Beginning in 1951 and accelerating in 1952, the Communists began to deport from Budapest those they considered 'unreliable'. In registers at schools and places of work the population was divided into four categories: workers (the best category), peasants, intellectuals, and those due to be expelled. Panic spread through the city until people discovered the meaning of the categories; then only those in the last category had reason to fear. Friends told Ligeti that they had seen his name in the third category, but Vera, her mother and grandmother listed in the fourth. Before the war Vera's father had managed a large granary mill. Consequently, despite his having been murdered by the Nazis, the family was deemed to be bourgeois. At any moment they would be evicted and sent into the countryside to do forced labour, along with 150,000 others expelled from Budapest. It was 'bureaucratic stupidity', says Ligeti, 'deportation without trial, dependent on your ancestry'. But there was a reason. Since the war, the Communists had prioritised the rebuilding of bridges, essential infrastructure and heavy industry, rather than living accommodation. Nevertheless they wanted apartments for the new elite, many of whom were arriving from the provinces. Hence the requisitions. But, if one member of a threatened family was officially 'needed' in Budapest the whole family could stay. Ligeti asked at the Academy whether he was 'needed' and was told that he was.

The first evictions in 1951 were of families occupying the best flats. By the spring of 1952 Vera knew that their turn was near. Many of their acquaintances had already gone, woken in the early hours and given an hour to pack. 'We could not sleep,' says Ligeti. 'Even today I wake at 4 a.m. – it's ingrained in me.' Driven to a remote country village, the deportees were billeted with resentful and hostile peasants, forbidden to travel, denied telephone or mail, forced into physical work, whether child, adult or aged. Were Ligeti to marry Vera, she and her family would qualify for exemption as his dependants. Pondering this situation, a bizarre sequence of events precipitated a decision.

Ligeti had exhausted his voice through teaching large classes for twenty-four hours a week, and had been advised by his doctor to take a recuperative holiday in the warmer climate beside the Black Sea. Since only collective travel was allowed, the secretary of the Academy asked the Ministry of Education to place Ligeti in a group due to visit the Bulgarian coast. Through an administrative error, however, he found himself in July 1952 joining a party of seventy-five factory workers bound for the Baltic. This might not improve his larynx, he thought, but it was still the sea, which he had never seen; indeed, he had not yet travelled beyond Romania and Hungary. Their route took them through East Berlin, from which performer friends like Márta Kurtág had returned bringing information. Ligeti knew, for instance, that only some passports were checked on the subway trains that ran between all four sectors of the city. The S-bahn was a recognised route for refugees – the Wall had not yet been built – and he began to consider escape. Changing trains in the Berlin suburbs, the party was marshalled by the Stasi secret police, but on the Baltic they were left more to themselves. Ligeti and the three comrades in his dormitory discussed the possibility. They would all 'visit' West Berlin.

Returning through East Berlin, the miners were accommodated for two days in a large hotel, their time split between organised sight-seeing and the 'honour' of contributing half a day's labour to the huge building project of East Berlin's first new boulevard, Stalinallee. Both the Hungarian secret police and the Stasi were exceptionally nice, says Ligeti ('maybe they also hated the regime'), but they shepherded the party everywhere and counted heads meticulously. On the second day, however, whilst dividing the group into two, Ligeti was inexplicably overlooked.

It was 2 o'clock in the afternoon and I was asleep in my room. They had forgotten me! Suddenly there was the possibility of escape. I had a couple of East German marks, enough for a ticket, but no identity . . . nothing. I put on my trousers and went down to the lobby. One of the secret police asked, 'Aren't you going to work?' 'I slept and nobody woke me,' I said, 'What shall I do?' He was pleasant, and told me to 'just sit down'. Then, in a moment when I saw they were occupied, I went out. I knew from the map that there was a subway station very close. I went down, bought a ticket, passed through the ticket control onto the platform and heard the train coming.

Then I began to cry. I couldn't leave Vera and her family to be deported. Without thinking, instinctively I returned . . . shaking and sobbing. It was one of the most traumatic moments in my life, more traumatic than escaping from Hungary to Austria, which was risky. Now came a very dangerous moment, because I wasn't supposed to leave the hotel. How was I going to re-enter? By chance, it was a moment when the secret policeman wasn't looking; he didn't even know that I had gone. My God, what had I done! Then, again, in the railway station, as I put down my luggage, I was beside an entrance to the subway. I could still have disappeared, but I didn't. It was a challenge. Can you understand this state of mind? I knew I had to go back to Budapest for ever. I felt I was responsible, and the logical next step was to marry Vera. The decision was made in Berlin. [29]

Ligeti could not forget the decimation of his own family in the Holocaust. Though it might not end in death, the prospect facing Vera and her family was brutal. Had Ligeti escaped to the West in 1952, he would undoubtedly have gone to England where he had an uncle in Reigate, a mechanical engineer who had previously lived in Hamburg and left Germany only at the last moment before war was declared.

He would immediately have fetched me, so I would be a British citizen today. You and I would never have met, because I would have worked in a printing works in Reigate. With hindsight, I could say that, if I had taken the subway, then surely Vera would have followed me in 1956. But I would never have had the chance to be with the Cologne-Darmstadt people because Britain was very much apart, nor to meet Dr Bruno Karlheinz Jaja[30] [Gerard Hoffnung's wonderfully funny caricature of Darmstadt]. Mr Dadelsen, my student, who is absolutely against the avant-garde (he's a Bob Dylan fanatic), told me that it was a big mistake not to go to Britain. I would have been a part of swinging London!

In far-from-swinging Budapest, on 8 August 1952, Ligeti and Vera were married. It was a marriage entered upon with the understanding that, once the threat of deportation was removed, they would divorce. Following the death of Stalin conditions improved and, in 1954, Ligeti and Vera did divorce. But it was not a complete separation; their friendship continued and Ligeti's feelings towards Vera remained warm. His mother had also now arrived in Budapest, where she continued to live until Ligeti arranged for her to settle in Vienna in 1970.

In 1954 he made another visit to the Romanian capital, travelling via Cluj. He could not understand why before the aircraft left Budapest he had been stripped and searched – a commonplace humiliation – whereas on the flight from Cluj to Bucharest he was afforded deferential treatment and privileges. Only afterwards did he discover that the Hungarian Consulate in Cluj, having run out of the correct forms, had given him a diplomatic passport without telling him.

Professional isolation

In his role as a teacher at the Academy, Ligeti published two textbooks on traditional harmony (in 1954 and 1956), and an article on Bartók's chromaticism (1955). But he was as isolated from new music in the West as he was unable to investigate the work of his immediate predecessors. The music of the Second Viennese School went unplayed and undiscussed; his only acquaintance with it was via a score of Berg's *Lyric Suite* which he had seen in the Academy library. Nor had he any idea about the post-war avant-garde. When the opportunity to learn and branch out eventually arrived, many composers had lost the ability to reinvigorate their work. The few who did included Kurtág and another of Ligeti's friends András Szöllősy. Szöllősy also came from Cluj and was appointed to teach at the Budapest Academy in the same year as Ligeti. He too established his reputation in the 1960s, but remained in Hungary aware that, through reticence and patience, he had escaped the worst of the restrictions that had emasculated his younger colleagues. 'When they should have broken with socialist-realist ideology, not all had the courage and the strength to discard half their life-work and start again from scratch.'[31] Living under a dictatorship sapped one's energy, sowed distrust, stifled discussion and killed originality.

Despite working for the next six years under such severe censorship that his creative development was greatly retarded, Ligeti managed to compose some remarkable pieces. But circumstances dictated that they remained in manuscript and unknown. In the public domain he adopted a similar stance to that of Lutosławski and Panufnik in Poland, legitimising his role as a professional composer through reworking eighteenth-century and folk material. Music of experimental character he wrote solely for himself, to be stowed out of sight in a drawer. It had become inescapably evident that any serious voyage of discovery had to be private. The ambiguities of this double life bore heavily on the composer. In fact, contradictions had confronted him virtually since the day he was born; it is hardly surprising that his music developed a schizophrenic quality.

Ligeti's remaining years in Hungary were marked by a widening divergence between the relatively bland music he wrote for public performance and the radicalism of his secret compositions. The frustrations implicit in this contrary-motion counterpoint, leading to his eventual escape following the Budapest uprising of 1956, provide a backdrop to the music we shall examine in Chapter Two.

2

Night and Morning:
an East European Apprenticeship

[Schumann] created three critics, each one himself, but a
different self . . . Florestan was the personification of poetic
fire and impetuousness, Eusebius of dreamy melancholy,
Raro of reason and system. Three masks equally true to the
person they were masking. The student who ignored one
would fail to understand the man.
  Marcel Brion[1]

Knowledge is not enough; that which I have learned has to
gain strength and certainty by its application to life.
(Florestan)
It is characteristic of the extraordinary that it cannot be
easily understood; the majority is always attuned to the
superficial. (Eusebius)
Let the youth who composes be warned. Prematurely ripened
fruit falls from the tree. The young mind must often unlearn
theory before it can apply it. (Raro)
  Robert Schumann[2]

Just over fifty years before Ligeti entered the Budapest Academy of
Music, one of the great Hungarian musicians of the early twentieth
century, Ernő Dohnányi (1877–1960), had also enrolled there as a
student. Persuaded by Dohnányi to choose Budapest rather than the
more famous conservatory in Vienna, where he had been promised a
scholarship, Bartók (1881–1945), who was four years younger than
Dohnányi, soon took the same path and was joined, a year later, by
Kodály (1882–1967). These three composers graduated from the
Budapest Academy in the first decade of the twentieth century, fired
with creative energy, to exert an unprecedented impact on Hungarian
musical life. The Brahmsian character of the older composer's style
was replaced in the work of Bartók and Kodály by a passionate commitment to folk music, which they nourished by months of field

recording amongst the peasantry, an experience so heady and exciting that it seemed as if only folk music could hold the key to the development of a distinctive national style.

Two decades later, all three composers were invited to contribute to an event of symbolic importance for Hungary. Each was commissioned to write a work to mark the fiftieth anniversary of the union in one city of Buda and Pest. Despite Hungary's tribulations following the First World War, Budapest was a thriving capital, the fastest growing European city of the late nineteenth century, home to the world's second underground railway and its largest parliament building whose ·neo-Gothic extravagance rivalled that of London. Dohnányi's *Festival Overture*, which opened this celebratory concert in November 1923, the year of Ligeti's birth, is now rarely played. But its sequel, Bartók's *Dance Suite*, glistening with the fruits of his forays into folk music, was an instant success and eagerly taken up by orchestras all over the world. Yet it was the final work in the programme, Kodály's large-scale choral and orchestral composition, *Psalmus Hungaricus*, whose premiere had the most profound impact, especially in Hungary, where its noble mixture of folk-derived musical material and national subject matter struck many a heart. Conscious of his success in appealing to a wide audience, Kodály turned away from his earlier attempts at pure instrumental music in favour of a simpler, more direct and popular style, drawn from Hungarian roots, whose preferred medium was choral. His elevation of peasant to art music had its critics, even amongst his own pupils. But Kodály was undeterred. Throughout the years both up to and after the Second World War, his painstaking and methodical dedication to a new concept of musical education, based on a choral method based firmly in the vernacular, won him international admiration. Moreover, it established Hungarian musical education as a model for other countries, especially in the English-speaking world.

After the war, it was in the context of this flourishing, if traumatically interrupted tradition that Ligeti took up further study, not now in Cluj, but in Budapest. The choirs which reconstituted themselves were eager for new repertoire. So it is little surprise that many of his first compositions were choral, madrigalesque in character, simple and unadventurous in manner, even in the comparatively free climate of the immediate post-war years. Certainly, once the Communists gained ascendancy, writing conventional choral music offered one of the few possibilities of performance. Had the political situation been different, had Bartók lived and returned, a more vigorous music might have prevailed. As it was, it was the gentler Kodály, devoted to the development of amateur choral singing, who, having remained in Hungary throughout the war, continued to pursue his educational goals blessed by official endorsement. Dedicated to folk culture, he nonetheless hated aggressive nationalism. Correct and straightforward, he managed to remain 'clean' politically, actively protected the more vulnerable, and was revered as someone untainted by either pro-Nazi or Communist regimes, despite the Communists' attempts to use his status to their advantage.[3]

Early choral compositions

Although he had only a mediocre voice, at the Cluj Conservatory Ligeti had sung in the several small choirs which performed Renaissance, baroque and classical music as well as works by modern Hungarian composers. Many of his early compositions conform to this choral culture, two – as we have seen – being liturgical cantatas on Latin texts. But Ligeti had no inclination towards religion. Mostly he wrote a cappella settings of secular Hungarian poems, following the manner of Kodály and similarly drawing on popular material. So easily did he assimilate folk culture, that one can scarcely distinguish between his 'learned' folk style, like the gently soulful *Magos Kösziklának* (*From a High Mountain Rock*) written in 1946, and original compositions from the same period. *Idegen földön* (*Far from home*) of 1945–46 is an example of the latter. For three-part female chorus, it consists of four short pieces setting verses by the Renaissance poet Bálint Balassa and three folk texts. Ligeti's treatments have the simple, repetitive phrases, rhythmic vigour and narrow compass of folk music. There is a purity about their consonant harmonies and modal cadences far removed from the textural inventiveness of, for instance, Bartók's *Four Hungarian Folksongs* of 1930 – which, in any case, he did not know.[4] The poems are concerned with loss and Ligeti's music is gently nostalgic. Considering what he had experienced and the brutal death of four of his family, its manner is surprisingly restrained. But Ligeti was elated to be in Budapest. The war-ravished city was full of wonderful musicians and concerts. It seemed to him that 'life was bearable . . . everybody lived the same way. Although we all grieved for our vanished families and friends, there was a euphoric hope for a better future.'⁵

Idegen földön had no performance at this time, nor for a further twenty-five years, until taken up by Eric Ericson and the Swedish Chamber Choir in April 1971. Some of Ligeti's choral pieces of the late 1940s and early 1950s were performed in Hungary and also published, either in Cluj or Budapest, but others remained unheard until long after he had emigrated and choral directors in the West rediscovered them – those, that is, which survived.

Friendship with Sándor Weöres

Between 1945 and 1947 the artistic climate in Hungary remained free, but it was relatively isolated. Telephoning abroad from anywhere in Hungary was difficult and expensive, whilst the lack of money and passports put international travel beyond the reach of most people. By the time living standards, trade and mobility revived, for those behind the Iron Curtain it was too late. Stimuli had to be sought from within. *Magány* (*Solitude*), which Ligeti also composed in November 1946, shows how he might more rapidly have developed a personal style had conditions allowed. Inward and dreamlike, its dissonant chromaticism is bolder than in his other choral music of the time, due perhaps to its text by Sándor Weöres (1913–90). This great poet inspired Ligeti to attempt other more experimental settings, notably the *Three Weöres Songs* of 1946–47 and *Éjszaka* (*Night*) and *Reggel* (*Morning*) of 1955 for unaccompanied chorus. Amongst Hungarian intellectuals Weöres's inventive imagination and breadth were much admired; both Kodály and Farkas, Ligeti's first composition teacher, also set his poetry.

Soon after composing the *Three Weöres Songs*, Ligeti was introduced to Weöres by Farkas. Ligeti played his settings to the poet and, although considerably in awe of him, they became friends, despite quarrelling about Mozart whom Ligeti worshipped and Weöres despised. On one occasion, having drunk too much, their disagreement erupted into a minor street brawl, Ligeti – physically the stronger – coming off best and then feeling thoroughly ashamed. He admired Weöres's intellectual and moral stature; and learnt, if not from the poet's scornful dismissal of classical mores, then from his corresponding passion, equal but opposite, for things non-European. Weöres was immersed in the Orient, translated Indian, Byzantine and ancient

Chinese poetry and loved Balinese and Asian culture. In 1937 he had visited Manila, India and Vietnam, and the experience gave his poetry a self-abnegatory mysticism. His surreal metamorphoses of commonplace experience and playful reinvention of language appealed to Ligeti as much as the poetry's intrinsic musicality.

Magány was performed in 1946 by students of the Kollégium Bartók.[6] Ligeti, who sang in the performance, was invited to stay on in the college as a resident, but declined, preferring to retain his independence. Its madrigalesque style stems from his choral diet in Cluj, but its harmonic false relations are refreshingly uninhibited. Their piquancy dominates the triadic middle section as well as the reflective opening bars and the extended pedal points that conclude each of the outer sections. During the first of these closes, E flat and natural are repeatedly pitted against each other above a pedal G sustained for thirteen bars. The closing section is especially beautiful. The sustained C, underpinning its final cadence, is a sequel to the G of the first, sounding tonic and final until the basses unexpectedly descend further to A flat, above which the upper voices continue to hold their D and C unresolved. Thus both outer sections end enigmatically on unresolved discords. On 21 May 1948, *Magány* was sung again at the Hungarian Radio and broadcast the following month – just in time. By the end of the year, its harmony would have fallen foul of the Communist censors, making performance impossible.

Although indebted to Bartók, the *Three Weöres Songs* are more accomplished than anything Ligeti had previously composed. Originally there were to be more songs – indeed, he had in mind a series of Weöres settings. The manuscripts were lost when Ligeti escaped from Hungary in 1956, and they remained largely forgotten for years. In 1986, amongst Ligeti's personal papers, Friedemann Sallis found a draft for 'Gyümölcs-fürt, ingatja a szél' (A cluster of fruit, swayed by the wind) and was able to reconstruct a fair copy.[7] Two others he discovered written out complete in the composer's sketchbooks. On each Weöres's exoticism has left its mark. The accompaniment to 'Kalmár jött nagy madarakkal' (A merchant has come with giant birds) is driven forward by a clangorous mixture of octaves and semitones. Its left-hand ostinato rises and falls within minimal intervals, and the declamatory vocal line has a primitive directness. In the second song, 'Táncol a Hold fehér ingben' (The moon is dancing in a white skirt), alternating patterns speed by to depict the clock ticking and the moon disporting herself, whilst the bitonal relationship between melody and left-hand clusters conveys the eerie nocturnal light. During its forty-four bars, the piano part crosses six octaves. Then comes Sallis's reconstruction of 'Gyümölcs-fürt, ingatja a szél', conceived in simple heterophony. In this song, the pentatonic melody is doubled by the piano in stark octaves, but which are frequently deflected to become sevenths or ninths, all three lines embellished with ornaments. Ligeti's retrospective assessment is that this song is 'kitsch', a 'faked' oriental style written when he knew nothing about Indonesian music, other than what Weöres's quasi-Pacific folk poetry suggested to him: 'not very good music', he concludes.[8] But it is evocative, and interestingly prophetic of the haunting second piece in *Musica ricercata*, begun five years later. To create illusory worlds was similarly a part of Ligeti's character. The pseudo-gamelan style of *Galamb borong*, the seventh of the piano Études, shows how durable the dream has been. In fact, none of the Weöres songs needs an apology. They are tiny gems, compressed and aphoristic, illuminated by the first genuine glimpses of an individual style.

A polyphonic mobile

Amongst other compositions from the early 1940s are some short pieces for piano duet written when Ligeti was still a student in Cluj. One is an inconsequential, tiny Allegro, another a bushy-tailed 'Funny March' (*Tréfás induló*) of 1942, sounding as if it had stepped out of Prokofiev's *The Love of Three Oranges* – not that Ligeti had heard the opera. The most interesting is a *Polyphonic Study*, written in 1943 when he was twenty and had been studying privately for a year with Pál Kadosa. It is an intriguing curiosity. The music is governed by a single premise, the idea of superimposing four folk-derived melodies according to a simple durational formula in which they repeat at different rates, circling each other like a Calder mobile. Each of the four hands contributes its own melody, differing in length, choice of pitches and tonality. Throughout the forty-nine bars of the piece each of the four melodies is recycled several times without variation.

At the start they enter successively, beginning with the second pianist's left hand, whose melody is twenty-four beats long, after which the right hand enters with a melody of twenty beats. The first pianist follows with a left-hand melody of sixteen beats and a right-

Ex. 4 Part of the *Polyphonic Study* (1943)

hand melody of eight beats plus four beats' rest. The lowest melody employs six pitches in C major, the tenor a five-note pentatonic scale on F sharp, the alto six pitches in E major, the soprano a pentatonic scale on B flat. Because it is the shortest, the soprano melody (though entering last) is heard most often, eleven times compared with the eight statements of the bass. Finally, on the last beat of the last bar, each hand plays a chord – E and B flat majors (a tritone apart) from player one, C and F sharp majors (also a tritone apart) from player two – telescoping the four tonalities that have coexisted all along. Subsequently, Ligeti realised that, 'in its naive insistence'[9] his *Polyphonic Study* resembles the first of Stravinsky's *Three Pieces for String Quartet*. But the idea came to him from reading a paper on polytonality published by Darius Milhaud.[10] It is early evidence of Ligeti's exploratory bent and propensity for devising automatic mechanisms.

Caprices and inventions

Sándor Veress, Ligeti's composition teacher at the Franz Liszt Academy, had learnt the piano with Bartók and composition with Kodály. Although a man of 'total integrity' whom Ligeti greatly admired, he was a less skilled teacher than Farkas. Veress taught formal analysis and Palestrinian counterpoint, but appeared to know little more about its rules than his pupils, for whom Knud Jeppesen's famous textbook was the approved guide. Three of Ligeti's sketchbooks from this period are inscribed 'Jeppesen 1, 2 and 3'. He also pursued his own investigations, into the string quartets of Haydn, for example, on whose development techniques he wrote an unpublished paper; indeed, throughout his life Ligeti has turned to original models, as recently as the Violin Concerto studying solo violin literature by way of preparation – from Bach to Paganini, Ysaÿe and Szymanowski.

Keyboard pieces featured regularly in Ligeti's assignments, being, in Veress's view, an ideal medium for practising sonata and rondo forms, inventions and fugues. Ligeti's sketchbooks from 1945 onwards are full of such exercises, imitations of Bach and Handel, Couperin and Scarlatti, Mozart and Haydn, Beethoven and Schumann – none of them however containing any corrections or comments. In Cluj Ligeti played them to his mother, who would say whether they seemed stylistically convincing. Veress was also keen for his pupils to develop their own voices. In response Ligeti wrote *Capriccio I and II* (1947) and an *Invention* (1948), their mixture of Bachian and a more personal style being suggested by his teacher. Apart from Bartók the influence of Hindemith is evident, whose Second Piano Sonata Ligeti had chosen to perform for his piano examination. But the pieces go beyond mere exercises. Their structures grow effortlessly out of the material; the balance between contrapuntal dexterity and expressive nuance is skilful and satisfying. In these three compositions written a year or so after the Weöres songs, there are far surer signs of Ligeti's mature style. Even the description 'capricious' is significant. It would reappear in his next major piano composition, *Musica ricercata*, as well as in the Cello Sonata and String Quartet no. 1 – although we also should note its use by Bartók, for instance in the 'Allegro molto Capriccioso' movement of his String Quartet no. 2. Ligeti's compression of the sinuous opening of *Capriccio I* into a terse middle section becomes in his later music a favourite means of throwing placid textures askew. In *Capriccio II* the interplay between duple and compound metre, and hemiolic asymmetry in the left hand, are technical devices he would use in *Désordre*. *Invention* too contains premonitions. The fan-shaped chromatic expansion of its opening motif, answered by its opposite (a semitonal contraction), anticipates one of Ligeti's most habitual fingerprints: clusters which expand and contract, wedge-like, by semitones.

Ligeti dedicated *Capriccio I* and *Invention* to Márta and György Kurtág, who gave their first performance in Budapest on 22 May 1948. Much later, when the three pieces were published by Schott, he sandwiched *Invention* between the two *Capriccios* and reversed their order; although *Capriccio II* was composed first it is the most spirited and makes the best finale. This was an auspicious month for Ligeti, a deceptive spring of optimism before the onset of the long Communist winter whose censorious grip would eliminate such opportunities for the next eight years. The day before Kurtág played the piano pieces *Magány* was performed at Hungarian Radio.[11] Three days after, on 25 May, the Weöres songs received their first and only Budapest performance. The soprano, with Ligeti himself at the piano, was Edit Gáncs, who later became a member of Cologne Opera and sang in the premiere of Zimmermann's *Soldaten*. The long delay before any of these pieces were heard again (forty years before they began to be published) can only be excused by the understandable ignorance of musicologists as well as performers about Ligeti's Hungarian compositions, which the composer's neglect of them after he arrived in the West did little to dispel. He would refer to them laughingly as 'prehistoric Ligeti'. This lack of interest had its justification. The impact of his dramatic entrance, centre stage, into the theatre of the Western avant-garde in 1959–60, and an intense dedication to the new and exciting international career which this success opened up, took all his energy. The music he had left behind seemed of little importance, its gradual rehabilitation incidental to more urgent concerns. Once they reappeared, *Capriccio I and II* and *Invention* proved to be elegantly accomplished compositions well able to hold their own.

The Youth Cantata

Ligeti's graduation compositions from the Budapest Academy are a different matter. Given their public exposure, the alarming political situation and the danger of courting disapproval, it is hardly surprising that they are so uncharacteristic of his later development, so cautious and unsure stylistically. The most substantial is the *Cantata for a Youth Festival* mentioned in Chapter One. With its three movements scored for four vocal soloists, chorus and orchestra, it is the largest work Ligeti completed in Hungary. The left-wing idealism with which he embraced its anti-imperialist text was naive but genuine: 'I really believed colonial people had to be liberated. Today I'm not so sure.' Neither Ligeti nor Farkas, who encouraged his pupil to have the cantata performed at the 1949 International Youth Festival, had any idea the event would be stage-managed by the Communists. In fact, the cantata was well suited to the occasion. Mildly derivative of Britten and Kodály but completely diatonic, its imitative choral writing is reminiscent of Handel's popular style as exemplified in the *Dettingen Te Deum*.

The music is a curious mixture of youthful exuberance, contrapuntal academicism, affecting melody (in the second movement) and one brief hint of Ligeti's later cluster technique. The first and last movements begin in the same way, with upward flourishes in C major from the orchestra and declamatory responses from the chorus. Halfway through the first movement, Ligeti begins a pastiche fugue whose technical working out he viewed with some pride: 'I was very good at counterpoint,' he has remarked.[12] At the equivalent point in the last movement, this is replaced with an accompanied recitative for tenor and bass soloists, followed by the most interesting section of the work, an embryonic cluster, starting in the basses, then adding the altos, tenors and sopranos, like the beginning of *Éjszaka* (*Night*) and in very similar rhythm. Notwithstanding its routine style, much of the cantata is effectively direct and could be fun for a young chorus to sing. But, as a whole, it betrays its immaturity and there are passages where Kuczka's text has led Ligeti to write with embarrassing banality.

By the time he had completed its composition, the Communists had the country in their grip. With growing horror he began to hate the proletarian text and to despise himself for setting it. His anxiety and inability to prevent the performance made him ill. Rehearsals were organised in Tata, a small town not far from Budapest; but the premiere took place in the sumptuously gilded auditorium of the Budapest Opera, on 8 August 1949, given by the choir and orchestra of the Franz Liszt Academy conducted by Károly Melles. The following day the cantata was repeated at the City Theatre. In a letter written to Ove Nordwall in August 1965,[13] Ligeti describes how his Handelian fugue was criticised by Communist officials for its 'clerical reactionism' – for which reason even Bach's cantatas and Handel's oratorios were now banned. Ironically, he also found himself accused of 'formalistic modernism'. In the Opera House the chorus of around two hundred and fifty occupied the stage and the orchestra the pit. Unable to hear each other, when Melles began the third movement the orchestra entered a beat behind the chorus, and the result was cacophonous: 'more like Stravinsky than Handel'. The next day at the City Theatre everything went well – but only just. This time Melles forgot to bring the score of the last movement and had to conduct it from a summary of the time-changes hastily written out by Ligeti on the back of his student tram pass. At the last minute, noting the absence of a percussionist, Ligeti himself climbed over the rail into the pit to play the cymbals.

Although the festival left a depressing aftertaste, it provided some valuable new experiences. Apart from the inevitable left-wing youth groups invited from Western countries, there was a variety of Asian art including a 'wonderful performance' of Beijing Opera. Ligeti's interest in oriental music owes much to the impression this made. Immediately afterwards he began composing some 'pseudo-Chinese' incidental music for seven singers, flute, violin, piano and percussion, to accompany a production of Chinese folk tales called *Tavaszi virág* (*Spring Flower*) and staged by the National Marionette Theatre six weeks later. The manuscript is titled in elegant Chinese characters; but they were only decoration. Ligeti found them in a Chinese book and had no idea what they meant. That the autograph was also a working theatrical score is indicated by numerous alterations and scribbled directions relating the thirty-three short musical numbers to the scenario.

His final graduation piece was performed the following year on 4 September 1950, an *Andante and Allegretto* for string quartet which, some forty-five years later, has been published and recorded. This, too, is predominantly consonant, although its diatonicism is coloured by abrupt sidesteps into other keys. For a composer of twenty-seven it is disappointingly tepid and inconsequential. The modal linearity of the Andante eschews polarity or any hint of dialectic. It could scarcely be less characteristic of Ligeti's subsequent career, whilst the Allegretto second movement (to which he again adds the direction 'poco capriccioso') is strangely bland and reticent. If Ligeti felt that, for his graduation, he needed to demonstrate an individual voice, it seems that the conviction with which he had embarked on the *Youth Cantata* two years earlier had entirely ebbed away.

His music in folk idiom was at least unambiguous and could adopt the virile if predictable spirit of the genre. This was the formula for his longest work so far, *Bölcsötöl a sirig* (*From Cradle to Grave*), a cycle of Hungarian folk songs and dances in nineteen movements for soprano, bass, oboe, clarinet and string quartet, written in the autumn of 1948 and lasting some twenty-five minutes. Instrumental and vocal movements are interspersed, the soprano and bass alternating, nowhere singing together. The music is lightly scored, modal and innocent, with just a few moments of chromatic coloration. One such modulatory passage, for string quartet alone, shows that the romantic disposition evident in the *Little Piano Pieces* of 1939–41 had not disappeared (see Ex. 5). A performance of *Bölcsötöl a sirig* was broadcast by Hungarian Radio on 22 February 1949, apparently the work's only airing. In similar vein are a *Ballad and Dance* for two violins composed in 1950, which he subsequently orchestrated to become the first and second movements of his *Romanian Concerto*.

Orchestral and instrumental works

Ligeti continued to write a cappella choral pieces to satisfy the authorities, but he was becoming more interested in instrumental music. Before leaving Hungary, he completed three sets of *Duos* – for violin

Ex. 5 An instrumental interlude from *Bölcsötöl a sirig* (1948)

and cello, violin and piano, and for two violins – none of which he deems worthy of revival, a set of *Old Hungarian Ballroom Dances* arranged for flute, clarinet and string orchestra, the Sonata for Solo Cello, the *Romanian Concerto*, some occasional orchestral works (now lost), the *Six Bagatelles for Wind Quintet* and the String Quartet no. 1 *Métamorphoses nocturnes* – the most important and impressive of his works from behind the Iron Curtain, composed in 1953–54, when he had just turned thirty.

Of the two surviving orchestral scores, one tells us nothing about Ligeti's creative development, the other quite a lot. For *Old Hungarian Ballroom Dances* he adapted existing melodies by eighteenth- and nineteenth-century composers. Simultaneously and for the same reason Andrzej Panufnik was attempting to mollify the censors in Poland with his *Old Polish Suite* (1950) and *Concerto in modo antico* (1951). Premiered by the Radio Orchestra in February 1950, *Old Hungarian Ballroom Dances* was the work which most usefully earned Ligeti royalties (if relatively little) and contributed to his early reputation. But it was a reputation wholly misleading, since, as he remarks, 'I became famous for writing a piece which was not my composition.' During 1951 alone, as noted in his work list, the *Dances* were performed on twenty-one occasions.

Although in folk style, the *Romanian Concerto* is actually original. Completed in June 1951 and scored for double woodwind, horns, trumpets, percussion and strings, it had been intended for an army orchestra to play. But only the orchestra of Hungarian Radio sightread it in the studio and, rejected by the censors, it was never broadcast. Subsequently the score was lost. In the 1960s Editio Musica Budapest reconstructed this from the orchestral parts and without Ligeti's knowledge, a performance took place in Evanston, Illinois. Full of mistakes, the material was eventually purchased by Schott and Ligeti was able to correct it.

Fifty years after its composition the *Romanian Concerto* has finally been recorded by the Berlin Philharmonic under Jonathan Nott as part of Teldec's 'Ligeti Project'.[14] Its zesty folk energies at last unveiled, the work could become popular with orchestras looking for 'safe' but entertaining mid-twentieth-century repertoire. Ligeti still retains his affection for the music. It was his 'last compromise', he says, 'but quite surprising – good and bad at the same time!' There is little indication of this in the first two movements, adapted from the earlier *Ballad and Dance*, which are firmly in the mould of Kodály and Bartók (the *Romanian Dances* and *Dance Suite* come to mind). The third movement is similarly routine, although it hints at a wider exoticism with its use of 'untempered' horn harmonics (presaging the *Hamburg Concerto*), its bolder dissonance and wispy ending. But the finale is another matter. Eccentrically exuberant, it exudes the high-spirited and kitschy cheekiness which Ligeti so evidently enjoys: a sort of Keystone Kops meets Beijing Opera on the plains of Transylvania. This movement has some inspired orchestration, but mainly Ligeti's scoring is competent rather than exceptional. It would be two years or so before he came to know Rimsky-Korsakov's famous treatise on orchestration. Meanwhile he relied on his observations as a concertgoer, what he learned from classical scores, and his experience of orchestral texture from the inside whilst playing timpani as a student.

The *Romanian Concerto* was one of several works composed at the old Rákoczy Castle at Sárospatak in north-east Hungary, close to the

Czech (now Slovak) border. The castle itself had been half destroyed by Napoleon, but the fine Renaissance buildings nearby had been designated for short-term use by writers, composers and artists. Mrs Magda Szávai, the well-disposed secretary of the Composers' Union – to which it was obligatory to belong – arranged for Ligeti to stay for periods of two or three weeks. Although a Party member, 'she was an angel, who hated the regime, and did favours for people rejected by the officials'. The only cost was the train fare. It was quiet, nobody interfered with what you wrote, and it was warm. The apartment in which he lived in Budapest had no heat. Around 1950 the fire department demolished its chimney on the grounds that it was dangerous, and since only factory chimneys were being built, it could not be replaced. When the coal-fired boiler was relit, fumes and smoke seeped into the rooms and further use of the central heating was forbidden. Belonging to the Union brought further advantages, especially in 1956 when it gave access to otherwise censored material. At the Union he could play Stravinsky on the gramophone and see Czech and Polish experimental films screened for members.

The Cello Sonata banned

Ligeti's Sonata for Solo Cello is an impressive and eloquent piece, ill deserving the oblivion into which it was cast at the time of composition, remaining virtually unknown and unperformed for twenty-five years. Stylistically, however, it still draws on earlier twentieth-century Hungarian characteristics, and it is hard to comprehend how music so melodic and warm-hearted can have been denied performance.

The Sonata's first movement was originally conceived in 1948 as a single short piece, a gift to a fellow student, a cellist named Annus Virány with whom the composer was secretly in love. Alas, she neither understood the reason for the gift, nor did she play the piece. Five years later Ligeti met another more celebrated cellist, Vera Dénes, who asked him for a composition. To the existing Adagio he therefore added a more demanding sonata-form Presto, another 'Capriccio' in fact, although this time the description alludes to Paganini's violin caprices, whose mercurial brilliance Ligeti had encountered as a child. Despite their different styles, the two movements well complement each other. The first, called 'Dialogo', depicts a conversation between a man and a woman in which the four strings of the cello are employed successively to suggest individual voices. Its tempo is a fluid rubato, bar lines marking only the division between phrases, there being no regular metre. The 'Capriccio', on the other hand, maintains a vigorous 3/8, interrupted only once by a brief recollection of the first movement. Although of more modest proportions, this movement echoes the sonorous sweep of the final movement of Kodály's sonata; Ligeti similarly employs double stops and contrasting registers in rapid alternation to good effect.

From 1949, the newly established Composers' Union was required to vet all new scores and reject any which showed traces of bourgeois or modernist tendencies. The most influential assessor on its committee was the composer Ferenc Szabó, an implacably severe Communist who had spent the war years in Moscow. Being in the privileged position of a very young conservatory teacher, Ligeti was obliged to submit compositions to the committee or else lose his job. Everything from orchestral to small a cappella choral pieces had to be presented for scrutiny, some failing to gain approval for the flimsiest of reasons. One was vetoed simply because it contained a musical joke, another because it ended with a minor-second interval between mezzo-soprano and tenor.[15] The artistic climate in which a young composer was to cultivate his talents could scarcely have been more discouraging. Technical experiments, or music that came deeply from the heart, had to be kept out of sight. Ligeti later recalled the fate of the Cello Sonata:

Before the piece could be performed or I could be paid even a small commission, the sonata had to be passed by the Composers' Union, in this case one man who, it turns out, was a member of the secret police. I needed the money because I only had a small job at the Music Academy and was a freelance composer. Had I been expelled from the Union I would have been sent to work in a factory and dismissed from the Academy. Vera Dénes learned the sonata and played it for the committee. We were denied permission to publish the work or to perform it in public, but we were allowed to record it for radio broadcast. She made an excellent recording for Hungarian Radio, but it was never broadcast [I believe]. The committee decided that it was too 'modern' because of the second movement . . .[16]

The Sonata had to wait a quarter of a century before it received its first public performance, played by Rohan de Saram during the English Bach Festival in London in May 1979. As Ligeti realised the full implications of Soviet domination, his earlier idealism gave way to deepening despair.

In 1948 he had written another set of keyboard pieces, *Eight Little Marches*, one of which he orchestrated the following year. These and many other compositions from the late 1940s and early 1950s have been lost, amongst them a piece for small orchestra in pentatonic style called *Chinese Imperial Court Music*. Completed in September 1950 at Sárospatak, it was a reworking of the puppet theatre music composed a year earlier, which he believes to have been 'absolutely interesting'. Surviving from 1950 are a Sonatina and *Three Wedding Dances*, both for piano duet. The *Dances* Ligeti arranged from some recently completed settings for female voices and piano of Hungarian folksongs, one of them collected by Bartók. Both the vocal and piano-duet versions were broadcast by Hungarian Radio and the first of the piano-duet arrangements was included in a collection published in Budapest in 1952.

Although lively enough, the Sonatina is perfunctory, suggesting a composer unsure of himself, no longer convinced by either Bartókian routines or folk style. But we should not dismiss it. Not averse to rearranging pieces, Ligeti adapted its final movement from a solo piano set called *Ronggyszönyeg* (*Rag Carpet*) whose title is symbolic. *Ronggyszönyeg* is also the title of two cycles of aphoristic poems published by Sándor Weöres in 1941 and 1945. In them Weöres stripped away all the inessentials of his style in order to rebuild it from scratch according to the most rigorous discipline, exactly what Ligeti himself was about to do. He would rework the first two movements of the Sonatina for his own purgative self-examination, *Musica ricercata* for solo piano – and with surprising results. From the first of the piano duets, rather than expand his original, he removed all of the modulatory structure and much of the tonal coloration that had given it zest. Why this sudden austerity? We shall discover in a moment.

Wiping the slate clean

Following the example of Weöres, in *Musica ricercata* Ligeti strips down his own style to its primary ingredients. Surprisingly, this results in his first significant composition to merit a place in the regular concert repertoire. Around 1950 he had grown increasingly dissatisfied with the Bartókian idiom and decided to investigate the possibilities of treating sonic material as an intrinsically pliable organism, both textural and abstract.

It was then that I first conceived the idea of a static, self-contained music without either development or traditional rhythmic configurations. These ideas were vague at first, and at that time I lacked the courage and the compositional and technical abilities to put them into practice. Although traditional modes of thought appeared questionable, I still clung to regular, metrical groupings. In 1951 I began to experiment with very simple structures of sonorities and rhythms as if to build up a new kind of music starting from nothing. My approach was frankly Cartesian, in that I regarded all the music I knew and loved as being, for my purpose, irrelevant and even invalid. I set myself such problems as: what can I do with a single note? with its octave? with an interval? with two intervals? What can I do with specific rhythmic interrelationships which could serve as the basic elements in a formation of rhythms and intervals? Several small pieces resulted, mostly for piano.

Certain features of these problems and their solutions have something in common with the principles of serial composition. This is surprising, as I had approached them from totally different premises and a totally different route. At the time, I hadn't the faintest idea of the developments which led up to serial music and which were then evolving in Western Europe. I was even totally oblivious of Schoenberg's method of composition with twelve notes, not to mention Webern's procedures. My supposed self-liberation was, of course, doomed to partial frustration by the isolation in which I was working, for the worthy Bartókian idiom still came through, even though it was less marked than in my earlier music. So my works of that period strike me as being thoroughly heterogeneous in style, naive in their absence of orientation, inadequate and half-baked as solutions.[17]

Musica ricercata is the first fruit of this approach, although it took Ligeti two years to complete its eleven movements. Composed between 1951 and 1953 for a secretive 'bottom drawer', free from any necessity to please, his aim was to derive, concisely yet ingeniously, the maximum result from the minimum material. How well can one subsist on almost nothing? The first movement provides an answer. Lasting four pages, it is composed entirely of one note (A) plus its octave transpositions, until a 'resolution' on to D in the last four bars. Despite this limitation, Ligeti creates an exhilarating piece built on the thrust and counter-thrust between two motifs in the right hand and a quaver continuum in the left. It has even a motivic dialectic. Indeed, the fascination of *Musica ricercata*, as its title implies, is that all eleven pieces search for meaningful invention within the confines of the tautest discipline.

By resolving on to D, the first piece finally employs two pitch classes. The next has three, the third four, the next five etc., so that each piece contains one more pitch class than the last. In the eleventh and final piece we hear all twelve semitones, the conclusion being a dignified chromatic fugue whose theme fans out in ascending and descending semitones until it spans a major seventh, not unlike his earlier *Invention*. That is why the third piece – his reworking of the first movement of the Sonatina – is now shorn of modulation. In the scheme of *Musica ricercata* it is allowed only four pitch classes – C, E, G and E flat. But to compensate, Ligeti also reconstructs the other parameters. Drastically rationed in pitch content, his new version is rhythmically more pointed and incisive.

The eleven movements contain a wide variety of character. Two are again marked 'capriccioso'. The second of them (no. 10), composed with all but one of the available pitch classes, is a brilliant vivace full of clashing semitones. Sporting indications like 'burlesco, precipitando, feroce, insistent, spiteful', and 'as if mad', it points to Ligeti's gestural manner of the following decade. The three slowest movements (Nos 2, 5 and 9) are marked either 'mesto' or 'lamentoso', and have what he calls a 'Hungarian diction'. No. 9 is an impassioned memorial to Bartók, beginning with an evocation of low, mourning bells after which reversed dotted rhythms predominate – doubly dotted at the climax – to whose two stringendo passages Ligeti adds the direction 'as if panicking'. The other two slow movements start out as cantabile melodies, in which lie seeds destined to germinate thirty years later. Each has three phrases, the third being double the length of the previous two: i.e. 5 + 5 + 10 crotchets in no. 2, and 6 + 6 + 12 crotchets in no. 5. That this is a basic strophic formula common to folk music and to poetry in many languages does not reduce its significance as a source-component of Ligeti's later *lamento* motif, as we shall see in Chapter Thirteen.

In keeping with his compositional scheme, the haunting melody of the second movement uses only two pitches a semitone apart (E sharp and F sharp), a third note being withheld until halfway through. The entrance of this G in bar 19 is strikingly dramatic, as it accelerates into an outburst of violent reiterations above the stately lament of the melody. Years later, Stanley Kubrick used this movement, or part of it, four times on the soundtrack of his final film, *Eyes Wide Shut*, to accompany the scenes which are most disturbing. Interviewed for a

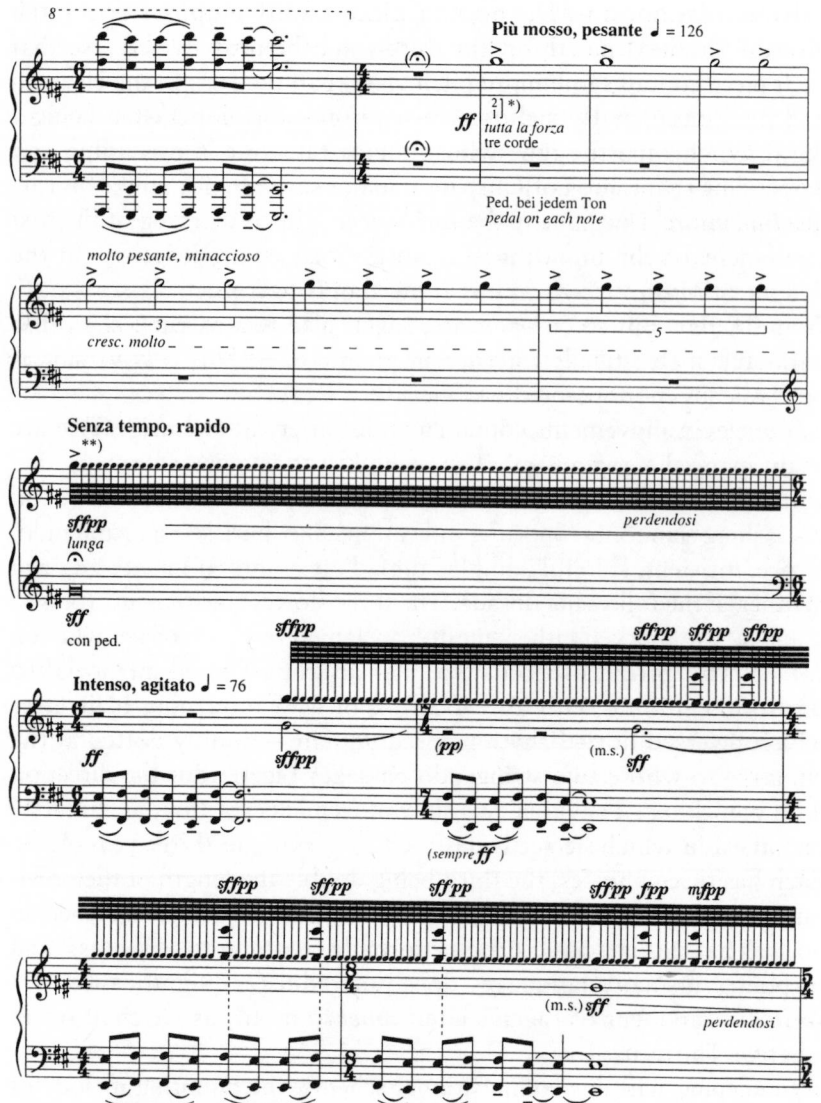

*) Mit beiden Fingern zugleich anschlagen / *play note with both fingers at once.*
**) Tonrepetition so dicht wie möglich / *repetition of tones as dense as possible.*

Ex. 6 Entrance of the third pitch in *Musica ricercata* No. 2 (1951–53)

© 1995 Schott Musik International, Mainz

posthumous documentary about Kubrick issued with a video collection of the films, Ligeti revealed that, as he composed the piece, the reiterated Gs had symbolised for him 'a knife through Stalin's heart'.[18]

Interspersed with the slow movements are pieces of delightful vivacity. No. 3 is the rewritten first movement of the Sonatina, now confined to arpeggios of C minor/major. None the worse for that, its fleeting wit reminds one of Prokofiev. No. 4 is a graceful waltz played 'with rubati, ritenuti, accelerandi, just as an organ grinder would play his barrel organ'. No. 7 is also fast, although its prototype in the Sonatina was a staid, chordal Andante. The new version is a gentle folk-style melody in B flat major (a hybrid of Serbian and Romanian idioms), soon shadowed canonically by a version of itself in E flat. The counterpoint flowers into three parts above an unsynchronised pentatonic ostinato – a much more inventive treatment than before.

Homage to Frescobaldi

The final piece refers directly to the seventeenth-century *ricercar* evoked by Ligeti's title. Its model is a 'Ricercar cromatico' from Girolamo Frescobaldi's *Messa degli Apostoli*, published in *Fiori Musical* of 1635 – hence the additional subtitle 'Omaggio a Girolamo Frescobaldi'. Like the Frescobaldi, Ligeti's first version was composed for organ. A colleague at the Academy, Sándor Margittay, had asked him for a composition and Ligeti responded by reworking Frescobaldi as an exercise in parody. But the connection goes deeper. In his *Introduction to the Early Works of György Ligeti*, Friedemann Sallis draws attention to an analogous stylistic renovation in both Weöres and Frescobaldi, for whom the word 'ricercar' implied a technical exploration. 'Oblighi' composition, as practised by Frescobaldi and his contemporaries and defined by the theorist Ludovico Zacconi (1555–1627), involved an 'obligation' to observe certain restrictions as a challenge to ingenuity. Thus Frescobaldi, in the eighth *Ricercar* in *Il primo libri di capricci* (1626), sets himself the task 'obligo di non uscir mai di grado' (never to use conjunct motion). With his schooling in Renaissance music and his study of the organ, Ligeti must have known of this practice; and, if it stimulated similar tasks in *Musica ricercata*, it probably also influenced his self-imposed 'rules' in the Requiem. Interestingly, both Frescobaldi and Ligeti use the term 'caprice'.

But the homage to Frescobaldi looks forward as well as back. Its subject and countersubject are twelve-note themes (although the countersubject is merely a chromatic scale). Ligeti arrived at this quasi-dodecaphonic writing on his own, rather than through an intimate knowledge of the twelve-note system established by Schoenberg. He had read about it, but little more. He even possessed a copy of René Leibowitz's famous post-war study, *Introduction à la musique de douze sons* (Paris 1949) which Vera had procured from friends in Vienna, smuggled in by a travelling chemistry salesman. But he had scarcely opened it, and it was buried somewhere in a 'chaotic' corner of his room. In fact, the 'Omaggio a Girolamo Frescobaldi' is not serially structured. Thematically it recalls Bach's 'Wedge' fugue and his (virtually) twelve-note B minor fugue subject in the first book of *The Well-Tempered Clavier*. Its fan-like expansion, already anticipated in Ligeti's *Invention* for piano, would figure extensively in his music after 1960 where it functions as an expanding cluster or a chromatic reservoir – rather than a row. A comparable fan-shaped row serves Nono in *Il canto sospeso*. In 'Omaggio' the row or subject enters twelve times at three-bar intervals, governed by the circle of fifths like the entries of the 'Kyrie' in the Requiem. Thereafter Ligeti develops it using stretto, augmentation and diminution. Near the end he presents the subject doubled at the fourth, similar to the chordal enhancement applied to the *lamento* melody in the sixth piano Étude, *Automne à Varsovie*. Another pre-echo of the Études is the sinking semitonal descent of the countersubject, which reappears speeded up as an unsettling subsidence in the ninth Étude, *Vertige*.

These are interesting premonitions. But on its own account *Musica ricercata* is a fine composition, as effective in any professional recital as it is a rewarding technical and intellectual study for students. Its clarity of purpose is matched by expressive contrasts and an accumulative structure of considerable power. There are transparent dances, sorrowful lamentation, grandiose bravura, the dignified homage to Frescobaldi. The listener can appreciate Ligeti's self-imposed restrictions in the context of the whole, and follow their gradual relaxation from rigid exclusivity into lyrical freedom – a progression from austerity to passion, reined in by the noble counterpoint of the final fugue.

Yet it is not difficult to see why Ligeti put the piano pieces behind him when he joined the Western avant-garde in 1957. Although *Musica ricercata* anticipates his original approach to sonority of the

1960s, its artisan craftsmanship would have seemed embarrassingly gauche amid the iconoclastic novelties and intolerant attitudes of his new associates. A performance at Darmstadt would have been inconceivable! As we have seen, he considered these Hungarian experiments to have been 'naive, inadequate and half-baked'. When he composed *Musica ricercata* he was approaching thirty. By the same age a precocious young Stockhausen had turned keyboard music on its head with his astonishing and epoch-making *Klavierstücke I–XI*. Boulez had completed his twelve *Notations* for piano when he was only twenty, in 1945, the year the war ended. Ligeti arrived in the West at the age of thirty-three. Until that moment he had been completely deprived of the creative camaraderie they enjoyed, his development arrested, as theirs had not been, by the adversities of the war and its aftermath. He was impatient to catch up.

But such comparisons are only relative. Copland produced his *Piano Variations* when he was thirty – similarly a musical turning point and comparable to *Musica ricercata* in their aim. Elliott Carter composed his Piano Sonata even later, at the age of forty, and the String Quartet no. 1, which can be regarded as his first mature work, when he was forty-three. In any case, Ligeti's intention was different from that of either Carter or Stockhausen. Whereas Stockhausen's *Klavierstücke* are pluralistic, Ligeti's aims are rigorously exclusive. It was the reductive thinking of *Musica ricercata* that would later bring about the chastened yet paradoxically glowing textures of *Atmosphères* and *Lontano* – from which all recognisable motivic or rhythmic configurations are finally excised. In Hungary he sensed such possibilities, but still needed traditional props. However experimental, each piece in *Musica ricercata* has a thematic and rhythmic discourse. Therein lies their delight.

Six Bagatelles and a truncated first performance

Musica ricercata received its first performance only in 1969, played by Liisa Pohjohla in Sundswall, Sweden; but as soon as Ligeti had completed the composition, he began to arrange six of the set for wind quintet, in response to a request from the eminent Jeney Quintet. The exercise appealed to him, but he had no expectation of a performance. If the Jeney Quintet hoped to receive a work they could play in public, this was not it, despite signs of a thaw following the death of Stalin earlier that year. Nevertheless, the quintet played the transcriptions privately for the composer and Ligeti was able to correct some details. His inner ear suggested to him that the greater characterisation and colour afforded by wind instruments would dramatise and alleviate the austerity of his original concept. In selecting six for this purpose, he omitted the first two because of their reductive pitch content, the Chopinesque Waltz because of its pianistic delicacy, the sixth presumably since it is the slightest of the piano set, and the eleventh because it would have made too academic an ending for the medium of wind quintet.

His scoring is felicitous, and it is hardly surprising that the *Bagatelles* were among the first works of Ligeti's Hungarian period to be resurrected after he had settled in the West. Even before he left Hungary, in September 1956, encouraged by a relaxation of the censorship, the Jeney Quintet played five of the movements in the Franz Liszt Academy – but not the last, which remained too 'dangerous'. This left the first complete performance to be given on 6 October 1969 by the Stockholm Philharmonic Wind Quintet in Södertälje – also in Sweden, and just six weeks before the premiere of *Musica ricercata*. In the years since, the *Bagatelles* have become a cornerstone of twentieth-century wind repertoire and one of the most frequently performed works by any living composer. To their musical content Ligeti made few changes. The semiquaver and demisemiquaver stringendo before the reprise in no. 1 (no. 3 in *Musica ricercata*) becomes a more dignified quaver-based rallentando for the bassoon; the end of no. 2 (no. 5 in *Musica ricercata*), which was originally based solely on G and its overtones, acquires new semitonal clashes to maintain the tension of the dissonances earlier in the movement. His most interesting alteration is to the duration of the long notes of the cantabile melodies in no. 3 (no. 7 in *Musica ricercata*), some of which are extended in the later work, in order to improve the phrase architecture of the movement as a whole.

In reassessing the *Bagatelles* for a programme note written in 1977, Ligeti rated this 'Allegro grazioso' as the most original movement on account of the way the melodic lines are coloured (e.g. the flute an octave below the oboe at bar 72, rather than, as more conventionally, above). In fact, his instrumentation frequently enhances qualities less evident in the piano original, notably at the end of no. 5 ('Béla Bartók in memoriam') where the trills and gradually arrested tremolos of the woodwind sound more fluid and mysterious than on the keyboard. The shimmering, a-metrical slowing down of this movement is the forerunner of many more extended examples of a textural process in later Ligeti, revealing however that their roots lie in Bartók.

More music for voices

Meanwhile, Ligeti continued to compose small choral works at the invitation of professional as well as amateur choirs, although less often than in the immediate post-war years. Another *Wedding Dance* for four-part a cappella choir, composed in December 1950, received no less than sixteen performances between its premiere on Hungarian Radio on 30 May 1951 and 5 June 1952, as noted in Ligeti's work list. His *Four Wedding Dances* for three female voices, or three-part choir, and piano (one of which Ligeti had reworked for piano duet) found favour with a gypsy band who arranged them for instruments and a single female singer. But performances of two SATB settings of Hungarian folk poetry, *Haj, if júság* (*Oh, Youth*) were forbidden, despite the fact that one of them had been published, because of Ligeti's 'adolescent recalcitrance'.[19] Adolescent? He was twenty-nine!

In 1953 another composition based on a traditional Hungarian ballad, *Pápainé* (*Widow Pápai*), suffered a similar fate, condemned for 'excessive dissonance'. *Kállai kettős* (*Double-dance from Kálló*), written at the same time as the *Four Wedding Dances*, received a number of performances, but the circumstances of its premiere were chilling:

József Gát, an outstanding piano teacher and choral director, asked me for a folksong arrangement for 'his choir', in 1950, without telling me what 'his choir' was called. He probably didn't wish to embarrass me, and I thought nothing of it at the time. A few weeks later I was summoned by the state security (called ÁVÓ in Hungary). At the stipulated time I had to report to the ÁVÓ headquarters at the infamous Andrássy út 60. I was led into an auditorium where József Gát and about fifty women and men were assembled, dressed in the state security uniform of the armed border troops. They sang my work.[20]

Ligeti was also writing songs. The *Three Attila József Songs* of 1950 received a broadcast the following year and ten more performances, either individually or as a group, up to 1953. More interesting are the

Five Arany Songs of 1952 for soprano and piano to texts by the lyric poet János Arany (1817–82). The first, with its fluent, linear chromaticism, approaches Ligeti's student ideal of achieving a 'Hungarian modernity' stemming from Bartók. Apart from the second song reconstructed by Sallis, the others all have character, although less than in *Musica ricercata*. The *Arany Songs* were given a private performance for members of the Association of Hungarian Musicians and received one broadcast, but their wider dissemination was obstructed.

Sándor Weöres was similarly denied publication. There arose in Budapest a culture of 'closed rooms' in which the majority of artists opted for 'inner emigration'. Ligeti, too, realised that the only possibility was to 'attend to my obligations as a teacher of harmony and counterpoint at the conservatory and compose for the drawer'. That everything the least bit experimental was banned 'merely served to increase the attractiveness of the concept of modernity for non-conformist artists. Books were written, music was composed and pictures were painted in secret, in what little free time they had available. To work for one's bottom drawer was regarded as an honour.'[21] Yet the distinction was not absolute, as Friedemann Sallis has revealed, for in due course all these 'secret' compositions were entered on a work-list maintained by the Composers' Union. It was the Union whose committee operated the censorship. But it was also the Union which assessed Ligeti's status amongst his peers.[22]

From developments beyond the Iron Curtain he remained almost completely isolated. Up to 1949 he had exchanged letters with his uncle in England, but thereafter it was too dangerous. The penalty for 'unreliable behaviour' was confiscation of one's apartment and expulsion from Budapest. News of serialism and electronic music came through sporadically; printed music, books and records from the West were all forbidden until restrictions were relaxed in 1955. The works of Thomas Mann were tolerated, until the Communists tried to suppress *Doktor Faustus* because of its exposition of twelve-tone music. Ligeti had acquired a copy in 1952 and, through eventually reading it, learnt more about twelve-note music and, indirectly, about Theodor Adorno, influential apologist for the Second Viennese School. Knowing of his interest, along with the Leibowitz book Vera obtained a copy of Adorno's famous *Philosophy of New Music*.[23] This he read immediately, and its impact on him was accompanied by a sense of awe. At this stage he failed to understand the extent to which Adorno's advocacy of Schoenberg was also an attack on Stravinsky. When he met Adorno in the West he was 'much less impressed'.

The String Quartet no. 1

The most important product of Ligeti's attention to his 'bottom drawer' was the String Quartet no. 1 composed between 1953 and 1954. The autograph manuscript is headed *Vonósnégyes [Metamorfózisok]* (*String Quartet [Metamorphosis]*), and the title *Métamorphoses nocturnes* dates from 1955, when Ligeti submitted the quartet for the Queen Elizabeth of Belgium Competition. He had learnt about the competition from Mrs Szávai, the supportive secretary of the Academy and Composers' Union who, says Ligeti, 'deserves an honourable place, fighting for forbidden music in an official party-controlled institution'. Mrs Szávai arranged for the Union to send the score, before which Ligeti revised the end, replacing precisely notated double stops in artificial harmonics with the glissandi harmonics now printed from bar 1059. But the quartet was too conventional to impress the Western jury and failed to be shortlisted even in the final ten.

Yet Ligeti had written nothing of such originality and freedom, nothing so strongly wrought. Nor had he attempted such an extended structure, whose many sections with their various expressive currents are welded into a single design of masterly accomplishment. The ideas did not come easily. His sketchbooks contain several false starts, four of them attempted in October 1953, the month when composition really got under way.[24] Inspiration came from studying the scores of Bartók's third and fourth quartets and Berg's *Lyric Suite* (no chance of actually hearing these 'dissonant' works performed) and from the classical model of Beethoven's *Diabelli Variations*. From Bartók comes the chromatically intense melodic and harmonic language of *Métamorphoses nocturnes* and the textural contrasts. More characteristic of Ligeti are the explosive and disruptive forces which threaten to overthrow orderly progression.

If 'nocturnes' describes the work's general mood, 'Métamorphoses' suggests a set of character variations. But there is no primary theme. Instead the music is built from a four-note melodic pattern consisting of two ascending tones a semitone apart. From this intervallic cell, Ligeti evolves a sequence of self-contained sections following each other without interruption. At first these short quasi-movements are clearly differentiated, each with its own thematic character. Later the transformations become more fluid; the motivic cells of the Prestissimo sections merge into an iridescent haze of flickering particles (*sul ponticello*), then into the slithering harmonics near the end. At this point the music parts company with conventional thematic language, moving towards the moulding of sound per se. Throughout the quartet, Ligeti's use of canon, already an established technique in his music, produces a dense texture of interlocking figurations rather than of contrapuntally distinct lines. Some passages (like that beginning at bar 746) occupy an intermediate stage between Bartókian imitative writing at the semitone, and the micropolyphonic canons of Ligeti's later Requiem.

At face value the quartet is a taut, logically argued composition, a single movement of almost symphonic dimensions, ostensibly in many different sections, but linked motivically as well as by the polarities of the 'sonata' principle. After the ternary exposition (whose opposition of *grazioso* and *capriccioso* themes subsides in a brief *dolente* passage, before resolving in a more diatonic and exhilarating Presto), we hear a warm chordal chorale beneath mysterious, nocturnal tremolos (Andante tranquillo at letter S) – the equivalent of a slow movement. The subsequent Tempo di Valse functions like a scherzo (letter V), and is followed by a concluding rondo-style finale whose subsections range from light-hearted joviality and mechanistic precision to the wild, lunatic Prestissimo of the end.

This is the quartet's urbane surface. Hidden beneath are more subversive forces: exaggerated 'theatrical' gestures, a 'filmic' juxtaposition between unlike sections, plus the growing tendency of later pages towards non-thematic textural fluidity. The logic of thematic discourse seems more inclined to disintegrate than to seek affirmation. Figurative passages accelerate into frantic mechanisms, whose destiny is to be abruptly cut off. *Métamorphoses nocturnes*, therefore, contains not only a figurative but a conceptual metamorphosis. Tentatively – it was hardly evident even to the composer – but building on the exploratory experience of *Musica ricercata*, he was moving towards a more kaleidoscopic plasticity.

Towards artistic and personal freedom

It was only after the completion of the String Quartet no. 1 that Ligeti began, in earnest, the search for a radically new music that would start from the malleability of the sonic material rather than from motivic logic. But the older techniques were difficult to discard. He began fragments of a Requiem, some variations for chamber orchestra and an oratorio, *Istar's Journey to Hell*, a setting of Sándor Weöres's epic poem *Istar pokoljárása* based on ancient Babylonian legend. Ligeti completed its prelude, a passacaglia on a twelve-note theme involving rhythmic layers in different metres. This mechanistic concept anticipates the three pieces for two pianos of twenty years later, but his description suggests a more physical approach: 'the bass was a twelve-note series and various versions of the series, moving at different speeds, tore into the bass line like a cogwheel.'[25] Texture is the starting point for two short choral pieces completed in 1955, *Éjszaka* (*Night*) and *Reggel* (*Morning*), setting telegraphic texts again by Weöres. In both, the melodies of the individual voices are simple, but their multiple superimposition produces a dense polyphony which Ligeti moulds onomatopoeically to illustrate the words. In the first, night is envisaged as an immense, thorny jungle shrouded in stillness and mystery. The second is a spirited contrast, in which the chiming clock tower and piercing cockcrows of dawn are portrayed. The overlayering of simple canons in *Éjszaka*, although still diatonic, is a further stage on the path towards micropolyphony. The montage is denser than anywhere in the quartet but still elementary compared with his works of the following decade.

Ligeti wrote little else in 1955, but the goal of a truly new way forward was beckoning, as a gradual seepage of information hinted at artistic achievements elsewhere. The forces welling up in his increasingly fertile and fantastical imagination pulsated the more because they were consciously experimental, they were of necessity clandestine (and therefore representative of a personal, anti-authoritarian credo), and because they coincided with a wider turbulence in society in which a resurgence of liberal aspirations, creative and personal freedom was suddenly evident all around.

These were highly charged days in every sense. The tenth anniversary of Bartók's death, celebrated in festivals and exhibitions during September 1955, unleashed a current of resentment, not only amongst musicians. In November, fifty-nine prominent writers and other cultural leaders, all recipients of either the Kossuth or Stalin Prize for artistic achievement, signed a protest against censorship, which was presented to a meeting of the Hungarian Writers' Union. Amongst their complaints was further suppression of *The Miraculous Mandarin*. Whatever credibility the Communists may have enjoyed, amongst Hungarian intellectuals it was fast disappearing. With the writer Istvan Lakatos, Ligeti himself set up an opposition group, but it was soon infiltrated by the secret police and he decided to keep his distance – wisely, perhaps, since Lakatos subsequently spent six years in prison.

During the winter of 1955–56 there was a noticeable easing of restrictions. Contacts with the West and other East European states opened up. On the black market one could buy cheap West German record players (there was still no Eastern bloc production) and, for the first time, have recordings mailed from the West. Relations of Vera living in Switzerland sent Ligeti parcels of records, and at last he was able actually to hear the third and fourth Bartók quartets, more Stravinsky, Webern's op. 5, Berg's *Lyric Suite*, Schoenberg's third and fourth quartets and *Pierrot Lunaire*. Following Khrushchev's historic denunciation of Stalin at the Twentieth Party Conference in Moscow on 18 March 1956 – although unreported in the media – there was a further loosening of the reins throughout East Europe. 'From one day to the other, foreign contacts became possible; scores, records, information on new musical ideas and changes came to Hungary. It's virtually impossible to convey how incredibly fast all this came about; it was as though air were rushing into a vacuum.'[26] *The Miraculous Mandarin* was revived at Budapest Opera. English and German broadcasts remained jammed until 23 October, but Ligeti could hear the Romanian language transmissions from the BBC which were jammed in Romania but not in Hungary.

At the age of thirty-three he began to learn what his contemporaries in the West had been up to. From Vienna he obtained a copy of Hanns Jelinek's practical textbook on twelve-tone composition,[27] which he immediately read and assimilated, and which awakened his interest in Webern. Late in the summer of 1956 he wrote to Karlheinz Stockhausen and to Herbert Eimert, director of the Electronic Studio of West German Radio in Cologne, as well as to Universal Edition in Vienna, publishers not only of the Second Viennese School but of leading representatives of the avant-garde. Not for a moment did he imagine he would go to the West; for a start he had no passport. But he desperately wanted scores. By the end of September he had received information about electronic music which particularly fascinated him, a score of *Structures* by Boulez and several by Webern. Ironically, in the confusion and excitement of the following weeks, there was no opportunity to study them.

Also in late September, the Franz Liszt Academy presented a first Festival of New Hungarian Music which attracted three noteworthy visitors from England. They were the composer Michael Tippett, musicologist John Weissmann – eager to collect information for a series of articles on young Hungarian composers for publication in *Tempo*, and to whom Ligeti gave copies of *Éjszaka* and *Reggel* as well as his work-list – and the emigré Hungarian composer Mátyás Seiber, who had lived in London since 1935. After Ligeti himself left Hungary, Seiber became a good friend, whose congenial company he enjoyed at the Darmstadt Summer Courses, and to whose memory he dedicated *Atmosphères* following Seiber's premature death in a road accident. During the festival, the Jeney Quintet gave the first public performance of Ligeti's *Bagatelles*, but minus the sixth movement, still deemed too dissonant on account of its minor seconds. Even so, the audience had little idea how to react. For, as the city witnessed an overwhelming return of vitality and optimism, there was also uncertainty and fear.

Ligeti's creative spirit was now bubbling like sparkling wine in a stoppered bottle. Briefly he experimented with a personal kind of serialism. He began another Requiem, this time using the twelve-note system. Interrupting it, he began and completed a *Chromatic Fantasy* for piano. Although Ligeti has called the piece 'serially orthodox',[28] its row is no more than a chromatic scale. This he uses to create fractured figurations and to assemble semitone clusters, including a climactic reiteration of a twelve-semitone cluster marked *ecstatico* (see p. 68). Because the row unfolds successive steps of the chromatic scale, using octave transpositions, these *martellato* passages involve so many major seventh and minor ninth intervals that the result sounds more like Schoenberg or Webern than anything else in Ligeti. But the technique is too obvious and the rhetoric lacks subtlety. Late in the summer he composed a more radical orchestral score called *Viziók* (*Visions*): textural, colouristic and non-serial. Tantalisingly, in view of its transitional significance, the manuscript appears to be lost; but it was based, Ligeti remembers, only on chromatic clusters, whose geometric organisation owed something to Ernő Lendvai's theory of golden sections in the music of Bartók. Ligeti doubted Lendvai's claims, but out of friendship had defended his book in an article pub-

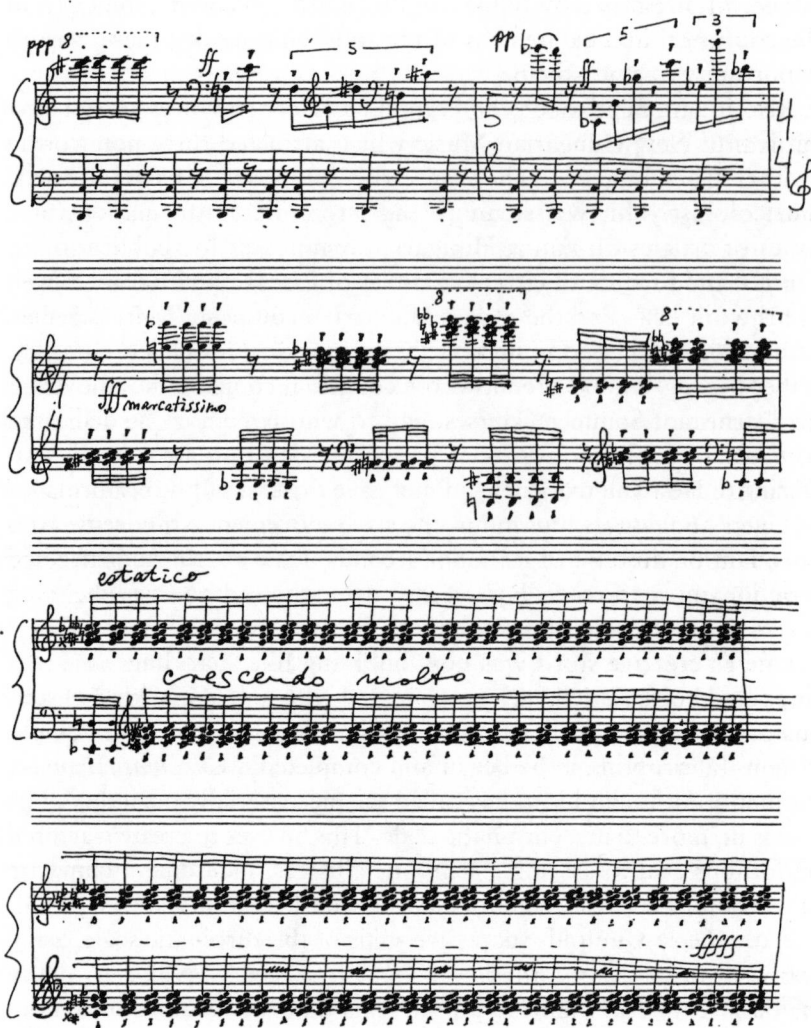

Ex. 7 Part of *Chromatische Phantasie* (1956)

lished in Hungary in 1954 – it somehow passed the censor – after Lendvai was attacked for his 'constructivist' analysis. Recast from memory, *Viziók* was to become the first movement of *Apparitions*, whose premiere at the ISCM Festival in Cologne on 19 June 1960 earned the composer his first spectacular success in the West.

Another orchestral sketch begun in the autumn does survive, called *Sötet és világos* (*Darkness and Light*). Its title could also be translated as 'Obscure and Clear' – or reversed, perhaps, as *Clair-Obscur*, a title Ligeti floated repeatedly thirty years later amongst his unrealised ideas for the piano Études. Lacking the lost *Viziók*, these four pages of unfinished score are fascinating.[29] Each consists of two twenty-two-stave sheets glued together to make a larger page of forty-four staves. The orchestration includes an enormous percussion section and strings spread across fifteen staves. The tempo is *Lento sostenuto* and the time signature 8/8. The work starts with a twelve-semitone cluster played by cellos and double basses, each divided into six, and lasting six slow bars. During this time, the soft opening becomes more active – marked *tremolo* and *sul ponticello* – and transfers to low muted brass. On the reverse of the second sheet is an earlier attempt at the same passage, but much compressed. Ligeti's realisation of just how long such textures could be sustained evidently came to him in stages. But the piece still deals in opposites. At bar 18 begins a biting, glittering Allegro for piccolos, E flat clarinets, xylophone and metallic percussion: a jagged, asymmetrical duo in high register. After a further nineteen bars the music peters out.

Escape

Dramatic events were unfolding. Nowhere would Khrushchev's policy of de-Stalinisation have a more catastrophic outcome than in Hungary, where the combination of economic change and unstable government fomented an undercurrent of popular unrest that the Communist party found itself unable to control. The dissatisfaction of intellectuals and of creative artists – abstract painters forbidden to exhibit, writers like Weöres unable to publish – added to the general resentment. On 23 October 1956 the people of Budapest rose against the Soviet presence. Barricades appeared in the streets, the massive statue of Stalin in the City Park was torn from its plinth leaving only his six-foot-high bronze boots. The next day the former reforming prime minister, Imre Nagy, who had been ousted in 1955, was prevailed on to return, promising sweeping reforms. Soon after, as the entire population embraced the fervour of revolution, a humiliated and hated Russian garrison quitted the city. On 1 November Nagy renounced Hungary's allegiance to the Warsaw Pact and appealed to the United Nations to recognise the country's independence and neutrality. It was a fatal act of defiance, and sadly ill timed, since Britain and France were deeply embroiled in their abortive, much-criticised attempt to reclaim the Suez Canal, and the General Assembly was preoccupied with the ensuing Middle East crisis. Two days later the Soviets resumed offensive positions around all of Hungary's major cities. Early on 4 November, two thousand Russian tanks re-entered the capital. The forcible removal of Nagy served only to fan the flames.

Shortly before, Ligeti received a letter from Stockhausen telling him that his latest electronic work, *Gesang der Jünglinge*, as well as the instrumental *Kontra-Punkte* would be broadcast at 11 p.m. on 7 November. When the time came Soviet tanks were patrolling the streets, whilst fighting, detonations and flying shrapnel erupted in every direction. One of Ligeti's most vivid memories is of emerging from a basement shelter to listen to the broadcast above ground, unjammed but surrounded by the noise of shells exploding. It was a symbolic breaking of the bonds of confinement, an easing of the cork. Moving fast to force the genie of revolution back in its bottle, the Russians reimposed totalitarian discipline, showing neither mercy nor restraint, unhindered by the condemnation of the West. Protesters fell to volleys of shells and bullets. But the vision shared, if briefly, by so many could not be instantly deflated. It bubbled over as some two hundred thousand refugees fled across the Austrian border to freedom.

Railway workers helped people to escape, running trains apparently as normal but secretly intended to assist refugees. Each evening you could find out from which of Budapest's four stations a train would leave early in the morning, although they stopped well short of the frontier. On 10 December, dangerously late in fact, Ligeti and Vera took a train towards the West. At Sárvár, around sixty kilometres short of the border, it was stopped by the Russian military police and many people were arrested, but there were too few Russians to surround every carriage. Ligeti and Vera slipped into the town and found shelter in the post office. The following day, with a few others, they continued forwards, hidden under the postbags of a single-wagon mail train. Deposited a safe distance from the station and a few kilometres from the border, they crossed on foot during the night, scrambling through mud from which mines had been cleared the previous year following prime minister Nagy's negotiations with Austria. Repeatedly exposed to view by army flares, they finally found themselves in Austria, welcomed by the Christmas tree lights in the frontier village of Lutzmannsdorf, destitute but free, as the Iron Curtain fell once more behind them and returned their country to imprisonment. A day later, on 13 December 1956, a car arrived to take them to Vienna.

So the cork was out. Within five years, an astonished Western avant-garde would be sipping Ligeti's post-Hungarian cocktail. His life and career turned 180 degrees. The cultural isolation, in which he had committed his most personal and important work to the dark recesses of a 'bottom drawer', was over. In Vienna, Ligeti and Vera were welcomed by Hanns Jelinek and introduced to its somewhat daunting new music elite. It included, however, a composer of similar age to Ligeti, Friedrich Cerha, who later founded 'die reihe' ensemble and would conduct the premieres of *Aventures* and the Chamber Concerto. It was an intoxicating new start. Ligeti had at last arrived. Morning had come. Prehistory had ended.

3
Catching Up

The ultimate freedom of atonality is only the semblance of freedom – it was converted into its very opposite, into constraints never before imagined, in the inexorable mechanics of the twelve-tone row.

György Ligeti, 1955[1]

To overthrow oppression is the highest aspiration of every free man.

Nelson Mandela[2]

Vienna and Cologne

In Budapest in the summer of 1952 Ligeti and Vera had married, only to divorce two years later. Soon after they arrived in Vienna they married again, once more influenced by external circumstances. Ligeti wanted to visit Cologne, but he didn't think he could afford to stay there. Like other refugees, they imagined they would make new lives in America or Canada. But their documents were inadequate. Vera had her Hungarian identity papers which showed that the marriage had been dissolved. Ligeti had lost his documents and had only his Hungarian army card, barely enough to prove who he was. The Americans at the embassy, dealing with hundreds of refugees, were kind but sceptical. They could not issue a joint visa to a couple who were no longer married. Perhaps they should go away, get themselves remarried, and present themselves at the embassy again.

This situation triggered Vera and Ligeti's remarriage in January 1957 in the Town Hall of Josefstadt, a suburb of Vienna. But their inner feelings were more complex, affected in part by turbulent historical events. Despite their divorce, there was, and continues to be a unique bond between them: Vera, as Ligeti reiterates, remains his closest friend. But his reluctance to be tied, independent spirit and overriding motivation as an artist were the forces determining his future life. In fact, the marriage took place but not the emigration. Ligeti would not see the United States for fifteen years. Vera found employment as a psychologist working with retarded children and completed her studies at Vienna University. For a long time they were extremely poor and had to rent inadequate and uncomfortable lodgings: at first just one room without even their own bathroom or running water.

There Ligeti lived when he was in Vienna. Later Vera was offered use of a room in the apartment of a well-off elderly Canadian named Maria Theresa Wood, who gave her considerable help. In the late 1960s she also gave Ligeti a Steinway upright piano; up until then he had to make do without one. Ligeti was loath to take Austrian citizenship in view of the country's Nazi past, and his status remained that of a refugee. This meant that to visit Cologne or anywhere else he had to obtain a visa. After he was invited to lecture at the Stockholm Conservatory, his visits there two or three times a year from 1961 brought in a little money and, around 1963, he and Vera were able to rent rooms in the same building. In 1966 their son Lukas was born, and his parents were concerned that he would grow up lacking any nationality. Ligeti decided, after all, to apply for Austrian citizenship. In any case, by now he increasingly needed a passport. This was granted in 1968. Much later, in 1982, he and Vera purchased an elegant small house on the edge of the city in the Vienna woods which was for sale cheaply since it was in a poor state of repair. Its purchase coincided with the receipt of a legacy, left to Lukas by Maria Wood, and with the help of another friend, an architect Lilia Praun, they were able to renovate it to become their Viennese home. As a musical centre, Vienna had relatively little to offer. Ligeti made some close friendships with composers, like Friedrich Cerha – although they properly got to know each other only at the Darmstadt Summer Courses. For fifteen years, none of the city's musical institutions offered him an official position. Culturally Vienna was a backwater, formal and aloof; the 'blank response' of the audience to the Austrian premiere of Boulez's *Le marteau sans maître* in 1957 was typical of its coolness towards the avant-garde.[3]

Ligeti's compositions had mostly been abandoned in Budapest. Only the most important could be carried on the hazardous journey across the border. This meant, of course, the String Quartet no. 1, but what else he took he cannot exactly recall. 'I think I had the Requiem fragments, maybe *Víziók*, maybe also the *Chromatic Variations* – but not *Musica ricercata*. I considered my old music of no interest. I believed in twelve-tone music!' Ove Nordwall, the Swedish musicologist who was closely in touch with Ligeti in the 1960s and published a monograph on the composer in 1968, asserts that Ligeti did bring out *Musica ricercata*, along with the *Bagatelles* for wind quintet, *Éjszaka*, *Reggel* and the *Chromatic Variations* – but does not list *Víziók*.[4] Perhaps the orchestral score was physically too large. Certainly in attitude, if less in achievement, Ligeti was already a radical, described by John Weissmann in his survey of Hungarian composers as 'the most adventurous and enterprising – i.e. dangerously "formalistic" – of his generation'.[5] But his view of serialism was ambivalent. On the one hand is his dismissive criticism published in Budapest's *New Music Review*, quoted at the head of this chapter; on the other are his several attempts at serial composition during the final months in Hungary. These were undoubtedly stimulated by receiving from Vienna a copy of Jelinek's guide to the twelve-note system. It seems, in fact, that Ligeti 'left Hungary a twelve-note composer and then became a non-twelve-note composer': the opposite of what some analysts have assumed.[6]

All his other manuscripts, apart from those already given to publishers or performers, he left stored in his mother's cellar; until, over a period of time (since their export was illegal), most of them were secretly retrieved by Nordwall to inform his monograph. In the late 1980s, Nordwall sold this collection to the Paul Sacher Foundation in Basle, but the transaction angered Ligeti, notwithstanding all Nordwall had done for him. Ligeti had agreed that Nordwall should keep the money from their disposal, but on condition that they were sold simultaneously with the sale of all his manuscripts. Because Nordwall failed to observe this condition, the relationship between Ligeti and Sacher was strained, and the transfer of Ligeti's other manuscripts to Basle delayed. The location of *Víziók*, his most experimental composition from his Hungarian years, if it survived at all, remains a mystery. Ligeti never imagined that it would be of future interest; if he did have it with him, having used it to compose another work, he thinks he may have given it away. Tantalisingly, there exists a tiny fragment (now in Basle) containing part of one chord. The page is torn and only the top half survives, but it is enough to show Ligeti deploying a fully chromatic cluster from middle to upper register with individual pitches notated for each of the strings. The corners of the manuscript have holes in, as if it had been pinned up for reference. Ligeti also regrets the loss of another score: a choral piece from 1947 called *Tavasz* (*Spring*) which he believes to have been 'one of his best'.

In Hungary, after his escape, all his published works were removed from circulation. He abandoned his personal books, and the scores of Webern and Boulez which had recently arrived but which, during the Revolution, he had been unable to study. None of this mattered compared with freedom, soon to be symbolised by the first performance of *Métamorphoses nocturnes* given in Vienna on 8 May 1958 by the Ramor Quartet, whose members had also fled from Hungary. Long before this took place, the centre of Ligeti's creative life had shifted. In February 1957, a few weeks after his arrival in Vienna, he left for Cologne which, with its pioneering electronic music studio, the patronage of West German Radio (WDR Köln), and the presence of Karlheinz Stockhausen and his circle, was at the crux of the Franco-German axis of the avant-garde, if not its very Mecca.

The story of Ligeti's arrival in Cologne has been variously embroidered, notably by Karl Wörner.[7] Ligeti's own account is less dramatic. At that time the train journey from Vienna to Cologne took two days and nights so that, like any other refugee, he alighted unshaven, hungry and exhausted. His first thought was to find a barber's shop. Here he received a shave; but the well-meaning staff, concerned that their dishevelled customer seemed on the verge of collapse, decided to call an ambulance. Despite his protestations, he was taken to hospital where he was soon discharged. From the hospital he caught a tram to the house of Herbert Eimert (1897–1972), founder and director of the Electronic Music Studio, to whom Ligeti had written from Vienna, and who had secured for him a four-month scholarship. Eimert gave Ligeti tea, and then accompanied him to the Stockhausens' spacious home at 6 Meister-Johann-Strasse. By chance the door was opened by Bruno Maderna, the charismatic and ebullient Italian who would become one of his closest friends and allies. Supremely gifted both as a conductor and composer, Maderna (1920–73) was a selfless promoter of the avant-garde, whose congenial and benign spirit did much to diffuse their disagreements. For the moment, it was a brief encounter and Ligeti would not see Maderna again for several months.

The Stockhausens' large flat in a two-family villa, situated in the gracious suburb of Köln-Braunsfeld, had been acquired by Karlheinz's first wife Doris, who, as the daughter of a highly esteemed and prosperous family, was gifted and generous in welcoming visitors. Their friends included poets, painters and publishers, besides the composers converging on Cologne from several countries and even different continents, amongst them Herbert Brün from Jerusalem, Earle Brown from the United States and (in 1958) the Korean-born action-artist Nam June Paik. Many were invited to stay, Earle Brown for one, Cornelius Cardew from England – who became one of the assistants who helped Stockhausen realise the score of *Carré* – and, later on, the Belgian Henri Pousseur. Ligeti especially liked the company of Franco Evangelisti, newly arrived from Rome, and of the young German composer Gottfried Michael Koenig, Stockhausen's colleague at the studio. To enter this invigorating intellectual milieu was an extraordinary tonic, all the more potent because such stimuli had long been denied him. For a wonderful six weeks he stayed with the Stockhausens, conversations extending far into the night as Karlheinz expounded *Gruppen* and his other scores, and the achievements and aspirations of post-war music underwent animated discussion. Evidently Ligeti himself commanded considerable respect. Tentatively, he showed Stockhausen his string quartet, and Stockhausen discovered in it 'two bars which he could accept'. Then Ligeti found somewhere of his own to live. It was a simple loft over a garage, but at least it enabled him to continue working in the Studio of WDR, learning its techniques under the guidance of Stockhausen and Koenig. After his scholarship ran out, Eimert gave Ligeti further work in the studio, although mainly unpaid. This he supplemented with occasional proof-reading and small-scale writing, like the analytical preface which he contributed to the Philharmonia miniature score of Bartók's String Quartet no. 5 published by Universal Edition in 1957. For most of the next two years Ligeti remained in Cologne, although barely able to subsist.

Eagerly though he absorbed new ideas, it was also a time for reflection, particularly concerning the implications of serial thinking, some of which he could endorse, some of which he could not. He was uneasy about so ruthless a rejection of the past. Ligeti's personal relations with Stockhausen and his circle were excellent; indeed Stockhausen, Maderna and Boulez (whom he met in December 1957) he regarded almost with veneration. But he recoiled from the narrow ideologies and intolerance which were adopted by many of the avant-garde – although not by Maderna. Despite his own recent serial experiments, it was hardly likely, so soon after escaping Communist cultural censorship, that he would submit to another set of strictures. From the politics and the intrigues of the Cologne composers he preferred to keep apart, especially after Mauricio Kagel arrived from Buenos Aires in September that year, and he and Stockhausen (both tall and of dominating physique) immediately became rivals. Yet, for all Ligeti's anti-establishment scepticism (and by now the avant-garde certainly was an establishment), in beating his own path he still wished to learn from others.

Sound synthesis: the new medium

Ligeti's interest in electronic music had been awakened in Budapest where, straining to listen amidst the noise of exploding shells and street fighting, he had tuned in to the premiere of Stockhausen's *Gesang der Jünglinge* broadcast by West German Radio on 7 November 1956. Herbert Eimert, director of the WDR studio, was a musicologist and critic who had proved himself by publishing, as early as 1924, a treatise on atonality.[8] Already, between the wars, Eimert had worked for the radio station, to which he returned in 1945 to direct its late-night new-music programmes. A calm, cheerful and generous associate, it was Eimert who in 1951 spearheaded the project which resulted eighteen months later in the establishment of the world's first studio dedicated to electrically generated music. The crucial ingredient which made this possible was the invention and marketing of the tape recorder around 1948; indeed, foundations had already been laid elsewhere, notably in Paris where Pierre Schaeffer, a French sound engineer and radio producer, was assembling collages using environmental sounds recorded on disc.

In 1949 Schaeffer was joined by Pierre Henry, who introduced more sophisticated techniques, as in their joint composition *Symphonie pour un homme seul*, realised in 1949–50. With other composers and engineers they founded the Club d'Essai studio at Paris Radio in 1951, using tape to develop more subtle manipulative processes so that sounds could be transformed further from their natural origins. Guest composers invited to work in the studio included Boulez, Messiaen and Stockhausen; but none of them could accept Schaeffer's unbending aesthetic with its dogmatic insistence on recorded source material. In his first and only *concrète étude*, composed in Paris in 1952,

Stockhausen virtually negated Schaeffer's approach by announcing that his study would depend entirely on many minuscule splicings of a single sound source. Then, whilst at work on it, he began to experiment with superimposing sine tones produced by the studio's frequency generator, an idea suggested by the Belgian composer Karel Goeyvaerts.

This line of exploration was also that of the Cologne group, whose studio was due to open in May 1953 – but it held no interest for Schaeffer. Still in Paris, Stockhausen weighed up the next task proposed by Schaeffer, a classification of prerecorded *concrète* sources. It did not attract him. Instead, he resolved to move to Cologne and pursue the 'purer' aim of creating music entirely through sound synthesis, with its greater mathematical precision. So arose the distinction between *musique concrète* and *elektronische Musik*, widely recognised in the 1950s and 1960s, until the infiltration of the two approaches by each other led to the adoption of a single umbrella term, 'electro-acoustic music'.

In Cologne, Eimert and Stockhausen presented their first results to the public through performances in the concert hall of WDR, demonstrations in various cities, and numerous radio broadcasts. Stockhausen's principal assistant at the studio was Gottfried Michael Koenig, who was of a similar age and who had joined them in 1954, remaining at the studio for twelve years before becoming head of the Institute of Sonology at the University of Utrecht. Working together every day for some fourteen months (and often through the night), Koenig had helped Stockhausen create both *Gesang der Jünglinge* and *Kontakte*, the first major artistic achievements of the Cologne studio. The extraordinarily meticulous documentation in the published score of *Kontakte* records the laborious, time-consuming detail which these projects necessitated. Not only was Koenig as dedicated as Stockhausen; his cultured intelligence, modesty and judgement won him wide respect, and it was he who became Ligeti's principal mentor. Ligeti assisted in the technical processes involved in Koenig's electronic *Essay* (1957–58), whose sonic fluidity so impressed him that he still regards it as the best example of the studio's montage work. Welcomed into this citadel of the avant-garde, he joined in vehement discussions about the techniques, opportunities and difficulties of the new medium – and about its legitimacy.

He also began to compose electronic music of his own, attempting to realise through synthesised means the new concepts of texture, stasis and movement which he had begun to conceive in Hungary. Characteristically, Ligeti focused on the communicative potential of synthesised sound as a quasi-language – evoking associations, images and implications – rather than as a technically precise vehicle for serial organisation. These extra-musical inferences are apparent in his first electronic work, *Glissandi*, composed in 1957. Influenced by Koenig's *Essay*, its sliding sinusoidal aggregates and filtered white noise flow as freely as the broad washes of a water-colourist. Neither technically nor artistically is this first study very sophisticated: it shows all too clearly the limited parameters with which early electronic composers had to grapple, and seems quite primitive beside Stockhausen's epoch-making *Gesang der Jünglinge* – a product of the latter's far greater studio experience. But *Glissandi* is significant for at least one reason. In this new medium Ligeti could create for the first time an amorphous sound-flow, freed from metre and pulse, which would become the defining trait of his return to instrumental music. It was an important extension of his horizons.[9]

An artificial language

Ligeti's second completed electronic composition, *Artikulation* (1958), is more refined. Here he manipulates synthesised sound with greater subtlety so as to simulate a quasi-verbal language, with its own artificial syntax. His starting point was the belief that music could be articulated 'in an analogous way to spoken prose', an idea fostered through reading extensively about phonetics, although he had thought about exploring the sound characteristics of speech even before leaving Budapest. Whilst working on *Artikulation*, Ligeti benefited from the practical help of Koenig and Cardew, but he was particularly influenced, as were all the composers of the Cologne group, by the ideas of Werner Meyer-Eppler (1913–60), director of the new Institute of Phonetics and Communication Research at Bonn University.

Originally a professor of theoretical physics, Meyer-Eppler was also an accomplished linguist and amateur pianist who, following the war, had transferred to the faculty of philosophy. His brilliant dissection of the scientific and acoustic fundamentals of sound – whether musical notes, speech or anything audible – encouraged composers like Stockhausen, who attended his lectures in Bonn, to pursue a radically new approach to its organisation. Meyer-Eppler was one of the first to envisage the possibilities of electronic music. He published a book on electronic sound in 1949, and was the first to describe and construct some of its early equipment. Indeed, it was his initiative that had brought the Cologne group together. The leading German exponent of the newly established American study of information theory, he was also familiar with the vocoder, an artificial speech apparatus invented in 1948, to which he had been personally introduced by its creator, the research physicist Homer Dudley from the Bell Telephone Laboratories in the USA. Meyer-Eppler's application of statistical methods derived from information theory also led him to the view that phenomena that appear orderly in broad terms may yet succumb to chance in their detail – so are effectively aleatoric. It was an early contribution to a debate that would only take fire after John Cage and David Tudor visited Europe in 1954 and 1958. Meyer-Eppler's testing of these theories in his lectures is recalled by Stockhausen in the second volume of *Texte*:

We tried to compose artificial texts, using cards, lottery, roulette or telephone directory numbers in order to determine their structure . . . we would take a newspaper and cut the text into smaller and smaller units – three syllables, two syllables, one syllable, sometimes right down to individual letters. Then we would shuffle the pieces like cards, arrange the new text and study the degree of redundancy . . . It is from such experiments that I derived inspiration to compose my first sounds with statistical characteristics.[10]

Meyer-Eppler's influence on Ligeti was less crucial than for Stockhausen, who considered him 'the best teacher I ever had'. But Ligeti heard him lecture and was impressed by 'this high-level analysis of phonetics and psychoacoustics'. It helped to liberate his thinking from the post-Bartókian language of the String Quartet no. 1, and provided a rationale for *Artikulation*. For the raw material of this second piece, he assembled small sound fragments and artificial speech components, using sine-wave, white-noise and impulse generators, plus filtering equipment. Ligeti grouped these source ingredients associatively into ten categories – grainy, friable, fibrous, slimy, sticky, compact etc. – cutting each sound into numerous short lengths of tape sorted into boxes. From these, in turn, bits of tape were extracted and spliced together to make 'syllables', 'words' and 'sentences', and the resultant 'language' subjected to the transpositions, reversals and overdubbing of standard tape manipulation. Ligeti's many sketches for

Artikulation show that his methods were part serial, part empirical, part aleatoric, but they clearly did not inhibit the spontaneous, even witty character of the finished piece. More differentiated than *Glissandi*, it features predominantly short events, cascades, rapid superimpositions, explosive exchanges, exclamations, sighs, simulated conversation, massed voices: a compendium of quasi-vocal mannerisms compressed into less than four minutes.[11]

Artikulation was completed quickly, and premiered in its original four-track version on 25 March 1958 in the 'Musik der Zeit' concert series at WDR Cologne. It was heard again in a programme presented by the Cologne Electronic Music Studio at Darmstadt on 4 September that year, the first of Ligeti's works to be performed at the Summer Courses. Stockhausen admired the piece, and it has coincidental similarities with work emanating from the studio established in 1955 by Italian Radio in Milan, where Bruno Maderna, Luciano Berio and Luigi Nono were making electronic transformations of the human voice. Like Ligeti's piece, Maderna's *Invenzione su una voce* (1960) uses artificial phonemes as raw material for a non-semantic, gestural composition. Berio differently develops an emotive combination of manipulated speech, vocalise and electronic sounds in works like *Thema: Omaggio a Joyce* (1958) and *Visage* (1961).

Moulding the sonic plasma is the bread and butter of electro-acoustic art. Sounds are energised, expanded and compressed, blown apart, cut up, regrouped, granulated, filtered, sprinkled through sieves. Purists, notably the pioneers of *elektronische Musik*, played down suggestions of any extra-musical meaning, arguing that a sonic construct should function on its own. Certainly *Glissandi* can be heard as an abstract piece, but less so *Artikulation*. Its material is synthetic, but its implication lingual, the music's metaphorical nature being confirmed by Ligeti's own explanation:

Certainly I have an aversion to everything that is demonstratively programmatic and illustrative. But that does not mean that I am against music that calls forth associations; on the contrary, sounds and musical coherence always arouse in me ideas of consistency and colour, of visible and recognisable form. And vice versa: I constantly combine colour, form, texture and abstract concepts with musical ideas. This explains the presence of so many non-musical elements in my compositions.

Sound-fields and masses that flow together, alternate with, or penetrate one another; suspended nets that tear or become knotted; damp, viscous, spongy, fibrous, dry, brittle, granulous and compact materials; threads, short flourishes, splinters and traces of all kinds; imaginary edifices, labyrinths, inscriptions, texts, dialogues, insects, states, occurrences, coalescence, transformation, catastrophe, decay, disappearance; all of these are elements of this non-puristic music.[12]

From so much laborious tape-splicing Ligeti wanted to create something poetic and iconic, having in mind the genial, surreal art of Joán Míro with its symbolic treatment of colour and line. Applied·to the orchestral medium, this textural pliability would make possible the achievements of *Apparitions* and *Atmosphères*, whilst his increasingly allusive treatment of sound became a rich narrative of psycho-acoustic suggestion. By the time of the String Quartet no. 2, composed in 1968, the articulative and gestural aspects of the music had become principal components of its structure.

In the orchestral works which followed *Artikulation*, Ligeti discarded motivic and tonal organisation as radically as any composer of the period. His preoccupation with texture was shared with Xenakis and Penderecki, who would pointedly call two of his compositions *De Natura Sonoris*. More often than theirs, however, Ligeti's music simulates spoken language: its rise and fall, compression and lingering, exclamation and response, an isolated solo voice against the bubbling of the many. *Artikulation*'s linguistic manner led directly to the two miniature semi-operas, *Aventures* and *Nouvelles aventures*, whose phonetic texts replicate dialogue but have no real meaning.

Darmstadt

No less important than Ligeti's work in the studio was the opportunity at long last to hear the music of his Western colleagues. He seized it avidly, listening to all he could by the post-war avant-garde. For the first time he discovered graphic and space-time notations and learnt ways of writing down non-metrical music which, whilst composing *Musica ricercata* and the String Quartet no. 1, he had not realised were possible. The liveliest forum for such encounters was the Internationale Ferienkurse für Neue Musik held annually in the German city of Darmstadt, to which most of Europe's progressive composers and theorists came. These summer courses had been established in 1946 by the musician and critic, Wolfgang Steinecke, cultural adviser to the city, whose aim was not only the regeneration of artistic energy and international dialogue after the war, but the creation of a sort of 'musical Bauhaus' in which music forbidden under Hitler, especially serialism, would be reinstated. Teachers in the early years included René Leibowitz from Paris, author of two seminal books on the Second Viennese School (one of which Ligeti had acquired in Hungary but had not read), the pioneering composer Edgard Varèse from New York, the German social theorist and philosopher Theodor Adorno, whose *Philosophy of New Music* Ligeti had read, and the leading French composer Olivier Messiaen.

Then in his mid-forties, Messiaen was probably the most revered composer-teacher in post-war Europe. His *Modes de valeurs et d'intensités*, composed at Darmstadt in 1949, one of an innovatory set of *Quatre études de rythme* for the piano, made a profound impact when it was circulated in recordings two years later – notably on Stockhausen. In that year, 1951, twelve-note music was chosen as the principal theme of the Ferienkurse, and the programme culminated in the world premiere of the 'Dance Round the Golden Calf' from Schoenberg's *Moses und Aron*. Composed according to serial principles, Schoenberg had begun work on his one full-length opera twenty years earlier, but completed music for only two of its three acts. A few days after this concert performance of the opera's most spectacular scene, Schoenberg died in Los Angeles, bringing to a close the momentous achievements of the Second Viennese School.

All this Ligeti had missed. It would be another seven years before John Cage, with his disconcertingly non-Western, anti-causal view of music, would make his first visit to Darmstadt. When he did, in 1958, his anarchic radicalism caused a furore, rekindling the debate about aleatoric music. Stockhausen, for one, was immediately influenced. But in Europe things were also changing. From 1959 onwards, concerts at Darmstadt were allocated specifically to music by the young, many of whom migrated there annually. Rarely, indeed, can it have seemed so de rigueur to hunt with the pack. Some, of course, particularly composers in countries on the fringes of Europe like Great Britain, failed to find their way. Some recoiled from what they perceived as an arrogant and intolerant hegemony, as did Hans Werner Henze. But for many Darmstadt was the crucible in which new ideas were forged, the latest compositions given searching scrutiny, and technical and aesthetic discussion engaged at the highest level.

When Ligeti made his first visit to the Ferienkurse in the summer of 1957, the original leadership was beginning to fragment, but Darmstadt remained magnetic. Ligeti took courses with Luigi Nono and the American pianist and friend of Cage, David Tudor, and quickly impressed and was admitted into its inner circle. He was in fact older than Nono, Tudor and their colleagues. In 1959 he returned to the Ferienkurse as a teacher, presenting a course in the techniques of Anton Webern, whose exquisitely integrated serialism was for Ligeti, as for others, an important inspiration. He had already presented some Webern analyses on West German Radio – a modest but useful source of income. Thereafter Ligeti continued to be one of Darmstadt's most engaging lecturers and intellects, accepting annual invitations to teach there up until 1970. He always attended Stockhausen's lectures, and sometimes Karlheinz came to his.

The crisis of serialism

In 1955 theoretical debate reached a wider audience when two new periodicals were launched in the same year, both devoted to developments in contemporary music. *Gravesaner Blätter*, edited by the conductor Hermann Scherchen and published in Switzerland, had the smaller circulation, in fact was relatively little known. The other, evangelically titled *Die Reihe (The Row)*, was published by Universal Edition, first in German and soon after also in English. The initiative of its joint editors, Eimert and Stockhausen, *Die Reihe* was first and foremost a mouthpiece of current thinking emanating from Darmstadt and Cologne. Volume One was devoted exclusively to Electronic Music, including articles by Eimert, Koenig, Meyer-Eppler, Boulez, Pousseur and Stockhausen. Volume Two concentrated on Craftsmanship, Volume Three on Anton Webern, Volume Four on Young Composers.

Almost immediately Ligeti arrived in Cologne, Stockhausen suggested that he undertake a substantial analysis with a view to its publication in *Die Reihe*. At first Boulez's *Le marteau sans maître* was mooted, but nobody could even begin to explain its internal working. So the plan changed to focus on Boulez's most uncompromising example of integral serialism, the two-piano composition *Structures 1a* composed in 1952, of which Ligeti had received a score before leaving Hungary. Compared to the opacity of *Le marteau*, the 'crystal-clear sobriety' of *Structures 1a* – although very different from Ligeti's own sensibility – offered a promising anatomy for the dissecting table. Ligeti had published some analytical studies whilst in Hungary, including contributions to the German music journal *Melos*, in the last of which – submitted around 1948 before censorship prevented further contact – he even speculates about whether serialism or a 'new tonality' will replace tonality.[13] As we have seen, he also wrote reviews and articles for the Hungarian journal *Zenei Szemle (Music Review)* and its successor *Új Zenei Szemle (New Music Review)* – reconstituted with a new board under Communist party control in 1949. Especially interesting are his 'Remarks on the Development of Bartók's Chromaticism', published in the September 1955 issue of *Új Zenei Szemle*,[14] since they closely anticipate his assessment of *Structures 1a* contained in the fourth volume of *Die Reihe*.

Before leaving Hungary, Ligeti had become more familiar with serialism, not only from Jelinek's treatise but also from reading Thomas Mann's *Doktor Faustus*. He knew about its extension by Boulez and others to the parameters of rhythm, dynamics and instrumentation. He had composed his entirely serial *Chromatic Fantasy* for piano, and started a twelve-note oratorio and Requiem and another serial piano piece, to be called *Chromatic Variations*. So it is curious to find him questioning serialist theory in two *Die Reihe* articles, in very similar language to that of his Bartók essay of 1955. In the Bartók study he rails against serialism's elimination of differences between 'attraction and resolution, consonance and dissonance', and its consistently 'high temperature'. By contrast, Ligeti applauds Bartók's refined chromatic architecture, his 'twelve-tonalism' being a higher synthesis of two contradictory systems, functional tonality and what he calls the 'distance principle' of symmetrical divisions laid out between opposite harmonic poles, as defined by Ernő Lendvai. 'Just as the germ of its own self-destruction was contained in the diatonic system', he writes, anticipating almost exactly the words of his second *Die Reihe* article, 'dodecaphonism carries within itself its own liquidation.'[15]

Published in 1958 but written in February and March 1957, Ligeti's analysis of *Structures 1a* is impressively thorough and penetrating. He had worked on it almost every evening after returning from the studio, Stockhausen as editor helping him to correct the German. No other analytical study in previous or subsequent issues of *Die Reihe* approaches it in the clarity of the questions asked or the detail of the evidence presented. It was an approach learnt from Lajos Bárdos's analysis lectures in Budapest, in which nothing was taken for granted. Initially Ligeti imagined that he would write about Boulez 'in the most admiring way'. But as he pondered the relationship in *Structures 1a* between decision-making and automation, doubts arose. These conditions he finds not to be alternatives at all, but crucially dependent on each other.

You stand before a row of automata, and are free to choose which one to throw into; but at the same time you are compelled to choose one of them. You build your own prison as you please, and once safely inside you are again free to do as you please. Not wholly free, then, but also not totally compelled . . . choice and mechanism are united in the process of choosing one's mechanism.[16]

Ligeti questions Boulez's application of the dodecaphonic principle not only to the twelve-note chromatic scale (where it is logical), but also to durations, dynamics and modes of attack (for all of which the number twelve has no intrinsic significance). Moreover, in Boulez's treatment of these other parameters, Ligeti detects inconsistencies and 'fields of inexactness', even momentary lapses in serial precision which undermine the prevailing technical rigour. Yet his assessment is far from one-sided or predominantly negative. Since practically everything within each section of the piece is predetermined, artistry must reside in the contrast and balance between sections. Ligeti observes how the tritone, which occurs between the last two notes of the pitch series and, similarly, between the first two pitches of the retrograde form, 'serves as an adhesive'; it illumines the ends of sections, then their beginnings, so that tritones 'help to organise the build-up of the piece'. This effect is enhanced by the fact that Boulez superimposes simultaneous serial threads in both pianos to form 'bundles'. Whichever transpositions he uses, all the pitch series begin or end with the unmistakable flavour of the tritone. 'The accumulations of tritones are produced automatically,' says Ligeti, 'yet they result from choice – choice of the tritone as the series's peripheral interval, choice of the series's simultaneity within the sections. Clearly the automatism of the serial loom can be artistically exploited, if elements and operations are well chosen.'

Then he returns to the constraints which one apparently free choice imposes on another, the way decisions become interdependent. Since the registral distribution in *Structures 1a* is not subject to any systemic permutation, theoretically the composer can place notes in whatever register he likes. In reality, as Ligeti demonstrates, such licence exists only in the two monodic sections. Where two or more different statements of the series occur together, there is always the possibility of their arriving simultaneously on the same pitch class – a well-rehearsed hazard of writing serial polyphony ever since the technique was invented. Like earlier serialists, Boulez avoids such simultaneities sounding in octaves, preferring to conceal them by placing offending pitches in unison with each other. However, 'the more simultaneous threads are present, the more likely are octaves to occur, and the choice of registers becomes increasingly fixed, to ensure that they are avoided as much as possible.' The number of serial threads in each section is predetermined. But this prior choice of polyphonic density 'affects the free choice of registers, because of the principle of avoiding octaves. Thus one choice inevitably imposes limits on all the decisions which follow it.' Indeed, Ligeti argues, the registral conformity produced by avoiding octaves has another outcome at variance with serial ideals: a piling-up of note-repetitions generated by several simultaneous threads being 'woven in fixed registers'.

Exploring the effect of these note-repetitions, Ligeti likens them to 'knots', by which the integrity of the system is compromised, as the supposedly independent threads get tied together. Despite, or rather because of Boulez's pre-compositional planning, unseemly coincidences occur. Only eight bars into the work near the start of the second section, the allocation of four different forms of the series to each of the pianists' four hands causes four E flats in middle register to sound in close proximity (two of them simultaneously, of which one is notated as D sharp) with only two other notes intervening; these both happen to be G sharps (see Ex. 8, p. 88).

Thus the note E flat becomes especially conspicuous, emphasised by the recollection of the E flat three octaves higher at the beginning of the first section. But one may not regard this note as a 'tonic' or central note – nothing of the kind can exist in this kind of music (since to compose 'serially' means the abolition of any hierarchy of the musical elements); the pile-up of this note, being a purely accidental result, has no harmonic function.'[7]

Cracks in Schoenberg's original law (forbidding the repetition of any pitch-class until all the other eleven had been sounded) became

Ex. 8 *Structures 1a*. Boulez's serial bundles deliver four sounding
E flats in close proximity.

evident as soon as simultaneous series were combined, Schoenberg
himself being the first to break the code. Later composers discovered
the elegant contrivance of 'combinatoriality' to overcome the problem. By choosing a certain type of series, one could combine, for
example, the first six notes of one form with the first six of another to
make up all twelve pitch classes without duplication. Combinatorial
series were employed especially by Webern who put pitch coincidence
to artistic advantage. For instance, in his elegant canonic structure in
the first movement of the Symphony op. 21, pitches are distributed
symmetrically around a central nucleus. The pitch-repetitions, produced by having four simultaneous forms of the row, are curiously
pleasing and beautiful, on the one hand proportioned with classic
refinement, on the other almost Asiatic in their contemplative stasis.
Symmetrical pitch and interval repetitions in Webern produce an
unmistakable impression of tonal focus, whose magnetic attraction is
enhanced by their interplay of sound and silence – what Boulez himself, in *Die Reihe* 2, calls 'respiration'. Nevertheless, Boulez is not
Webern, and Ligeti's comment about the impossibility of serial composition allowing any kind of 'tonic' is surely intended to be ironic. Or
is it? A few paragraphs later, he extols the 'charm' of the six-part

section III, in which all registers are fixed and the harmonic result is 'wholly static, nuanced by intensities and modes of attack.'

So what is Ligeti's conclusion regarding *Structures 1a*? For the moment it is cautious. There is the paradox that 'interacting decisions lead automatically to automatism, determination creates the unpredictable; and vice versa, neither the automatic nor the accidental can be created without decision and determining'. Ligeti grants that 'the beauty of a piece like this lies in quite new qualities', but points out that its composition is less 'artwork' than research into newly discovered relations within the material. On the other hand, the self-imposed 'dry-severity' of *Structures* was a necessary discipline before Boulez could break away into 'the sensual, feline world of *Le marteau*' which, despite baulking at its analysis, has for Ligeti always retained a primacy amongst Boulez's compositions. Indeed its score lay on Ligeti's table when I visited him in Hamburg in February 2000, because, Ligeti said, he wanted to study it again.

During the 1960s and 1970s criticisms and rejections of serialism multiplied. But Ligeti's remarks remain trenchant. He had not consulted its subject, whom he met only when Boulez conducted *Le marteau* in Vienna in December 1957. For a while Boulez was friendly, until, it seems, he read the English translation of the *Die Reihe* article in 1958. Boulez made no comment, but Ligeti sensed his displeasure and for a decade or so there was a coolness between them. Yet Ligeti's most pertinent observations are applicable to much new music, including his own, since they address the way musical perspective affects our sense of structural relationships.

Seen at close quarters, it is the factor of determinism, regularity, that stands out; but from a distance, the structure, being the result of many separate regularities, is seen to be something highly variable and chancy, comparable to the way a network of neon lights flashes on and off in a main street; the individual lamps are indeed exactly controlled by a mechanism, but as the separate lights flash on and off, they combine to form a statistical complex.

Seen from a greater distance, these light-complexes merge to form a higher unit, which is also significant in its own way; so, too, does the structure of this music when heard often. Our perception, which at first only noted the accidental details, then penetrates gradually to deeper levels, till it discovers the overall coherence and proportions. It is just these latter that give the piece its artistic value, which can hardly be grasped by listening in a traditional way.[18]

Degrees of distance, between microscopic detail and misty organic whole, provide the perspective shading in the orchestral scores to which Ligeti was now turning. His focus in the Boulez analysis on linear 'threads' and 'bundles', on 'knots' of harmonic coincidence, had direct bearing on his own technical thinking in the micropolyphonic works of the following decade. What mattered more was the dramatic character one could achieve without the nullifying constraints of serialism. He preferred to listen to his inner ear and trust where it led: the stranger and more rarefied, the more in tune with his deeper vision. *Artikulation* had simulated language. Through a tactile manipulation of orchestral sound Ligeti could indulge the fantasies which had flooded his mind since childhood – surreal hallucinations, imagined landscapes, sonic clouds, bizarre cartoons – using his knowledge of serialism only to assist in holding things together.

Towards textural composition

When his first major orchestral works, *Apparitions* and *Atmosphères*, received their world premieres in 1960 and 1961, it was the creation of liquid texture out of meticulous detail that gave them their novel magic. This approach arose partly through working with electronics. Preceding *Artikulation*, Ligeti had begun another electronic study which he intended to call *Atmosphères*. In it he proposed to blend forty-eight layers, using only combinations of pure sine waves, from which composite sounds would emerge and recede like shadows within a fluctuating yet generally sustained texture. But as he began work on it in the studio, he realised that it was 'a quite illusory idea'. Never completed on tape, his graphic plan for the piece can still be studied in a published facsimile, entitled *Pièce électronique* no. 3. It must have been the only electronic work to exist in score but not in sound until, using computer technology, it was realised by Kees Tazelaar and Johan van Kreij at the Institute of Sonology (now relocated at the Koninklijk Conservatory in the Hague) and performed there on 2 February 1996. The result is not impressive, and *Pièce électronique* no. 3 remains a curiosity which Ligeti prefers to omit from his work-list. By now he knew that what he was seeking could be achieved more effectively with orchestra. The title and aesthetic concept of *Atmosphères* he would restore to the domain of acoustic music.

Although its impetus came from electronic music, *Atmosphères* owes a debt to other scores written in the late 1950s in which textural considerations came to the fore; works like Penderecki's *Anaklasis*, Stockhausen's *Carré* and, before that, *Gruppen*. In explaining *Gruppen* to Ligeti, Stockhausen had described the statistical processes he was exploring:

I showed him the relative variability within what I called *Gruppen*'s time fields. For example, within a given interval – what I call a certain musical complex or texture – I'd determine a spiral movement. All the instruments that were participating, according to a predetermined number, had to go in irregular but directionally upward movements; spiralling insofar as they rise and then come down again; go a bit higher, come down again, then go still higher until, reaching the top pitch, they start again from the bottom.[19]

Ligeti was attracted to processes which eschewed thematic figurations and which realised so effectively some of the textural ideas about which he had speculated in Hungary. Indeed, the premiere of *Gruppen* on 24 March 1958 was influential for many composers, not least a new generation of Poles, whose radical treatment of orchestral sound emerged as an important artistic movement in the cultural thaw following Gomulka's return to power in 1956. In *Gruppen*, Stockhausen seemed to have stepped beyond the limitations of serialism, most of all in his spatial treatment of sound. Scored for three orchestras which surround the audience, the notoriety of the premiere was enhanced by the presence as joint conductors of three leaders of the avant-garde, Boulez, Maderna and Stockhausen himself.

In certain respects, *Gruppen*'s statistical processes had been anticipated, both theoretically and musically, by a relatively little known Greek. Trained in Athens as an engineer, forged in the fire of anti-fascist resistance (whose violent street demonstrations left him with a serious facial injury and under a sentence of death, only rescinded in 1974), Iannis Xenakis had escaped to Paris in 1947, where he joined the architectural practice of Le Corbusier. In this role, he designed the Philips Pavilion for the 1958 Brussels World Fair, for which Edgard Varèse created his classic of *musique concrète*, *Poème électronique*, and for which Xenakis himself made a short electro-acoustic composition. When in the early 1950s Xenakis began also to compose, albeit from a wholly unorthodox standpoint, his radicalism involved applying to the morphology of sound the so-called 'vitalisation' of architectural form (through mass, surface and line) which preoccupied Le Corbusier and his colleagues. Xenakis's expertise as an engineer focused on the load-bearing capacity of pre-stressed concrete, understanding which made possible the plasticity of the new structures, of which the Philips Pavilion, with its audaciously curved surfaces, was a spectacular example.

He had already applied similar concepts to his first composition *Metastasis*, completed in 1954. Written for sixty-three solo instruments, mostly strings and each with its own stave in the score (a practice which Xenakis seems to have invented, but which Ligeti and others would independently adopt), *Metastasis* moves in clouds of sound, featuring huge avalanches of string glissandi sliding at different inclinations. The resultant textural mass appears to bend, expand and contract. Volcanic streams of energy activate the individual lines differently, but their directional 'tendency' is definable. This pioneering work, composed at exactly the same time as Ligeti's String Quartet no. 1, ushered in what many regarded as a new abrasiveness in musical composition. Its controversial premiere at the Donaueschingen Festival in October 1955, conducted by Hans Rosbaud, produced a well-publicised scandal during which opposing factions in the audience jeered or applauded. But generally Xenakis's maverick contributions were not well known. Ligeti himself only heard *Metastasis* performed after he had composed *Apparitions* and *Atmosphères*, but he had heard its successor *Pithoprakta* (1957).

Serial rigour or sonic plasticity?

In July 1955, three years before Ligeti's first *Die Reihe* article, Xenakis had published his own essay on 'The Crisis of Serial Music' in the first issue of *Gravesaner Blätter*.[20] In it he too exposed what he regarded as the delusion of serialism, asserting that the distribution of all twelve notes across the whole spectrum produced not the audible polyphonic logic claimed for it, but rather a meaningless, indeterminate mosaic. A better organisational principle, Xenakis argued, would be not that of arithmetic series, but the calculus of probabilities.

Ligeti returned to the issue himself in the seventh issue of *Die Reihe*. Although published in 1960, this substantial essay, which he titled 'Metamorphoses of Musical Form', was written in November and December 1958, and is an impressive testament to the thoroughness with which he had assimilated the literature and methodology of post-war Western music during the two years since he had left Hungary. It remains one of Ligeti's most significant contributions to aesthetic debate and a remarkably shrewd assessment of developments in the late 1950s, written with the insight of one operating close to the work-face. Not surprisingly, *Die Reihe*'s editors, Eimert and Stockhausen, gave it pride of place.

In this second article, Ligeti reinforces the criticism of serialism he made in *Die Reihe* 4. Both tonal architecture and serialism, he asserts (echoing the words of his Bartók article), 'at birth harboured the seeds of their own dissolution'. The expansion of the serial principle so as to govern global categories, like register and density, led to the sacrifice of the very pitch systemisation which had initiated the process: 'as the larger form-categories came under serial control, the serial ordering of the elementary parameters became looser and looser'. Concentration on textural density resulted in a decreased sensitivity to internal pitch relationships, what he calls 'an erosion of intervallic profile'. Yet this shift of emphasis also revealed new possibilities, particularly the way one type of textural character might impinge on another. Thus *Gruppen* escapes censure because of Stockhausen's success in achieving bold interactions between its three orchestras, and strong transitions from one dominant timbre to another, so counteracting the levelling tendency of serialism.

More generally, Ligeti condemns a widespread indifference towards the automated character of early serial music, which insidiously infected every parameter with its fatal entropy. Now that so many elements 'have been turned over to the tender mercies of serial distribution, it becomes increasingly difficult to achieve contrast. A flattening-out process has begun to absorb the whole musical form.' Typically, he finds a telling metaphor:

Let us take an illuminating analogy: playing with plasticine. The distinct lumps of the various colours gradually become more dispersed the more you knead the stuff; the result is a conglomeration in which patches of the colours can still be distinguished, whereas the whole is characterised by lack of contrast. Knead on, and the little patches of colour disappear in their turn, and give place to a uniform grey. This flattening-out process cannot be reversed. Similar symptoms can be discerned in elementary serial composition . . . the finer the network of operations with pre-ordered material, the higher the degree of levelling-out in the result. Total, consistent application of the serial principle negates, in the end, serialism itself. There is really no basic difference between the results of automatism and the products of chance; total determinacy comes to be identical with total indeterminacy.[21]

Why then have serial manipulations at all? Is it to achieve organic integrity through a network of preformed choices and limitations? Ligeti offers this straw of comfort without much conviction, but stops short of dismissing serialism outright. We must remember the extraordinarily dominant position serialism had come to occupy in the Western musical establishment during the 1950s, and the unlikelihood of even Ligeti dismissing it absolutely. He is too discerning, too aware of the contradictory forces of history.

Instead, he turns to how contrasts of texture evoke visual and tactile sensations, pointing to similarities with the plastic arts, especially painting. This is less relevant to the narrative manner of tonal music, in which the present is experienced in relation to what has been heard, and to a conditioned expectation of the future. But once form becomes dependent upon texture, colour and surface, 'the succession of events is a mere exposition of something that in its nature is simultaneous . . . as one's glance wanders over the canvas of a painting'. Temporal relations become spatial relations; interest arises from the way phenomena melt into each other; functions are superimposed at different levels of perception.

These tendencies do not paralyse the flow of time itself, but do succeed in completely dissociating it. In the literary or pictorial field they can be seen to correspond with the manipulation and interpolation of events (and thoughts) in Joyce's *Ulysses*, or with the 'temporalization' of space in Picasso's 'simultanistic' paintings.[22]

Ligeti began this important essay with the view that a generally new feeling for musical form seemed to be emerging. What is necessary, he finally concludes, is 'to try and achieve a compositional design for the process of change'.

Already Xenakis had done so. From *Pithoprakta* all traces of serial thinking have disappeared; instead the composer-architect employs probability theory, aggregating individual pitches to create differentiated sonic 'characters'. Xenakis cites parallels between such mass effects in music and statistical phenomena in the natural world: swarms of bees, flocks of birds, clouds billowing across the sky. Although the premiere of *Pithoprakta* at the Music Viva concerts in

Munich, on 3 March 1957, produced an even greater uproar than *Metastasis*, its significance eventually had considerable impact. Scherchen's Paris performance in 1960 was a huge success. And when Xenakis's music was introduced to the Darmstadt Summer Course and Warsaw Autumn Festival in 1962, both the music and its theoretical basis met with an enthusiastic response. At this time *Metastasis* and *Pithoprakta* were important models for Ligeti as well. That year he wrote to Xenakis, asking him to send a score and recording of *Metastasis*, having chosen to analyse it at Darmstadt in consequence of knowing *Pithoprakta*.

There are musical textures and new sonorities in this work which serve more adequately than any other music as typical examples of the technique of global composition and of the destruction of the individuality of voices . . .[23]

Composers both sides of the Iron Curtain in the early 1960s had found a new vision of massed sonority that would rejuvenate jaded concepts of orchestration, and create widespread interest in the early 1960s. Ligeti was to be a leading figure in this development, although others were on a similar path. In 1960 he made his own spectacular debut. Overnight it removed him from his role as an obscure Austro-Hungarian theorist to become, in the eyes of the world, one of Europe's most fascinating and original composers.

4

The Watershed of 1960:
International Debut

The machinations of ambiguity are among the very roots of
poetry.
William Empson[1]

Reinventing the orchestra

Ligeti was thirty-seven, *Apparitions* his first substantial orchestral
score. Its world premiere on 19 June 1960 not only brought him his
first real success as a composer; it also signalled a fundamental change
in the direction of contemporary music. The performance by the
North German Radio Orchestra under Ernest Bour took place during
the World Music Days, the annual gathering of the International
Society for Contemporary Music (ISCM) which in 1960 happened to
be in Cologne, and was received with spontaneous enthusiasm by the
delegates – many of them dulled, no doubt, by the usual dreary sub-
missions of national committees. Ligeti's sculptural, elemental shaping
of the music sounded refreshingly direct and original. The audience's
excitement at hearing a work so different from the predominantly
serialist repertoire of the 1950s was heightened by the antics of the
final section, then quite novel: brass players striking their mouthpieces
with the hand, glockenspiel clusters played with rulers and the third
percussionist wielding a large hammer above a sack of empty bottles.
In the engraved score which soon replaced the original facsimile, the
player is instructed to take a tray of porcelain and hurl it violently into
a large chest lined with hard metal. 'Wear protective goggles,' suggests
the composer in a considerate note.

After this flamboyant action, *Apparitions* expires in a dying string
glissando and an exhalation of breath from the brass. From a later perspective, we know how commonplace such mildly anarchic gestures
became, as music adopted more elements of theatre and performance
art – not to mention popular culture and left-wing politics – during the

96

'liberated' 1960s. Indeed, Ligeti's percussionists have destroyed innumerable further trays of crockery (for example in *Nouvelles aventures* and in the first scene of *Le Grand Macabre*, at the moment when the drunken Piet, descending into a grave to collect Nekrotzar's instruments of death, collides with Amanda, one of the two lovers, coming out). And there were more subversive precedents. Kagel's *Anagrama* of 1957–58 calls for whispering, hissing and screaming from the chorus and wild noises from the instruments. Also present in Cologne in 1958 was a Korean, Nam June Paik, who had attended Cage's lectures at Darmstadt and was influenced by Marcel Duchamp and Kurt Schwitters. Nam June Paik's *hommage à john cage* of 1959 incorporated live actions involving eggs, toy cars and a motorbike, whilst *étude for pianoforte* of 1960 required the mutilation of two pianos, cutting Cage's tie and shampooing him without warning, then rushing from the room and telephoning the astonished audience to announce that the performance was over. Paik went on to become European organiser of the Fluxus group with which, as we shall see, Ligeti was fleetingly involved in the early 1960s. But on the whole, if Ligeti did such things he did them for reasons of genuine acoustic exploration. How to bring to an end the increasingly wild and frenzied second movement of *Apparitions* was a real issue. A moment of music theatre seemed an apt denouement.

Apparitions, however, is impressive for more substantial reasons, and was so greeted by critics and commentators. Noting the 'frenetic applause' of the audience, Wolfgang Steinecke wrote in his review of the ISCM Festival for *Neue Zeitschrift für Musik* that 'a great compositional talent was revealed that had lain hidden only because of exceptional circumstances'.[2] The international constituency of the ISCM audience was advantageous. Particularly enthusiastic were a group of Swedes, including the composers Ingvar Lidholm and Karl-Birger Blomdahl, whose subsequent recommendation led to Ligeti's fruitful involvement in Swedish musical life during the 1960s. A little over a year later, Ligeti's second large orchestral score *Atmosphères* received its world premiere at the Donaueschingen Music Festival on 22 October 1961, its reception no less newsworthy. It had not gone well in rehearsal. The conductor Hans Rosbaud had not grasped its shape, but 'was unbelievably friendly and open'. Ligeti talked with him for ten minutes and explained that '*Atmosphères* is from beginning to end like a bow, which has a closed form. It must not be broken up. He understood very well. He spoke with the orchestra for a few minutes and then they tried it out. It was perfect!'³ Between them, these two epoch-making orchestral pieces established Ligeti's reputation as a composer of bold, provocative, extreme imagination, and far-reaching resonance.

The performances of both pieces occurred only through happy accident, the first due to the action of Mauricio Kagel, the second to the inaction of Luciano Berio. More disposed to pressurise than Ligeti, Kagel was trying to persuade the ISCM committee to include his *Anagrama* in the 1960 World Music Days, despite the fact that it had not been proposed by the Argentinian national section in Buenos Aires – the normal procedure – from whom he was now geographically separated. The selectors told him they would consider an individual submission, but only if it were not alone. The solution was obvious: encourage Ligeti to submit the orchestral work on which Kagel knew he was working. A year later a similar stroke of luck occurred. Berio had been invited by Heinrich Strobel, head of music at South-West German Radio and programme director of the Donaueschingen Festival, to compose a new piece for 1961, but it had not been completed. To fill the gap somebody suggested Ligeti, who promptly responded with the score of *Atmosphères*. For its inclusion Ligeti received DM1000, the first payment for a composition he received in the West; a proper commission fee would have been twice as much.

Music as texture

In *Apparitions* and *Atmosphères* Ligeti created his trademark, the unmistakable 'Ligeti sound' that would define his music for the next two decades. Both works, but especially *Atmosphères*, deal with the global character of the orchestral mass. The microscopic activity of each player's part is mapped out with immense care; but instead of single lines, we hear only the homogeneity of the whole. Sometimes the resultant cloud hangs motionless; elsewhere it trembles with energy, buzzing like a beehive. Ligeti moulds its inner detail to achieve effects of growth and decay, contrasts of register and timbre, moments of wild violence next to others of mysterious, echoing stasis. Coloration gradually changes. Textures merge imperceptibly, are abruptly juxtaposed or suddenly cut off. Clusters pile up ominously, or are squeezed and attenuated until they disappear.

This sculptural approach to sound was shared by other composers who had toyed with serialism, before being drawn into the comparative freedom of textural structures. Orchestral composition suddenly became popular again, whereas, in the post-war period, the very institution had been decried as tired, inflexible and moribund. Many examples of the new spirit appeared in 1960, notably Lutosławski's *Venetian Games*, which introduced a completely new era in the music of this established Polish master, organised through a succession of textural and timbral blocks. For the younger Penderecki, 1960 was also an exceptional year. By the end of it he had completed *Anaklasis*, *The Dimensions of Time and Silence*, his String Quartet no. 1 – a brittle, abstract exploration of the no man's land between pitched sound and noise – as well as the most celebrated work of his career, *Threnody for the Victims of Hiroshima*. Although Penderecki and Ligeti soon became associated in the public mind, their technical approach was significantly different. Penderecki emphasised broad washes, generalised clusters, glissandi and noise effects, Ligeti a far more intricate micropolyphonic web in which every part is individually shaped. But in the early 1960s this distinction was less apparent. In the central section of *Anaklasis*, for example, Penderecki uses a microrhythmic structure for unpitched, percussive sounds similar to that used by Ligeti towards the end of *Apparitions* (second movement, letter E) – each doing so unaware of the other's work.

When the premiere of *Anaklasis* took place at the Donaueschingen Festival on 16 October 1960, four months after the premiere of *Apparitions*, it seemed to vindicate the proposition that one could compose simply by using differentiated sound and noise patterns. Sandwiched between Yoritsuné Matsudaïra's *Suite di danze* and Messiaen's magnificent celebration of 'the colour of time', *Chronochromie* – all of them commissioned by Strobel – it was the more radical *Anaklasis* that excited a response. It was immediately encored, the sort of reception associated with first performances in the nineteenth century. The previously obscure names of Penderecki and Ligeti were now on everyone's lips. When *Threnody*, with its formidable tone-clusters, was premiered at the Warsaw Autumn Festival in September 1961, it too made an indelible impression on the public and was hailed as a symbolic milestone in the recent development of Polish music. Penderecki's later retreat into characterless neo-Romanticism was then unimaginable. In the 1960s his reputation as an innovator was high, his style much imitated. Both *Threnody* and *Atmosphères* quickly received further broadcasts and live performances in other countries. Dealt a mortal blow by this newly fashionable treatment of the orchestra, the downfall of serialism seemed to be assured.

First and second versions of *Apparitions*

In fact, *Apparitions* was only in part a reaction to Ligeti's West European encounters – serialism and electronic music being to the fore – since he had conceived important aspects of it before leaving Hungary. Its roots go back to his childhood dream of a dense tangled web, shaken and torn by entrapped insects (see p. 7), an image absorbed into the non-thematic, textural music he began to envisage in 1950. At that stage he could hear the sound in his head, but lacked the technical experience to notate it. During the summer of 1956 Ligeti made renewed attempts. With the confidence of having completed *Musica ricercata* and the String Quartet no. 1, he drafted *Viziók* for large orchestra, his most radical score so far. Having arrived in the West, he soon decided that, measured by Cologne standards, *Viziók* was unsatisfactory both technically and structurally, and recast it for chamber orchestra, attempting to strengthen its internal relationships by adding a second and third movement. Renamed *Apparitions*, this thorough revision was scored for twelve solo strings, harp, celesta, harpsichord and piano. Frustratingly, since the score of *Viziók* is lost, we cannot compare the two treatments, but the revised first movement also develops ideas from *Sötet és világos*, the orchestral fragment from 1956 which has survived. Both are marked 'Lento sostenuto' and begin in similar manner to the final version of *Apparitions*, with a sustained semitone cluster played by double basses, joined by the cellos, then passed to the harp (in the preliminary sketch of *Sötet és világos*). By the end of the new movement, the low cluster has slowly ascended into the top register of the violins, just as in the final version, and dies away on a diatonic cluster of four notes (D, F, G and A). In the middle are faster passages played by the harp and three keyboards.

Celesta and string dispositions apart, the instrumentation of this chamber version is exactly that used by the Swiss composer Frank Martin in his *Petite symphonie concertante*, a work written in 1944–45 which won notable international success. Ligeti had heard it during the 1947–48 concert season in Budapest, and had favourably reviewed

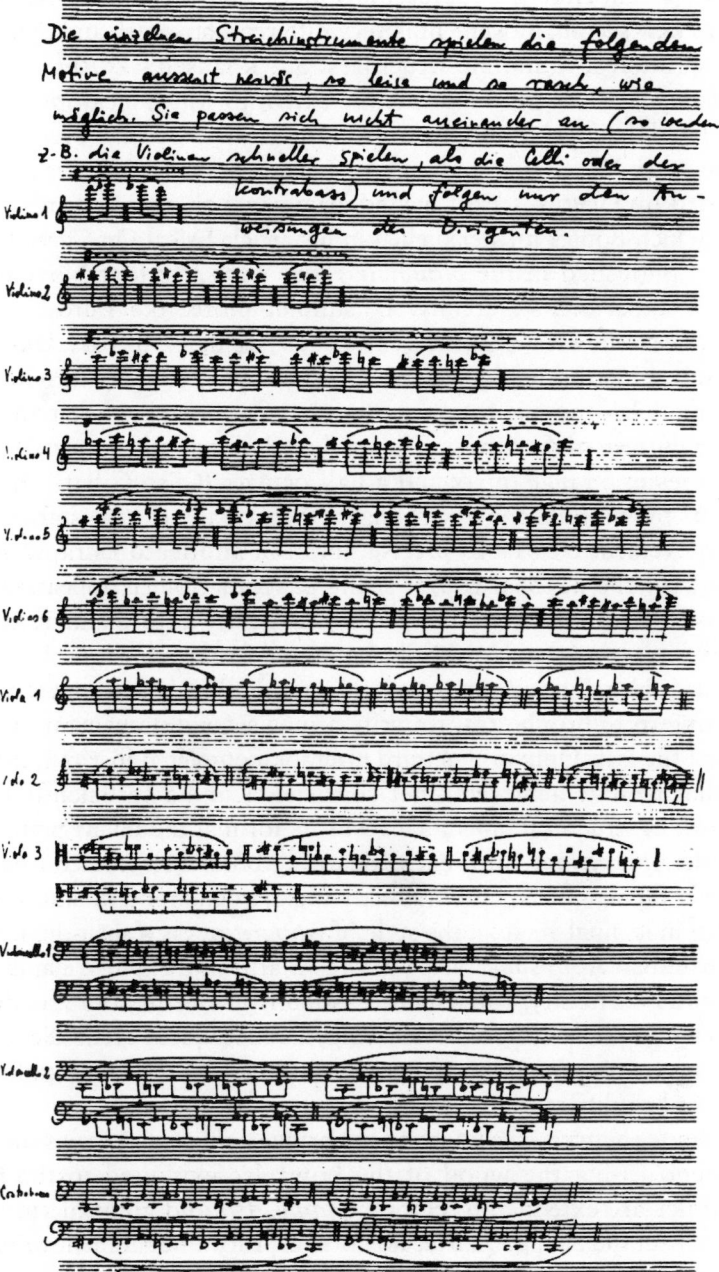

Ex. 9 Second movement of the first version of *Apparitions* (1957)

it for both Austrian and Hungarian music journals (in which he also deplored Schoenberg's representation by only *Verklärte Nacht*).[4] Ligeti's new second movement is very different, however, and reveals a fleeting interest in mobile structures. Stockhausen's *Zeitmasse* and *Klavierstück XI* of 1956 indicate the extent to which aleatoric issues, stimulated by Cage's example, were in the air. The German premiere of *Klavierstück XI* at Darmstadt in 1957 – the first of the summer courses attended by Ligeti – set off heated arguments about performer freedom, which Boulez further fuelled in his article 'Alea: On Chance and Music' published in the *Nouvelle revue française* that November. Ligeti's experiment is relatively simple, more like Lutosławski's 'aleatoric counterpoint' of the early 1960s (see Ex. 9, p. 101). Directed by the conductor, the twelve string players enter playing unsynchronised modules, ranging from a pattern based on two pitches in the top part to thirteen in the lowest. The total pitch distribution covers all the semitones in a range of six and a half octaves (C^1 to G flat^7). But as none of the module content changes, the overall effect is static. The final movement returns to precise notation and features rapid figurations for the keyboards over string *pizzicati* – but it appears to be unfinished. Still dissatisfied, Ligeti subsequently gave the manuscript of this version to Ove Nordwall as material for his monograph.

By now he had decided to recast the original *Viziók* section yet again reverting to full orchestra, to write a new second movement and to discard the last. Only in this third attempt, completed in 1958, did he feel that he had 'achieved inner consistency and a sufficiently tight network of structural links'.[5] This was its form at the ISCM premiere, the title *Apparitions* (in French) denoting both the sonic concept of ephemeral phenomena and indirectly Ligeti's childhood dream.

Even in its final version, the style of *Apparitions* is transitional. Less cohesive than *Atmosphères*, it is more volatile and explosive and also of greater difficulty, for which reasons it has been comparatively neglected in the concert hall. As in Ligeti's subsequent orchestral compositions, textural detail is defined with precision. The string players are asked to differentiate between five types of *pizzicato* and to vary the distance between the bow and the bridge, whilst techniques such as *col legno* (using the wood of the bow) are exploited to the full. Dynamics are extended to embrace *pppp*, *ffff* and all gradations in between. In the String Quartet no. 1, except for one moment of barely audible insect-like scurrying, Ligeti had stretched the normal

conventions by only one step in each direction, i.e. to *ppp* and *fff*.
Occasionally in later works he would go as far as *pppppp*, or even (as
in the Cello Concerto and Piano Étude no. 13) to *fffffffff* – a wholly
unrealistic ideal, one might think. But these are exceptions. At the time
they were written, orchestras were 'unaccustomed to playing less than
mezzo forte', unlike today 'when there are no rehearsals but they
know how to play pianissimo, so that some of my pieces you can't
even hear!' – but he has not revised their dynamics. In *Apparitions* and
thereafter, Ligeti differentiates between *pp*, *ppp* and *pppp*, charging
even the quietest of sounds with nuances, so that nothing is nondescript: the music remains vital and intense, however soft. To ensure
that such minute gradations of timbral and dynamic balance remain
audible requires exceptional tone control, especially from the wind
players in pianissimo, and an acute ear from the conductor.

In *Apparitions*, all the string players are allocated separate lines in
the score, making a total of forty-six staves when all play together.
Ligeti had been moving towards such multiple subdivision in both
Viziók and *Sötet és világos*, unaware that it had been pioneered two
years before by Xenakis. Separate staves facilitate notation, especially
where in *Apparitions* clusters in the lower strings span over an octave
of adjacent semitones, or all players have different patterns. Pitch
choices derive from a reservoir of semitones rather than from any
serial ordering, the few discernible melodic lines being freely atonal.
The work's broader proportions were influenced by constructivist
dogmas emanating from Cologne, as well as by Ernő Lendvai's identi-
fication of golden section structures and Fibonacci numbers in Bartók
– although in retrospect, Ligeti felt that he 'could have applied any
other principle of proportion just as well'.[6]

Micropolyphony: an 'intricate labyrinth of sound'[7]

In the second movement of *Apparitions*, for the first time in Ligeti's
music, we find an example of what he has christened 'micropolyphony', a technique with which he became strongly identified in the
1960s and 1970s. Micropolyphony is microscopic counterpoint, an
internally animated yet dense texture in which large numbers of
instruments play slightly different versions of the same line. At its core
can be a three- or four-part counterpoint of different melodies, but
with each multiplied by perhaps a dozen or more variants of itself,

resulting in an intricately complex web. Although micropolyphony may simultaneously employ every instrument in the score, more characteristically, bands of instruments enter and leave, and the composer's skill is in keeping timbral coloration in flux. Spinning the web, sculpting its expansion and contraction, controlling its direction, are all part of the art. Ligeti has cited the influence of Ockeghem, whose music he studied as a student, and one may think of micropolyphony as a distant descendant of Flemish polyphony, overlaid upon itself many times, with certain registral bands blocked out, as if removed by the filter-banks of an electronic music studio.

Usually instruments or voices start together or in succession on a single note. Frequently – although not in *Apparitions* – they enter so softly that they appear to grow out of an indefinable mist, rather than from definable pitch. Often the microscopic lines gradually diverge, the slow-motion expansion from a nucleus being one of Ligeti's most famous and magical hallmarks, subsequently much imitated. In *Apparitions*, however, the technique makes a more exuberant first appearance. Twenty-four violins simultaneously play exactly the same melodic pitch sequence, but each instrument has its own pattern of durations so that no two are rhythmically identical. The eight violas follow another pitch sequence, as do the fourteen cellos and double basses. The dynamic is *fff*, and the effect is of a seething mass of melodies, some more frenzied than others. Amongst the twenty-four violinists, the most active (the principal second violin) gets through forty-four notes in seven bars, whilst the least busy (the twelfth first violin) plays only twenty-three. However many notes a player dispatches before the micropolyphonic texture comes to an end, each draws from the same angular pitch sequence,[8] although Ligeti adds a note saying that 'verve is more important than completely accurate intonation'. Each player is to exert the utmost force, playing as intensely as if he or she were a soloist.

An absence of pulse

An equally significant development, apparent in both *Apparitions* and *Atmosphères*, is the removal of metre and pulse. Metrical rhythm was entrenched in the String Quartet no. 1, except for its prophetic last four pages in which glissandi of artificial harmonics accompany slithering melodic phrases, marked *sempre rubato, senza misura*. It was the beatlessness of the music forming in his mind in the early 1950s that had defeated his attempts to notate it. In *Apparitions* Ligeti tries two solutions. One is the composition of clustered textures which have no regular pulse, but are scored for convenience mainly in 4/4. This is his approach in the second movement, and it would serve for many more pieces. The other is to position the clusters, interspersed with more volatile events, in a sequence of changing time signatures, as in the first movement. Constant variation of metre occurs in other composers' scores in the 1950s and was motivated, in part, by a distaste for the rhythmic regimentation of martial music played incessantly during the Second World War. Executed with the sophistication of Boulez in *Le marteau sans maître*, changing bar-lengths and subdivisions create a wonderful elasticity. But for performers the counting of fractional tempo relationships can be inhibiting. This is hardly a problem in the first movement of *Apparitions*, because of its extremely slow tempo of crotchet = 40. Nevertheless, there is a different time signature in nearly every bar, and the music itself is awkwardly disjunct. The means influence the concept, as they are also dictated by it. Ligeti would not employ such constantly variable bar-lengths for a large group of players again.

There is no serial ordering in *Apparitions*, but to organise the material Ligeti employed a concept of 'scaling'. In the first movement this involves a 'repertoire of durations' planned with serial precision, but from a more logical standpoint. In standard duration series, where all gradations appear with equal frequency, longer durations dominate, simply because they are longer. Pitch series have no such hierarchies, but to a duration series they are endemic. To avoid this potential disadvantage, in *Apparitions* Ligeti created a 'system of apportionment [in which] the length of the shortest element, multiplied by the number of times it appears in the piece, matches the total length of the longest'.[9] The model for this approach was verbal language, in which letters like 'x' and 'z' occur infrequently whilst others appear more often. Any verbal language can be defined by the statistical frequency with which its component letters appear; whilst the way they are associated – the syntax – is at the behest of the user and accounts for his uniqueness of utterance. It is the method of 'scaling' in the first movement of *Apparitions* that results in its constantly changing bar-lengths and makes the music sound unpredictable. The same system had governed *Artikulation*. But its attraction for Ligeti was short-lived.

After 1960 he lost interest in predetermined repertories in favour of syntactical connections.

Already, the second movement of *Apparitions* reveals a different approach. It is as rhythmically fluid as the first, and no less textural, but the effect is achieved through simpler means. The movement has three sections, each using a different technique. The first is polymetric, the second micropolyphonic, the third a sequence of sonic blocks spawning fragments of melody. The first grows out of short clustered tremolos punctuated by rests, soon to encompass runs, cascades and brief fanfares. Beginning with the strings, its separate timbral layers are assigned different subdivisions of the beat (3, 5, 6, 9, 10 etc.), although the metre itself remains constant. The layers interact with much rapidity, the prevailing soft dynamic interrupted by sudden surges and explosions. The second section, entering ferociously in triple forte, is the micropolyphonic texture already discussed. It is in two segments, the second abruptly terminated 'as if snatched away', leaving behind an airy (and eerie) fluttering, as the wind and brass lightly tongue their instruments in unpitched polymetric patterns. There follow some scarcely audible tremolos, momentary swooping glissandi from the strings and trombones, and fragile strands of melody – a series of musical 'incidents' culminating in the third per- cussionist's *coup de théâtre*. The character of this movement is a prelude to the restless, fragmented manner of *Aventures, Nouvelles aventures* and the third movement of the Requiem.

Although most of those at the premiere of *Apparitions* reacted with enthusiasm, some demonstrably did not, including members of the North German Radio Orchestra who showed their contempt by refus- ing to stand to acknowledge the applause. *Apparitions* continued to provoke mixed reactions. At the Munich Music Viva a year later, the audience tittered with amusement and greeted the composer's arrival on the platform with boos and catcalls. 'Ligeti took the unfriendly reception with a smile,' wrote one critic, 'knowing that the problem- atic nature of his *Apparitions* cannot be concealed by applause.'[10]

Colour and harmony in *Atmosphères*

More than *Apparitions*, the premiere of *Atmosphères* in October 1961 was a defining moment in the establishment of Ligeti's mature style. From its opening fifty-nine-note cluster, entering pianissimo and gradually fading during the first minute without change of pitch or any other activity, the listener is drawn irrevocably into a mysterious new world of sound and sensibility. Yet, compared with the geometric scores of the Polish school and mathematically driven works of Xenakis, there is something directly emotional about *Atmosphères*. Ligeti's sensitivity to the expressive potential of pitch prevents his abandoning harmonic structure so completely. Despite its novelty, the piece owes more to the past. Like Boulez, Ligeti was fascinated by the fluidity of Debussy's late ballet score *Jeux*, which many of Debussy's contemporaries had considered to be incomprehensible, added to which its premiere in May 1913 had been upstaged by that of *The Rite of Spring* two weeks later. But by the 1950s *Jeux* had become widely admired amongst the avant-garde. In a radio talk in 1954, Stockhausen analysed Debussy's score in terms of sonic blocks, densities, mass, and their statistical tendencies,[11] claiming it as a prototype for the textural compositions of the 1950s. Equally influential for Ligeti were Schoenberg's *Five Pieces for Orchestra* which he also discovered around this time – notably the shimmering third movement, 'Farben'. And there were more distant precedents. At the start of Beethoven's Ninth Symphony and frequently in Bruckner the music begins with an atmospheric tremolo, as if defining the nature of the acoustic space into which the themes will be projected. *Atmosphères* explores only this void. Identifiable melodies and rhythms never emerge from its gaseous clouds. But the empty vessel never stagnates. As in Debussy, pitch, timbre and texture fuse together, animating the space.

A novel aspect of Ligeti's technique is the dynamic and timbral phasing that occurs within otherwise static clusters, changing their coloration and even their apparent harmony. The opening cluster in *Atmosphères* covers five and a half octaves and lasts for three quarters of a minute.[12] During this time the wind instruments gradually fade, the disappearance of their glowing sub-cluster in mid-register leaving a barely audible halo of divisi strings. The following cluster is played by violas and cellos, spans only an octave and a fifth and sounds noticeably 'cooler'. This is succeeded by a huge chromatic cluster at letter B, played by every instrument in the score and sustained for a whole minute. During this time groups of instruments crescendo and diminuendo in turn: first the trumpets, trombones and double reeds, then the flutes, clarinets and horns, finally the strings. As a result, not only do we hear timbral change; we seem to hear a chord progression, although in reality no pitch changes occur.

But the non-existent chord progression is not complete fiction. By highlighting different groups within the whole, Ligeti creates an illusion of four successive harmonies. The first is the cluster at letter B, sounding intensely soft but weighted towards the top. From this emerge and fade two brighter entities, chosen from the wide range of pitches already present. Both are diatonic chords but tonally opposed, as the spotlight shifts from a white-note aggregate (trumpets, trombones and double reeds) to a black-note pentatonic aggregate (flutes, clarinets and horns). After these also fade, there remains the cool afterglow of the strings playing *sul tasto* (on the fingerboard): pallid, drained of colour. The strings, too, apparently play a new cluster containing all the semitones spanning four and a half octaves. In fact these pitches have been sustained ever since letter B. Through timbral and dynamic shading Ligeti has caused different subgroups selectively to catch the light.

The technique of selective highlighting becomes far more sophisticated in *Lontano*, in which the timbral-dynamic phasing is extremely subtle. In *Atmosphères* most of the pitch structures are not conceived chordally at all, although they have a role in shaping the music. After the passage just discussed, the flutes, clarinets and strings (except the double basses) animate the sustained textures through a gradual introduction of tremolos. No two of these fifty-six tremolos are exactly alike, but they nearly all encompass minor thirds so that one senses a minor third identity within the chromaticism of the whole. Later (at letter H), there occurs a passage of micropolyphonic counterpoint for all the strings. As we observed, Ligeti first properly attempted a micropolyphonic texture in *Apparitions*, where it unleashed a ferociously energetic display. This second instance, the only passage of micropolyphony in *Atmosphères*, is different. The micropolyphonic web enters extremely softly, increasing in volume only in the last four bars. Each part has a stepwise pitch sequence except where octave shifts are necessary. What starts as a huge net stretched across five octaves winds down into the centre, the upper lines descending, the lower ascending. Gradually compressed, the fifty-six strands twist ever tighter into a dense knot, tied together by a minor third. Cut off at their maximum dynamic, we are left with a narrow cluster, sole residue of this many-layered polyphony, softly rotated by flutes,

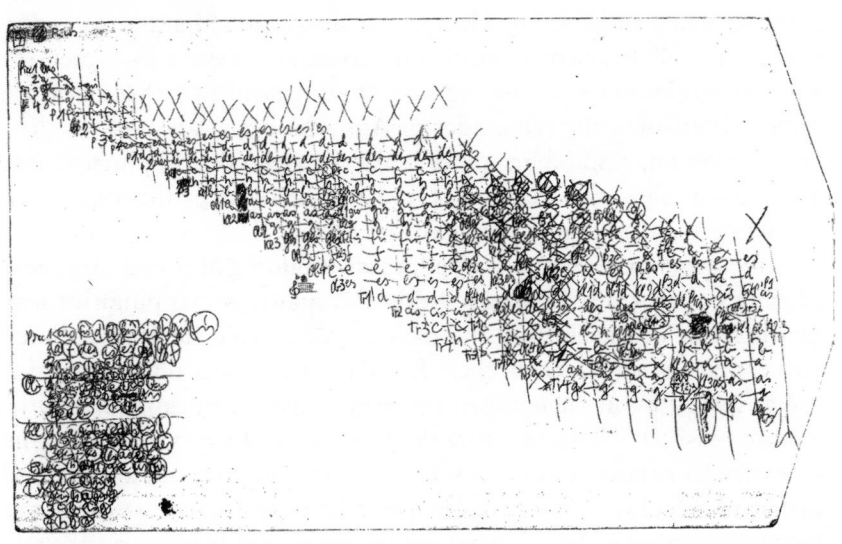

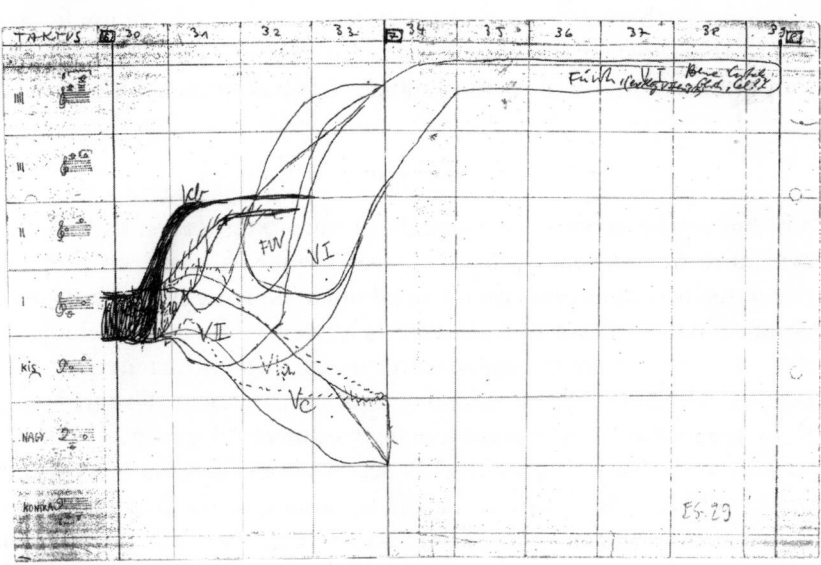

Ex. 10 Planning *Atmosphères*

clarinets and a single horn. The fan has slowly closed until it is barely pencil thick. A moment later, this quietude is dispelled by a metallic surge from the brass in low register, braying stridently through their mutes. Thereafter, the remainder of *Atmosphères* floats away in delicate flutters and vapid harmonics hardly recognisable as pitched. Just audible is a minor-third cluster played as harmonics by the four flutes, rolling up to another and dying away.

Atmosphères is essentially a sculptural moulding of sound. Amongst Ligeti's sketches are drawings, grids and matrices mapping the geometric shape of the clusters and their physical evolution through time (see Ex. 10, p. 109). From these it is clear that many of the minutiae are governed by mathematical, perhaps statistical rules. Tonal architecture must have been far from the forefront of Ligeti's mind. But the shadow of a harmonic subplot suggests that schooling and instinct had not been entirely overthrown. The presence of selective aggregates and recurrent intervals, the alternation of white- and black-note groups, the contrast between clustered constellations and their nuclei are things that exist in Debussy, if very differently – like the incessant minor-third motto in his piano Prélude, *Des pas sur la neige*.

Serial and electronic influences

Nor has serialism wholly disappeared from *Atmosphères*. Its legacy is evident in the micropolyphonic weave at letter H, where each of the twenty-eight violins plays an identical pitch sequence but with its own unique rhythm. The sequence itself is a twenty-four note melody, or two slightly different twelve-note series, descending across two octaves. The first of them extends a four-note segment (F sharp, G, F, E) by sequential transposition (the next segment is D, E flat, D flat, C) to fill the twelve-note gamut. The second does likewise but using a marginally different pattern. At the beginning of the passage all the violins enter together, starting on successive notes of the pitch series, proceeding from the principal first violin at the top to the fourteenth second violin at the bottom. Thus we hear the series both in linear and vertical form, except that for the twenty-eight violinists there are only twenty-four pitches, so four pairs share the same entry pitch. Meanwhile violas and cellos play a similar ascending twenty-four note series, sounding like an inversion of the violin series, but built in fact from retrogrades of each four-note segment in turn. Here, too, all the players enter together, each starting on the next note of the pitch series. Effectively this is a huge forty-eight-part canon combining tra-\ ditional retrograde and inversion techniques. Its purpose is chromatic saturation: a serial means to a non-serial end. Each line (fifty-six of them once the basses enter) is expressively charged, but none can be isolated. Individuals are subsumed in the crowd.

Atmosphères, as we recall, originated as an unrealised electronic score, *Pièce électronique* no. 3. Although nowhere can the electronic and the orchestral score be correlated, both are concerned with timbral phasing. Because it was conceived as an exercise using only sine waves, the orchestral piece has no place for percussion, apart from two players sweeping the strings of a grand piano, notably at the end. Oboes, which Ligeti had omitted from *Apparitions* because of their inappropriateness to the 'unreal' ghostly sound he sought, are now restored, but play for only nine bars. Neither piece has the elegance of later Ligeti. He was still working out the syntax of the new language and the results are somewhat idiosyncratic. Apart from cluster transformation, other facets vie for attention, especially in *Apparitions*: clock-like mechanisms, abrupt juxtaposition, flamboyant gestures. These he would differently emphasise throughout the 1960s. Some pieces focus on one approach, like *Lontano* and *Continuum*; others, like the String Quartet no. 2 and Chamber Concerto, mix or alternate these styles.

International excursions

Like *Anaklasis* the year before, *Atmosphères* was received so enthusiastically at its first performance in Donaueschingen on 22 October 1961 that it was immediately encored. Its reputation quickly spread, assisted by new vigour in the promotion of contemporary music. In Britain William Glock had become Controller of Music at the BBC. His programming of the Henry Wood Promenade Concerts, and of a new series of Invitation Concerts begun in 1959, initiated the BBC's boldest years of commitment to the European avant-garde. The BBC's Third Programme became essential listening for all aware musicians. The first relays of Ligeti's and Penderecki's orchestral novelties generated widespread interest and discussion, their sculptural treatment of sound instantly etched on the memory in striking contrast to the pointillism of Boulez and Stockhausen – let alone the late products of Stravinsky, by now an ageing camp follower of serialism.

Eastern Europe had become less remote. Whereas for Hungary the end of 1956 had been disastrous, in Poland Gomulka's cultural thaw allowed contacts with the West, enabling the Warsaw Autumn Festival to be established that year as one of the most important platforms for new ideas. With the increasing impact of America and growth of international travel, the authority of the Darmstadt–Cologne avant-garde diminished, undermined by its own fragmentation. During the winter of 1962–63 Stockhausen himself went to live for six months in a villa on Long Island, where he got to know many of the New York artistic elite and attended the first pop-art exhibitions by Andy Warhol and Roy Lichtenstein. Three months later, Xenakis also crossed the Atlantic to lecture at Tanglewood, finding that in the USA he was already a celebrity, even if few understood his music.

Ligeti was yet to make any significant impression in America. In January 1964 Leonard Bernstein introduced *Atmosphères* to New York, though it was not, in fact, the American premiere. A year earlier, the Cuban composer Aurelio de la Vega had organised a performance at the San Fernando Valley State College (later California State University, Northridge) where he had become professor of composition, and wrote to Ligeti to tell him about it. Unsurprisingly, in the wider circles of North American music, this performance went unnoticed.

Although Ligeti had settled in Vienna and would not visit America for another ten years, he was invited to lecture in Europe and Scandinavia. In 1959 he visited Stockholm and delivered (in German) two lectures on Bartók and Kodály. Mátyás Seiber had recommended him for a permanent post at the Royal Swedish College of Music. Ligeti did not get it, but in the autumn of 1961, he was asked back as a guest lecturer at the instigation of Lidholm (a pupil of Seiber) and Blomdahl (newly appointed chair of composition). The invitation was repeated, and Ligeti became a regular visitor returning every year until 1971, his visits helping to stimulate a new era in Scandinavian music. In 1962 he went for four weeks, but usually it amounted to a fortnight two or three times a year, providing him with a welcome source of income. His principal role was to direct the composition seminars which the Royal College organised as an adjunct to individual lessons. Besides the obvious choices of Debussy, Webern, Stockhausen and Cage, he lectured on Kagel's *Sonant*, Cerha's *Mouvements* and Cardew's electronic *Second Exercise*. His discussions of Romantic orchestral technique (especially Mahler's Sixth Symphony) led on to Schoenberg's use of *Klangfarbenmelodie* followed by his own approach as exemplified in *Apparitions*, *Atmosphères* and the Requiem. Some of the colouristic exercises written by his pupils, who included Folke Rabe and Arne Mellnäs, were reproduced in a booklet printed in Stockholm, in which Ligeti described the content of the seminars he had held in 1962–63.[13]

The work of the textural composers was observed by Boulez with polite but withering scorn. In 1963 he published *Boulez on Music Today*, written at Darmstadt and intended to fuel its polemic, observing not only that clusters and glissandi were too elementary for his liking, but that 'their recent abuse has rapidly turned to caricature. This quickly "parcelled" material is no guarantee of great acuteness of conception; it suggests, on the contrary, a strange weakness for being satisfied with undifferentiated acoustic organisms.'[14] In attacking a lack of differentiation, texturalists and serialists were now accusing each other of exactly the same defect!

Following Cage's European excursions, 'happenings' and the Fluxus phenomenon had also crossed the Atlantic from New York. The firecrackers they ignited, plus a few damp squibs, are subjects for the next chapter.

PART TWO
Fantasy and Technique

5

Distorting Mirrors:
Humour and Antilogic

For me the most powerful Surrealist image is, I must admit,
that which displays the highest degree of arbitrariness –
which takes longest to translate into practical language either
because one of its terms is mysteriously missing, or because it
promises to be sensational and then appears to fizzle out, or
because it suddenly narrows its field, or because it is hallucinatory by nature, or because it finds in itself some ridiculous
formal justification, or because it quite naturally makes the
abstract masquerade as concrete, or because it implies the
negation of some elementary property or, finally, because it
touches off laughter.
    André Breton[1]

The huge plunge into the depths near the middle of *Atmosphères* is an
instance of extreme dislocation which, if it sits a little uncomfortably
amongst the otherwise gradual transformations, is nonetheless wholly
typical of the composer. Four screeching piccolos ascend to their highest cluster, spanning a minor third although too shrill to be identifiable
as pitch. Suddenly the piccolos give way to a thunderous cluster six
octaves lower played by the double basses, as if the music had disappeared from the top of the frame and reappeared at the bottom. The
shock of this juxtaposition belongs to a different facet of Ligeti's
musical character, his taste for sudden disruptions and disorientating
contrasts. Such volatility had characterised *Artikulation*. During the
early 1960s Ligeti resumed this kaleidoscopic approach to structure,
encouraged by an anarchic climate emanating from America, with its
resurgence of Dadaistic, anti-art tendencies that seemed to remove any
obligation to preserve conventional logic and which Ligeti, with his
natural impishness, love of the absurd and self-mocking wit, was more
than ready to share.

Cage and Fluxus

The admiration of Hungarian intellectuals for ironically fantastic humour found a natural corollary in Ligeti's liking for its English-speaking equivalent, as embodied in the writings of Edward Lear and Lewis Carroll, or in the *New Yorker* cartoons of the émigré Romanian satirist Saul Steinberg. Carroll was a surrealist in all but name. The illogical nature of Alice's encounters might almost be a route map for the non-sequential 'happenings' that became fashionable in New York around 1959–63. Their immediate antecedent, however, was a 'concerted action' staged at Black Mountain College in North Carolina in 1952 by John Cage, who, with the pianist David Tudor, dancer Merce Cunningham, painter Robert Rauschenberg and others, presented an unprecedented collage of music, dance, painting, recitation, actions, recordings, films and slides – entirely unrelated to each other. It was the first (and now historic) post-war mixed-media event.

In the wake of this and similar spectacles, 'theatre' – as Cage defined it – spilled over into many unsuspecting corners of everyday life, apparently rigid boundaries disappeared, and ideas of what was admissible changed for ever. By the end of the decade another Californian composer now resident in New York, La Monte Young (b.1935), was leading the way in extreme performances. His compositions of 1960 reveal a touchingly humanitarian streak along with a subversion of normality. *Piano Piece for David Tudor* no. 1 instructs the performer to bring a bale of hay and a bucket of water on to the stage so that the piano (too long an ill-treated workhorse, one might think) can 'eat and drink'. Another piece calls for butterflies to be released into the performance area, but with the proviso that they must be allowed to fly away outside at the end. Returning to first principles is the single injunction of *Composition* no. 10 – 'draw a straight line and follow it' – whilst less potentially disruptive but no less momentous is *Composition* no. 7, with its two pitches (B and F sharp) followed by the simple instruction: 'to be held for a very long time'. This piece became the credo of La Monte Young's entire career: an opening of ears and minds to an unobserved universe of inner frequency relationships and psychoacoustic perception, revealed through the medium of infinitely long drones.

In 1961 Cage published his remarkable book *Silence*.[2] It contains nuggets of Zen wisdom, mushroom-gathering anecdotes, statements of belief, simple stories, essays (on Satie, Varèse and Rauschenberg), and the text of lectures Cage had delivered during the previous decade, laid out on the page with bewildering artistic licence to emphasise their role as compositional processes, mobiles, simultaneous events etc. Three of these lectures – entitled 'Changes', 'Indeterminacy' and 'Communication' – were attended by Ligeti at the Darmstadt Summer Courses in 1958. Highly idiosyncratic in their discontinuity, they are more thought-provoking than informative. The third contains only rhetorical questions relieved by assorted quotations, which include remarks about information theory, lines such as 'Every day is a beautiful day' and 'I have nothing to say and I am saying it', and finally, a philosophical story from Kwang-Tse.

For impressionable minds – Ligeti being one, the Italian composer Franco Donatoni (1927–2000) another – Cage's extreme subversion of Western maxims was both exhilarating and disturbing. One can see similar traits in these three unalike composers: their charm, spirit, generous encouragement of others, debunking humour and, particularly in the case of Cage and Ligeti, gift for communicating ideas through memorable metaphors. Ligeti got to know Cage at Darmstadt and was also present at the European premiere of *Concert for Piano and Orchestra*, its remarkable graphic score as much an icon of the visual as of the musical avant-garde. He was attracted to Cage as a person but dubious about his ideas. Thirteen years later, in conversation with Pierre Michel, he would say despairingly 'I really like Cage; I admire what he does, but . . . his attitude!'[3] Following the initial allure of Cage's permissive philosophy, neither Ligeti nor Donatoni allowed its deconstructive force to destabilise, at least for too long, their own creative bent. But inevitably, Cage's influence remained subliminally present. In August 1961, Ligeti demonstrated his Cagean credentials at a European Forum held at Alpbach in the Austrian Tyrol, where leading practioners and theorists had gathered to discuss the future of their art forms. Invited to contribute, Ligeti had misgivings:

From the first, when I was asked to discuss the future of music before an audience of academicians, I had grave doubts, because what can, in fact, be said about the future? However knowledgeable one is, there is only one thing which is certain, and that is that the future will be something completely different from one's prophecy. In order not to deliver untruths, I decided to say nothing.[4]

The organisers had assured Ligeti that he could say, or do, what he liked. He decided to give not a lecture but a 'musical provocation' for 'non-speaker' and audience. He mounted the stage, set his stopwatch for the allotted ten minutes, and began to take notes recording the behaviour of the audience, occasionally breaking off to write in different colours on the blackboard such incitements as: 'Please don't clap or stamp your feet', 'Crescendo', 'Più forte', 'Silence', 'Don't let yourself be manipulated!' As Louis Christensen reported:

After one minute the first hissing began and various cries and foot stamping increased, but at about four minutes the audience seemed to tire (the slow movement). After five minutes the impatience grew, and when an indignant professor banged the auditorium door as he left shortly after the sixth minute, it became the signal for something like an opera finale, with lots of action, solo, and choruses 'performed with perfect ensemble'. After eight minutes some 'soloists' approached the podium in a threatening manner and removed Ligeti, claiming that he had used up half an hour![5]

Ligeti's impromptu performance matched Cage's definition of 'theatre' being all around us. Two years later, some American manifestations were gathered in a collection edited by La Monte Young and called *An Anthology*.[6] Its table of contents is arranged as a graphic montage so as to list in no particular order, 'chance operations, concept art, anti-art, meaningless work, natural disasters, indeterminacy, improvisation, plans of action, stories, diagrams, poetry, essays, dance constructions, mathematics, compositions'. Apart from La Monte Young, contributors included Earle Brown, Yoko Ono, Toshi Ichiyanagi, Nam June Paik, Terry Riley, Christian Wolff and, naturally, Cage himself.

This unique publication contains unconventional typography, pages perforated with holes like Emmental cheese, envelopes with enclosures, and many novel examples of music notation, the whole book printed on variously coloured sheets. Its designer was a Lithuanian called George Maciunas (1931–78), whose family had settled in New York in 1948. Trained in art and graphic design, in 1960 Maciunas and a fellow Lithuanian, Almus Salcius, opened a small gallery on Madison Avenue, at much the same time as they resolved to launch a cultural magazine for émigré Lithuanians, for which Maciunas invented the name 'Fluxus'. The exhibition space was christened the AG Gallery after their two first names, although some thought it stood for 'avant-garde'. Unfortunately, the ultra-modern art failed to sell, the gallery was little visited and the journal, although announced in the papers, never appeared. Meanwhile, Maciunas had been attending composition classes given by a pioneering electronic composer, Dick Maxfield. At Maxfield's instigation, Maciunas decided to turn the AG Gallery into a centre for concerts, initiating a lifelong habit of making master plans: in this case a five-year programme of new and very old music, art performances, poetry readings and publications – its grandiose ambition modelled on Soviet Five-Year Plans, of which Maciunas was an admirer.

In this milieu Maciunas met Cage, Ono, Young and many who would feature in the Fluxus movement. But the literary and musical programmes incurred huge losses. By the end of 1961 the gallery was bankrupt. Leaving *An Anthology* in its design stage, eventually to become a source book for Fluxus and the new arts, Maciunas flew to Wiesbaden in Germany, where he took a job as an architect and designer for the US Air Force and began to court the European leaders of the avant-garde. Stockhausen was an obvious target, having just created his own happening in imitation of Cage, named *Originale*, which had been given twelve performances in the Theater am Dom in Cologne during October. For this, Stockhausen organised a structure of eighteen scenes, its duration determined by a performance of *Kontakte* cut up into segments, between which bizarre sequences were presented simultaneously on different planes by some twenty other participants, many of them painters, theatre people and notable 'originals' from Cologne, including an attendant from the monkey house at the zoo and a newspaper vendor known for her witty street-cries. David Tudor and Christoph Caskel, the percussionist, appeared in a variety of outlandish costumes. But the most outrageous actions were those of Nam June Paik:

Moving like lightning, [Paik] threw peas up at the roof over the audience, or straight at them. Clad in a dark suit, he smeared himself all over with shaving cream, emptied a bowl of flour or rice over his head and jumped into a bathtub full of water. He submerged, then ran to the piano, began playing a sentimental salon piece, tripped over and banged his head several times on the keys. Paik's absurd actions changed every day . . . Once, when he knew that the 'informal' painter Karl Otto Götz was in the audience, he poured inky water over his head, ran out to the toilet, flushed it and came back wiping his hair with a toilet roll.[7]

Ligeti took no active part, but witnessed the event from the (relatively) safe distance of the auditorium. In no time *Originale* became a civic scandal and, with ten performances still to run, the city withdrew its subsidy.

In Paik, Maciunas had found a ready-made Fluxus collaborator. When Maciunas mounted the world's first Fluxus Festival the following autumn in Wiesbaden, Paik became his principal associate. Its fourteen concerts grouped over four weekends in September 1962 contained, in fact, some perfectly serious compositions, like Stockhausen's *Klavierstücke* IV and Toru Takemitsu's *Vocalism A-I*. Others on the programme read more intriguingly: Philip Corner's *Passionate Expanse of the Law*, Frederic Rzewski's *Three Rhapsodies for Slide Whistles*, George Brecht's *Word Event* and Luc Ferrari's *Étude aux accidents* and *Tête et queue du dragon*. Ligeti had also been prevailed upon to take part. As he recalls, 'George Maciunas had informed me that I belonged to Fluxus, with the simple argument: "Ligeti, I want you." So, since I was already a member, as well as a friend of Nam June Paik . . . I suggested or performed numerous Fluxus pieces in the following two years.'[8] The piano composition which Ligeti provided for the Fluxus Festspiele in Wiesbaden had been written for David Tudor at the same time as his Cagean lecture, but was even better suited to the Fluxus environment. Entitled *Trois Bagatelles*, or 'musical ceremonial' for a pianist, it contains only one note, after which all is silent. The score instructs the performer not to play from memory, and there is an optional encore consisting of one semiquaver rest. Surprisingly, Ligeti says that he did not know about 4'33", which Cage had 'composed' in 1952, otherwise he 'would not have dared to make this joke'. Three months later *Trois Bagatelles* was repeated at another 'Festum Fluxorum' in Paris, to which the public was enticed by an explanatory subheading on the poster, promising 'Poetry, Music and Anti-music, Concrete and Sensational Occurrences'.

As a reaction to more earnest endeavours in Cologne, it is hardly surprising that Ligeti should have been attracted to Fluxus; but he was more amused than inclined to take it seriously. Fluxus was a comparatively short-lived phenomenon in Europe, but it had disciples in New York, Scandinavia, Japan, and even in England where the young John Cale, still a student at Goldsmith's College, organised a Fluxus-inspired concert so provocatively insane that the distraught music staff could hardly decide whether to summon help from the police or a lunatic asylum. Ligeti's name continued to appear on 'Festum Fluxorum' programmes, until Maciunas unexpectedly returned to the States in 1963. He was never part of its inner sanctum but was attracted to its openness, as he had already been by Cage.

During 1961 he completed only one other composition, really nothing more than a sketch – a *Fragment*, as its name indicates, of only eleven bars. Lasting for between seven and ten minutes, *Fragment* is Ligeti's strangest piece – an ironic pastiche of *Apparitions*.[9] Scored for three double basses, double bassoon, bass trombone, contrabass tuba, harp, piano, celesta (all in low register), tam-tam and large drum, it was written ostensibly as a sixtieth birthday tribute to Alfred Schlee, the director of Universal Edition in Vienna, and publisher of *Apparitions* and *Atmosphères*. Much of it consists of a single chord on the double basses, spelling out the musical notes in Dr Schlee's name, which is to be sustained uninterrupted for up to four minutes. In fact, Ligeti was upset that Schlee had attended neither of his orchestral premieres. Schlee had published *Atmosphères* only because Donaueschingen needed the material quickly, and apparently knew nothing of its success. UE already boasted Boulez and Stockhausen in its catalogue and was currently negotiating to add Berio and Pousseur. For Schlee, Ligeti's music held no further interest – although he was later to regret this judgement. Nonetheless, UE issued an engraved score of *Fragment*, giving the piece a cachet which Ligeti had never intended.[10] Thereafter he took his work to Peters in Frankfurt and, from 1967, to Schott in Mainz. Schlee was also absent from the premiere of *Fragment* on 23 March 1962, but the occasion was distinguished by a rare ascent of Ligeti himself onto the podium in order to lead the members of the Munich Philharmonic Orchestra through the performance. This was one of only three times in his life when Ligeti has attempted to conduct. The last was a performance of *Atmosphères* at the Musica Viva concerts in Munich in 1963, at the insistent invitation of Karl Amadeus Hartmann, who died before the concert took place leaving Ligeti with a sense of obligation, despite his earlier protests. His apprehension was well founded, since the experience proved terrifying. 'I was helpless with the orchestra . . . my God. Never more!'

Volumina

The first performance of Ligeti's final Fluxus composition, his grandiloquently titled *Poème symphonique* for 100 metronomes, happened in the most bizarre circumstances any Fluxus activist might desire. But before he had even thought up the idea, he was invited by the head of the Music Section at Radio Bremen, Hans Otte, to write an organ work for Bremen Cathedral. Also commissioned were two other composers who, like Ligeti, had trained as organists: Mauricio Kagel and Bengt Hambraeus, a Swede five years younger than Ligeti, who had worked with distinction in the WDR studio in Cologne as well as the new electronic music studio in Milan. In wishing to transfer to the organ the clusterous manner of his new orchestral works, Ligeti was aware of Hambraeus's *Constellations* I–III for organ and tape (1958–61), in which a virtuoso use of the stops contributes as much to articulation as to colour. As his first commission in the West, Ligeti turned energetically to his new composition, to be called *Volumina*, completing it in just over a month. Alas, despite his entirely serious intent, a whiff of Fluxus anarchy lingered in the air and, dogged by disasters (whether 'natural' or man-made it's hard to say), its broadcast premiere had some of the attributes of a 'happening'.

Ligeti was attracted less to the organ's nobility of utterance than to its shortcomings – its 'stiffness, clumsiness and unwieldiness' – and its unexplored possibilities of tone colour. Given the instrument's ability to sustain, to mask individual 'attack' through registration, and the oily ease with which sounds can be rolled up and down the keyboard and across the manuals, it seemed an ideal medium in which to explore the textural fluidity he had developed in *Apparitions* and *Atmosphères*. *Volumina* is composed entirely of clusters, some static, others trembling with internal movement, pyramiding, dissolving, shifting in register. The rapid addition or subtraction of pipes causes fluctuations of volume as well as of density. Timbral transformations are achieved by rolling clusters between manuals. There being a single performer (albeit with one or two assistants to operate the stops) and therefore no problem of ensemble coordination, Ligeti decided that in this piece he would use graphic symbols, following the cluster notation originated by the Polish musicologist Felix Wrobel,[11] and exemplified in Penderecki's *Threnody*. A vogue for graphic scores had rapidly arisen, led by composers like Kagel, the Italian Sylvano Bussotti, Polish-born Roman Haubenstock-Ramati and Bulgarian-born Anestis Logothetis. Both these last Ligeti knew well, since like him, they had spent time working with electronics before taking up residence in Vienna.

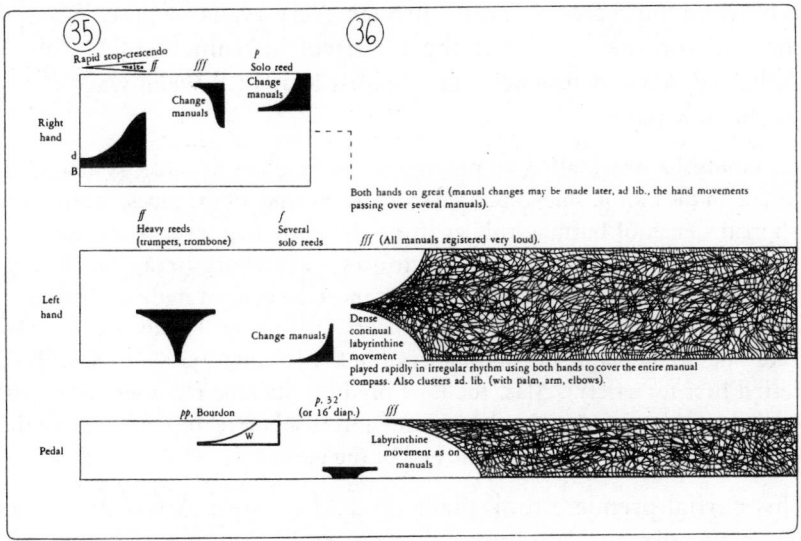

Ex. 11 Ligeti's graphic notation in *Volumina* (1961–62)

Although *Volumina* is the only score in which Ligeti uses graphic symbols, for this piece they are entirely appropriate. To realise his concept of an amoebic sonic mass, detailed pitch definition is less important than the moulding of larger shapes. Yet the performed result is less imprecise than one might think. The organist can play individual passages at whatever speed he or she chooses, but the duration of each page must average forty-five seconds. The piece is timed to last sixteen minutes, and the overall impression of any two performances sounds much the same. *Volumina* is also an apt title, for as in *Atmosphères*, the music seems to probe the distant reaches of musical space. 'Strange contortions of sound', says Ligeti, create 'an empty form of immense expanses and distances, an architecture consisting only of featureless façades, in which figures appear without faces, as in the paintings of Chirico.'[12]

Ligeti had tried out techniques for playing clusters on a mechanical organ in the Vienna Conservatory. They ranged from small, dextrous movements of the palms of the hands to chromatic clusters embracing the entire keyboard, produced by both arms between them depressing every key. That, indeed, is how the piece starts, with all stops drawn and coupled before the motor is turned on, gradually gathering wind to blow an unprecedented tutti through every available pipe. What no one had foreseen was that the electrical instrument of Göteborg Cathedral in Sweden, where the organist Karl-Erik Welin was practising the new piece,

. . . would be overloaded by playing so many pipes at once. When Welin turned on the motor, smoke poured from the vicinity of the pipes, followed by a horrid stench of burning rubber (from the insulating layer of the electrical wires). When the news of the 'burnt-down' Göteborg organ reached the Bremen church council, they decided to cancel the concert in the cathedral . . . So the 'premiere' was heard in a concert on Bremen Radio, from a tape recording Welin had made on the organ in the Johanniskyrkan in Stockholm (tested first for safety). Alas, the tape used on the tape recorder at Swedish Radio had been too short, and we found only just before the performance that a few minutes were missing at the end of the piece.[13]

This partial premiere took place on 4 May 1962. A few days later, Welin performed *Volumina* complete and without accident at the Westerkerk in Amsterdam. In 1966–67 Ligeti made a revised version which Welin also premiered. Meanwhile Welin had been enlisted by George Maciunas to share with Frederic Rzewski the four concerts of piano music with which the first Fluxus Festival opened in Wiesbaden on 1 and 2 September 1962. It is a nice irony that, while in *Volumina* he had activated thousands of pipes simultaneously, in *Trois Bagatelles*, which he performed in Wiesbaden, Welin had only to play one note.

Ceremonial with metronomes

Ligeti did not attend the Wiesbaden concerts and was unaware that they included an interactive piece for metronome and three or more performers, *Music for Electric Metronome* (1960), by the Japanese composer Toshi Ichiyanagi.[14] It is indicative of the widespread resurgence of Dada, however, that independently, Ligeti should also think up a piece for massed metronomes, in this case all mechanical. With its splendidly inappropriate title, on the face of it *Poème symphonique* is

subversive anti-art. In reality, it was also an experiment in indeterminate rhythmic counterpoint, furthering Ligeti's exploration of
micropolyphonic textures. As a Fluxus diversion, it had the entertain-
ment value of guessing which of the stalwart participants would stay
the course the longest. As music, it offered the interest of individual
clockwork mechanisms heard together and gradually thinning out,
the stuttering hocket of the last survivors making an amusing and
unpredictable epilogue. Whereas Ichiyanagi's composition required
just one metronome, Ligeti planned to use a hundred, all wind-up
pyramid metronomes whose ensemble performance would be acousti-
cally and visually engaging. For the moment he had no performance in
mind and no idea how to obtain the metronomes.

The opportunity arrived the following autumn when Ligeti took
part in the annual Gaudeamus Music Week in Holland, a series of
courses and concerts (still important in the new music calendar),
intended to provide openings for young professional composers, for
which he had been asked to provide a piece. All he had ready was the
Poème symphonique which, he nervously suggested, was hardly suit-
able. But the organisers were not to be put off. With such a title, it was
surely the ideal choice for the final civic reception, to be held on 13
September 1963 in the impressive surroundings of Hilversum City
Hall. The occasion turned out to be alarmingly formal. Ligeti's instructions read with deceptive propriety, directing the ten performers and
conductor to wear evening dress, file soberly on and off stage, and
return at the end to take a dignified bow. But in between was provocation. He has enjoyed retelling the tale many times since. Hosted by
the mayor in his ceremonial outfit complete with silver sabre, attended
also by the Spanish ambassador similarly attired and with brightly
coloured cockade – both of whom made speeches praising 'the sublime
value of musical art' – the distinguished guests included the elderly and
venerable Willem Marinus Dudok, the City Hall's modernist architect.

Walter Maas, the leader of the Gaudeamus Foundation and a legendary figure
in the world of new music, had ordered the 100 metronomes on loan from the
Wittner company in Isny in Allgau (Germany). He took on the costs of the
loan, transportation and insurance. As to what I intended to do with the 100
metronomes, he did not ask . . . In Hilversum the piece was set in motion by
ten performers, eight men and two women, all composer participants in the
Gaudeamus music week. My directions stated that the executants were to
appear in tails or evening dress. So on the afternoon of the reception, the eight

gentleman composers drove to a tuxedo rental shop in Utrecht. As I was to participate as conductor, they brought me tails too, but there was no time to try them on. Only when the evening was already under way did I discover that the stiff tuxedo shirt was several sizes too large – so my appearance fitted the Fluxus image.

I couldn't try my clothing on because there was a more pressing problem: 100 metronomes lay in a distant corner of the city hall, packed safely for shipping in ten wooden crates nailed tightly shut. I stood all alone in front of these wooden boxes, armed with a hammer and a pair of pincers. Opening the crates was child's play, but the metronomes (all brand new) had been delivered wound up, every last one. So the first thing I had to do was open them and set them in motion to run them down. I had no idea at the time that even at the fastest setting it takes a fully wound-up metronome a good half-hour to completely unwind. Then there was the added difficulty that the wind-up key was taped securely to the bottom of each device. So first I had to liberate the 100 keys and then screw each one individually into its keyhole.

It was already September, but the sun was still blazing hot. I was covered with sweat, alone, and panic-stricken. How on earth was I going to get all these preparations done before the beginning of the reception – how was I going to get the 100 metronomes set up on pedestals in the banquet room of the city hall before the guests arrived, and cover them with black cloths so that the public would have no idea what kind of music was going to be performed? Somehow I managed to finish at the very last minute; the ten musicians arrived and fairly flew off to the hall, metronomes in hand. Some composer friends rubbed me down with a broad terry cloth, and I had to jump into my waiting tails, half dry. But nobody knew how to fasten the unfamiliar buttons and clasps, nor how to tie a real bow tie.

In the meantime, Dutch Television trucks had arrived with television cameras . . . Following the official speeches, the premiere proceeded according to plan. Since the audience had never heard of Fluxus, and since John Cage, too, was as yet completely unknown to the invited nobility and citizens of Hilversum, the last tick of the last metronome was followed by an oppressive silence. Then there were menacing cries of protest . . . Two days later – I was still Walter Maas's guest in the curious Gaudeamus Foundation house, which was shaped like an open grand piano – we sat in front of the television awaiting the scheduled broadcast of the filmed event. But, instead, they showed a soccer game . . . the programme had been prohibited at the urgent request of the Hilversum Senate.[15]

Notwithstanding the scandal, it is the acoustic quality of *Poème symphonique* that continues to be interesting. Its superimposition of pulsation grids – a *moiré* effect familiar in physics – results in a rhythmic evolution whose properties Ligeti would variously exploit in subsequent compositions. At the start, the grids are so numerous that they coalesce, sounding disorderly and blurred. To achieve adequate textural density, he needed large numbers of metronomes. A hundred had been an estimate. Ligeti had never dreamed that someone would actually put them at his disposal. 'That required the tenacity and deeply lovable naivety of Walter Maas.'

As soon as some of the metronomes have run down, changing rhythmic patterns emerge, depending on the density of the ticking; until, at the end, there is only one, slowly ticking metronome left, whose rhythm is then regular. The homogeneous disorder of the beginning is called 'maximal entropy' in the jargon of information theory (and in thermodynamics). The irregular grid structures gradually emerge, and the entropy is reduced, since previously unpredictable ordered patterns grow out of the opening uniformity. When only a single metronome is left ticking in a completely predictable manner, then the entropy is maximal again – or so the theory goes.

Since 1963, *Poème symphonique* has been performed many times. In later performances I dispensed with the Fluxus ceremony altogether, which is really rather superfluous. The piece can be set up by a few performers – even by just one. The metronomes should be started before the audience enters the concert hall, so that the piece truly runs like a machine: metronomes and audience are confronted with each other without any human mediation.[16]

In that the running down of their separate mechanisms takes time, *Poème symphonique* charts successive stages in a polyrhythmic counterpoint that is differently perceived by every listener; for the interpretation of acoustic (and visual) patterns is to a degree subjective. Ligeti's basic idea for the piece had germinated over many years, originating in his childhood reading of Gyula Krúdy's tale of a house full of clocks, and the memory of his uncle's printing works in Dicsőszentmárton. Although an interest in pulsation grids was also shown by others, the metronome experiment – with its Pythonesque humour – remains unique.

Absurd adventures

Poème symphonique was committed to paper (a single typed sheet of instructions) towards the end of 1962. Most of Ligeti's attention in the previous six months had been devoted to another project which, like other novelties of the 1960s, had taken root a decade earlier. Whilst still in Budapest, he thought of composing music simulating speech; soon after arriving in Cologne, he expounded the idea during a walk with Stockhausen. Stockhausen suggested realising it in the medium of electronic music, and so *Artikulation* was born. But ideally, the concept needed live performers to act out the theatre of communication (and non-communication) Ligeti had in mind. In the early summer of 1962 he returned to the idea: by December, he had completed *Aventures*, the first of two concentrated works of stylised music theatre. He had intended to write just one piece, but the novelty of its disjointed structure had to be worked out from scratch: there were no precedents. Sensing that such capriciously schizophrenic music could not be long sustained, he chose to break off after a bleak, isolated alto solo, by which point he had composed a loose-linked chain of episodes lasting around eleven minutes. In this form *Aventures* was premiered in Hamburg, on 4 April 1963, by Friedrich Cerha's Ensemble 'die reihe' of Vienna, in a concert promoted by North German Radio. Ligeti then turned to composing the Requiem which had been commissioned by Swedish Radio – the 'Dies irae' movement was a direct outcome of the frenetic, disjunct manner of *Aventures*. Three years later, after completing the Requiem, he took up the left-over sketches of *Aventures*, restarting where he had left off, to create a companion piece of similar length called *Nouvelles aventures*. Despite differences in emphasis – *Nouvelles aventures* has two linked movements and is more parodistic – the pieces ideally complement each other and have habitually been performed together.

Looking at their scores, one is drawn to the intricacy of detail and idiosyncrasies of notation, designed to convey innumerable gradations between sung and half-voiced pitches, whispering and exclamation, exhalation and inhalation. Both scores use the International Phonetic Alphabet, with its 120 or so different symbols. Both are also a forest of verbal instructions, indicating the shades of characterisation between which singers must differentiate – performing if possible from memory. One can hardly imagine these facsimiles of Ligeti's highly personal handwriting being typeset without losing their individuality. But what most distinguishes *Aventures* and *Nouvelles aventures* from other music theatre of the time is that, despite the profusion of detail, neither piece has any specific scenario, nor intelligible text. Beneath the gestural surface is no actual meaning. By using an artificial language and stylised behaviour, Ligeti suggests relationships that are realistic, funny and disquieting. We observe a drama of the emotions. But what has triggered these violent exchanges we can only guess. We witness the vicissitudes of imaginary persons on an imaginary stage, whose extravagant behaviour seems all the more truthful because it is archetypal and has no location. The spirit of Fluxus is never far away. Moments of Dadaistic hilarity rub shoulders with Ionesco-like absurdity and Beckettian fatalism. It is a collage of psychological caricature, a hall of distorting mirrors that squash, stretch and mock, turning agonised grimace into salacious laughter, in all of which we may recognise ourselves on the verge of, if not quite, losing control.

The music operates on various levels. One is constructive: for instance, vowels are gradually transformed into nasals, dentals into palatals. This phonetic dimension is extended to the instruments, whose interjections are never just punctuation, but a counterpart to the human sounds and a means of casting them in relief. Another is a skeletal pitch organisation, ensuring a measure of consistency where pitch is only one component amongst many. Both pieces centre on D, from which notes radiate more or less symmetrically. The process can be observed at the opening of *Nouvelles aventures*, briefly at its return in bar 21, again in the 'Hoquetus' at bar 28, and loosely at bar 63 ('Commérages'), as well as in the opening of its second part and the spare, two-part counterpoint of the 'Chorale' (II, bar 19). A third level is emotional. By defining five types of emotion (following the precedent of *Artikulation*) as 'humorous, ghostly–horrific, sentimental, mystical–funereal and erotic', Ligeti creates a display in which 'all five areas or processes are present, all through the music, switching from one to the other so abruptly and quickly that there is virtual simultaneity. Each of the three singers plays five roles at the same time.'[17]

Aventures and *Nouvelles aventures* are in effect miniaturised operas, each containing a sequence of highly compressed 'scenes'. Sections are subtitled 'Conversation', 'La Serenata', 'Action dramatique', 'Commérages' (gossip), 'Communication', 'Les horloges démoniaques' (satanic clocks). There are several solo cameos: an excited outburst from the baritone, as if he had just arrived with an important message; a precipitous 'Grand Hysterical Scene' from the soprano (see Ex. 12, pp. 132–33); a disoriented monologue from the alto (at the end of *Aventures*), sung with 'increasing anxiety and desperation; her questions go unanswered, she is completely alone'.

FANTASY AND TECHNIQUE

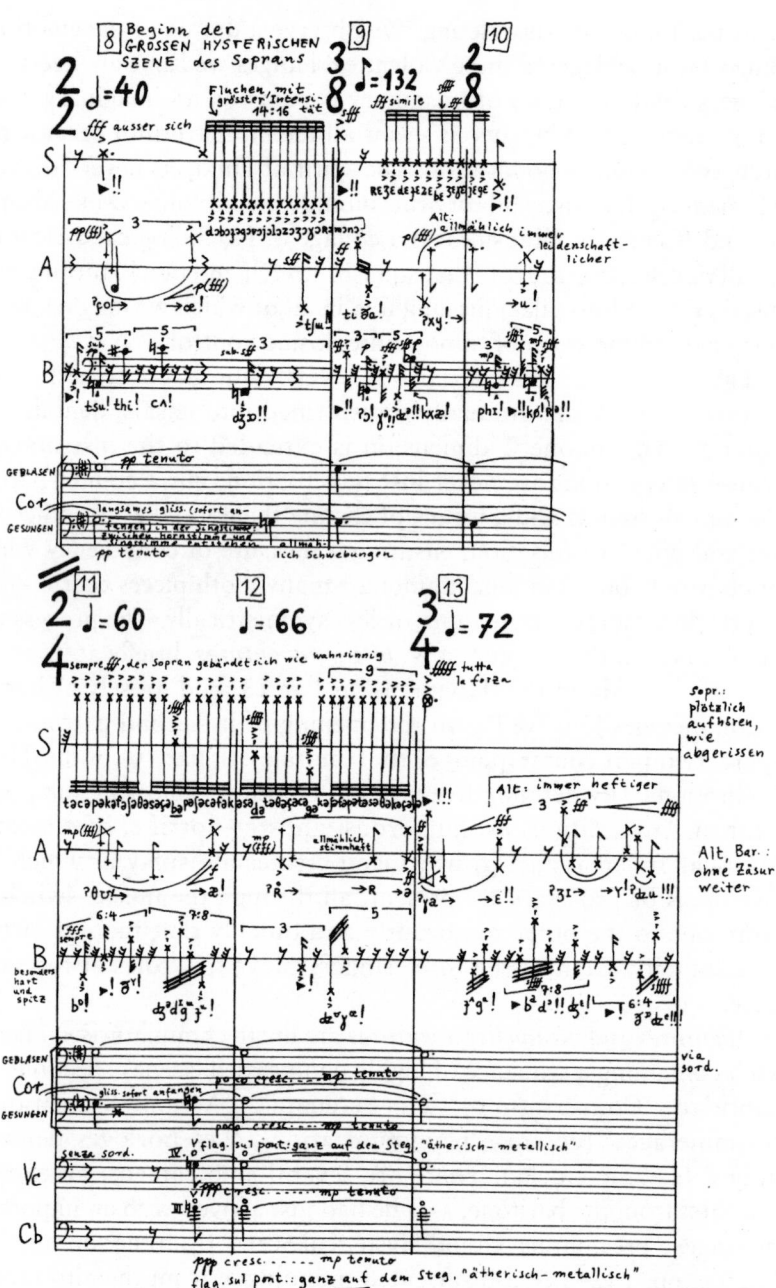

Ex. 12 Part of *Nouvelles aventures* (1962–65)

DISTORTING MIRRORS

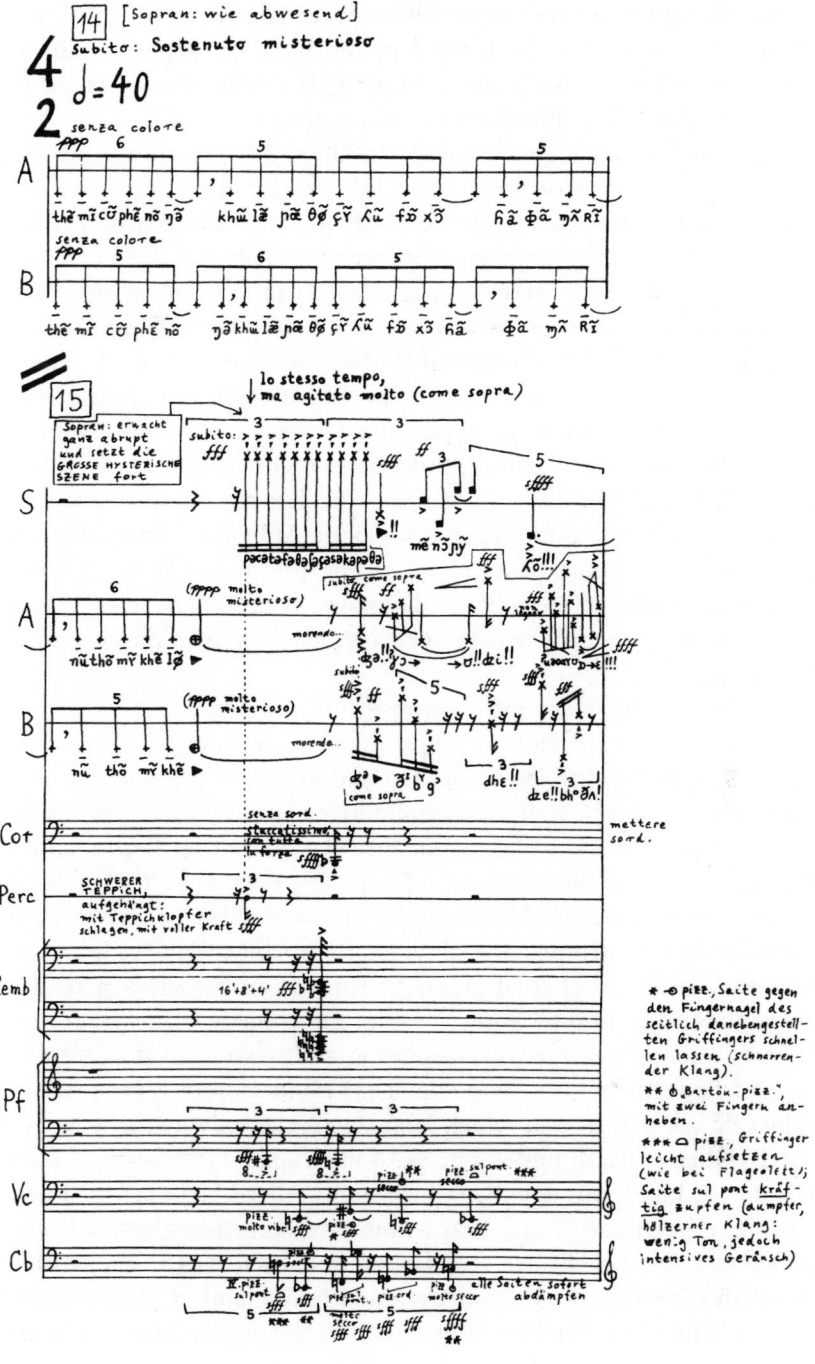

The instrumentalists share in this neurotic tension, to which the percussionist contributes by tearing paper, beating carpets, breaking crockery, and activating a croaking toy frog – now, alas, rescored for plastic cup, due to a shortage of croaking frogs!

Many influences came together in their composition. One was Ligeti's recollection of how, as a child in the Hungarian town of Dicsőszentmárton, he was astonished to hear its Romanian police shouting in a strange language. Another was his knowledge of Dadaist poetry; of Kurt Schwitters's *Sonate mit Urlauten* and Hugo Ball's invented word patterns. And there were the musical examples of Stockhausen's *Carré*, premiered in October 1960, and of Kagel's *Anagrama*, performed at the ISCM World Music Days in June 1960 a week before the premiere of *Apparitions*. For his spatial music for four orchestral and choral groups, Stockhausen composed a text using a graduated scale of vocal sounds from voiceless consonants to vowels, also notated in the International Phonetic Alphabet. *Anagrama* was even more radical. Through assembling phonemes from different languages, Kagel creates absurd dialogues, entirely devoid of syntax. As we noted earlier, its first performance made a deep impression on Ligeti.

Similarly, Ligeti's abrupt juxtapositions and non-causal structures relate to the widespread development of experimental theatre and film during the 1950s, led by Beckett and Ionesco – a Romanian compatriot whose work Ligeti especially loved. In Paris in 1957 he had attended performances of *La cantatrice chauve* and *La Leçon*, part of the anarchic canon that Ionesco subsequently defined as 'theatre of the absurd', after the critic Martin Esslin had coined the phrase in 1961. Here actions are stripped of reality; familiar mannerisms recur drained of meaning; the clichés of language turn into obstacles, instead of being aids to communication. Despite the comedy of his stagecraft, Ionesco's sombre emphasis on isolation and separation is as bleak as that of Beckett, whose *Endgame* (1958) and *Happy Days* (1961) – fables of self-delusion in which language is the only action – veil the inevitability of death under a mask of ill-tempered formality and trivial chatter. Ligeti was equally influenced by Alfred Jarry (1873–1907), the main precursor of post-war avant-garde theatre, whose *Ubu-Roi* was revived at the Théâtre des Nations in Paris in 1958. The work of Swedish film director Ingmar Bergman had a similar, if less lasting impact. His films dominated art cinemas during the late 1950s and

Ligeti saw most of them. *Wild Strawberries* (1957), for example, begins with a surreal image of an old man walking in an empty street and confronted with a clock face without hands, then opening his pocket watch to find that it, too, has frighteningly lost them. The dislocation of time, which became a frequent characteristic of Ligeti's music after 'Les horloges démoniaques', also occurs in Alain Resnais's seminal film *Last Year in Marienbad* (1961), whose ambivalent treatment of time fascinated many viewers while infuriating others. Ligeti was in neither camp, since he never saw it.

Staged productions

The premiere of *Nouvelles aventures* took place in Hamburg on 26 May 1966, preceded by *Aventures*. Ligeti's programme note referred to 'a new genre of art, in which text, music and imaginary stage action completely merge and form a collective compositional structure'. He had planned to give an introductory lecture on 'imaginary music theatre', but was suddenly taken ill with a perforated intestine, a serious condition requiring emergency surgery.

In the autumn, Ligeti's friend Friedrich Cerha, who had conducted the first performance of *Aventures*, repeated both pieces in a staged performance at the Württemberg State Theatre in Stuttgart, directed by the pantomime artist Rolf Scharre. The composer was convalescing and kept his distance. He attended a rehearsal, but disliked its pantomime style. He decided to write his own scenario with detailed stage directions, providing roles for mime artists, dancers and extras besides the three singers, and doubling the length of the performance through pauses and scene changes.[18] But it has never been produced, at least not as he intended. In February 1970 *Aventures* and *Nouvelles aventures* were staged again, this time in the Orangerie, a small theatre in the suburbs of Darmstadt, in a double bill with the first performance of Bruno Maderna's *From A to Z*, with Maderna conducting. The action was set amongst waxworks viewed by a party of tourists, and Ligeti was able to work with the director Harvo Dicks. Other productions followed, but with varying success. At the Styrian Autumn Festival in Graz that October, Hans Neugebauer, who had directed the world premiere of Zimmermann's opera *Die Soldaten*, directed another version. The set featured a pedestrian crossing, and the performance opened with the soprano and alto helping a blind man across the road so that he fell into the orchestra pit. Later a love scene was interrupted by a number of gangsters emerging from a car stopped by traffic lights, only to be clubbed down by one of the mimes and resuscitated by the singers. At various points a silent policeman arrived to place parking tickets on everything from a discarded bunch of flowers to a collapsed long-distance runner. As a theatrical experience all this was entertaining enough, but Ligeti thought it superficial and over-dependent on mimes and extras. Somebody made a film version in which the composer himself appeared. The pieces were even produced in Budapest in January 1972, but in a relatively low-key manner, in the National Marionette Theatre performed by puppets.

By the early 1970s, Ligeti decided to discard his scenario, preferring that the music should stand on its own. Kagel had made better scenic jokes in his extraordinary *Staatstheater* of 1967–70, a work which has entered the mythology of music theatre, although it has never been revived. In fact, *Aventures* and *Nouvelles aventures* have little need of visual gags. Within the detail of their scores is plenty of scope for anarchic dark humour, to which theatrically minded instrumentalists can contribute with restraint. A good performance intensifies the exaggerated emotional language through understatement, like the deft strokes of a skilled cartoonist. An inspired concert staging toured by Ensemble Recherche of Freiburg in the early 1990s achieved exactly this ideal.

The Cello Concerto

In the development of a contemporary solo repertoire, the interaction between composer and executant has often been formative. In 1960 the German cellist Siegfried Palm premiered Zimmermann's Sonata for Solo Cello – then regarded as the most adventurous solo work for the instrument – and became a magnet for commissions by avant-garde composers from Kagel to Xenakis. His repeat performance of the sonata at the ISCM Festival in Amsterdam in 1963 made a powerful impression, especially on the composers present. One of them, Krzysztof Penderecki, proceeded to write no less than three compositions for Palm during the next five years. The first of these, a Sonata for Cello and Orchestra premiered at Donaueschingen in October 1964, opts for a homogeneous integration of soloist and orchestra in a two-movement structure: the first quiet and speculative, the second a nimble burlesque of rapidly changing effects.

This is also roughly the format of Ligeti's Concerto for Cello and Orchestra, commissioned by the Sender Freies Berlin – also for Siegfried Palm, who gave its first performance in Berlin in April 1967. Eschewing opposition between soloist and orchestra, Ligeti builds up a montage of timbral and gestural effects, from clusterous and confined, to capricious and volatile. Originally, he planned a one-movement composition in twenty-seven overlapping and merging sections. But as he worked, the first section grew into a separate movement. The second is a much-elaborated variant of the poised *sostenuto* of the first, containing all the other links in the chain from which the first became detached. Both movements begin with pitch clusters expanding, but at completely different speeds.

Despite the existence of such adventurous instrumentalists as Palm, oboist Heinz Holliger and flautist Severino Gazzelloni, the solo concerto had found little favour since the Second World War. More than any other classical form, it carried too much romantic baggage, its elevation of the individual above the mass seeming unattractive for much the same reason that foursquare rhythms were anathema following their military manipulation in the war. Maderna, however, had already written five solo concertos by 1967, and Ligeti can have felt little inhibition about using the term. His four solo concertos contain some of his most innovative music. Nevertheless, the Cello Concerto (the first of them) so minimises the soloist's traditional dominance that the part is barely distinguishable from the rest of the ensemble. Were it not for the soloist's visual presence and a phrase or two of *espressivo* melody, one would hardly know that the first movement even belonged to a concerto. In the score the solo part is notated amongst the other strings; and in performances where the orchestral string parts are played one to a part (as Ligeti prefers), all become soloists. Even when exposed, much of the solo part is so soft and nearly immobile that it seems to be frozen, as with the opening long-held E – marked *pppppppp*, Ligeti's most extreme soft dynamic. In this movement, the gradual pitch expansion takes place more slowly than in any other work by Ligeti, recalling in its rigour the first of the *Musica ricercata*. More than a minute and a half elapses before the opening E embraces its closest neighbour, F. During this time, delicate articulations take place, a true *Klangfarbenmelodie* that involves timbral changes alone without any alteration of pitch. This intense and magical evolution continues for the six minutes or so of the movement. At its heart is a gradual opening of the harmonic cluster in both directions, illuminated by timbral transformations of individual pitches, moments of melodic highlighting, and such care for instrumentation that the chromatic clusters have a calculated timbral imbalance – as, for example, in bars 28 to 36.

Octaves rehabilitated

The arrival on B flat is simple but striking: B flat appears not as an addition to the evolving chromatic clusters, but by itself, multiplied across six octaves. Open octaves in Ligeti (here played by all the strings, muted) are always significant. They had the added attraction for him of having been banished by the serialists, a restriction continued after the Second World War.[19] Yet earlier in the century, octave doublings were an essential part of every composer's palette. Ligeti's fondness for misty, mysterious octaves, as well as tritones, links him to the Impressionists. They begin to reinstate themselves in the 'Lacrimosa' of the Requiem, and its sequel, *Lux aeterna*. His readiness to use unencumbered plain intervals in prominent positions, and avoidance of the more angst-laden major sevenths and minor ninths, indicates a distancing from Schoenberg. As Ligeti had remarked of Boulez's *Structures 1a*, such intervallic 'signals' function as pivotal anchors, and provide moments of stasis and polarity. It was the gradual rehabilitation of a fundamental harmonic vocabulary that would lead Ligeti, in the 1980s, to rediscover major and minor chord structures, yet without any sense of neo-Romantic reaction. In the late 1960s he risked only tentative allusions, but by the 1980s he had lost all scruples. The second of the piano Études, for example, *Cordes à vide*, is saturated with Debussyan perfect fifths, whilst the fourth Étude, *Fanfares*, has bar after bar of triadic harmonies, but played so fast that their acoustic effect is polytonal.

The second movement of the Cello Concerto is, like *Aventures* and *Nouvelles aventures*, a linked chain of gestural mannerisms. Some are little more than snapshots, like the twenty-one-note hocket at bar 63, which is an expanded replica of the hocket at bar 29 in *Nouvelles aventures*, both based on rising chromatic scales. As in those pieces, the music grows increasingly volatile, arriving at an alternation between what Ligeti describes as 'extremes of ferocious impetuosity and alienated clockwork-like rigidity'. The one has wildly oscillating passages in which octave transpositions dismember chromatic scales, the other superimposes different rhythmic grids, like tiny segments of *moiré* patterning cut out of *Poème symphonique*. Throughout the movement, the soloist has outbursts of exaggerated virtuosity; but so, to a lesser extent, do the other players. Their relationship is less that of celebrant and congregation than a collective: joining, separating and regrouping like a company of dancers. The 'Whispering Cadenza' which concludes the music is like a mime sequence, a negation of conventional cadenzas in that the cellist appears to busy himself with rapid passagework, but to no avail. After a while, only his pattering left-hand fingers remain audible. This disappearance of sound back into the belly of the instrument mirrors the 'inaudible entry, as if emerging from nothingness' with which the concerto opens, and also the end of the first movement where the solo line is left 'suspended at immeasurable heights above unfathomable basses, its dangerously thin, piping harmonics eventually breaking'. Ligeti's suggestion that this conveys 'aloneness and a sense of being lost'[20] is characteristic of the psychological symbolism underpinning his musical language.

Being so introvert and understated – virtually a non-concerto – the Cello Concerto does not communicate easily in large concert halls. The sustained clusters in the first movement are less eventful than subsequent versions of the same process, in the Chamber Concerto for example. If the first movement is self-denial, the exhibitionism of the second is almost breathless in its brevity. Only near the end is there virtuosity characteristic of the genre. Does the Cello Concerto betray a post-Fluxus uncertainty in the handling of structure, a reluctance to cast its soloist in a traditionally dominant role? Certainly all Ligeti's other concertos have more movements and give their protagonists more meat, although still within a spirit of integration. Amongst Ligeti's six concertos, the Cello Concerto most requires intimate performance conditions. It also postdates Ligeti's largest score of the 1960s, to which we must now return.

6

Distance and Enchantment

'Tis distance lends enchantment to the view,
And robes the mountain in its azure hue.
Thomas Campbell, 'Pleasures of Hope'

The same that oft-times hath
Charm'd magic casements, opening on the foam
Of perilous seas, in faery lands forlorn.
John Keats, 'Ode to a Nightingale'

The Requiem: a cry for humanity

The premiere of Ligeti's Requiem in Stockholm on 14 March 1965 was a shattering experience for all who heard it, making an impact without parallel in Swedish concert life. The musicologist Ove Nordwall recorded that 'for weeks afterwards the music critics of the newspapers continued to refer to the performance and, as one of them remarked, "for a while all other music seemed impossible"'.[1] Another wrote of its 'enormous expressive force . . . a shout from all living things'.[2] William Mann, music critic of *The Times*, commented similarly after the London premiere in 1971 that its effect was so compelling that 'I would gladly have forgone Beethoven's ninth symphony after the interval'.[3] The Requiem was awarded first prize by the International Society of Contemporary Music (ISCM) in 1966 and the Beethoven Prize from the city of Bonn in 1967. Although its technical difficulty meant that performances in other countries did not occur immediately, it was quickly perceived as a masterpiece, an outcry of humanity haunted by the Holocaust, but whose relevance is actually timeless and non-specific, like that of *Aventures* and *Nouvelles aventures*.

The achievement of the Requiem set a seal on Ligeti's reputation in the West. However, the success with which Ligeti harnessed his new technical language to its monumental vision arose from the fact that, of all the creative ideas that had been germinating during his time in

Hungary, this one had been in his mind the longest. For many years, even from before the war, the Last Judgement had been a preoccupation, 'the fear of death, the imagery of dreadful events and a way of cooling them, freezing them through alienation, which is the result of excessive expressiveness'.[4] One of his own drawings made after the war shows the Archangel Michael on the Day of Judgement weighing souls on a balance from a butcher's shop; the Devil in the shape of a spider catches the souls, netting them like butterflies (see plate No. 7). His first encounter with Thomas of Celano's Sequence for the Dead – the 'Dies irae' – was through Mozart's Requiem. After the war, whilst a student and then teacher at the Franz Liszt Academy in Budapest, Ligeti twice developed plans for setting the Requiem. The first, worked out for chorus with harps and percussion, was inspired by a performance in Budapest of a work by the medieval composer Pérotin in which, lacking original instructions, the conductor chose to double the voices with assorted percussion, including glockenspiels and bells. 'Pérotin was transformed into a mixture of church music and fairground music.'[5] Had Ligeti continued with this idea, it would have been a Requiem with 'cuckoo accompaniment', but 'a serious work, not a joke'.

Instead, during the early 1950s he began a second version, composed in a kind of 'pentatonic serialism' prompted by hearsay about Schoenberg and Webern, although he had not at that time heard or seen any of their scores. Influenced by having witnessed a performance of Beijing Opera in Budapest in 1949, to two pentatonic scales Ligeti attached two *pien* notes – which, in Chinese music, are secondary notes filling the gaps between the five notes (e.g. a fluctuating F/F sharp, or B/B flat, attached to CDEGA) – so arriving at a twelve-note scale. Around the same time, he began to plan an oratorio on a related subject, Sándor Weöres's epic poem *Istar's Journey to Hell*, which also remained unfinished. A letter from Ligeti to John Weissmann written on 25 January 1957 – providing information for Weissmann's third 'Guide to Contemporary Hungarian Composers', published the following spring in *Tempo* – reveals that upon arrival in Vienna, Ligeti was still contemplating the composition of a Requiem, but now for the victims of the Hungarian Uprising.[6]

To these several prototypes we should add *Aventures*, the composition which immediately preceded the Requiem and whose wildly gesticulating manner reappears, enlarged, in the music of its 'Dies irae'.

In the early 1960s, many composers became interested in large-scale choral works which explored the purely sonic potential of voices and text. One was Kagel's *Anagrama*, another Stockhausen's *Momente* (1962–64), a sequel to *Carré* which Ligeti had heard in Hamburg in October 1960. Penderecki's *St Luke Passion* had its premiere in Münster Cathedral in 1966, a year after Ligeti's Requiem, but the Stabat Mater for three a cappella choirs, which Penderecki incorporated in the *Passion*, was completed and performed in 1962. Perhaps the most remarkable of these choral soundscapes was Lutosławski's *Trois Poèmes d'Henri Michaux* (1962–63), whose second movement employs whispering, shouting, cries and screams – every method of producing sound short of actually singing – across an abstract canvas of tremendous dynamic energy, the musical equivalent of a Jackson Pollock.

For Ligeti, the visual arts provided an important impetus, although from a very different quarter. During 1961 he visited Madrid, where he had been invited to lecture about electronic music, of which he was then considered a significant representative. In the vast Museo del Prado hang many of Goya's greatest paintings, his searing documents of war and darkly pessimistic series of 'black paintings', in violent contrast to the graceful idyll of the early tapestry cartoons for the Spanish court. Here, too, Ligeti saw the work of two artists whose macabre and disturbing paintings would affect him deeply. Hanging at opposite ends of a highly charged room of Flemish art are *The Triumph of Death* by Pieter Breughel the Elder (c.1525–69), a merciless and horrific canvas, and *Garden of Earthly Delights*, the exotic and grotesque fantasy by Hieronymus Bosch (1462–1516) – whom Jung called 'master of the monstrous . . . discoverer of the unconscious'. These surreal and satirical allegories would seed not only the Requiem but also Ligeti's opera *Le Grand Macabre*. In fact, the fundamental subject-matter of these two major compositions is inextricably related, both having their genesis in Ligeti's early life.

From 1961 Ligeti began regular visits to Stockholm, travelling two or three times a year to teach at the Royal Swedish College of Music. As early as 1961 the suggestion was made of commissioning Ligeti, as well as Lutosławski (who responded with his string quartet), along with some Scandinavian composers, to compose new works for the tenth anniversary of the 'Nutida Musik' concert series of Swedish Radio, due to fall in 1965. Ligeti's tentative suggestion of a Requiem was accepted and he set to work on what he fully intended to be a complete setting of the text, writing for full orchestra (including harpsichord), soprano and mezzo-soprano soloists, and two large choruses. In the Requiem's final form the choruses are amalgamated into a single twenty-part choir consisting of sopranos, mezzos, altos, tenors and basses, each divided into four.

He began the composition in 1962. Many of the sketches were written – as Schubert might have done – in the spacious comfort of the coffee houses, the traditional 'second home' of Viennese citizens. Much warmer than Ligeti's apartment, the coffee houses provided congenial composing conditions throughout the winter months until they acquired televisions. At home he had no piano (and accordingly wrote no piano music) until Vera's Canadian friend, Maria Theresa Wood, gave him an upright Steinway in the late 1960s. Only in 1973 at the age of fifty, following Ligeti's appointment as professor of composition at the Hochschule in Hamburg, could he afford to purchase a grand piano.

The 'Introitus' of the Requiem was quickly completed, but his numerous attempts to perfect the complex counterpoint of the 'Kyrie' took nine months. It was a 'utopian indulgence' that he thought could never be repeated. (But it was: the first movement of the Piano Concerto took many times longer.) The 'Kyrie' involved the most complicated polyphony Ligeti had ever composed. Inspired by Nono's serial rigour in *Coro di Didone* and *Il Canto Sospeso*, he strove to make his own twenty-voice polyphony equally 'correct'. Following the teaching of Jeppesen, he gave himself strict rhythmic and melodic rules, like the 'oblighi' techniques of Frescobaldi echoed in *Musica ricercata*. For instance: two successive semitone steps in the melody must never be followed by a third; or, in the vertical harmony, there must always be at least one minor second between the voices. Musical sense, however, remained paramount.

Ligeti wrote the final 'Lacrimosa' only in January 1965, just two months before the work's premiere. By the middle of 1964 the chorus was already rehearsing the earlier movements under the gifted Swedish choral conductor Eric Ericson, and grappling with its huge difficulties of intonation. They were well prepared, having spent earlier rehearsals on Lars Edlund's *Studies in Reading Atonal Music.*[7] But, in the late summer, Ericson sent Ligeti a desperate telegram: 'Please come at once to Stockholm: we can't learn your piece!' Ligeti arrived to find chorus and conductor 'all terrified'; but his presence reassured them, especially when he decided to sanction passing imperfections in the choral intonation of the 'Kyrie', even of their melodic and rhythmic precision, allowing that the choir 'could not sing it exactly' but that the resultant 'dirty patches' and microtonality actually enhanced the total effect.[8] The sections of the score to which this licence is granted are indicated by extended lines above or below the stave. Despite the technical challenges, the chorus members took the flamboyant and charismatic composer to their hearts – 'as a son', although 'a very curious animal' – continuing to work with great commitment. Once combined rehearsals began with the orchestra, everything went excellently.

That Ligeti's Requiem is only a partial setting is due to a number of factors. Most significant were questions of structural continuity which, following their radical rejection of the past, composers had to work out anew for every piece. Ligeti's awareness of such problems is made clear in a lecture he gave at the Darmstadt Summer Courses a few months after the premiere.[9] He observed that 'each new work obeys its own rules', but that in most of them, individual events are 'isolated and unconnected to other events'. Although contemporary music deploys its material functionally in all sorts of contrasting and merging formations, it lacks 'unambiguous signals' to indicate that the music will go in any particular direction. Its structures are many and manifold, like those in architecture: 'single rooms, vast empty buildings, winding subterranean labyrinths, isolated homes spaced out in a landscape'. The dislocated continuity of his own *Aventures* and *Nouvelles aventures* resulted in two compressed pieces of highly experimental structure, one of eleven minutes, the other twelve. Apart from the Requiem, they were the longest compositions Ligeti had produced since leaving Hungary. Though he might wish to create a Requiem on a grand scale, the intense concentration of the music he had written since 1956 made it unlikely. Conscious of this problem, Ligeti was beginning to use specific interval groups as 'signals' to articulate longer structures. For the Requiem, he drew together virtually all his current techniques, so that at nearly half an hour, the finished work was the most extended he had ever composed.

Ligeti sets approximately half the traditional text: the opening 'Introitus', the 'Kyrie', and the long sequence of the 'Dies irae' – but detaching its final stanza, the 'Lacrimosa', to make a separate fourth movement. The remaining five sections he omits. Each of the four movements manifests a different approach, covering between them the principal musical types which absorbed his thinking in the early 1960s – with the exception of one, the '*meccanico*'. The 'Introitus' is seamless and clusterous, a gradual iridescent brightening out of darkness into light; the 'Kyrie' is a huge architecture of micropolyphonic textures; the 'Dies irae' is a wild, gesticulating sequence of kaleidoscopic images performed with exaggerated contrasts of manner by all the participants; finally the 'Lacrimosa' takes a hushed backward look at the previous events, what Ligeti calls a 'decoding' of their intervallic and harmonic content, performed only by the soloists and an ever-dwindling orchestra, as if losing themselves in a numbed, glassy twilight. Each movement goes to extremes to achieve its aim. Although there is no exact reprise of early material, the 'Lacrimosa' completes a powerfully expressive structural arch, after which it would be difficult to imagine any sequel. This must have become evident as Ligeti grappled with the form of the composition which, in its integration of organic and disjunct writing, certainly achieves a more complex and shrewdly proportioned balance than anything he had written in the West. During another lecture given in 1969 on the Requiem itself, Ligeti likened his treatment in a characteristic analogy to 'brutal surgery on a splendid silk: the material is carefully smoothed and stroked ("Introitus"), crumpled and unravelled ("Kyrie"), completely destroyed and torn like a cobweb ("Dies irae") and, finally, the pieces are tentatively rejoined ("Lacrimosa")'.[10]

If Ligeti's depiction of the 'Dies irae' draws on the *stile concitato* extravagance of *Aventures*, he turned for the great cry of supplication in the 'Kyrie' to his deep love of Flemish polyphony, particularly the example of Ockeghem's mensuration canons, refracted and multiplied through the technique of micropolyphony. As we have seen, during his student days in Hungary, Ligeti had become a skilled contrapuntalist, immersing himself in the discipline of Renaissance polyphony, whose rules could be paradoxically liberating compared to the stifling strictures of censorship. In his interview with Péter Várnai in 1968, Ligeti spoke of the 'unceasing continuity' which attracted him to Ockeghem in preference to Palestrina, 'because his music does not tend towards culminating points. Just as one voice approaches a climax another voice comes to counteract it, like the waves in the sea.'[11] Only in Vienna, before writing the Requiem, did Ligeti see a score of Thomas Tallis's forty-part motet, *Spem in alium*, although he had long known of its existence. But the sense of immensity in the 'Kyrie' comes from another influence: Bach's double-choir motet, *Singet dem Herrn* – a work which, Ligeti says, 'had an extreme impact on my imagination'.

Compositional technique in the Requiem

Micropolyphony also occurs in the opening 'Introitus', but here the essential idea is a transformation from the purgatorial darkness of 'Requiem aeternam' (eternal rest) to the lustrous glow of 'lux perpetua' (eternal light). The process is effected through a gradual shift upwards in the distribution of the twenty-part choir, starting with the basses and ending with sopranos, mezzos and altos. The chorus is divided into five plaits or bundles (soprano, mezzo, alto, tenor, bass), each plait consisting of four interlaced strands. The strands weave to and fro across each other, sharing the same narrow compass, creating a barely perceptible fluctuation within otherwise static harmony. Nowhere do more than three plaits (i.e. twelve parts) occur together. Meanwhile, the role of the orchestra is primarily to support and transform these sonorities, not least through the changing coloration of its connective tissue which, from time to time, hangs suspended in space during the few bars where the chorus falls silent.

In the 'Kyrie', the almost imperceptible movement of the 'Introitus' becomes sinewy and impassioned. Its structure is canonic and fugal, but with the 'subject' multiplied by so many variants of itself that we hear a dense, seething mass of voices from which no individual line can be detached. In this movement Ligeti's use of micropolyphony is especially apt, conjuring up an immeasurable tide of imploring humanity. Just as one can separate no individual from the crowd, nor is there reason to imagine their number any less than infinite. The chorus is again divided into five plaits, each comprising four strands; and although the movement begins just with altos and tenors, it quickly builds to twenty parts. The technique derives from traditional canon and fugue, but there are also elements of serial thinking in Ligeti's self-imposed procedural rules. As each plait enters, its four constituent strands follow the same sequence of 112 notes or their inversion, weaving a long melisma to the words 'Kyrie eleison'. Within each plait, each of the four parts presents its own rhythmic treatment of the pitch sequence – as in *Atmosphères*. They are alike, however, in having similar durations at the same time, i.e. longer durations at the start and towards the end of any sequence, increasingly compressed towards the middle. The pitch and duration sequences bundled together in each plait are exactly replicated in all the others, except that (as in traditional fugal structure) they enter successively at different transpositions and two are in inversion (basses and sopranos). A minor practicality is the adjustment Ligeti makes to the soprano lines in bars 23 and 24 to avoid what would otherwise be a descent to low A sharp.

As in a conventional fugue, there is a countersubject, here associated with the 'Christe eleison'. Preliminary versions occur at the beginning of the movement in the four tenor parts, beneath the 'Kyrie eleison' subject in the altos, followed by the four mezzo parts to accompany the subject in the basses. Ligeti marks these at an extremely low dynamic of *pppp* so that the 'Christe' countersubject begins almost as a tentative shadow. During the central part of the movement (beginning at bar 60) it comes to the fore, sung by the upper twelve voices rising in a huge crescendo. In this section the 'Christe' theme settles into its real shape (see Ex. 26e, p. 296). Now it is treated similarly to the 'Kyrie' subject; except that it appears not only in prime form and inversion, but also at the climax of the movement (bar 102) in retrograde, sung by the sopranos in their highest register.

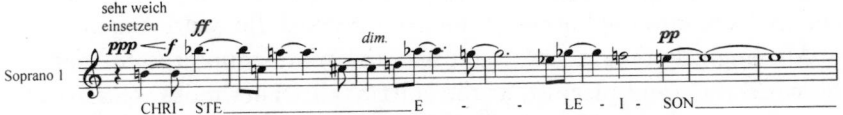

Ex. 13 Retrograde of the 'Christe' countersubject in the Requiem (1963–65)

Whereas the 'Kyrie' subject moves entirely in semitones and tones, the 'Christe' countersubject opens out simultaneously in both directions, encompassing ever larger leaps (the process being reversed in the retrograde). It starts as a twelve-note series, and is extended by swinging backwards and forwards through the row's last six notes. Ligeti uses this pitch sequence also to provide the first note of each entry of both subject and countersubject in his quasi-fugal design.

In the Bachian architecture of the whole movement, 'Kyrie' and 'Christe' themes eventually achieve parity. The orchestra emphasises the contrapuntal structure. The central fabric of 'Christe' motifs in the upper voices and strings contrasts with the huge wailing of the final pages. Here the brass and winds pierce through with strident and gleaming held notes, like harmonic pillars supporting an intricately ribbed fan-vault. It is an impressively grand concept, in which Ligeti develops his micropolyphonic technique to effect seamless textural and timbral transformations. Its inspiration may derive from Ockeghem but its outcome is a sophisticated contrapuntal and tonal edifice worthy of the Baroque.

The entry upon this canvas of the 'Dies irae' is marked by violent contrasts between frenzied activity and frozen immobility, an explosion of the emotion locked inside the vast sweep of the 'Kyrie'. The style of the music is gesticulatory and disintegrative, its abruptness conveying both shock and fear. Different types of musical character cut across each other in a vivid and harrowing sequence, prompted by the graphic pictorialism of the text; Ligeti is as ready to break off in mid-sentence as he is to arrest the music in mid-flow. Amid the turbulence are sustained sections, some anguished and tense, others poised and elegiac. As this stark and dramatic movement unfolds, gentler passages subdue the volatile. When a final cluster in the high voices dissolves upwards into nothing, to be replaced by a soft low C sharp sustained by the double basses, by the hollow sound of flute and piccolos and by simple two-part movement in both instruments and solo voices, we sense the beginning of the 'Lacrimosa' and a withdrawal of energy back into the hushed stillness with which the work began.

Although there is no exact reprise, the spare counterpoint shared between flute and piccolos at the start of the 'Lacrimosa' recalls the first eight pitches of the 'Christe' motif in the second movement. It is really a synthesis of both 'Christe' and 'Kyrie' motifs: a contrary-motion chromatic expansion beginning from a C sharp pedal and moving outwards through all twelve semitones. In this slightly different shape there are traces of the *lamento* formula of Ligeti's later years – or its first two thirds – each drooping fragment entering fractionally higher than the phrase before.

Aesthetic questions

Ligeti's extremely intricate polyphony in the 'Kyrie' raises awkward questions. Why compose with a precision that cannot be heard? Why write choral music of such difficulty, then absolve the singers from achieving exactitude? Ligeti himself confronted this paradox in a conversation recorded with Josef Häusler two days before the premiere of *Lontano*.[12] But the issue involves not only Ligeti. Similar but more problematic questions are posed by the music of other modernists, notably Xenakis and Ferneyhough. A predictable reaction was the emphatic rejection of complexity by many composers during the final decades of the twentieth century, leading to such simplified styles as minimalism which were already taking root at the time of the Requiem's first performance.

Is Ligeti's exacting yet inaudible detail misconceived? If the choral writing is impracticable should it not have been written differently? Judged as craft, the answer might be 'yes'. Judged as art, it could be that means and ends are linked: the effort required intensifies the sense of supplication, the integrity of each anonymous strand authenticates the whole. Judged as history, there is ample evidence for thinking that any accuracy unobtainable in 1965 will subsequently be achieved. There are many examples of intellectual fantasy weaving webs that are not easily perceived. Consider Bach's puzzle canons in *The Musical Offering* and Schumann's cryptic ciphers. Consider how Gothic stonemasons carved sculptures so far aloft that few mortals could see them. The miracles of colour and pattern in the rose windows created by medieval glaziers contain iconography whose detail is overwhelmed by the glory of the whole, although fully to appreciate their pictorial symbolism you need binoculars – invented long after the glass was installed. Whether for the greater glory of God or the inner satisfaction of the artist, unseen craft strengthens the visible achievement.

In his discussion with Häusler, Ligeti compares his own technique with the 'generalised notation' used by Penderecki, whose individual string parts are rarely soloistic but more like droplets in a cloud. For Ligeti's critical ear such a method is inadequate. He wants to 'steer the course of each separate part' himself, arguing that, although the individual parts are 'not immediately audible, we hear not the polyphony, but the result'. If he were to notate in an undifferentiated way, 'the result would not be the same'. In transferring his intuitive vision into the concrete structure of a musical score, Ligeti becomes increasingly prescriptive. But in performance the reverse occurs: there is a shift back to the sensory and generalised. 'It is precisely this tension between the rational, constructed element on the one hand, the visionary on the other, that plays such an important role in composing.'[13]

Illness and *Lux aeterna*

Following the first performance of the Requiem, Ligeti finalised his revisions to the score and changed his provisional title, 'Four Movements from the Requiem', into the single description 'Requiem'. Even up to composition of the 'Dies irae' he had maintained his intention of setting the full text. So when, in the summer of 1966, he accepted a commission for an unaccompanied choral work for the Schola Cantorum Stuttgart and its conductor Clytus Gottwald, it was to one of the remaining sections of the Mass that he turned, the 'Lux aeterna'. Gottwald's letter reached Ligeti at the time he was seriously ill in a Viennese hospital, recovering slowly from the emergency operation for his perforated intestine, during which it seems he had come 'close to death'. He was so heavily sedated with morphine that he remained addicted to it for three years afterwards; and for two months, was so little aware of reality that he was not allowed to go alone into the street. But if *Lux aeterna* is 'psychedelic music composed in a drug-induced trance', he had not lost his analytical faculties. Almost at once, after reading Gottwald's letter, Ligeti had a vision of 'extremely clear' euphonious harmonies, and wrote an outline of the pitch structure. He decided to put aside the Cello Concerto, which he had just begun, in order to work on *Lux aeterna*. Short though it is, this ethereal composition, with its slowly evolving harmonic clusters, instantly made a strong impression. After the premiere in November 1966, it was quickly issued on a recording, along with other compositions with which Ligeti had made his name in the West.

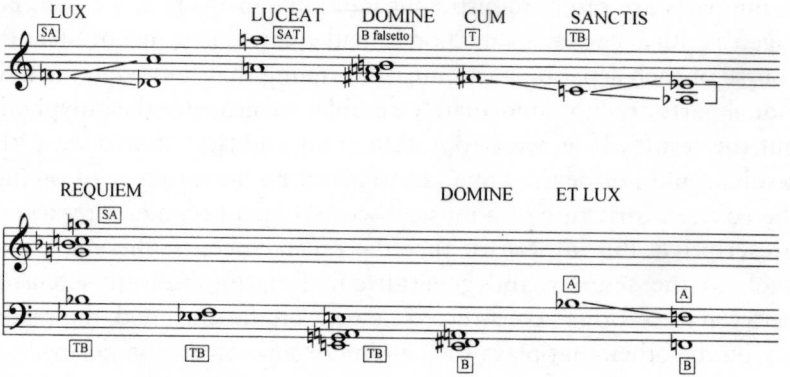

Ex. 14 Ligeti's first outline of the pitch structure in *Lux aeterna* (1966)

Indeed, *Lux aeterna* is exceptional among Ligeti's works for its purity. It has none of the gesticulating character of the 'Dies irae' or of *Aventures* and *Nouvelles aventures*. The choir is divided into sixteen parts, a refinement of the clusterous micropolyphony of the 'Introitus' in the Requiem. As in that work, each vocal group is subdivided, each bundle or plait consisting of four canonic strands. All sixteen parts draw on exactly the same pitch sequence, but each in its own rhythm. None of the vocal groups sings throughout, and where each enters, it adopts whatever section of the pitch sequence has been reached at that moment. That this central thread was conceived as a melody is confirmed by Ligeti's sketches, in which the pitch sequence is notated as a *cantus firmus* underlaid with text. This cantus as barred by Ligeti is shown in Ex. 15 (see pp. 156–57), except that my example reverses its second and third sections in order to make a comparison with *Lontano*.

After completing the Requiem, Ligeti had turned to the fourteenth-century Guillaume de Machaut, wanting to study his celebrated *Messe de Notre Dame*. Thus the concept of mensural notation, as used by both Machaut and Philippe de Vitry, is echoed in *Lux aeterna*. Here it is allied to Nono's practice (observable in the choral movements of *Il Canto Sospeso*) of assigning durations based on the ratio 3–4 –5 to fractional subdivisions of the beat, associating the different fractions with separate voices, and maintaining these allocations throughout the composition. In *Lux aeterna*, the first soprano part moves only on triplet subdivisions, the second soprano on quintuplet subdivisions, and the third on semiquaver (quarter) subdivisions. The scheme is repeated down the other thirteen voice parts from fourth soprano to fourth bass, so that, although barred in 4/4, the music sounds always fluid. Not only are there no accents; to render imperceptible the transitions between sound and silence, consonants at the end of held clusters are deleted. A curiosity of the texture is that the sequence of notes in each part is mostly punctuated by tiny rests, producing a delicate if irregular sense of pulsation. All of these details were worked out by Ligeti on pre-compositional matrices. For a few bars the voice-leading is legato; otherwise the micropolyphonic and canonic web continues without any major disturbance other than through changes of register. But these are striking. Vocal compasses are exploited to their limits, requiring expert control at both extremes. Entries at these extreme registers occur mostly in unison; others articulate fledgling chords – signposts guiding us through the ether.[14]

The *cantus firmus* and its canons are divided into three sections, in between which are sustained clusters, the 'extremely clear' chordal harmonies that had occurred to Ligeti in hospital. Mostly they consist of a perfect fourth enclosing, for example, a minor third and major second. Such an entity he came to identify as a 'typical Ligeti signal'.[15] Examples occur at bars 37 (F sharp, A, B) and 61 (G, B flat, C), between bars 87 and 90 (although here, due to the very low register of the divisi basses, they sound less clearly), and again at bar 100. Indeed, the harmonic structure of *Lux aeterna* is altogether less chromatic than in Ligeti's previous scores, drawing on the relatively stable harmonies in the final 'Lacrimosa' of the Requiem and on diatonic elements in the pitch sequence. Intriguingly, the whole *cantus firmus* is reused in *Lontano*, with surprising ramifications.

Perspective and opalescence: *Lontano*

After the last notes of *Lux aeterna* have faded, Ligeti writes in the score a further seven entirely empty bars, enigmatically marked 'tacet'. At the indicated metronome mark of crotchet = 56, they amount to half a minute of complete silence. This is no Cagean invitation to environmental sounds, but is intended to focus on the void into which the dying strains of music have disappeared. Following its rarefied, ever-so-gentle drift of choral clusters, such stillness seems appropriate. There has been no drama. *Lux aeterna* is the most seamless and unruffled piece Ligeti had yet written. The dynamic scarcely rises above soft, mostly very soft. The score is prefaced with the instruction: 'sostenuto, molto calmo, "wie aus der Ferne" [from afar]'. So it is no surprise to find Ligeti's next composition, after *Lux aeterna* and the Cello Concerto, venturing even further into the mysterious reaches of musical space and exploring again a sense of infinite remoteness. This single movement for orchestra, called *Lontano* and completed in May 1967, is in effect a recomposition or expansion of *Lux aeterna* in the manner of a sixteenth-century parody mass. Like Palestrina's Missa 'Assumpta est Maria', *Lontano* is based on a 'motet', embedding the original in an otherwise new and extended composition.

But the work is in other ways unique, even for Ligeti. No piece of his combines so sensuous and strange a voyage with such an absence of incident or definition. It is the furthest he would take this element in his music, indeed just about as far as one could go, although the technique has had many imitators and indirect descendants, like the spectralists in France (notably Tristan Murail and Gérard Grisey). Its unity of form and content, craft and spirit, assures it a place amongst the masterpieces of twentieth-century orchestral music; although, like Sibelius's *Tapiola* which at times it resembles, it is also a *ne plus ultra*, the end of a line. *Lontano* is a study in opalescence, in slowly evolving timbral and harmonic transformation heard through polychromatic mists of sound. Within these vaporous textures, timbres and harmonies ebb and flow. Sometimes the sonic mists almost clear, to reveal for a moment tangible chordal shapes, before slowly enveloping them again as other shapes coalesce in sharper focus, before they too recede. As in *Atmosphères*, there are no themes, no audible rhythms, no overt melody (although more of this in a moment). The sense of floating and voyaging is absolute. Ligeti controls this fluidity with immense skill, so that its huge resonances become an intoxicating vision, like the sun streaming through the stained-glass windows of Saint-Chapelle in Paris – one of several inspirations.

The textural flow operates in two main domains. One is timbral, a subtle blend of instrumental hues whose coloration changes constantly. Behind is the harmonic, which is itself not a single plane but a series of layers of greater or lesser prominence stacked behind each. The 'phasing' attempted in *Atmosphères* is far more subtle here. It is the depth of perspective and sense of sonic entities emerging from far away, then receding and diminishing, that is implied by Ligeti's title 'Distant'. Despite the space race between the Russians and Americans which dominated the 1960s, cosmic space was apparently not in Ligeti's mind. Yet of all his works, it is *Lontano* which seems to extend beyond earthbound horizons towards a greater infinity. It could be Rilke's mystical quest, the inspiration of George Crumb's *Makrokosmos III* – 'And in the nights the heavy earth is falling from all the stars down into loneliness. We are all falling. And yet there is One who holds this falling endlessly gently in his hands'[16] – were it not that Ligeti, despite his setting of the Requiem Mass, is no believer in deity. Nor does he care for Rilke. It was not Rilke but Keats, to whose lines from 'Ode to a Nightingale' (which head this chapter) he returned time and again as he composed the music[17] – an unlikely choice for a contemporary composer, one might think.

Lontano, like *Lux aeterna*, is barred in 4/4 throughout, but again only to assist synchronisation, never to imply accentuation. There is no beat. As Ligeti says in his preface to the score, 'the music must flow smoothly, and accents (with a very few, precisely indicated exceptions) are foreign to the piece.' The micropolyphonic rhythms are notated within regular bar-lengths without any loss of plasticity. Fifteen years earlier he had imagined such textures, but been unable to write them.

Because *Lontano* has no audible metre and few landmarks, reading its score is a challenge. What exactly do we hear? Where in the score is what we hear? The work is an object lesson in how to blend instrumental sounds, and the craft is in the detail. In order to articulate the first note, Ligeti has fourteen instruments enter on the same pitch, at their softest possible dynamic, one after another. Each then crescendos in successive waves, but very slightly, then falls away. The music appears to come out of nowhere, but once arrived the opening pitch glows with minute pulsations. Its colour changes imperceptibly before any other movement takes place, yet the ear can hardly discern how or why. When the pitch changes at bar 6, it too is concealed in a haze of overlayering. Later in the score over sixty separate lines contribute to the texture simultaneously, each following its own path, each promoting in its small way the organic evolution of the music yet hidden in the mass. Only rarely do single colours or groups emerge. Nevertheless, Ligeti's handling of chiaroscuro is masterful. There is the first identifiable timbre, the oboes at bar 13, whose brighter hue matches the emotional lift of the first open interval in the pitch sequence, a rising perfect fourth. There is the way that shafts of light seem momentarily to illuminate the trumpets, or where the texture of strings starts to flutter and tremble. There is the one brief instance when the four horns play in unison to highlight a three-note phrase (bars 73–75) – it is the perfect fourth enclosing a minor third 'interval signal' from *Lux aeterna*. Most surprising is the incident, some forty bars into the piece, where the burgeoning sound mass is suddenly excised, and we sense a gaping void of seven octaves, a mysterious 'black hole', its vastness located between two pitches so extreme that they sound like remote whistling. One is the lowest possible note of the orchestra, D flat^1, sustained by a muted contrabass tuba; the other is virtually the highest, a stratospheric C^7 harmonic from a solo violin.

The hidden melodies in *Lux aeterna* and *Lontano*

In the following section, luminous transformations wax and wane across wide octaves and a dense texture of numerous contrapuntal strands. So it comes as a shock to look more closely at the score, and discover that it is reducible throughout virtually the whole composition to just one line, a single pitch sequence. At its heart *Lontano* is a monody. This fact seems so unlikely that few analysts have given it much attention, and most have failed to notice it. Virtually the whole score is generated through canonic replication as in Ligeti's earlier micropolyphonic scores. Yet as essays in colour, none of them approach the sophistication of *Lontano*; nor is their micropolyphony so all-pervasive and unified. It is near miraculous that this most fluid and subtle of textural compositions should be but the elaboration of a single thread. Furthermore, this monody is melody. And melody is something we often assume to be absent from an overtly textural concept.

That its pitches are no casual sequence is demonstrated by their derivation from *Lux aeterna*. Ex. 15 (pp. 156–57) shows the sequence as it occurs in both works, plus the principal 'interval signals' which separate the cantus into three sections. The first sections of both melodies are identical, apart from the transposition up a minor third in *Lontano*. But the second and third sections of *Lux aeterna* are reversed in *Lontano*, as well as being transposed, and by different intervals. Additionally, the second section of the cantus in *Lontano* has two extra segments (one of nine notes, one of three), whilst the first fourteen pitches of the final section also generate canons in inversion. These begin at letter Y in the score, building towards the blinding climax at letter AA. Ligeti has described the passage graphically, referring to a painting that inspired it:

. . . the music seems to shine, to be radiant. Dynamically this is emphasised by a crescendo, and [in] pitch by a gradual ascent into higher and higher regions, until a single note, a D sharp, very high up, emerges and stands there, as if this musical light were at first diffuse, but slowly the diffuseness disappears and there is a single directed beam. I am expressing all this by the association of images. At the moment when the high D sharp is there, forming the concentrated 'pencil' of the musical beam, suddenly there yawns an abyss, a huge distancing, a hole piercing through the music. It is a moment that has an irresistible association for me with the wonderful painting by Altdorfer, *The Battle of Alexander* in the Alte Pinakothek in Munich, in which the clouds – these blue clouds – part and behind them is a beam of golden sunlight shining through.[18]

Ex. 15 The hidden melodies in *Lux aeterna* and *Lontano*

The *cantus firmus* in *Lux aeterna* is shown barred and with text underlaid as in Ligeti's preliminary sketch, except that he notated it in minims, and I have exchanged the middle and final sections to clarify their relationship to the melody in *Lontano*. Note that the last three pitches in section C of *Lux aeterna* are as they appear in the sketch; the finished composition ends differently. The *cantus firmus* in *Lontano* is shown as it is traceable throughout the orchestral score.

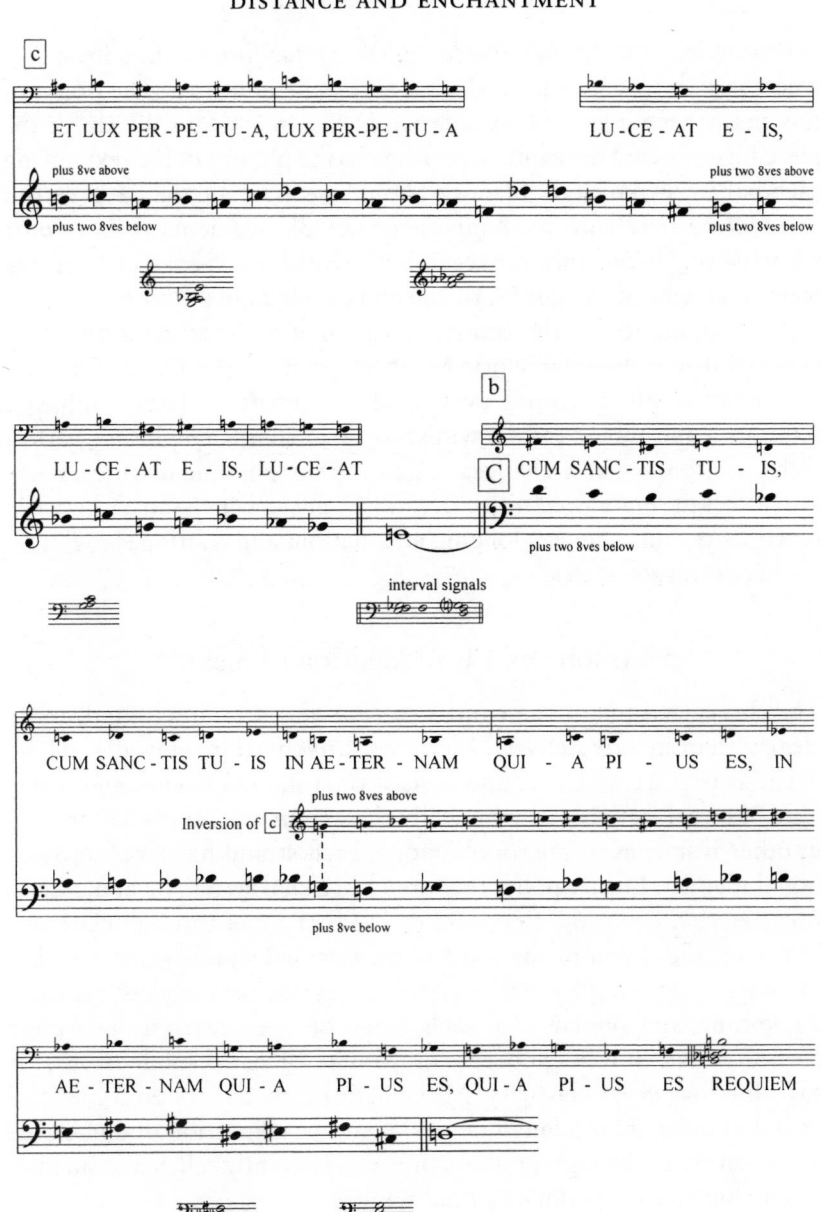

During its path through the score, the *cantus firmus* shifts from segments in flats to segments in sharps, and some in neither. The origin of this characteristic lies in *Lux aeterna*. In his preliminary sketch for the piece Ligeti barred the cantus according to the phrases of the text, giving each bar its own melodic identity. Should we associate the Latin text of the *Lux aeterna* with the equivalent melodic segments in *Lontano*? Clearly not. Undeniably, however, both works are visions of light: the 'perpetual light of the saints', the piercing sunlight of Altdorfer.

An examination of the cantus reveals that its quasi-tonal modulation is linked to intervallic prioritisation. At the beginning of *Lontano* for instance (although not exclusively) segments in flats emphasise semitones and minor thirds, whilst those in sharps emphasise perfect fifths and tones. These changes colour the surrounding texture as they also affect the emotional trajectory of the music, which moves between tenebrosity and radiance, longing and elation, and continues to fluctuate between such states.

Harmony as a prolongation of melody

The three sections of the cantus in *Lontano* are punctuated, more clearly than in *Lux aeterna*, by two relatively static episodes. These begin at bars 41 and 112, and consist of sustained pitches and three-note 'interval signals'. Rhythmically the cantus has no prime form; as in other instances of micropolyphony, each strand has its own durational identity. Ligeti applies the same fractional system he had used in *Lux aeterna*. From the first note of the first flute, through clarinets, bassoons and down to the third horn, metrical subdivisions are allocated part by part, the top given quintuplets, the next triplets, the third duple time, and similarly for each group of three instruments. In any part, rhythmic movement occurs only on its allocated subdivisions, yet each line has great elasticity. Movement rarely occurs on a metrical beat and there are innumerable ties. A similar allocation of durational units continues throughout the score: an apparently schematic method producing an extraordinarily fluid texture.

In the opening section up to bar 41, the melody spawns more and more canonic images of itself, each following the same pitch sequence but all varied in rhythm. The modulatory structure of the cantus creates an implicit tonal architecture. One can hear, for instance, the 'E major' flavour of its central segment, enhanced by repetition and prolongation, an inescapable consequence of composing multiple canons. 'Polyphony is what is written,' says Ligeti, 'harmony is what is heard.'[19] But it is also obscured. The melody breeds so many delayed reflections that different segments are present simultaneously. Successive pitches in the melody are aggregated into clusters and chords, but these remain elusive and are surrounded by a soft halo of more alien resonances. Throughout the opening section sustained harmonics in the cellos and basses preserve traces of earlier tonalities to cloud their successors. In this way the 'E major' aggregate around bar 17 dissolves, but only after the leading canonic strands have reverted to flats: an 'A flat, B flat, D flat, C' aggregate preceding the staggered arrival of all instruments on high octave Cs. Cloudiness and ambiguity characterise the whole piece. It is as if, from out of a huge expanse, objects almost solidify, fuzziness comes nearly into focus – but never completely.

The unexpected seven-octave void halts the melodic flow, and the next nineteen bars have only static formations, a momentary clearing of the micropolyphonic mist. A similar stasis with sustained 'interval signals' separates sections two and three (bars 112 to 122). Around these interludes, the three sections of the *cantus firmus* are treated very differently: varied according to instrumentation and register, by the amount of octave doubling and the extent of canonic elaboration.

The first interlude ends with a tritone (E–B flat) stretched across four and a half octaves. As it sinks into a resumption of the micropolyphonic flow at bar 60, we have the impression of a more sumptuous counterpoint with a separate bass part. Except for the first four bars, this is an illusion. Seemingly independent lines are really successive phrases of the cantus heard simultaneously and in different registers. The multiple voice-leading still derives from one melody. In this middle section, undulating and contrary currents spread out across the sonic space. The cantus is refracted both temporally and spatially, some segments multiplied many times merely through octave doubling. Despite a sense of exoticism and mystery, the lines are inexorably sinking. The descent grows darker. It narrows to a sequence of falling whole-tones, played in repetitive cycles by the strings and in different modes of bowing, finally by six solo double basses.

The third section begins weightily on a D, the cantus replicated across three octaves but now in low register. There is less temporal displacement; the melodic singularity of the whole concept is here more evident.

In this last section the melody has three distinct phrases. The first starts at bar 122, played by the dark timbres of alto flute, cor anglais, clarinets, bassoons and lower strings, and descends stepwise occasionally twisting back on itself. This is answered at bar 127 by its inversion on the brighter winds, plus trumpets, trombones and violins, building to the climax. Here *Lontano* comes closest to the quasi-fugal technique of the 'Kyrie' in the Requiem. But there are no countersubjects, only the counterpoint of canonic reflection. Altdorfer's blinding sunbeams are quickly extinguished, and the music disappears in a few furtive strands, the final phrase of the cantus ebbing away amongst the violas.

Lontano is an extraordinarily far-reaching product of canonic technique. The idea of turning a single line into a sonic aurora appears to be unique. Multiple canons do exist in the work of other contemporary composers: for the Italian Aldo Clementi (b.1925) rotational canons have been an obsession, but they are like acoustic musical boxes, audibly systematic and timbrally uniform, playful but austere. In *Lontano* the reverse is true: the original melody is chaste, its treatment indulgent and capricious.

Nonetheless, the different directional flow of its three sections, and the careful positioning of focal pitches and half-concealed harmonies, ensure that *Lontano* has satisfying shape in a genre lacking formal precedents. As for its 'romanticism', in his discussion with Josef Häusler,[19] Ligeti acknowledged *Lontano*'s expressive kinship with the nineteenth century, especially with the spatial qualities of Bruckner and Mahler:

We grasp the work only within our tradition. If one were not acquainted with the whole of late Romanticism, the quality of being at a distance . . . would not be manifest. The piece is in a sense traditional, but not literally as with Stravinsky; it does not treat exact quotations from late romantic music, but certain types of late romantic music are touched upon.[20]

And *Lontano* is conservative in other respects. It has no harps, keyboards nor percussion. It has no unusual notation, no extended instrumental techniques. Ligeti preferred to use means familiar to orchestral players, believing that to achieve such soft nuances and balance the texture was challenge enough. The neo-romantic label, however, he firmly rejects. Asserting that he believes 'in always making innovations in art . . . *Lontano*, contrary to appearances, has in reality nothing to do with the "retro" movement.'[21]

The prolongation of melody to produce harmony occurs in subsequent works by Ligeti as well as in other composers. Indeed, a synthesis of the vertical and horizontal is a legacy from both Debussy and serialism. Berio's *O King* is a quasi-serial example, his tribute to Martin Luther King incorporated into the *Sinfonia* (1968). The spectral composers developed a more complex blurring of timbral and harmonic elements based on their analysis of the acoustic properties of sounds, treating linearity as a prolongation of the vertical. In his *Die Reihe* article, 'Metamorphoses of Musical Form', Ligeti draws visual analogies. Music which juxtaposes textures, colours and surfaces has to be experienced all at once, he says, like a painting. Succession becomes simultaneity. But if *Lontano* is an ideal representation of this principle, it is also significant for its reinstatement of melody. From being hidden in the mist, melody would gradually return to the foreground, eventually (in the Horn Trio) bringing with it motivic narrative.

Stanley Kubrick's *2001*

On 22 October 1967 *Lontano* was premiered at the Donaueschingen Festival – and a few months later, Ligeti had a considerable shock. One day he received a letter from a friend in New York congratulating him on his contribution to the soundtrack of Stanley Kubrick's new film *2001 – A Space Odyssey*. Astonished, he attended its Vienna premiere and discovered that Kubrick had helped himself to large sections of three of Ligeti's recently recorded compositions. Parts of *Atmosphères*, the 'Kyrie' of the Requiem and *Lux aeterna* join Johann Strauss's *Blue Danube* and Richard Strauss's *Also Sprach Zarathustra* on a soundtrack distinguished as much by its sustained use of silence as by its choreographic cutting of science-fiction images to pre-existing music. In the room scene near the end of the film there is also a short section of *Aventures*, although unacknowledged in the credits and treated electronically almost beyond recognition. The extensive use of Ligeti's music contributed hugely to the atmosphere of mystery in a film that would change the history of cinema. As the director Tony Palmer says: 'Before Stanley Kubrick, music tended to be used in films as either decorative or as heightening emotions. After Stanley Kubrick, because of his use of classical music in particular, it became absolutely an essential part of the narrative, intellectual drive of the film.'[22]

The extracts from the Requiem, *Atmosphères* and *Aventures* play continuously for sixteen out of the film's final twenty-one minutes, during which there is no spoken soundtrack and no other music. Most effectively they accompany Doug Trumbell's 'star-gate' sequence, in which light patterns hurtle out of infinity and rush past the viewer on all sides. Palmer, who already knew Ligeti's music, recalls 'seeing *2001* and thinking: I'm hearing things. This cannot possibly be Ligeti in a Hollywood film. But sure enough it was and, of course, it makes the sequence utterly unforgettable.'[23]

Yet neither Ligeti nor his publishers had been asked for permission, nor had any warning of this cavalier disregard for their copyright. In fact, Kubrick had considered many possibilities for the music before making his choice, and Ligeti was not the only composer to be upset. Screening some early footage whilst working on the script with Arthur C. Clarke, they had played numerous recordings ranging from Mendelssohn to Carl Orff, from whom they briefly considered commissioning a score. But, when it came to a viewing by the MGM executives, Kubrick's proposal to use recorded music was rejected. Instead Alex North, with whom Kubrick had worked on *Spartacus*, was engaged. Kubrick sent him recordings of Ligeti's works to imitate, but there was no creative synergy. A few months later, when North had composed his own music and it had been played and recorded, he was invited to the New York preview and was 'shattered to discover that Kubrick had discarded his score totally, and restored his prerecorded classics'.[24]

At least North was paid. So were Karajan for conducting *Also Sprach Zarathustra*, Maderna and the Darmstadt Chamber Music Players who performed *Aventures*, and the Bavarian Radio Chorus and Orchestra, soloists and conductor Francis Travis in *Atmosphères* and the Requiem. But not Ligeti. He wrote to complain and lawyers were engaged, his publishers contracting the best Berlin specialist in authors' rights. The lawyer threatened to take MGM to court, and proposed a payment of $30,000. MGM's reply was 'shrewd', says Ligeti:

'Please sue! You must start in Vienna and Frankfurt [the respective homes of Ligeti's publishers Universal Edition and C. F. Peters]. Undoubtedly, you will win. Then you have to go to London. Again, you'll win. The process will continue in Los Angeles. There, too, you'll win. But we think it will take twenty years. Would you prefer $1,000 now?'

After a six-year wrangle, in 1973 MGM paid $3,500 – 'a despicable amount' says Ligeti. Out of this his lawyer received $1,000, but Universal Edition and Peters graciously waived their shares. A quarter of a century later, Ligeti was staying as a guest artist of the Paul Getty Foundation in Santa Monica, California, and met a member of MGM's legal staff at a house-concert, where Pierre-Laurent Aimard was playing his piano Études. 'Do you know about my bad story with Metro-Goldwyn-Mayer?' he asked. 'Yes,' replied the lawyer. 'Everybody knows it, and everybody thinks you were stupid to engage a German instead of a Hollywood attorney.' Ligeti's indignation has not softened, but is tinged with irony:

I liked the film. The way it used my music I accept artistically . . . In the 1970s I saw a book on the making of *2001* and read there that Ligeti had successfully sued MGM for taking his music. But it's not so. I never sued them. MGM wrote me such nice letters. They said Ligeti should be happy; he's now famous in America.[25]

Not only in America. The worldwide success of *2001* generated an interest in Ligeti's music which crossed over many perceived boundaries. In Britain, his music was played not only on the BBC's classical music programme, but also on John Peel's popular late-night show on Radio 1, alongside Captain Beefheart, T-Rex, the Velvet Underground and punk. Peel enjoyed sharing his exceptionally wide interests. The hypnotic, surreal character of Ligeti's music suited a programme filled with surprises both ear-bending and subversive; for despite its cult following, Peel's selections were so eclectic that he 'expected to be sacked every week'.

Although the settlement with MGM was humiliating, from recordings of the soundtrack Ligeti received substantial royalties. In retrospect he concluded that Kubrick, whom he never met, may have been unaware that he was not paid, confusion having arisen in the offices of MGM because one composer had been: Alex North. Speaking on BBC Radio's *Desert Island Discs* in 1982, Ligeti was asked to reveal the truth about the incident. His account was reported in the press and Kubrick – now living in England – wrote a pained letter demanding that he retract. Ligeti replied asking Kubrick to 'furnish a copy of the contract' – and heard no more. But, by now, Kubrick was using more of Ligeti's music, with permission and paying handsomely. In *The Shining* (1979) there is a short passage from

Lontano. In *Eyes Wide Shut* (1999) the second piece of *Musica ricer-cata* is played four times as an increasingly hypnotic accompaniment to its most unsettling episodes. Always impressed by professionalism, in Kubrick Ligeti recognised a willingness to explore and take risks, a tireless concern for detail and obsessive pursuit of perfection similar to his own. When *Eyes Wide Shut* received its German premiere in Hamburg at the end of 1999, Ligeti attended accompanying Kubrick's widow.

Ironically, during the early 1960s when he particularly needed an income, he had been invited to compose film music without any stylistic preconditions. He refused, believing from his experience assisting Ferenc Farkas that the role of a cinematic composer (providing specific moods, composing with a stopwatch) is always corrupting. Rather than compromise he preferred poverty. In 1968 when *2001* appeared, Ligeti was still relatively poor. But the previous year he had found a new publisher, Schott of Mainz, whose engraved score of *Lontano* began a collaboration that has continued up to the present. In 1968 Ligeti composed three hugely successful pieces, all of them published by Schott and all of them commissioned.

Sliced clusters

Continuum, completed in January 1968, is shorter than the String Quartet no. 2 and the *Ten Pieces for Wind Quintet* (whose kaleido-scopic structures are explored in the next chapter), but it earned a handsome fee from its instigator, the Swiss harpsichordist Antoinette Vischer. Vischer had already elicited works from Henze, Berio and Earle Brown, and was discussing with Cage the proposal that would result in *HPSCHD*. But amongst her thirty-eight commissions, it is *Continuum* that has secured the most durable position in the repertory. Like other works of the period, it was written for the sturdy 'modern' two-manual harpsichord with 16', 8' and 4' stops, whose use was standard in the middle of the century, before the early music revival led to its eclipse by 'period' instruments. The piece's simple premise is that for most of its four minutes, both hands play opposite or complementary groups of pitches on different manuals, as fast as possible. At the correct tempo, each hand depresses sixteen to seventeen keys per second. Apart from the extremely fast pulsations there is an incessant whirring of jacks and plectrums, and *Continuum* could hardly sound more different from the liquid flow of *Lontano*. Actually a clusterous expansion does take place, but it is chopped up like a landscape being viewed through a slatted fence from a moving train.

In *Continuum* Ligeti develops the *meccanico* character that had appeared briefly in *Nouvelles aventures* and the second movement of the Cello Concerto. Although related to the metronome experiment, the idea also derives from working with Koenig in the Cologne electronic studio. Whilst exploring psychoacoustic effects, Koenig had discovered that a succession of pitches spliced together to sound at a rate of more than twenty per second are no longer heard as melody, but coalesce into chords. Ligeti decided to treat the harpsichord as a machine for producing a similar effect. 'How about composing a piece', he thought, 'that would be a paradoxically continuous sound, something like *Atmosphères*, but consist of innumerable thin slices of salami?'[26]

Rhythm in *Continuum* operates on three levels. The foreground pulses clatter incessantly. A secondary level relates to the rate at which the patterns repeat. This varies according to the number of pitches in each pattern: i.e. patterns containing few notes repeat more frequently; those with more notes repeat less frequently. Then there is the speed at which the pitch choices (rather than their quantity) change. The pace of such harmonic change results in a corresponding third-level rhythm.

It is through the second level that the music breathes. During the first page of the score the pattern-repetitions decelerate. When the opening two-note ostinato of G and B flat acquires an additional F, the rate of repetition automatically slows down by fifty per cent. As the ostinato grows to five notes, the repetitions slow down further. On the second page the process is reversed: the number of notes in each ostinato reduces and the apparent tempo speeds up, returning to a two-note pattern like the opening (but now F sharp and G sharp). Throughout *Continuum*, ostinato groups wax and wane like phases of the moon, until they finally arrive at rapid reiterations of a single pitch alternating between the manuals.

Beneath these expanding and contracting cycles, the third-level harmony pursues its slower course. From the initial clusters comes the surprising arrival of two consonant triads (B major and B minor). Thereafter the pitch content of each hand floats apart. Harmonic change accelerates to the point where the right-hand pattern changes at each repetition. There is a delicious whiff of dominant-seventh kitsch before the music heads into the highest register where the pulsations sound like disembodied electronic bleeps. No harpsichord piece had achieved such an effect before.

An interesting footnote to *Continuum* is the adaption of the piece for barrel organ, made by Pierre Charial some twenty years afterwards in 1988. Ligeti was delighted with the result, which initiated a repertory of adapted barrel organ pieces, created by Charial at a time when Ligeti was addicted to the music of Nancarrow. A disadvantage of the barrel organ is its limited range of forty-two pitches. Its virtue is the superhuman speed with which it can read the perforated rolls. The recorded performance of the barrel-organ version of *Continuum*[27] takes only three minutes twenty-two seconds, instead of the four minutes allowed for human players. The headlong tempo creates a splendid 'coalescing', whilst the shifting patterns of second-level rhythm are actually clearer.

7

A Gestural Kaleidoscope

Composition consists principally of injecting a system of
links into naive musical ideas.
  György Ligeti[1]

At first, his dreams were chaotic; somewhat later, they were
of a dialectical nature.
  Jorge Luis Borges, 'The Circular Ruins'

Asked in 1978 by the Hungarian musicologist Péter Várnai to single
out the most important composition in his output,[2] Ligeti pointed to
the String Quartet no. 2 of ten years before as the work that embodied
his ideas most clearly, in which one would find all the techniques he
had used up to that time. This work was written for the LaSalle
Quartet, whose famous interpretations of Schoenberg, Berg and
Webern, and of new works by Kagel, Lutosławski, Penderecki and
others, placed them at the forefront of contemporary music ensembles.
Ligeti worked on the piece between February and August 1968, following his composition of *Continuum*, but it was over a year before
the LaSalle had sufficiently mastered its immense technical demands,
to give the premiere in Baden-Baden on 14 December 1969. Until then
most of the music Ligeti had composed in the West had been, like
Lontano and the Cello Concerto, laid out in single or perhaps paired
movements. The second quartet has five. Up to a point, each movement is a different way of looking at the same material; each reaches
towards a supra-unity from its own technical starting point. But the
second quartet is also a work of striking contrasts. In it Ligeti adopts
a kaleidoscopic approach to structure, using a repertory of elements
that are repeatedly shaken up and reassembled. In the quartet he combines this concept with passages of more consistent texture. The *Ten
Pieces for Wind Quintet*, composed immediately after during the
autumn and winter of 1968, depend almost entirely on the kaleidoscopic principle.

This volatility of 'manner', for all its apparent novelty and technical invention, has links with Ligeti's music of before 1956, in which *capriccioso* is a frequent indication. The five-movement structure of the second quartet allowed Ligeti to refine the schizophrenic tendencies that had resurfaced most dramatically in *Aventures* and *Nouvelles aventures*. In his search for a non-motivic, non-sequential language, he had embraced a hectic, freakish, disjunct irregularity. 'Music should not be normal, well-bred, with its tie all neat,' he remarks to Várnai.[3] At the same time, he was seeking ways of transforming these frantic, disorderly tendencies – the super-expressive gesticulation of his mini-operas – into something cooler, 'as if a pane of glass, or sheet of ice, separated us from the blazing heat of expression'.[4]

The second quartet is a summation, a thesaurus of Ligeti's expressive vocabulary of the 1960s all the richer for the variety of ways in which he treats its syntax. In the second movement, Ligeti revisits the densely woven micropolyphony of his orchestral and choral works, attempting to apply this technique to the textural confines of chamber music. The already purified micropolyphony of *Lux aeterna* provides its starting premise, although now, given the greater precision of string playing, Ligeti makes the pitch domain microtonal. In the third movement he indulges his delight in the 'ticking of malfunctioning machinery', an ironic caricature of technology, automation and bureaucracy already presaged in 'Les horloges démoniaques' from *Nouvelles aventures* and, of course, the *Poème symphonique*. Much of the fifth movement is a study of superimposed tremolos and of extremely fast, precise yet 'weightless' scurrying lines, played at the point of the bow and *sul tasto*, a wilder but similarly ghostlike version of the final pages of the first quartet. So we have the floating quality of *Atmosphères*, the *meccanico* grids of the metronome piece, a 'cooled expressionism' derived from *Aventures*, and echoes of the Bartókian style of Ligeti's Hungarian period as well as of the inflamed, clandestine intimacy of Berg. For, whatever Ligeti has said about freezing the hot-blooded volatility of Expressionism,[5] the second quartet remains an impassioned and impulsive work, full of impromptu changes of feeling, abrupt juxtapositions, stylised attitudes, theatrical extremes.

How can such a gestural music be knitted together?

Structural parallels

It is no idle question. The second quartet is not only a defining achievement of Ligeti's mature style, but undoubtedly one of the great string quartets of the second half of the century, no less effective and relevant now than when first performed. Although it rejects all pitch and other 'systems' both old and new (including serialism), its development of a repertory of mannerisms and contradictory directional energies, rather than of straightforward thematic logic, is symptomatic of its time and place. Par excellence, the quartet is an archetype of sensibilities and attitudes that were widespread in the 1960s and 1970s. It should be possible to crack the code and understand, at least in part, how it works.

Analogies from outside music may help us. As we know, Ligeti was already drawn to the Gothic landscapes of Bosch and Breughel, whose rich tapestry of bizarre detail would provide stimuli for his forthcoming opera. His impressionable antennae were no less affected by the non sequiturs of absurdist theatre, the Fluxus movement or Lewis Carroll, of cinematic art with its tradition of surrealism going back to Buñuel, the loose association of ideas in Kafka, Joyce or Krúdy, and labyrinthian paths in Jorge Luis Borges (another favourite author). A compendium of musico-visual incidents was concurrently being assembled by Kagel, whose *Staatstheater*, completed in 1970, would profoundly influence Ligeti in his attitude to writing opera and which includes an extended 'scenic concert piece' significantly called 'Repertoire'. One might cite also the subconscious spontaneity, and loosening of cognate relationship between shape and colour, in the work of artists like Kandinsky, Klee and Miró; although it is Cézanne whose influence Ligeti acknowledges in relation to the quartet, for his demonstration of how colour can replace contour, and how contrasting volumes and weights create form.[6] All of these models provide maps and metaphors for Ligeti's gestural kaleidoscope. They may define or intuit their structural premises, as it were, on the spot; yet none is chaotic.

Ligeti's involvement with phonetics and electronic music clearly influenced his ideas of continuity and vocabulary. The huge field of linguistics might provide a syntactical framework with which to explain the relative significance of different elements, except that linguistic analysis and semiotics seem often contrived in their application to music, even where the assumption is that musical articulation is rational, and therefore subject to a definable grammar. For music that eschews semantic structure and conventional logic, a theory of signs should be helpful; what, if anything, its audible symbols mean is then less encumbered by any referential context. It is a debate too complex, and so far inconclusive, to enter here. For the moment, in our attempt to understand the structural dynamics of the second quartet, I offer one further analogy whose relevance is that, like music, it is a medium fundamentally abstract but which unfolds sequentially in time.

Intuitive choreography: a dialectic of stasis and movement

In the sibling performance art of contemporary dance can be found illuminating parallels. Modern dance-theatre has its roots in Martha Graham (1894–1991), but it was her protégé Merce Cunningham (b.1919) who most emphatically rejected narrative in favour of abstract inventions, stimulated by his association with John Cage and the latter's advocacy of chance. In the work of such later European choreographers as Pina Bausch (b.1940) and Anne Teresa de Keersmaeker (b.1960) we find energies and flow patterns strikingly analogous to music, even when danced to speech or in silence. Both de Keersmaeker and especially Bausch integrate the most improbable sequences of imagery, mime, stage movement, episodes of storytelling and anecdote, through loose-knit cycles and apparently unpremeditated collage. The structural rationale of these epic creations has an inherent musicality. Conversely, where synaesthetic suggestion is as strong as in Ligeti's music, heard events can conjure in our minds a virtual chore-ography, as if on an imaginary stage. The counterpoint of dance and the choreography of music are remarkably alike.

The combination of collective as well as individual experience means that within any unique genetic inheritance are common formu-lae for making connections. Ligeti's words quoted at the beginning of Chapter One[7] – so like Robert Schumann's in writing to Clara – could be those of artists in any discipline, although some might proclaim a more detached objectivity. In Pina Bausch's strangely polyglot dance language, collections of images and memories are their own justifica-tion. During an interview with Helen Dawkins shortly before her company's return to London after an absence of seventeen years,[8] Bausch said, 'What I start with in a piece is a feeling – what I want to do, what I want to find. I'm working with a lot of questions.' Her dancers invent the answers, fragments of movement, story, even song, which Bausch juggles incessantly, uncertain how the piece will begin until she finds instinctively what she knows is right, 'a form waiting for her to discover it in the welter of detail'. Out of this interplay of feeling, incident and imagery, an expressive language is born, truthful and intelligent yet perplexingly indefinable. The result 'doesn't have a point, it has lots of points. It is as complex, even contradictory, as the world outside the theatre.' Her interviewer notes how Bausch's 'conversation has its own choreography – bursts of arm-waving animation, then quieter, more muted passages'.

Arm-waving and quietude: it could be a summary, if a simplistic one, of Ligeti's music in the second quartet. For without either themes or conventional logic, the quartet retains at least one attribute from classical tradition: dialectic – at its most basic a dialectic between stasis and movement. In fact, nothing in Ligeti's music lacks polarity, in the sense that his material always exposes contrary tendencies within the musical space. Even in *Continuum*, *Lontano*, *Lux aeterna* or *Monument–Selbstportrait–Bewegung* – those pieces in his output which are most nearly monolithic – divergent tendencies remain. In *Selbstportrait*, despite the reference to Reich and Riley in the title, there is no attempt at a Reichian purity. Ligeti has never sought the cool, undisturbed liquidity of, for example, *Music for Mallet Instruments, Voices and Organ*. Processes he has, but not without subversive currents to lead them astray; and when, as in the second quartet, they set off contradictory exchanges, we have an implicit musical drama with the probability of resolution.

Structure of the String Quartet no. 2

In the light of the preceding paragraphs we may interpret the second quartet in a variety of ways. It is exaggerated melodrama. It is a language of gestures and mannerisms. It is a repertory of techniques and types. It is a behavioural kaleidoscope. It is dreamlike non sequitur. It is deep-frozen expressionism. It is the confrontation of opposites. It is immediacy and memory. It is the young science of phonetics and new technology of electronic music applied to the old art of the classical string quartet. It is a wild zigzag trajectory catapulted out of furious energy into a state of graceful stasis, choreographed in five movements.

The listener's first impression is of a profusion of unpredictable, disconnected incidents. But their outcome is less haphazard than might appear. If the music seems to oscillate between crazy impulse and more durable continuity, it is a precarious balance which eventually favours the latter. In fact, the mercurial juxtapositions of the first movement are, in the other four, progressively distilled into music of more lyrical pacifity. The technical novelties of Ligeti's most extravagant manner give way to echoes of an older Bartókian tradition. The microtonal mysteries and rootless, scurrying semiquavers, wheeling and diving like flocks of birds through the early pages of the score, lead eventually to reposeful tremolos and the resonance of remembered chord structures in which there are no microtones at all. Through all its surprises and confrontations, the music proceeds to a psychological resolution, an experience still strange and dreamlike but with its centrifugal tendencies largely diffused.

The first movement is the most volatile and changeable; the last the most consistent, its limpid tremolos leaving a relatively stable atmosphere much less disturbed by extraneous events. In between, the second movement is concentrated and clusterous, a relatively tranquil oasis, despite some explosive outbursts. Its exotic coloration is striking, through many subtleties of left-hand technique, bowing and microtonal pitch movement. All these effects emerge from a confined cluster. Later in the movement the texture liquefies in a profusion of trills and tremolos, anticipating the relaxation that will overtake the last movement. When this second movement ends in a passage of sustained Bartókian voice-leading and a few notes of shared chromatic melody (albeit played with the wood of the bow and in spectral harmonics), we recall the end of the first movement and the melancholy feel of its strangely dislocated melody played in octaves by all the instruments. Ligeti has described these connections between movements as 'rhyming'. The third movement is a mechanistic ticking of unsynchronised *pizzicati*, the fourth a sort of scherzando in which the opposition between ferocious down-bow chords and calm, soft resonances is at its most brutal. Mediation is accomplished by the minor-third tremolos and more translucent harmonies of the last movement which, give-or-take a few darting shadows, maintain their aura of mild gentility before vaporising into nothingness.

Unlike *Aventures* and *Nouvelles aventures* or the 'Dies irae' of the Requiem, from which it is directly descended, the quartet surprisingly contains no silences, apart from the brief gaps which articulate the hard-hit chords at the end of the fourth movement. Other than between the movements there is not a single break, let alone a general pause. Instead of violence confronting frozen tableaux and icy immobility (as in *Aventures* and *Nouvelles aventures*), whenever the wild energies of the quartet are arrested we hear a background of soft sounds: calm, harmonious, enigmatic. Thus there is a dialectic of layers: on the one hand the frenzied activity of the foreground, on the other a gentler pool of limpid harmony which we momentarily glimpse behind. This occurs throughout the quartet and is implicit in its very first gesture, an abrupt pizzicato exploding out of silence and leaving as its residue the almost imperceptible sound of a tremolo. These nervous, microscopic tremolos soon become sustained, flutelike echoes, cool recesses in the surface turbulence – recalling the diatonic chords in *Lux aeterna*. They are evident in the fourth movement where aggressive chords played at the heel of the bow are repeatedly stilled by very soft sounds marked 'molto calmo'. The tense second movement also softens into a warmer sequence of stepwise voice-leading, a consequence of the expanding cluster with which it begins, although here it is surrounded by some of the most brittle and bizarre sounds of the whole quartet.

This 'softening' affects the impetuous semiquavers whose texture pervades so much of the composition. They occur in many forms: otherworldly in high harmonics (the opening), heavy and ominous in low register (movt I, bars 17–18), trampolining across the strings 'as though crazy' (movt I, bars 62 and 72), 'suddenly bursting out' in a ferocious, single-minded tutti (movt IV, bar 37), airily dismembered across four octaves (movt V, bar 20). Midway through the first movement is a section (bars 52–61) where their scurrying slows down and notes lengthen into bounding, elasticated melodies, as graceful yet athletic as dancers. By the last movement the impetuous semiquavers have become gentler; bowed tremolos are now fingered tremolos across a minor third, marked 'legatissimo' and 'mildly', oscillating between all the instruments. The harmonic expansion of this interval is liquid and Arcadian, whilst the end of the movement returns to the same minor third (a rare reflection of earlier material in this capricious music) whose resolutional significance is now clear.

The components of Ligeti's dialectic are complex, hidden by the colouristic and gestural inventiveness of the quartet's surface, but the originality and stature of the work was immediately evident. One critic hailed it, Bartók aside, as 'the most important and remarkable work since Alban Berg's *Lyric Suite*'.[9] Another, writing of a later performance in 1972, declares it 'the masterpiece of the century for string quartet', remarking that 'without being torn out of their traditional character . . . the instruments speak a new language'.[10]

Ten Pieces for Wind Quintet

Ligeti would return to the five-movement form of the second quartet in the Piano and Violin Concertos, although both these works were premiered with only three movements, indicating that their five-movement design was not easily achieved. For the moment, his development of different technical procedures based on the concept of 'repertory' led to a profusion of movement types, but all comparatively short. His next composition doubles the number of movements in the second quartet by having ten. This was commissioned by the Stockholm Philharmonic Wind Quintet, who had given the first complete performance of the *Six Bagatelles* (in Ligeti's absence) in Södertälje, a town just south of Stockholm.[11] According to Nordwall[12] Ligeti had harboured for some time the idea of writing a wind quintet in which each player would take turns to be a soloist. A few days after completing the quartet he plunged eagerly into the completely different sound-world of wind instruments, and by mid-August 1968, two and a half movements were written. He thought he would have the whole piece finished within a month. But suddenly the political equilibrium of central Europe was thrown into disarray by an event which affected him profoundly. On 21 August Soviet and Warsaw Pact tanks entered Czechoslovakia, bringing to an end the liberal reforms promoted by the Czech leader Alexander Dubcek during the 'Prague Spring'. Living comparatively nearby in Vienna, Ligeti felt acutely the agonising repetition of what he had experienced himself during the Hungarian Uprising twelve years before. For several weeks composition seemed impossible. Then early in November, he visited Stockholm to rehearse the first five movements, and the experience of working with the musicians rekindled creative ideas. A few days before Christmas he completed the final movements, and returned to Stockholm in the New Year to prepare for the premiere in Malmö on 20 January 1969.

Like the *Six Bagatelles*, the *Ten Pieces* have proved both accessible and delightfully characteristic of their composer. He decided to alternate the virtuosic 'concertino' pieces, one featuring each player, with five purely ensemble movements, thus creating the effect of a spirited divertimento. The even-numbered movements successively present as protagonist the clarinet, flute, oboe, horn and bassoon. In the odd-numbered movements coloration is enhanced by the use of doubling instruments. Alto flute and cor anglais, for instance, darken the clusterous texture in no. 1; in no. 9 the more piercing tones of the piccolo join oboe and clarinet in their highest registers to play a strident three-part canon exploiting the phenomenon of 'difference tones'.

The style of the *Ten Pieces* is intentionally kaleidoscopic, following the manner of the second quartet but with a nod towards *commedia dell'arte* – or, in Ligeti's analogy, *Tom and Jerry* cartoons. The music is quirky, epigrammatic, comic; rarely are the deeper currents of the quartet evident. If there is resolution, this time it is the impish burlesque of the bassoon that has the last word. The concluding pages emphasise the music's underlying humour, as the hollow low register of the piccolo mockingly parodies the squeaky high register of the bassoon. The bassoon responds scornfully. 'Ex abrupto . . . con violenza', writes Ligeti in nearly the last of numerous character indications provided throughout the score. But it is not quite the last. After the bassoon's final note, there is a quotation:

> . . . but –'
> There was a long pause.
> 'Is that all?' Alice timidly asked.
> 'That's all,' said Humpty Dumpty. 'Good-bye.'

The Chamber Concerto: motion and melody

The second quartet and *Ten Pieces for Wind Quintet* are each based on the idea of juxtaposing variegated 'repertories'. Ligeti repeats this approach in his Chamber Concerto for thirteen instrumentalists, written a year later, which assumes a character midway between the exuberance of the *Ten Pieces* and the darker demeanour of the string quartet. But although many of its techniques had by now become Ligeti mannerisms, the Chamber Concerto is far from being merely imitative of these earlier pieces. Familiar technical processes produce different results. There is a new delicacy and gentleness about Ligeti's handling of texture that unfolds bar after bar of magical coloration. The transparency of scoring and sensitivity of the transformations give a special luminosity to the Concerto.

The work was composed for the Ensemble 'die reihe' which had been co-founded by Ligeti's friend Friedrich Cerha, and which gave a first partial performance with Cerha conducting on 11 May 1970 in Vienna. This performance lacked the fourth movement, which was separately commissioned by the Berlin Festival, where the complete Concerto was premiered on 1 October. On 13 January 1971 David Atherton and the London Sinfonietta introduced the Chamber Concerto to Britain. But the score and material arrived late, the style was unfamiliar – this being the first of Ligeti's instrumental works composed for an ensemble of such proportions – and, due to insufficient rehearsal time, on this occasion too only three movements were performed. Since then, the Concerto has become a cornerstone of contemporary ensemble repertoire, despite the fact that its instrumentation deviates slightly from the norm for ensembles of this size. There are four woodwinds, but they include clarinet and bass clarinet (doubling second clarinet) instead of bassoon. There are parts for horn and trombone but no trumpet. Ligeti writes for two keyboard players, covering between them piano, celesta, harpsichord and Hammond organ (or harmonium), but there are neither harp nor percussion. A string quintet makes up the complement of thirteen soloists, in which no single instrument dominates and a similar virtuosity is required of all.

More than in the string quartet, the movements of the Concerto explore different aspects of a whole. Each movement seems to grow organically, the different character of its successor sounding like an inevitable consequence. All four movements are based around ideas of motion, starting from a web of close-knit clusters that flower into more variegated polyphony. The patterns within these opening textures grow into externalised melodies of surprising grace and shapeliness, like butterflies emerging from their chrysaline constraints.

The first movements of both the Cello and Chamber Concertos make an interesting comparison, since their technical and expressive trajectories are remarkably alike. Both extend an initial colouristic idea by prolonging the opening pitch, or group of pitches, for a minute or even longer. In the Cello Concerto this is a single pitch. In the Chamber Concerto it is an iridescent cluster reminiscent of the minor third at the start of *Continuum* (and with the same span, G to B flat), except that here the intervening semitonal steps are filled in, and below them is an additional semitone. Around these five pitches (F sharp, G, A flat, A and B flat) Ligeti weaves a more transparent version of his full orchestral micropolyphonic technique: there are now, of course, fewer instruments. The web spins, surges and sparkles. Micropolyphony here is still a fluid network of entwining strands, but autonomous melodies are beginning to be revealed.

In both the Cello and the Chamber Concertos the initial pitch cells expand with calculated restraint. In the Chamber Concerto the process takes two and a half minutes to arrive at a perfect fifth (G to D). But within these confines are timbral transformations, an ebb and flow of perceived tempo and alternations between diatonic and chromatic movement. In both movements, the basic pitch structure is audaciously simple, nothing more than a rising chromatic scale. When E flat arrives in the Chamber Concerto, it rings out in wide octaves, at much the same point as octave B flats occur halfway through the first movement of the Cello Concerto. In both cases the octaves are mysterious and arresting, and a platform for further divergence. In the Chamber Concerto they lead to a brief sequence of 'spectral' harmonies, a momentary vision of those strange upper partials in the Violin Concerto. Characteristic of Ligeti's growing interest in line, the defining point in the Chamber Concerto movement is a six-note melody, also played in octaves by eight of the thirteen instruments (bar 49). After this, the texture loosens up, scalic phrases leap athletically and the rhythmic counterpoint grows more animated. A moment later it is stilled.

Although the beginning of the second movement is gentle and sustained, it too becomes more melodic. Via a soft passage of liberated micropolyphony, eight separate instrumental melodies emerge sharing the same repertory of pitches, but desynchronised to the point where several have no bar lines. At bar 40 there is an extended melody played by three winds and two violins in identical rhythm, but with their pitches laid out in canon to produce a dancing melody of chords. In the third movement synchronisation is further discarded. More radical than the equivalent movement in the second quartet, it is a veritable mayhem of disruptive ticking at different metronomic speeds, using every metrical subdivision from duplets to septuplets. After the *Poème symphonique*, this is the piece that most vividly conjures Ligeti's childhood memories of his uncle's printing works and Gyula Krúdy's surreal story of a house full of ticking clocks. Here there is no linearity, only a counterpoint of idiosyncratic clockwork.

The final movement is a bustling Presto, again modelled on the Cello Concerto, this time its second movement. It could be a continuation of that piece, but with a greater proclivity for comedy. Near the centre, the pretty chinoiserie of harpsichord, piano and cello is suddenly hijacked by a crazy cadenza from the pianist, 'hammering like a madman', then stopping abruptly 'as though torn off' (one of Ligeti's favourite imperatives), before a thunderous scratching takes over from the double-bass player. This movement gives birth to an arching melody more liberated and impassioned than any we have heard so far. It is the single unison line beginning at bar 23 in the horn, then passed to strings, oboe and piccolo. That it commences as a twelve-note series seems to be of no consequence. That it coincides with the pianist's crazy cadenza is inauspicious. The darting piccolo tries avoiding manoeuvres, but the weight of piano hammering grows overwhelming. The melody is obliterated, but its legacy remains in the graceful spiralling upwards of the final arpeggiated patterns into a shimmering tritone (A–E flat), dominated, with blinding intensity, by the high register of the oboe. It is strange that the timeless tritone, despite so many associations, can still sound mysterious in Ligeti's sound-world. Meanwhile, from the combat between melody and mayhem, melody has temporarily withdrawn. But it is not defeated.

8

Spider's Web:
The Labyrinth of Melodies

The more accurately you approach nature by way of imitation, the better and more artistic your work becomes.
   Albrecht Dürer[1]

Tying and unravelling knots

Ramifications is a single movement for strings with a specific experimental purpose. Ligeti's ideas for it date from 1967, but detailed
work on the composition was postponed until the winter of 1968–69,
following completion of *Continuum*, the String Quartet no. 2 and the
Ten Pieces for Wind Quintet – all of them pressing commissions – but
before the Chamber Concerto. *Ramifications* had a commission too,
awarded as a Koussevitzky Prize in 1965, and is dedicated to the memory of Serge and Natalie Koussevitzky. Its title comes from the word
'ramify', meaning to branch out, since part of Ligeti's intention is to
explore ways in which densely netted polyphony can be dismembered.
Most of the piece consists of such ramifications and fusions, unravelling and re-knotting, presented in two main sections separated by a
static interlude. In each half, whirring ostinati fan out and expand,
rather as in *Continuum*, except that in *Ramifications* these tightly
meshed plaits are prised apart so that their tendrils open out and
diverge, only to be bundled afresh in some new collection.

Ligeti's music between 1960 and 1974 (the year he completed *San
Francisco Polyphony*) reveals a gradual change of emphasis from the
massed anonymity of micropolyphony to the individualism of multiple
melodies. In the String Quartet no. 2, the *Ten Pieces for Wind Quintet*
and the Chamber Concerto, the branching of the web into tentative
melody becomes an expressive and structural force, as relationships
between texture and line are variously explored. *Melodien* and, to a
lesser extent, the Double Concerto go much further, the once fettered
and fragmented threads of micropolyphony drawn out into long

179

lyrical arcs – superimposed waves of melody in *Melodien*, a few lonesome solos in the Concerto. *San Francisco Polyphony* is the flamboyant climax of this stylistic development, although its liberated melodies still belong to a fundamentally contrapuntal texture.

Ramifications also has its melodies, but they are concentrated near the end (bars 96 to 102) where the unravelling tendrils suddenly assert their freedom in an outburst of impetuous rhetoric. Otherwise there is only one moment of half-hidden melody, starting at bar 54 and played in octaves (and briefly tritones) by divided violins and double bass. It is a stepwise descent with a kink in it (A, G sharp, F sharp, E, F and E flat) lasting ten bars. Is this an unconscious echo of the cantus in *Lux aeterna*, or a pre-echo of the *lamento* motif of Ligeti's late works? At any rate, it is soon lost in the resurgent ostinati. Melody here is not the point.

Microtonality and the organ Études

The experimental nature of *Ramifications* belongs in a different domain. During the 1960s, Ligeti had become interested in alternatives to equal temperament, possibilities which he would explore further in the Double Concerto and with spectacular outcomes during the 1980s and 1990s. Just as temporal fluidity was one of his aims in the early 1960s, now he found its vertical equivalent in another concern: a hyperchromatic treatment of harmony.

Ligeti had already toyed with microtonality. In the 'Kyrie' of the Requiem he authorised microtonal deviation as a practical solution to a choral problem: that of maintaining accurate intonation in complex chromatic counterpoint. More playfully, with Gerd Zacher, then organist of the Lutheran Church in Hamburg-Wellingsbüttel, he probed the 'shortcomings' of an instrument already teased from its familiar mould in *Volumina*. Three years later Zacher moved to a prestigious post at the Folkwang Academy in Essen, and began to perform avant-garde organ music (including his own) at various European new music festivals, which he also promoted in a series of recordings. His approach was to treat the organ as a quasi-synthesiser. We should remember that Ligeti himself was no novice on the instrument, which he had studied keenly for a short period during his pre-war student days in Cluj.

Harmonies, the first of his two organ Études composed in 1967, requires a 'consumptive' organ with reduced air pressure, in order to produce microtonal intervals not otherwise available. For its first performance, in the spirit of Fluxus, Zacher disconnected the motor and hooked up a vacuum cleaner to the wind-chest, in order to achieve Ligeti's concept of 'pale, strange, vitiated' sounds. On paper, *Harmonies* appears to be not only equal-tempered, but more systematic than anything else by Ligeti. The score contains a ten-note cluster (five notes in each hand) held for 231 bars, whose only change is that one of the ten pitches shifts up or down a semitone in every bar. It looks as if, for once, Ligeti has written a piece unremittingly monolithic and methodical. Indeed, the gradual process of pitch change outlined by the five parts in each hand is inversely symmetrical, implying deeper mathematical proportions – not only of pitch, but of duration – whose presence as a formal geometry has been advanced by the American composer-theorist Pozzi Escot.[2] Ligeti, however, has no recollection of devising such a structure.[3] Furthermore, in performance *Harmonies* sounds nothing like its appearance in the score. In the first place the registration, performed by an assistant, is completely random, except that stop changes must be frequent, continuous, and as far as possible, imperceptible.[4] Secondly, Ligeti instructs the organist to make all the bars of uneven length, so that the piece sounds not at all rigid or metrical, but fluid and amoebic, like *Volumina*. Finally, by minimising the wind pressure, each pipe is starved of wind, particularly as more stops are drawn, so that they rarely sound at the notated pitch, or even speak properly. The harmonies are 'tainted', says Ligeti, and 'more or less diverge from the written text'. Fluctuations of intonation, timbre and volume are the music's essence, as if the composer meant to replicate the luminous transformations of *Lontano* (rather as *Volumina* replicates *Atmosphères*), but using methods specifically appropriate to the organ.

Harmonies can only be performed, of course, on mechanical organs where the gradual drawing of a stop has a progressive effect; on electrical instruments the switching is either 'on' or 'off'. Subsequent performances dispensed with the vacuum cleaner, since there are other ways of achieving the intended result. The CD recording for the Sony Ligeti Edition was made, as Ligeti explains, 'on the most tidily built organ I have ever come across, in Olten – Swiss precision craftsmanship. Zsigmond Szathmáry played, his wife pulled the stops, while Marcus Herzog and I (temporarily) impaired the organ. We removed the (precision Swiss) stone weights from the wind reservoir; and in their place I pressed down with all my weight, changing the position of my upper body as Szathmáry played.'⁵ Occupying a ghostly no man's land between normal and degenerate sound, a performance of *Harmonies* sounds eerily vaporous and unstable, quite unlike any other organ music one has heard, even *Volumina*. But, for the analyst, it is something of an enigma – a greater paradox than that posed by the imperceptible detail in the Requiem. Did Ligeti really compose geometric symmetries, only to make free with bar lengths and to 'denature' both pitch and tone, so rendering them impotent? Possibly – since the relationship between order and chaos is an instinctive pre-occupation – but if so, it was unintentional.

The second of the Études, *Coulée*, was completed two years later than *Harmonies* and premiered by Zacher in Graz, during the Styrian Autumn Festival in 1969. Its technical basis harks back to *Continuum*, in that the whole study consists of even (but non-metrical) quavers played extremely fast in both hands whilst the pedals contribute long-sustained background chords. Registration is left to the player, although Ligeti asks that it should sound 'sharp and colourful' so that, despite their extreme speed, individual attacks (or their key action) do not fuse together, but create the impression of a 'very fast time-grid'. As in *Continuum*, rhythm is perceived on three planes: the minuscule pulsations of the grid, the variable content (and therefore variable duration) of the repeating ostinati, and the more spacious but irregular rate of chord change. Harmonically *Coulée* runs its own course, starting with an open perfect fifth (the same pitches in both hands), and continuing in an even more seamless and unruffled manner than *Continuum*. Yet the distinctive character of organ articulation makes it a fascinating complement to the harpsichord piece. Devised by the same clockmaker, their mechanisms are similar, their music quite distinct.

Originally Ligeti had intended to write four organ studies. In another called 'Zero', he envisaged going even further than *Harmonies* by using the sounds of escaping air, totally without pitch. A fourth would involve one player at the keyboard and another manipulating the pipes inside the instrument, like an organ equivalent of the 'prepared piano'. Both ideas were closer to Fluxus and other experimental fashions, in which conventional sound was being variously erased or impaired. Disinclined to continue anything beyond its useful life,

Ligeti felt that he had done enough, and the third and fourth studies were never composed.

Coulée employs the mechanics of the organ normally and has no microtonality. Already, however, Ligeti had adopted a more strategic use of microtones in the second and third movements of the String Quartet no. 2, where they are used to produce smaller gradations within a narrow, clusterous pitch expansion. In the quartet he adopts a conventional quarter-tone notation, but instructions in the score make clear that these are not quarter-tones, but narrower deviations 'of a not precisely determined size'. They are used only when there is time to savour their effect, or to add further discrete steps to slow-moving conjunct polyphony, never when the music is fast, volatile or disjunct.

In *Ramifications* Ligeti maintains a microtonal climate from beginning to end. The idea was a direct result of hearing the 'Kyrie' of the Requiem. The music is laid out in two groups each of six parts, one for four violins, viola and cello, the other for three violins, viola, cello and double bass. Although the printed score describes the piece as playable by orchestra or soloists, nowadays Ligeti prefers solo strings. Instruments in the first group are tuned a quarter-tone higher; or rather, slightly more than a quarter-tone, to counteract the tendency for the intonation to equalise. Here, too, Ligeti means an approximate rather than a precise pitch deviation, but the effect is striking: nowhere else does his music sound quite so like swarms of insects. Moreover, even simple chords sound rich. They 'smell high', what Ligeti calls '*un goût faisandé*', as if putrefaction had set in. When the process of ramification eventually explodes in a fantastic contortion of expressionist counterpoint, it is like the shock of finding a seething mass of maggots in a decaying carcass. Influenced by serialism, all the individual lines are palindromic sequences lasting between seven and eleven notes, but they sound wildly uninhibited, the sudden rush into atonality heightened by their angularity. Almost as quickly the tumult expires, leaving a few residual reflexes surrounded by soft harmonics.

Multiple melodies

Ramifications ends in characteristic manner, 'suddenly, as though torn off', followed by five empty bars, the music vaporised in a measured silence lasting almost half a minute through which the conductor continues to beat. For *Melodien*, composed after the Chamber Concerto, Ligeti writes nothing so abrupt, drawing instead on the gentle liquidity of the Concerto. Commissioned by the City of Nuremberg to commemorate the quincentenary of Albrecht Dürer's birth in 1471 and dedicated to Ligeti's wife Vera, *Melodien* is an exceptionally organic score. Also in one movement but lasting around twelve minutes, it signals a change in outlook. The shift in emphasis, from cluster composition and woven nets towards a loosening of line and harmony, opens door upon door to subtleties of orchestration, and seemingly to deeper currents of sadness and melancholy. It is a score rich in allusions – to Ives, Mahler, Brahms – and in figurations, melodies and incidents whose variety is enhanced by contrasting tempi and perspective. There is no hint of the grandiose; rather, *Melodien* is an exquisite study in delicacy. But the bar-to-bar process is symphonic, a narrative of transformation compressed into one short movement. Dürer, who like Ligeti, was of Hungarian parentage but resident in Germany, immersed himself in the relationship between scientific theory and art, a theme which he developed in a learned treatise on proportion published in 1528. Although Ligeti felt honoured by the association, a stronger inspiration was the 'metallic shimmering' of Gustav Klimt's mosaic paintings. And, in that *Melodien* is a procession of figures across an eventful canvas, it again evokes Breughel: not now the dark horror of *The Triumph of Death* but his *Series of the Months*, in which humans, animals and birds pursue their work and play amidst awesome and dignified landscapes, each a microcosm of daily life.[6]

In *Melodien* Ligeti sets aside – at least until *Le Grand Macabre* – the schizophrenic, gesticulating manner of *Aventures* and *Nouvelles aventures*, adopting instead a dreamlike metamorphosis characteristic of the 'Lacrimosa' in the Requiem, *Lux aeterna* and *Lontano*. The sense of spatial recession cultivated in *Lontano* is a primary model, for *Melodien* too explores the hinterland between foreground melody and background texture. Here the foreground is filled with an elaborate web of independent figures of differing character, tempi and direction, everything from brief snatches to long, expressive arches. In the middle-ground are subordinate ostinato patterns marked *corrente* (running), but also in places running down – pattern becoming melody, as figurations expand and take flight in lyrical lines. Behind, as in *Lontano*, is the noble drift of the harmony defined by slower horizontal lines, 'anchor' chords and pedal points. Yet the more closely one studies the score, the more miraculous seems to be the opalescent unity of the whole.[7]

Occasionally in *Melodien* we hear a fully-fledged melody, like those in the solo violin part between bars 46 and 50 and from the tuba at bar 64. Generally only short phrases separate themselves from the polyphonic mass, just as individual colours and harmonies rise momentarily from the micropolyphonic mists of *Lontano*. From the arpeggiated wisps of ostinati, individual phrases grow in amplitude and duration to sail gracefully over two or more octaves, elastic in rhythm, relatively harmonious in pitch content, using the 'open' intervals of perfect fourth, perfect fifth, major and minor sixth. Most of them draw from the same store of figurations, but no two are exactly alike. They soon fall back into the prevailing drift of the overall texture, until later in the score they grow more animated, propelled by capricious roulades of demisemiquavers.

Form and content in *Melodien*

What gives *Melodien* its exceptional quality is the subtle interaction between soloistic detail and the spacious sweep of the whole. Framed by two waves of upward-running chromatic scales, the harmonic foundation of the music falls away, like a wide valley, to rest on a pedal C at bar 72 where the music is at its most Mahlerian,[8] before rising again on the other side. 'Hunters in the Snow' from Breughel's *Series of the Months* describes a similar inverse arc, the winter landscape dropping into the middle of the canvas before lifting to distant peaks, a calculated movement from left to right. Each side of the arc, each half of *Melodien* concludes with a horn duet, similar in their ascending phrase-shapes as well as in intervallic character. Marked in *rilievo*, these evocative duets recall classical horn calls and their hunting origins. The first (bars 60–66) is answered by the melody for tuba – its only prominent solo – whilst the second (bars 136–38) fades in a gentle dissolution. Similar duets occur in later works by Ligeti, notably in the first movement of the Trio for Violin, Horn and Piano.

As we observed, the three-dimensional landscape of the music involves a busy polyphonic foreground set against a slower background harmony. The background harmony in the first half of *Melodien* is underpinned by a slowly sinking chromatic scale. This is not traceable in any single part but passes between the lower instruments in an otherwise predominantly high tessitura. Beginning on E at bar 22 in the trumpet, the line passes to bassoon in bar 23, first horn a bar later, back to the bassoon at bar 27, then oboe, first violin, trombone, clarinet etc. Some steps in this chromatic scale are contributed by instruments dipping to a low note in the midst of their own lyrical phrases. In this way, the oboe A flat and the first violin G in bar 28 carry forward the process of descent from the bassoon's A natural in the bar before. Meanwhile, higher strands of melody flower with delicate expressivity. Many of them also fall through arpeggiated triads, as in the flute part in bars 33–34 and 37–38 and the piano in bars 40–41. Ligeti had already decided to employ triadic components as an escape from the confined chromaticism of cluster technique, and had used them to this end in *Lux aeterna*, where a perfect fourth enclosing a minor third stands as an 'interval signal' calming the micropolyphonic flow. In *Melodien* the third is major (F and A, bar 13) at the juncture between the opening *corrente* passage and the start of the scalic descent spawning its melodic canopy. To this warmer major third are added first a tone below (E flat), then F sharp, B and D, and below them a G (bar 19): a seven-note aggregate formed from the ostinato patterns in flute, xylophone, celesta and first violin. It is a combination of two dominant seventh chords on G and B, their roots also a major third apart. But there is no tension. Rather the effect is of a soft homogeneity, as if some bitonal pounding from *The Rite of Spring* had become a shimmering constellation in the night sky.

Ligeti's firmament is typically cloudy. But the veiled bitonality of bar 19 is the first in a succession of harmonic pillars of increasing depth and solidity. It and other 'focus' chords are strategically sited throughout the composition. At bar 45, the polyphony temporarily exhausts itself in a lone piano chord of similar astringency. It signals a change to more animated music, whose material has been 'anticipated' (*à la* Brahms) in the upward thrust of violin, viola and trumpet three bars before. Below them the chromatic descent continues, now heard as a series of staccato patterns moving progressively lower. At bar 57 they arrive at a still darker harmonic complex, complete with decay characteristics (the higher frequencies fade most quickly), like a tolling bell whose resonances linger through the next twelve bars. Now comes a codetta to the first half of the score, during which the horns play their cadential formula.

So the first half of *Melodien* consists loosely of four sections defined by a series of 'focus' chords. First are the ascending cascades of the opening *corrente* texture floating upwards to a single high A. Then come three contrasting paragraphs above a descending bass line. The first sets the mood with its wave upon wave of mostly falling melody; the second enlivens the music with mercurial solos and brittle ostinati; finally comes the repose of the codetta in which, besides the horn duet, we hear further descending arpeggios from flute and clarinet enveloped in a mysterious sheen, until all resolve on octave Cs.

The second half has three more or less differentiated sections. The first (starting at bar 73) contains the most varied and liberated counterpoint in *Melodien*, notable for its Ivesian diversity and rhythmic independence. The second is introduced at bar 99 by another aggregate chord, this time in the strings and coloured by a propensity for minor sixths and perfect fifths. From here, double-stopped string chords flow into the third and final section – a recapitulation, at least in feeling, of the *corrente* passage at the opening. So the music comes full circle. As before, the ascending scales decelerate. Indeed, *Melodien* is marked by a repeated tendency for energy to dissipate, followed by a rewinding of the mechanism, a renewed burst of activity, until the process repeats.

Melodien is scored for single woodwind and brass (except for the two horns) plus percussion, piano doubling celesta, and strings. Ove Nordwall suggests that Ligeti originally considered amalgamating three Swedish chamber music groups from the Stockholm Philharmonic Orchestra: the wind quintet for whom he had composed the *Ten Pieces*, a brass ensemble and a string quintet, plus percussionist and keyboards.[9] Certainly, this reduced orchestra allows endless subtleties of instrumentation. Unfortunately, at the first performance of *Melodien* on 10 December 1971, apparently neither the Nuremberg Orchestra nor Hans Gierster the conductor could 'cope with its great difficulties'.[10] The American premiere, given by the Los Angeles Philharmonic on 13 April 1972, was hardly any better. Ligeti relates that the conductor Zubin Mehta knew the score so superficially that, during rehearsal, he failed to notice the presence of the second horn. Ligeti was angry and refused to go forward after the performance to shake Mehta's hand. By contrast, Seiji Ozawa's performance a month later with the San Francisco Symphony delighted him. On the strength of it he promptly agreed to their request that he should write a new work for the orchestra.

But it was Michael Gielen's direction of *Melodien* with the Amsterdam Concertgebouw Orchestra, given on 24 June 1972, which so illuminated the intricate beauties of its inner texture that Ligeti came to regard this as the 'authentic' premiere. In 1965 Gielen had conducted the first performance of the Requiem in Stockholm, preparing it while also working on the world premiere production of Zimmermann's *Die Soldaten* in Cologne, and commuting to rehearsals between the two cities. Despite this exacting schedule, despite also having a car accident, his direction of the Requiem had been 'wonderful'. Gielen had recorded the Cello Concerto and conducted the first performance of *Ramifications* in Berlin in April 1969, and knew Ligeti's style intimately. For *Melodien* in Amsterdam he used solo strings, achieving a transparency and radiance which, in the words of one critic, 'one would hardly have thought possible'.[11] Ligeti was thrilled, and now prefers that all his chamber orchestra pieces except for the Piano Concerto should be performed with solo strings.

It is a slight impediment to the study of *Melodien* that the published score exists only in a reproduction of the composer's manuscript – in some places verging on the illegible, with bar lines bent from the vertical to accommodate his minuscule figurations. Several of Ligeti's scores which were first issued in facsimile have since been engraved. In the case of *Melodien*, he has never yet had time to correct its text and re-scrutinise every detail. Awaiting that authority, it remains untypeset; a compensation is that Ligeti's handwriting is endearingly indicative of the way he thinks.

Teaching

For much of the period between 1969 and 1973 Ligeti resided in Berlin, following the award of a year's stipend under the DAAD 'Berliner Künstlerprogramms'. *Ramifications* had been premiered there by the Berlin Philharmonic Orchestra, likewise the complete Chamber Concerto at the Berlin Festival in October 1970. Then the festival decided to commission Ligeti to write a work for the Berlin Philharmonic, with Karlheinz Zöller and Lothar Koch – two of its principals – as flute and oboe soloists. This was the Double Concerto on which Ligeti began work in 1971, and which received its first performance conducted by Christoph von Dohnányi on 16 September 1972. Soon after, it was played in Royan, Vienna and Eindhoven, and

Ex. 16 A page of *Melodien*

in Glasgow where Ligeti's music was featured at the 1973 Musica Nova with the composer in attendance.

Throughout the productive 1960s Ligeti had become increasingly sought after, not only as an articulate and amusing apologist for his own music, but as an inspired analyst of classical repertoire as well as of early twentieth-century composers. His lectures on Wagner, Mahler and Debussy focused, as one might expect, on the textural 'perspectives' in their music, their elevation above his own work having less to do with modesty than with Ligeti's exceptional interest in other musics. Besides his visits to Stockholm and the Darmstadt Summer Courses, at which he was one of the most charismatic lecturers, he delivered composition and analysis courses in Finland, Germany, Holland and Spain. On an early visit to Stockholm, he found himself sitting beside Shostakovich in the Konserthus. Believing that Shostakovich and his music were representatives of Soviet Communism, he avoided being introduced. Much later, after reading *Testimony* and hearing *The Nose* and the Fourth Symphony, he completely changed his view, deeply regretting that he had behaved coldly.

First visit to America – encounters with computer music

The most interesting of these many teaching engagements arose from an invitation to be Visiting Lecturer and Composer-in-Residence at Stanford University. It was Ligeti's first experience of America and a hugely enjoyable time, shared with Vera and their seven-year-old son Lukas. Relatively few performances of his music had occurred in the States. Lukas Foss had made an impression by including *Poème symphonique* in four 'Evenings of New Music' in Buffalo in March 1965, designed to showcase his new Center for the Creative and Performing Arts, and in 1971 Seiji Ozawa and the San Francisco Symphony introduced *Atmosphères* to the West Coast. The invitation from Stanford was instigated by John Chowning, its director of Computer Music and Acoustic Research, and his pupil and colleague Martin Bresnick, who had studied at the Vienna Music Academy with Cerha, and had met Ligeti. Ligeti knew nothing about Stanford's computer activities, but accepted because he thought it would be warm and sunny and he needed time to work on his commissions. To begin with he could barely understand the Californian accent, let alone its vocabulary. 'I was hopelessly forlorn, but the students were so nice and made no

criticism. After three months I could speak "techno" very badly.'
Predictably, he began his teaching with Debussy.

The six months spent in California in the first half of 1972, during
which Ligeti continued to work on the Double Concerto, brought
valuable new stimuli. For instance, there was his first contact with
minimalist music. He had already met Terry Riley in Stockholm in
1968, warming to him as a person, although at that time he knew
none of his music. In Stanford he heard recordings of *In C* and of Steve
Reich's *Violin Phase* and early tape piece *It's gonna rain*. Back in
Berlin, he met Reich himself. But he was equally impressed by another
encounter, for it was in Stanford that, for the first time, Ligeti realised
the vast power of computers and their apparent potential to revolu-
tionise artistic media. John Chowning (b.1934) had established
Stanford as one of the world's leading centres for computer music and
sound synthesis, years before Pierre Boulez's creation in 1976 of his
Institut de Recherche et de Coordination Acoustique/Musique
(IRCAM) in Paris. It was several weeks before Ligeti visited the
Stanford laboratory, but when he did, Chowning explained his work
and a lasting friendship developed. In his small office Chowning
played Ligeti his *Sabelithe*, the first work ever composed using FM
synthesis. Chowning taught Ligeti Fortran and Ligeti attended the
premiere of Chowning's *Turenas*, the first computer-controlled composition to move sounds in a 360-degree soundspace. No sooner had
Ligeti returned to Europe than he was advocating Chowning's work –
indeed, within days and to Boulez, no less. By chance, the day after
Gielen's performance of *Melodien* in Amsterdam, both turned up at
the Institute for Sonology in Utrecht where Gottfried Michael Koenig
was now director. Ligeti had not previously seen the Institute and
wanted to visit his friend; Boulez was seeking ideas and advice for his
own research powerhouse. Ligeti spoke of what he had found in
Stanford. In Berlin he recommended Chowning for a DAAD grant and
arranged for him to be invited to the Berlin Festival and to the
Darmstadt Summer Courses.

Six years earlier, Ligeti himself had been invited by François Bayle
to work in the Centre de Recherche of Radio France. He thought
seriously about creating a piece of *musique concrète* but illness had
intervened. His encounter at Stanford with a sophisticated means of
sound generation, far superior to the tedious procedures of analogue
studios, caused him to think again about returning to electro-acoustic

composition. Indeed, the promise of establishing similar facilities at the Hochschule in Hamburg was influential in persuading him to accept a permanent teaching post there in 1973, rather than offers from other institutions. Alas, after his appointment, despite many discussions with the conservatory authorities, the money failed to materialise and the equipment never arrived. Had it done so, Ligeti might have become an altogether different animal: an 'electronic computer composer'. True, his artistic disposition made it unlikely. Scepticism gradually returned. He imagined that it would take at least a year to learn the necessary computer programming. As time went by and he heard the first products of IRCAM, he decided once again that as far as his own composition was concerned, he preferred the superior quality of live instrumental sound.

Whilst living in Palo Alto in Silicon Valley, Ligeti made frequent visits to San Francisco, surrendering happily to the charm of the city with its benign climate interrupted only by its famous fogs. There could scarcely be a composer more interested in observing them! One could be sitting in a café in full sun on the fiftieth floor of the Bank of America, watching the fog glide under the Golden Gate Bridge and invading the rectangular pattern of the streets far below.[12] Grids and mists were already fundamental ingredients of his music, and the experience of watching them mingle from above influenced Ligeti's approach to his two largest orchestral works of the 1970s, *Clocks and Clouds* (which includes female chorus) and *San Francisco Polyphony*. On 14 May 1972, an all-Ligeti lecture-concert was presented at Stanford, including *Artikulation*, *Poème symphonique*, *Lux aeterna* and *Ten Pieces for Wind Quintet*. The reporter from the *San Francisco Chronicle* remarked that Ligeti appeared to be shy and very nervous, but that he 'seemed to be having a wonderfully good time. So did the rest of us.'[13]

Before leaving California Ligeti took the opportunity of visiting Harry Partch (then living at Encinitas) and the University of California at San Diego, where Partch's unique instruments were kept and Ligeti was able to play them. One of the century's most extraordinary musical pioneers, Partch had spent a lifetime (he died two years later) building an ensemble of instruments to his own sculptural designs and forty-three-note scale. In the 1970s Partch was little known in Europe, nor in America outside some university campuses and a loose confederation of similarly minded composers. Ever attracted to outsiders and mavericks – the more detached from any establishment the better – Ligeti was intrigued by Partch, as he would later be by Nancarrow and Vivier. But he was less interested in the music as such, than in its microtonal harmony based on ostensibly rational tuning systems.

All those real major chords, dominant sevenths and ninth chords, major thirds which are tighter than in equal temperament . . . The way Partch uses his instruments, all tuned differently, is that each produces perfectly pure sound with natural harmonics but, from the point of view of equal tempera-ment, they are outrageously out of tune in relation to one another. That is what interested me, the effect of music where the tuning systems clash; it is like a body in a state of gradual decomposition.[14]

The Double Concerto for flute and oboe

In fact, there is little of Partch's direct influence in the Double Concerto, whose first movement was completed before Ligeti met him. And whereas Partch's microtonality was calculated mathematically, Ligeti's is entirely empirical, governed solely by his ear. A greater inspiration – apart from the precedent of *Ramifications* – was Bruno Bartolozzi's widely read technical manual, *New Sounds for Woodwind*.[15] In the Concerto micro-intervals are played by the soloists and selectively by members of the orchestra. For practical advice Ligeti consulted Heinz Holliger and Karlheinz Zöller, flute soloist at the first performance. As a result, he decided to suggest fingerings only in the flute parts, mostly for the production of harmonics. Other micro-tonal deviations, he concluded, are better achieved by changing the embouchure – relying on individual technique and sensitivity to the harmonic context – than by alternative fingerings. Multiphonics, a major subject of Bartolozzi's study, Ligeti rejected as 'too unstable', despite their popularity following publication of the book.

Like the Cello Concerto, the Double Concerto is composed of two movements, contrasting slow-moving clusters in the first movement with rapid figurations in the second. It is an old Hungarian formula found in gypsy music and in the *Hungarian Rhapsodies* of Liszt. In both concertos the second movement is the structural consequent – or in Ligeti's term, 'variant' – of the first movement; and the first is virtu-ally monodic, in that clusters are but horizontal projections of the melody (as in *Lontano*). Through the opening pages of the Double

Concerto, the texture expands and contracts between judiciously placed unisons and open octaves – one of them, at bar 29, also containing a perfect fifth, and again (as not infrequently in the Ligeti of this period) reminiscent of Mahler. The second movement replicates the busy tempo of the Cello Concerto, but only briefly its wild frenzy. There is no parading of musical types, instead an evolution of trembling, clock-like ostinati, revolving at infinitely variable speeds in the manner of *Ramifications*. Here they generate more in the way of melody, all the more striking when microtonally inflected as in the solo oboe at bar 75. In this movement, the texture shimmers like patterns of light on water. The solo flautist is rarely an instigator, more often on a par with the winds of the orchestra. Only near the end does Ligeti offer the soloists a few virtuosic flurries – to the disappointment of the work's original protagonists, who had expected more prominent roles, each with its own cadenza.

For the most part, this is music about the art of togetherness. Ligeti's unusual community of instruments produces rare timbral combinations. There are just four brass and only lower strings – i.e. no violins. But rather than omit orchestral flutes and oboes in order to highlight the soloists, he multiplies these instruments by scoring for triple orchestral woodwind. The blending of solo alto flute with the three orchestral flutes and soft-toned clarinets in the opening bars is particularly lovely. In contrast, the four oboes in upper register sound dazzlingly bright. Ligeti ends the movement with the solo flautist playing bass flute, the pitch-bending of its deep hollow tones giving the passage a musky sweetness. Earlier he achieves an extraordinarily rich coloration, by combining with low brass and strings all the deeper woodwind, including oboe d'amore, cor anglais, bass clarinet and contrabassoon. In the second movement a generally high tessitura ensures that its continuous oscillations sound airy and effortless; even the double basses' entry at bar 32 is in the treble clef. The music maintains its luminous sparkle. Rarely in the whole work do the strings uniformly assert a lower compass. Of the few occasions where they do, the most telling is a dominant seventh on F in the first movement, played by all the strings, between bars 39 and 42. Not only is Ligeti's partial rehabilitation of a clichéd chord the foundation from which flows the remainder of the movement; its half-concealed warmth, below the twisting microtonal clusters of solo oboe and wind, is strangely tantalising, lingering in the mind's ear well after the chord itself has vanished, like the bloom of a perfect complexion glimpsed in a crowd. Ligeti's consolidation of a diatonic as well as a chromatic vocabulary coincided with his renewed exploration of microtones. It is a Janus-like mix, reflective and innovative at the same time, but entirely pragmatic, groundwork for the more complex microtonal adventure of the Violin Concerto composed twenty years later.

In April 1972, between semesters at Stanford, Ligeti made another visit which, had he known what he learnt later, might have been very influential. This was to Mexico City where he was the guest of the Goethe-Institut and was able to meet different generations of Mexican composers. Nobody mentioned Conlon Nancarrow, the American refugee from McCarthyism. Although Nancarrow had been living in Mexico for over thirty years, creating complex polyrhythmic compositions for the resourceful but private medium of player piano, he was little known and had not been admitted to the circle of Mexican composers, who were by disposition tacitly anti-American. Ligeti, too, had never heard of Nancarrow. His 'discovery' of this most isolated of twentieth-century composers occurred eight years later.

9
Dis(c)loc(k)ation and Transformation

'I wish you wouldn't keep appearing and vanishing so
suddenly: you make one quite giddy.'
  'All right,' said the Cat; and this time it vanished quite
slowly, beginning with the end of the tail, and ending with
the grin, which remained some time after the rest of it had
gone.
  Lewis Carroll, *Alice's Adventures in Wonderland*

The Sinbad stories refer to real and possible metamorphoses:
at one point Sinbad changes into a sprig of mistletoe and
contemplates turning into a comb. This sense of shift is
reflected in Krúdy's syntax . . . [his] long rolling sentences are
held together by sentiment, sensuality and dream, but for all
their sense of gentle flux, something is breaking them up.
They are open-ended affairs . . . Tenses change continually.
The subject-verb-object structure is subverted, in much the
same way as a hierarchy or social order might be, from
within. Before the reader knows it, the language has come to
pieces in his hands, leaving a curiously sweet erotic vacuum,
like an ache without a centre.
  George Szirtes's introduction to Gyula Krúdy's *Adventures of Sinbad*[1]

A dynamic labyrinth

The orderly yet often capricious behaviour of man-made mechanisms
has intrigued Ligeti since childhood. His uncle's printing works in
Dicsőszentmárton, his encounter with the stories of Gyula Krúdy, and
later with Chaplin's film *Modern Times*, nurtured a delight in hypnotic and recalcitrant machinery. Clocks and automata worked a special
charm. In the printing presses and in Krúdy's tale of a house full of
clocks reside the origins of Ligeti's *meccanico* music. But Krúdy's significance went further. For Hungarian literati, his fantastic and ironic
excursions into an idealised past fed a melancholic nostalgia for a

country untainted by the political aftermath of the First World War. Amongst many literary influences – Joyce, Proust, Borges, Vian and other modernists, and perennially Lewis Carroll – it is the dreamlike discursiveness of Krúdy, his ability to turn simple narrative into an illusory (indeed, Joycean) association of unrelated ideas,[2] to which Ligeti feels closest.

In authoritarian societies, malfunctioning mechanisms and Dadaist nonsense become metaphors for the inefficiency and stupidity which, one hopes, may eventually unseat bureaucracy and oppression. But if gawky automata delighted the Surrealists for their implicit promise of anarchy, it was also because they touched a vein of childish naivety and playfulness. Idiosyncratic machines appear in the paintings of Duchamp, Picabia, Ernst, Miró and Klee. The mechano-sexual psychology underpinning such cornerstones of early twentieth-century art as Duchamp's *The Bride Stripped Bare by Her Bachelors, Even (Large Glass)* (1915–23) is relatively remote from Ligeti; but the primal innocence evident in Miró and Klee, with their rhythmic invention based on non-Western primitivism, are much closer to him, as is also Magritte. Jean Tinguely's motorised sculptures, with their creaky movement and penchant for self-destruction, provide another parallel; for Ligeti adores Tinguely, whose work he first saw in the early 1960s at Amsterdam's Museum of Modern Art in an exhibition named 'The Dynamic Labyrinth'. Cogs and mechanisms inhabit the wider modernist revolution that includes Cubism's play upon prisms, triangles and pyramids. It is interesting to observe that Braque and Picasso's twin paintings of guitarists, *Le Portugais* and *Ma Jolie* (both from 1911) look less like guitars and people than like refracted metronomes. Similarly Picasso, in his *Tête* of 1913, renders the head of a woman as a white pyramid, with arc and pendulum, upon a brown perch.

Such is the grist of Ligeti's metronomic mill. Dada and Fluxus may have been the subversive catalysts for *Poème symphonique*, but the idea had a serious intent, continued in the *meccanico* movements of the Chamber Concerto and String Quartet no. 2. In each of these pieces Ligeti subjects patterns of ticking clockwork to progressive dislocation. *Continuum* and *Ramifications* explore other rhythmic stratifications, whilst the sequence of orchestral works that occupied his attention during the early 1970s, culminating in *Clocks and Clouds* (1972–73) and *San Francisco Polyphony* (1973–74), comprises more complex musical landscapes in which relationships between pattern and fluidity, *meccanico* order and liberated melody, undergo many transformations. When the Kontarsky brothers asked Ligeti to compose a two-piano work, Ligeti viewed it as an opportunity to focus exclusively on rhythmic patterning, now with a fraternal nod towards the American minimalists. In the States, for the first time, he heard music by Terry Riley and Steve Reich, although only on recordings. But work on the two-piano piece lay further ahead. First he had to complete his choral and orchestral commissions. Clocks and clouds? Their parallel in the visual arts might be Salvador Dali (*The Disintegration of the Persistence of Memory*, perhaps), except that Ligeti's dislike of Dali's 'megalomaniac dandyism' amounts to artistic revulsion. No connection was in his mind.

Mists and mechanisms

In fact the genesis of *Clocks and Clouds* came from a quite different quarter. In 1972 the philosopher Karl Popper (1902–94) published an influential collection of essays under the title *Objective Knowledge*.[3] Amongst them was the text of the second Compton Memorial Lecture, which he had delivered at the University of Washington in April 1965, called 'Of Clouds and Clocks: an Approach to the Problem of Rationality and the Freedom of Man'. In it Popper confronts the dichotomy between physical determinism, the ruling faith of post-Newtonian physics, which asserts that everything is explicable according to preordained rules, and its apparent opposite, indeterminism, which gained impetus from quantum mechanics and admits the existence of randomness and uncertainty. What attracted Ligeti to Popper's paper, as it enlivens the issue for the general reader, is the philosopher's choice of metaphor to explain his thesis, an uncannily Ligeti-like opposition between clocks and clouds.

The problem addressed by Popper has since become central to linear dynamics – popularly known as chaos theory – and would also influence Ligeti and other creative artists during the 1980s and 1990s. Popper's conclusions pre-date but are not incompatible with this more recent science. Like many of his contemporaries, Popper was an indeterminist. But the gist of his argument is that determinism and indeterminism are reconcilable. Clocks, judged rigorously, are less perfect than they appear, and clouds (like weather in general) are predictable up to a point. Popper concludes by considering the influence upon our 'clock-like' physical conditioning of our 'cloud-like' mental states, an example being the challenge of mind over body, familiar to all who play a musical instrument. In seeking 'something intermediate between perfect clouds and perfect clocks', he also anticipates a recent view, that 'if quantum mechanics is correct about indeterminacy on the smallest scales, on macroscopic scales of space and time, the universe obeys deterministic laws . . . sufficiently large quantum systems lose nearly all their indeterminacy and behave much more like Newtonian systems'.[4] Humans, however, like horses, remain unpredictable because 'living creatures have their own hidden variables, such as what kind of hay they had for breakfast'.[5]

Ligeti was attracted to Popper's title, but he was also deeply impressed by the whole paper, which he read soon after its publication, and which appealed to his scientific mind. He particularly empathised with Popper's analysis of the laws of nature, and his idea of a scale between precision and imprecision. Popper's conundrum is that not only are all clocks cloudy (i.e. to a degree imperfect, so possessing the seeds of their own destruction), but clouds should be regarded as clandestine clocks (only appearing to be clouds because we are ignorant about the interaction of their particles). This paradox reappears in the polarity between order and disorder in Ligeti's piano Études. For the moment, he was attracted to the concept of clocks melting into clouds, and the reverse, clouds solidifying into clocks. Using his musical transformation techniques, he wanted to write the slowest and smoothest of metamorphoses.

The opportunity came with the commission by Austrian Radio for a work to be performed at the Musikprotokoll festival in Graz. *Clocks and Clouds* (Ligeti reverses Popper's title), for female chorus and orchestra, was conceived in San Francisco, completed in Europe, and premiered in Graz on 15 October 1973. Ligeti dedicated the score to the musicologist Harald Kaufmann, co-founder of Musikprotokoll and one of his closest friends, who died in 1970 at the age of forty-two. Kaufmann had helped Ligeti correct the primitive German in which his first *Die Reihe* article was written; his aesthetic and structural analyses of new music Ligeti held in great regard. Less than a month after the premiere of *Clocks and Clouds*, another of Ligeti's friends died prematurely. Bruno Maderna was already struggling with terminal cancer when he conducted a concert of Ligeti's music at the

1973 Holland Festival. After his death in Darmstadt on 13 November he was buried in the city with full civic honours. Maderna's authoritative and inspired dedication to the work of his colleagues had constantly taken precedence over his own composing. His generous enthusiasms held the avant-garde together. From now on, they increasingly diverged.

For music to glide smoothly between clockiness and cloudiness it must be liquid. So *Clocks and Clouds* contains none of the manic ticking that occurs in the String Quartet no. 2 and Chamber Concerto, nor has it any of the melodic profile of *Melodien*. It is far more homogeneous, following the example of *Lontano* and *Lux aeterna*. Everything happens gradually, right up to the ending which, in this piece, fades slowly to nothing. Ligeti's starting point is a watery undulation of flutes and clarinets, almost a replica of the passage beginning at bar 48 in the second movement of the Double Concerto. Now, however, he scores for no fewer than five flutes and five clarinets, and the mesmeric rippling of this well-blended sub-group continues for thirty-nine bars before any other instruments enter. During that time, the figurations speed up and slow down, and the pitch aggregates change from diatonic to entirely chromatic (bar 29 onwards), then to the momentary stability of a C major scale (bar 49) prefacing the entry of the voices.

Having devised an abnormal orchestration for the Double Concerto, in *Clocks and Clouds* Ligeti goes further in emphasising selected timbres and deleting others. In all, there are seventeen woodwinds, but only two trumpets, and no other brass. Violins are again excluded from the strings. Glockenspiel, vibraphone, celesta and two harps have important roles, and the twelve solo vocalists have material which is essentially the same as that in the orchestra, but sung in phonetics chosen to blend with the instrumental sonority. Quarter-tones are used to provide intermediate stages between major second and minor third, minor and major thirds, and the major third and perfect fourth. The lingering, quasi-canonic treatment of these microtones gives the work its misty yet noble luminosity.

The harmonic structure of *Clocks and Clouds* is created by a device which Ligeti had used repeatedly in the past – a 'fan', or 'wedge', opening ever so gradually through contrary-motion chromatic expansion – but had never previously extended to the point where it defines virtually the entire composition. The hypnotic elongation of the upward drift arises from the fact that, unlike the process in all his previous pieces except the second quartet and the Double Concerto, many of the rising steps are now quarter-tones. As a result, it takes seventy bars, from the initial two-note cell of D-E, for the expansion to stretch to a single octave on B, typically bisected by the tritone F. The lower edge of the fan opens even more slowly than the upper, because in several places Ligeti arrests the descent altogether in favour of long pedal points. This increases expectation, as the tension of the rising clusters exerts pressure on the bass to recoil in a contrary direction, not unlike processes of suspension and resolution in baroque and classical harmony.

More than in *Lontano*, the course of *Clocks and Clouds* is measured by its harmonic progression. As the outside parts stretch towards their registral extremes, the harmonies develop an opulent sensuality suggestive of Strauss or Scriabin – or Klimt, already an inspiration behind *Melodien*. An example is the chord at the end of bar 125, a mixture of F sharp major and E flat major triads above an F–C pedal, although the upper harmonies are immediately intensified by further quarter-tone inflections. The expressive import of this one chord is underlined by the fact that it is the only harmonic change in *Clocks and Clouds* which the whole ensemble articulates together (not, however, with any suggestion of regular beat). There are other coordinated harmonic shifts, but never for the full complement of performers, either because some are left out, or because some are allowed to trail pitches from preceding bars, 'clouding' the moment of change.

At these points, clocks are submerged by clouds. Twice the clock-like ostinati of the opening return, once to initiate the final section of the music, transitions between one state and the other coinciding with the changes in harmonic direction and pace. For above all, *Clocks and Clouds* demonstrates Ligeti's acute sensitivity to harmonic rhythm and tonal architecture. It is one of his deepest musical instincts. In the few works (*Aventures, Nouvelles aventures*, the 'Dies irae' of the Requiem) in which tonal architecture appears to be absent, it is only in abeyance. In others (*Atmosphères, Lontano*) it is veiled, but significant – especially in *Lontano*. In *Clocks and Clouds*, because the voice parts are in canon as in *Lux aeterna*, they create a similar misty and opaque polyphony. Nevertheless, Ligeti gives careful attention to the work's underlying harmonic rhythm. Consider, for example, the durations of the sustained pedal points which arrest the movement of the harmonic bass. After the opening cluster has expanded to its first octave, the tritonal B-F-B is sustained low down in the strings for a further fifty-two bars (i.e. for nearly two and a half minutes) whilst the remainder of the ensemble entwines itself in continuing ascent. By the end of it expectation is high. The upper parts shift with growing urgency, so that when at last the bass is released, it steps forward eagerly. Three and a half bars later, the low E (established in bar 122) moves up to F, underpinning the only instance in the work where all parts re-enter or change pitch together. Four bars later the bass shifts again, now to G flat, drawn on by the sumptuous chords above. But here begins a deceleration of harmonic rhythm, the G flat now held for thirty-nine bars, well beyond the climax. Thereafter it drops to E flat (held for twenty-four bars), slides microtonally to D (held for six bars) and finally down to a low C sharp, which fades into inaudibility as the upper instruments float ever higher. In all of this, the progress of the bass results in only one passage of relatively rapid movement, stimulated by a growing restlessness in the upper voices, and strategically placed to propel the music with increasing ardour towards its climax. For the rest it moves in long pedal tones, either generating or dissipating tension as harmonic aggregates above accumulate and disperse.

It is because the canons are identical in pitch but free in rhythm that Ligeti is able to commit them to the single moment of unified articulation in bar 125. But the canons in *Clocks and Clouds* hardly qualify as melody. Unlike *Melodien*, it has no liberated 'tunes'.[6] The essence of the music is texture, harmony and pulsation, the merging of pattern and haze, of rocking oscillations and an indefinable mistiness. Ligeti's integration of instruments and voices touches on Steve Reich's practice in *Drumming* (1971), but the broad arches of accelerating and decelerating patterns dissolving into sun-drenched clouds are far more sensuous. The power of pattern, within a luminous chord flow (e.g. between bars 160 and around 220), is more a precedent for the first movement of *Harmonium*, composed by John Adams (a real Californian) for the San Francisco Symphony Orchestra and Chorus eight years later.

West Coast hedonism

After *Clocks and Clouds* Ligeti composed a tribute to the city whose vibrant lifestyle and spectacular setting had so much appealed to him.

During his six months at Stanford he had been impressed by the performance of *Melodien* given by the San Francisco Symphony Orchestra under Seiji Ozawa, particularly in contrast to Zubin Mehta's in Los Angeles, five weeks earlier. He was surprised by the clarity Ozawa managed to achieve on only two rehearsals. Even someone as demanding as Ligeti was prepared to admit that, 'with the Ozawa performance, the theory that two rehearsals are not enough for new music is cancelled out'[7] – but he was yet to hear Gielen's revelatory reading with solo strings on 24 June with the Amsterdam Concertgebouw Orchestra. In the interim, following Ozawa's success, Ligeti enthusiastically accepted a commission from the San Francisco Orchestra Association (funded by two patrons, Dr and Mrs Ralph Dorfman) to write a work to commemorate its sixtieth anniversary. It 'would be somewhat like *Melodien*, but even more graphical, more transparent . . . nobler . . . I want to dabble with this idea of controlling pitches simultaneously, but then giving the possibility of different meters, different tempi.'[8] Up to a point it would be aleatoric.

Ligeti likes functional titles which combine the poetic and technical aspects of a composition. *San Francisco Polyphony*, which he began in 1973 and completed a year later, is no exception in that its title prepares us for a piece that celebrates the charisma of the city and is audaciously contrapuntal. Lasting barely eleven minutes, the work is constantly eventful, even ostentatious, and is one of his most exhilarating pieces. Tunes and textures crowd through the score in profusion. The material is abnormally proactive, even for Ligeti, generating multidirectional transformations both swift and dramatic. The music has an anarchic fecundity, redolent of the 'swinging sixties' for whose exuberant youth culture San Francisco had been the permissive heart. In its Ivesian plurality it is quite unlike the single-minded focus of *Lontano* and *Lux aeterna*. It is also the work in which Ligeti comes closest to Berg. Intended to develop further the melodic potential of *Melodien*, he decided, however, that *San Francisco Polyphony* would bring to an end this particular stylistic line. It was his first composition for large orchestra since *Lontano*, but would also (up to the time of writing) be his last. All his subsequent orchestral scores are much smaller, partly because of his wish to write soloistically for the whole ensemble – a preference already evident in *San Francisco Polyphony* – but most of all because of Ligeti's dissatisfaction with the often inadequate rehearsal provision of large orchestras.

As with *Melodien*, the role of melody – temporarily suspended in *Clocks and Clouds* – is paramount, but here the melodies are 'drier, sharper and more graphic'.[9] Unlike his earlier micropolyphony, the simultaneous melodies in *San Francisco Polyphony* exhibit a bravura independence, although derived from a common harmonic frame. The interplay of motifs is most complex at the beginning. Here a mass of some twenty separate lines are all marshalled in the foreground, played with 'heightened *espressivo*', so that one then another becomes audible, despite what appears to be 'an untransparent web of parts'. As the texture grows more polarised, melodies thrust themselves forward. The unison violin line at bar 79 (marked *col legno* but not easily articulated with the wood of the bow), is a powerful presence, its elasticated rhythm and impulsive surges indicative of Ligeti's style throughout the work. It also demonstrates how his more flamboyant lines still consume the gamut of twelve notes without being intentionally serial.

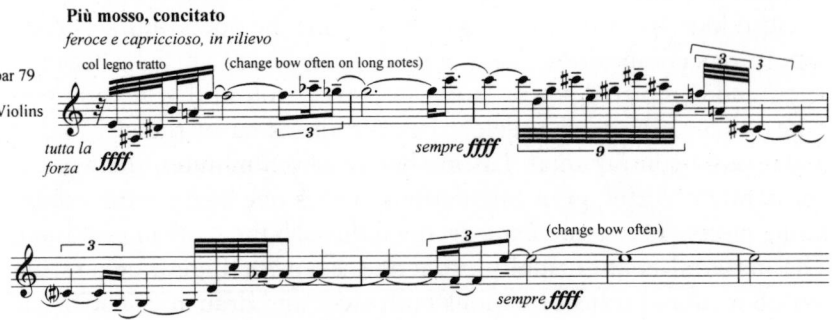

Ex. 17 Tutti violin melody in *San Francisco Polyphony* (1973–74)

Despite the variety of their bounding rhythms, these many lines are all notated with reference to one set of bar lines, and so are theoretically controllable by a single conductor. In places, however, Ligeti instructs individual players to accelerate and decelerate regardless of the conductor's beat, at the end of which each player is given a brief rest – a moment of reorientation – assisting their return to the fold. This adds layers of metrical divergence; and since other details of instrumental balance are also variable, some conductors have come to regard the score as problematic. It is certainly an extreme challenge to collective clarity. The timbral kaleidoscope is that of *Lontano*, except

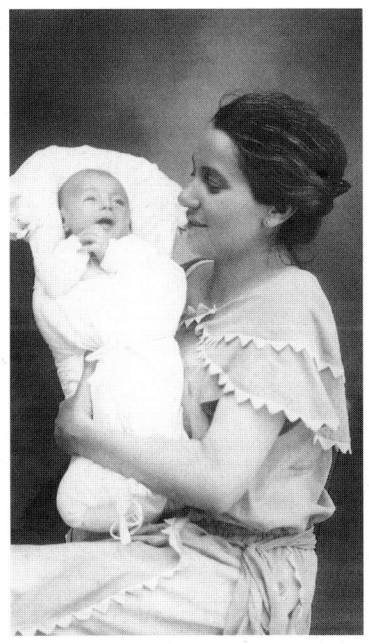

2. With his mother.

3. Ligeti's mother after moving to Vienna.

4. Luc Ferrari, Franco Evangelisti, György Ligeti, Yoritsune Matsudaïra and Luigi Nono at the Darmstadt Summer Courses in the late 1950s.

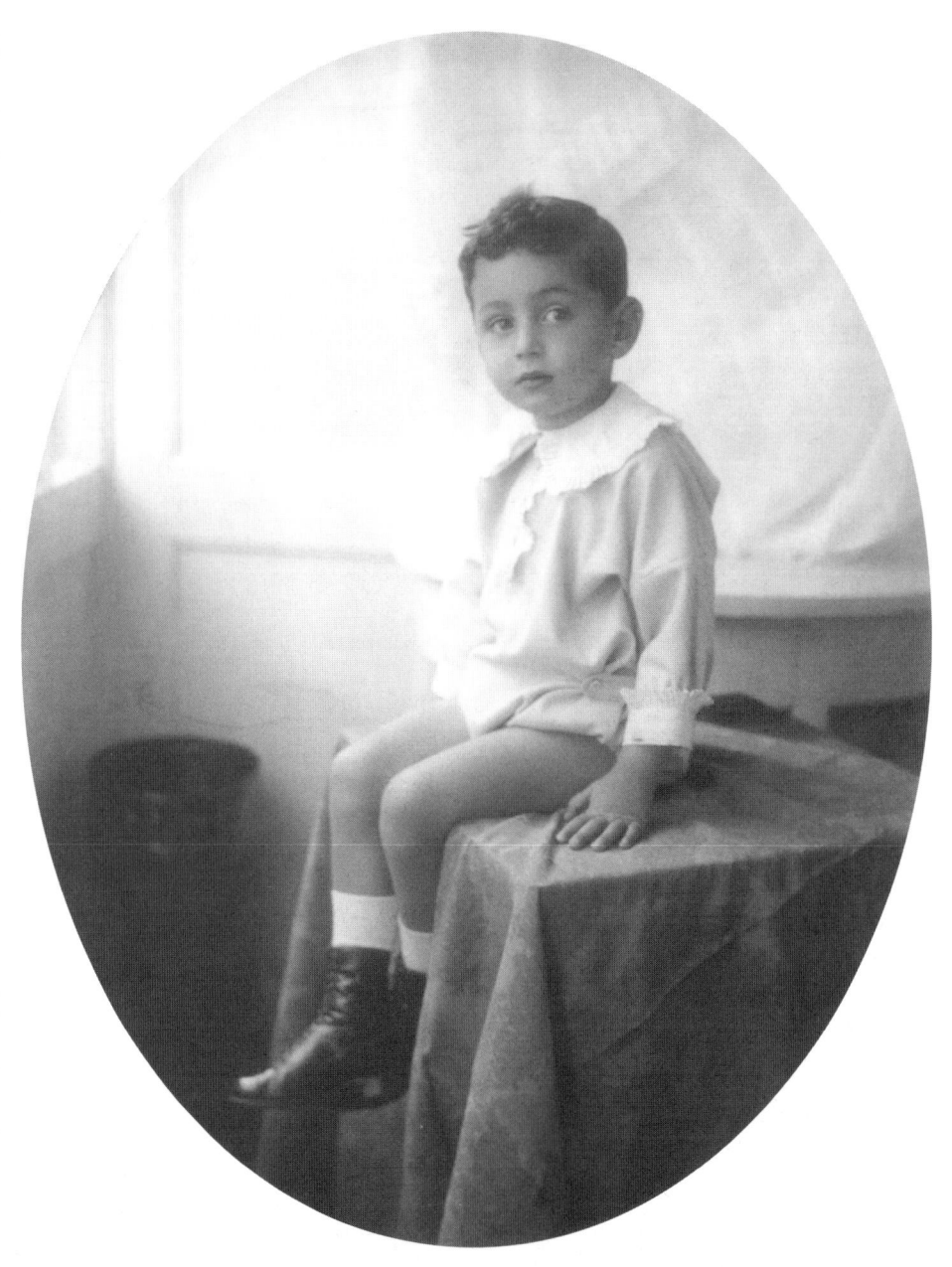

1. The small boy.

Uncharacteristically also, Seiji Ozawa conducted the first performance using a score, an understandable deviation from his usual practice, given the music's enormous proliferation of detail. Ligeti himself was absent. He was at home in Hamburg working hard on his opera, but – more to the point – amazingly he had not been invited. 'People were frightened because I come along with meticulous lists. But for *Melodien* I was present and was friendly. I would very much have liked to go.'

Escher, phasing and minimalism

In 1971, the year before Ligeti visited California, an exhibition was organised in San Francisco of woodcuts and lithographs by the Dutch graphic artist Maurits Escher (1898–1972). Escher was then seventy-three and had only a year to live. Belatedly the exhibition spread awareness of a unique mind whose work was still hardly known outside Holland. Some years earlier, when Edison Denisov wrote from Moscow to tell Ligeti that his music had a lot to do with Escher, Ligeti had wondered what he meant. In the laboratories at Stanford he saw copies of Escher's pictures, which typically appealed to the computer minds of Silicon Valley. Ligeti was also fascinated. Pattern transformation had been one of his major preoccupations ever since *Métamorphoses nocturnes*. Here was Escher's *Metamorphoses* showing a process – in this case a square of lizards changing into a hive of bees, then into fish and butterflies – remarkably similar to what Ligeti was attempting in music. In *San Francisco Polyphony* pattern transformation plays an important role, especially during the final Prestissimo *meccanico* section from bar 132. Talking to Pierre Michel about this work, he likened to Escher the manner in which 'a clear image is corrupted, an interval is gradually transformed, then a new interval transformed in its turn'.[11] But if the spirit of Escher hovers in the background of *San Francisco Polyphony*, it is central to Ligeti's next composition, written for the Kontarsky piano duo and called *Monument–Selbstportrait–Bewegung*. Ostensibly three studies in rhythm, these are really 'pattern-illusion experiments'. Like Escher, they deal with the metamorphosis of interconnected lattices.

The brothers Alfons and Aloys Kontarsky were members of Stockhausen's inner circle of trusted performers. Since Aloys Kontarsky had played the tam-tam in the premiere of *Mikrophonie I* that here every line is many times more active. Instead of sustained colours momentarily waxing and waning, there are numerous simultaneous mini-cadenzas, sparkling and scintillating like an open jewel box. To achieve an ideal balance between individualism and communality is difficult. Luca Pfaff, who has conducted *San Francisco Polyphony* with at least four orchestras, remarked to the author that 'every performance is different'. To this, Ligeti replied:

I can imagine. I have never heard a correct performance. Zender's European premiere in Amsterdam (with the Hilversum Radio Orchestra) was catastrophic. Afterwards I sat alone in the Keyzer coffee house crying, because it had nothing to do with my piece. The best performances were by Gary Howarth in Stockholm and Stuttgart – it's on the Wergo recording. Having relatively enough rehearsals, it's more or less OK. I can accept it. The only accurate recording was made by Haitink with the Concertgebouw Orchestra, but I was not invited and didn't know about it. With Ligeti present, it could have been perfect![10]

This gloomy assessment was made some time after Ligeti had attended the concert performance and recording of *San Francisco Polyphony* by Esa-Pekka Salonen and the Philharmonia Orchestra in 1996–97, with which he was also deeply dissatisfied, refusing to allow the recording to be released (see Chapter Fifteen). He could not forsee that he would again be present when *San Francisco Polyphony* was prepared for a public concert by Jonathan Nott and the Berlin Philharmonic in December 2001; nor that the recording of this live performance by Teldec would at last vindicate the technical daring of the score, demonstrating with clarity and precision its pluralistic vision. Its difficulty lies in the fact that, although written for large orchestra, this is really soloistic ensemble music. Paradoxically, being a synthesis of Ligeti's mature techniques, it is also an instructive model of large-scale polyphonic orchestration.

For the world premiere on 8 January 1975 in San Francisco itself, Ligeti wrote a programme note uncharacteristically in the manner of a travelogue: 'low clouds sailing slowly from the ocean . . . the presence of water and salt everywhere . . . student musicians between the red bricks of the old chocolate factory . . . the view of the red towers of the Golden Gate . . . the turning of the cable car'. It reflected his affection for the city. Later programme notes omit all of this, but the *joie de vivre* of San Francisco and the bay is at the music's heart.

5. Lecturing in Berlin in the 1960s.
6. Much later, contemplating a performance of *Poème symphonique*.

7. Ligeti's drawing of The Last Judgement, based on Memling's altar-piece in Danzig.
8. Erik Saeden as Nekrotzar and Sven-Erik Vikström as Piet in the Stockholm premiere of *Le Grand Macabre*, 1978.
9. Roland Topor's design for Scene II of *Le Grand Macabre*, Bologna 1979.

10. Ligeti in his studio in Hamburg 1982.
11. Sarah Leonard, Linda Hirst and Omar Ebrahim perform *Aventures* and *Nouvelles aventures* in Huddersfield, 1993.

12. Rehearsing the Violin Concerto with Saschko Gawriloff.

13. Addressing the audience at Huddersfield Contemporary Music Festival 1993.
14. In discussion with the conductor Elgar Howarth.
15. Pierre-Laurent Aimard.

16. Simha Arom, Pierre-Laurent Aimard and Ligeti with the Banda-Linda pipe orchestra and pygmies from the Central African Republic, Châtelet Theatre, Paris, December 1999.

17. Receiving the Kyoto Award, November 2001.

in 1964, his friendship with Stockhausen had deepened. Both he and his brother were remarkable pianists, Aloys especially. In 1966 he gave the first complete performance at Darmstadt of all of Stockhausen's *Klavierstücke I–XI*, a recital of amazing technical and mental accomplishment during which, after the interval, he returned to the platform with wrists bandaged (so that his playing of its innovatory glissando clusters would not bloody the keys), to render note-perfect, and from memory, the phenomenally difficult thirty-minute long *Klavierstück X*. This tour de force was soon repeated in other countries.[12] In 1970, Stockhausen composed *Mantra* for the Kontarskys, playing two ring-modulated pianos, his first work based on a melodic 'formula'. The relaxed, even humorous pluralism of *Mantra*, so different from earlier two-piano pieces like Boulez's *Structures* and Goeyvaerts's Sonata (1951), signalled Stockhausen's return to melody, and similarly reflects the liberated social and artistic climate that influenced *San Francisco Polyphony*.

Friends since the late 1950s, the Kontarskys had asked Ligeti to write a piece for them, but he was now working intensively on his long-planned opera. Nevertheless, during 1976 he temporarily put aside the opera, and embarked on his three pieces for two pianos, completing them in just three months. The achievement was matched by the Kontarskys' learning their complex rhythmic language in time to give the first performance only four weeks later, on 15 May, in the concert hall of WDR Cologne.

The Three Pieces were Ligeti's first return to the medium since leaving Hungary. It will be recalled that he did not possess a piano until the end of the 1960s. Although *Musica ricercata* eventually received its premiere in Stockholm on 18 November 1969, few people knew that Ligeti had written any piano music at all. He was known to be at work on an opera, but its premiere was scheduled for a year away (it turned out to be two). Thus the stylistic direction of *Monument–Selbstportrait–Bewegung*, and particularly the enigmatic full title of the second piece, 'Self-portrait with Reich and Riley (and Chopin in the background)', elicited much curiosity, most of all about Ligeti's flirtation with American minimalism, an issue which dominated articles and interviews with the composer. Originally he planned to call this movement 'Still Life with Reich and Riley'; but thinking that 'still life' (and its French equivalent, '*nature morte*') might be taken as a slur on the two composers, he changed it to 'Portrait', and then 'Self-portrait' in view of the music's relationship with his own *Continuum*. In the context of the opera, it is evident that Ligeti's approach also reflects his regard for classical and Romantic pianism, just as the much more surprising novelties of *Le Grand Macabre* are similarly the old made new, albeit in extravagant and garish dress. As for his acknowledgement of the minimalists, from the vantage point of the later Études, it seems but a passing pleasantry, a recognition that their styles had briefly impinged.

The reference to Reich and Riley is attached to the second piece. But the opening of *Monument* concentrates so exclusively on rhythmic phasing that the manner of early minimalism is strongly suggested. Its statuesque demeanour matches its title. Overall, the three pieces progress from reductionist austerity towards a more gracious lyricism. By the end of the first piece, the jerky hocket of the opening has become continuous pulsation. The stuttering first section of *Selbstportrait*, with its novel use of non-sounding keys, evolves into a flood of arpeggiated passagework, played *sotto voce* but in octaves, *à la* Chopin. In *Bewegung* (*Flowing*), legato arpeggios wash over the texture, through which strands of melody float, flower and grow insistent, until they finally detach themselves in chorale-like chords.

Monument is more rigorously controlled than any previous work by Ligeti. It begins with six superimposed layers of palindromic rhythm, each articulated on a single pitch, and development comes about only through an interaction between the pulses and the addition of more layers. At the start, three layers (or lattices) enter in each piano successively. The pulses in each lattice are separated by rests, whose duration increases and decreases systematically – hence the impression of unsteady beating. In the first lattice (starting *ff* on octave As in Piano I) the number of semiquavers separating successive pulses is:

16   17   18   17   16   15   14   15   16   17   18   etc.

A similar ebb and flow characterises the other layers. Some layers are greatly compressed, like the second lattice which enters fourteen bars later in Piano I with much shorter durations:

6   7   8   7   6   5   4   5   6   7   8   etc.

Some are just marginally compressed, as in the third lattice which enters at bar 27:

13   14   15   14   13   12   11   12   13   14   15   etc.

Piano II has a similar collection, but laid out in 6/8, instead of the 4/4 of Piano I. The simultaneous use of simple and compound time signatures, applied to the rhythmic ebb and flow of each lattice, creates an asymmetrical machine of considerable complexity. Already dissimilar in pitch and rhythm, the lattices are further differentiated by being played either in double or quadruple octaves and by different dynamic levels. Some pulses coincide, and these chordal simultaneities increase as more lattices are added using shorter duration patterns. What began as a hocket turns into a continuum, as patterns coalesce into composite textures. Squeezed together, they produce a clatter of semiquavers, still sounding asymmetrical because of the irregular accents. Harmonically, there is an audible if constrained development, as the first six lattices give way to others, and the chordal conjunctions become richer. Finally the chords themselves collapse, and *Monument* ends with a pattering of high pulses, like the end of *Continuum*.

Blocked keys

It is in *Selbstportrait* that Ligeti consciously combines his own treatment of lattices with Riley's pattern transformation and Reich's phase-shifting. Here, like Reich, he allows the number of pattern repetitions to be determined by the performers themselves, albeit within certain controls. Added to this is his use of 'blocked keys'. This idea surfaced during experiments Ligeti and Karl-Erik Welin made together when working on *Volumina* and the organ *Études*. They were further explored by Henning Siedentopf, whose article on the technique Ligeti acknowledges in his preface to the score.[13] In *Selbstportrait* each pianist uses his left hand to depress and hold silent clusters. Meanwhile, the right hand plays fast continuous quavers criss-crossing the depressed keys. Since keys depressed do not resound, the flow of performed quavers emerges as a pattern of sounding and silent notes. Both pianists have similar material, but differences in detail and synchronisation produce fluctuating and uneven combinations. Halfway through, their tumbling cascades are played in canon, the second piano instructed to echo the first, culminating in a short canonic phrase in each player's left hand. The figurations settle, and their pitch content slowly reduces to the same rotating cluster played by both pianos together, on the notes G, D flat and E flat.

These pitches commence the last section of *Selbstportrait*, a whirling succession of arpeggiated figurations in 12/8, played *una corda* and in octaves. Although the note sequence is Ligeti's own, it is an intentional parody of the last movement of Chopin's Sonata no. 2 in B flat minor, itself a highly original essay in perpetual motion. Also in 12/8 and in octaves, Chopin's patterns begin sequentially, but sweep so freely over the harmonic landscape that they achieve a Ligeti-like multi-tonality. One could almost substitute one for the other, were it not for Chopin's cadential resolution on the chord of B flat minor. Typically, Ligeti's version retains some of the jerkiness from earlier in the movement, as occasionally loud interjections from one piano interrupt the other's pianissimo.

It is not until the beginning of the third piece, *In zart fliessender Bewegung* (*In a gently flowing movement*) – to give it its full title, that a consistent legato is achieved. Ligeti describes it as a 'liquefied variant' of the first. Here both pianos begin with descending scales which expand harmonically to become arpeggios. Piano I has triplets whilst Piano II has duplets, and this metrical difference is replicated in the melodies which each player projects out of the arpeggiated background, by sustaining selected pitches in the manner of Chopin or Schumann. Like the lattices in *Monument*, the melodies in *Bewegung* are asymmetrical and follow each other canonically between the keyboards. Disarmingly gentle at first, the texture builds to a climax whose cascades sweep up and down across seven octaves with their melodic accents now dramatically synchronised. This splendid summation is not so much Chopinesque as Lisztian, until in Ligeti fashion the figurations vanish off the end of the keyboard, leaving the melodic threads to be gathered into a quasi-chorale that is suddenly cold and astringent. The melodies become mirror canons, doubled first in four, then redoubled in eight parts. Rhythmically simple and with repeatedly superimposed tritones, these final phrases restore the austere tone with which the work began. Their mood is that of the acidic chorales which the offstage chorus sing in *Le Grand Macabre*, a part of the opera which Ligeti had already completed before he started the Three Pieces.

Aside from his use of 'blocked keys', Ligeti employs none of the avant-garde playing techniques then in fashion, such as playing inside the piano. It was enough to explore the variety of polyrhythmic and metrical phase-shifting inherent in writing for two keyboards, and what he calls 'second-order' illusory effects produced by the interaction of divergent patterns. These he equates with stroboscopic and kinetic phenomena, and the projection of holograms. It was an interest to which he would return in the Piano Concerto and Études.

Hamburg

At the end of his six months in Stanford, the Dean of the Faculty invited Ligeti to consider a permanent appointment. His teaching was liked as well as his personality. But Ligeti wanted to return to Europe, not least because he knew that a composer working in an American university can be isolated by the huge distance between cities, whereas in Europe it was easy to know what colleagues were doing and to attend premieres, whether in Paris, Amsterdam or Berlin. Besides, Europe had its subsidised radio stations and many new music festivals.

Thus in the late summer of 1972 Ligeti again took up residence in Berlin. Nevertheless, he badly needed a permanent teaching post to provide adequate income. Sándor Veress, who emigrated from Hungary eight years ahead of Ligeti, had done his best to secure his former pupil a conservatory position in Switzerland during the years after Ligeti arrived in the West, but without success. Not even Stockholm could offer permanent employment. At first he was too little known; then he was too famous. Four institutions offered posts almost simultaneously: the conservatories of Berlin, Hamburg, Cologne and Vienna. Ligeti might have been expected to choose Vienna, but for some time now he and Vera had lived mostly apart. He decided to accept Cologne because of the presence of Stockhausen and Kagel, its enterprising cultural life and many excellent musicians. Unfortunately the conservatory failed to resolve a misunderstanding about Ligeti's pay and duties, and the idea foundered. The invitation from Vienna, his second choice, also went cold after its institution appointed a new director. As for Berlin, Ligeti felt uneasy about the city's geographical position surrounded by the Eastern bloc, and the inconvenience and discomfort of the 'air corridor' whose flights were frequently overbooked. Impressed by a gracious approach from the Hamburg Hochschule für Musik, in 1973 he decided to accept an appointment there to teach composition and analysis. At first he divided time between Hamburg and Vienna. Gradually Hamburg became his principal home. Except when he was absent for performances and engagements, Ligeti dutifully discharged his termly teaching commitments for the next sixteen years, until he retired at the age of sixty-six in 1989. Since then Hamburg has remained his home and professional base, although he has frequently considered moving and always spends part of every year in Vienna.

Later Ligeti felt that his choice of Hamburg had been a mistake. His contract was honoured but the city's cultural life proved to be stagnant, whilst the verbal promise made to him by the Hochschule of purchasing a 'big computer' was never realised. He could still accept invitations to lecture elsewhere, as in the summer of 1973 when he returned with Vera and Lukas to America to lead a fortnight of masterclasses at the Berkshire Music Center in Tanglewood. They travelled out via Canada, where Ligeti gave the CAPAC-MacMillan lecture at the University of Toronto and attended a 'portrait' concert presented by the Canadian Broadcasting Corporation. At Tanglewood, Ligeti held his classes in a wood-panelled room in The Red House, once a residence of Nathaniel Hawthorne, and marvelled at the idyllic New England countryside in which Ives had composed *The Housatonic at Stockbridge*. At the end of the Tanglewood fortnight he flew to France to attend an exploratory conference held at the Abbaye de Sénanque near Avignon, convened by Boulez to advance his plans for a new institute of electronic and acoustical research. Boulez had invited computer scientists, architects, musicologists and composers from several countries for six days, during which papers were presented and organisational issues discussed. Fired by his enjoyment of travel and interest in geography, Ligeti asked to be excused the final afternoon devoted to pedagogy, so that he could explore the French Alps – a region he had not previously seen. Boulez refused. Somewhat disaffected, Ligeti spent the session drawing a doodle to satirise the exchanges, a lonely alp (or possibly a volcano) depicted in the background (see p. 115).

Besides Chowning from Stanford, whom Ligeti had recommended, also present in Sénanque was the French pioneer of computer sound synthesis Jean-Claude Risset, destined to be head of the computer department of IRCAM between 1975 and 1979. Ligeti's acquaintance with Risset dates from this meeting, and Risset's computer-generated acoustic illusions – analogous to Escher's visual illusions – would have an important influence on the piano Études.

In September Ligeti spent several days at the Musica Nova Festival in Glasgow, where the Double Concerto received its UK premiere. The following summer he directed a composition course at the Accademia Chigiana in Siena. Everywhere he lectured, his charm and vivacity, self-deprecating humour, lack of dogma, perspicacity and lucidity won him affection and respect. Then he decided to limit composition teaching to Hamburg, giving up Darmstadt after 1976 and breaking the rule only once to lead a course in Aix-en-Provence during the summer of 1979. In Hamburg, Ligeti taught at first at the Hochschule, but later held classes in his apartment. His seminars were democratic and informal – indeed, anybody could come, whether enrolled or not. But it was not until the late 1970s and 1980s that the most interesting students arrived. One of them, a Puerto Rican called Roberto Sierra who studied with Ligeti between 1979 and 1982, came to the weekly sessions bearing recordings of music from all over the world – exotic musical dishes to feed Ligeti's insatiable appetite for ethnomusicology.

Another composition interrupted work on the opera, but it was the briefest of distractions, conceived and completed during one sleepless night in the early summer of 1976. Indeed it is curiously out of character for so established a composer, a throwback to ten years earlier. *Rondeau* is a monodrama for actor and tape recorder, and dedicated (as is the opera) to Ligeti's son Lukas. It contains no music and is instead an 'absurdist' conversation between actor and tape – assisted by a few props – and between the actor and himself as a corpse. *Rondeau* was given its first performance by Wolfgang Höper, together with new stagings of *Aventures* and *Nouvelles aventures*, in the Stuttgart Kammertheater on 26 February 1977, and was revived by the Theater am Hexenturm in Coburg in March 1984 alongside three other music theatre 'monologues' by Michael Leinert, Mauricio Kagel and Dieter Schnebel. But *Rondeau* is more its interpreter's creation than the composer's. Today Ligeti regrets that he wrote it, admitting that he 'was in an especially stupid mood!'[14] Although it lasts around twenty-five minutes, it is the slightest of sketches from the waste bin of his theatrical workshop. The magnum opus which he had been pondering for a whole decade, and actively composing for the last three years, was a completely different affair. Furthermore, it was nearly ready to be staged.

PART THREE
The Grand Illusionist

PART THREE

The Grand Illusions

Alice in Breughelland:
A Grotesque Carnival of Sex and Death

The threat of collective death is always present but we try to
eliminate it from our consciousness and to enjoy to the maximum the days that are left to us.

Ligeti in conversation with Claude Samuel[1]

. . . talking about comprehensible things only serves to weigh
the mind down and to warp the memory, whereas the absurd
exercises the mind and makes the memory work.

Alfred Jarry

Birth of an opera

The first performance of Ligeti's *Le Grand Macabre* in Stockholm, on
12 April 1978, took place in an atmosphere of intense excitement. The
opera had taken thirteen years from initial commission to completion.
The premiere had already been announced for April 1977, then postponed for a year – not only because of the time needed to learn so
difficult a work, but also, it was rumoured, because of objections to its
pornographic libretto, whose supposed sexual excesses had been
eagerly seized upon by the more prurient members of the press. With
a hundred and fifty invited critics from all over the world in attendance, few twentieth-century operas can have been anticipated with
such eager curiosity.

For Ligeti himself, *Le Grand Macabre* was both a summation and a
step forward. Opera, one might argue, was the ideal, the only genre
able to embrace his cornucopia of musical styles. What else could
encompass the humour and seriousness, fantasy and frustration, complexities and contradictions of contemporary life? The precedents he
had accomplished in the tape piece *Artikulation*, the huge choral
lament of the 'Kyrie' in the Requiem, the witty and neurotic exchanges
in his two mini-operas, *Aventures* and *Nouvelles aventures*, the sumptuous textures of *Clocks and Clouds* – all these different approaches to

vocal technique and to text indicate that Ligeti was well equipped to negotiate the broad sweep of a full-length opera. From his earliest compositions he had conceived music visually, almost as much as aurally. To realise the imaginings of his inner eye on stage was an obvious next step.

What few expected, and what particularly won praise at the premiere, was the revelation of attributes nobody knew that Ligeti possessed – not even, until he discovered them, the composer himself.[2] *Le Grand Macabre* is much more than a synthesis of what he had been writing during the previous twenty years. It reveals an ability to compose musical numbers of almost traditional operatic charm: Verdian ensembles, imposing melodramatic set pieces. Beside his avant-garde credentials, Ligeti now showed himself to be a gifted parodist, cunningly adept at pastiche, who could, astonishingly, write real 'tunes' – for the extended stylistic vocabulary of *Le Grand Macabre* is also the start of Ligeti's rehabilitation of his Hungarian years. The splendid Passacaglia finale, for example, has roots in works like *Musica ricercata*. Some of the opera's most telling moments of melodrama, like Nekrotzar's ominous prediction of the end of the world in Scene 1, stem from the unforgettable impression made on Ligeti by his first theatrical encounters with Mussorgsky and Verdi in pre-war Cluj. For all its ribaldry and extravagance, the opera has deeper currents, drawing from ancient wells of music drama. The critics who were less convinced focused their censure mainly on the structure and dramaturgy, especially on the extensive passages of spoken dialogue which Ligeti has since mostly deleted. Their irritation was excusable. Since the premiere was performed in Swedish, few of the international visitors could understand a word. Nevertheless, the grandeur, humanity, wit, lyricism and sheer musicality of this multifaceted score were widely recognised and applauded.

Ligeti was elated with its success. At once he began to plan more theatrical projects, including a treatment of Shakespeare's *The Tempest* which, in the early 1980s, he tentatively promised to English National Opera in London. Meanwhile *Le Grand Macabre*, so long nurtured in the womb, rapidly came of age in a bewildering series of new productions across Europe. Within two decades it received more than twenty different stagings, a remarkable achievement for any modern opera. (See the appendix, pp. 378–79, for a full list of productions.) But for the composer the experience proved sobering. Ligeti has stoically borne what has seemed like the repeated misinterpretation and obfuscation of his intentions. His anguish culminated in bitter distaste for Peter Sellars's imposition of a completely alien scenario for the 1997 Salzburg premiere of his meticulous revision of the score. If the composer's concept of locale and manner can be so peremptorily set aside, the trappings of Breughelland and the libretto's mocking humour discarded on a whim, why write more operas?

A winding road to Breughelland

To have his theatrical vision changed into something utterly different was galling, considering how long and laborious was Ligeti's journey towards a choice of scenario and the creation of its text. When Göran Gentele, director of the Royal Swedish Opera, approached him following the premiere of the Requiem in March 1965, *Aventures* and *Nouvelles aventures* were fresh in their minds. Ligeti thought that a new opera should also be non-narrative, perhaps, like them, using a meaningless artificial language; but to extend the disjointed, collage manner of his two mini-operas to a full-length work for a large theatre seemed problematic. At first he planned an opera to be called *Kylwiria*, the name of the imaginary country he had invented in childhood. 'It would be crazy, demoniacal but also humorous.'[3] Two years later he discarded this idea, feeling that, after all, some degree of narrative was necessary and that he should use a familiar story. Aware of its potency for composers as diverse as Monteverdi, Gluck, Offenbach and Stravinsky, he turned to the Oedipus myth, devised a scenario and sketched some music, some of which eventually found its way into *Clocks and Clouds* and *San Francisco Polyphony*. It would have a narrative structure, but with a non-semantic, collage text. He would devise 'a non-existent language of sounds and real words'; it would be a 'fun' treatment of the Oedipus story in the manner of Charlie Chaplin and the Marx Brothers, involving 'actors, acrobats and midgets as well as singers',[4] and he hoped that Saul Steinberg, the Romanian-born New York cartoonist, would design the sets.

For the next four years Ligeti devoted considerable time to the Oedipus idea, but he was also busy fulfilling concert commissions. Then an event occurred which brought the project to a halt. In 1972 Göran Gentele became director of the Metropolitan Opera in New York. Since it was understood that he would still produce Ligeti's opera, he invited the composer to New York to discuss it. Tragically, before the meeting could take place, whilst on holiday in Sardinia, Gentele was killed in a car accident. The loss of his principal mentor not only arrested Ligeti's progress; it also brought to a head more substantive doubts about the direction in which the work was heading.

A year before Gentele's death, Mauricio Kagel's extraordinary *Staatstheater* had been staged in Hamburg, a work which seemed to cross all boundaries and establish entirely new concepts of instrumental and gestural theatre. Ligeti, like others who saw it, was deeply impressed, regarding it as the ultimate 'masterpiece of "musical anti-theatre"'.[5] After *Staatstheater*, writing a 'real' opera seemed less sustainable than ever. The styles both of *Staatstheater* and his own *Aventures* had been fully explored. But, if one could have 'anti-opera' why not also an 'anti-anti-opera'? In a Houdini-like contortion, Ligeti concluded that since two successive 'antis' cancel each other out, an 'anti-anti-opera' must be . . . well, opera!

Ligeti was still contracted to compose for the Royal Swedish Opera where a production team had already been installed. It consisted of Michael Meschke, director of the Stockholm Puppet Theatre, as director, the German stage designer Aliute Meczies, and the British conductor Elgar Howarth, whom Ligeti himself requested after hearing Howarth's expert direction of his orchestral scores. A date was set for director, designer and composer to meet in Berlin, together with the musicologist Ove Nordwall, specifically to reconsider from scratch both subject matter and libretto. When they met, Ligeti explained his concept of something 'cruel and frightening based on the pictures of Breughel and Bosch and writers like Jarry, Kafka and Boris Vian'. Ideas were tossed back and forth, amongst which was Aliute Meczies's inspired suggestion of *La Balade du Grand Macabre*[6] by the Flemish dramatist Michel de Ghelderode, which is set in an imaginary Breughelland. Ligeti recalled that Ghelderode had already been proposed to him by a young Belgian composer over drinks one night in Darmstadt.

Michel de Ghelderode

Born in 1898, Ghelderode was the son of an archivist, a scholar of medieval tales who was principal clerk at the Archives Générale in Brussels. His mother was 'rich in proverbs, in forgotten songs, in haunted stories'.[7] From her Ghelderode derived a taste for the super-natural; from his father his love of the past: documents, ancient churches, old-fashioned theatres, marionettes, carillons, rites, processions, funerals. The memory stayed with him all his life of being surrounded, as a child, by parchments, seals and priceless relics: bundles of letters from Peter Paul Rubens, proclamations bearing the signatures of kings and queens, the register of the Duke of Alba's Tribunal of Blood containing the names of the condemned. Whilst employed as an archivist himself, Ghelderode began to write plays, some based on marionette theatre texts which he had written down and saved from oblivion, others in the manner of writers like Edgar Allan Poe. In 1927 he began an association with the Flemish Popular Theatre, but after three years withdrew into a more solitary life. His work was virtually unknown outside Belgium until after the Second World War, when he was 'discovered' by avant-garde directors and achieved some prominence, before dying in 1962.

The Renaissance held Ghelderode in thrall because he saw in it 'an infinitely complex and contradictory humanity', given to excess and sublimity, stretched between extremes: 'the ecstasy of living and the horror of living'.[8] Like Ligeti, Ghelderode was much affected by the work of his Flemish forebears Bosch and Breughel; indeed Breughel's *The Triumph of Death* had been a direct inspiration for *La Balade du Grand Macabre*. Just as influential were the fantastic and macabre carnival paintings of the Belgian James Ensor (1860–1949), whose portrayal of masked revellers and grotesque, fighting skeletons carries forward the gruesome satirical humour of Bosch, Breughel and Goya. Ghelderode also loved the music of the Flemish contrapuntalists. And he was widely read, influenced by Poe, Baudelaire and Jarry and aware of the work of his own contemporaries. The mentality which went into the making of *La Balade du Grand Macabre* was uncannily close to Ligeti's.

Concept and libretto

Ligeti in turn was attracted to the notion that Ghelderode's text could provide the basis for a theatrical form akin to Jarry and Ionesco. Ghelderode's ironic retrospection had, perhaps, some of the qualities which had drawn him to Krúdy. It would be an Absurdist opera with, he said,

. . . a very colourful, comic-strip-like musical and dramatic action. The cartoons of Saul Steinberg were my ideal: characters and situations should be direct, terse, non-psychological and startling – the very opposite of 'literary' opera; . . . the dramatic action and the music should be riskily bizarre, totally exaggerated, totally crazy. The novelty of this style of music theatre should be manifest not in the external properties of the production, but in the inner quality of the music.[9]

For the music, as for the staging, he set himself a precise but ambitious challenge: to draw upon the operatic precedents he admired, yet remain original. The texture

. . . should not be symphonic. The musical and dramatic conception should be far removed from the territory of Wagner, Strauss and Berg – nearer to Monteverdi's *Poppea*, Verdi's *Falstaff*, Rossini's *Barbiere*, yet still different; in fact, owing nothing to any tradition, not even avant-gardism.[10]

An immediate task was to create a libretto; but before that, he and Meschke had to resolve the issue of language. Hungarian, Ligeti's mother tongue, he considered too idiosyncratic. Ghelderode had written in French; German was the foreign language in which the composer was most fluent, but Italian and English he regarded as ideal for opera. However, the premiere had to be in Swedish! Eventually they agreed that Meschke would make a German prose version of the original, 'Jarryfied' at Ligeti's suggestion to replicate the terse, direct speech of *Ubu Roi*. After this libretto had been further compressed, Ligeti began intensive work on the composition in December 1974. As he worked on the music, he changed most of Meschke's prose into rhyming verse, using a dictionary of synonyms and rhymes to bolster his limited German vocabulary. This composed text was translated into Swedish by Meschke and became the basis for translations into the various languages needed for the opera's subsequent productions, notably English, French, and Italian, all of which Ligeti has proclaimed to be better than the German original. Finally, Ligeti opted for English as the primary language of his 1996 revision, as sung at the 1997–98 Salzburg and Paris performances and on the Sony CD – although for any staged production the language of the audience is still to be preferred, particularly if they are to enjoy the libretto's bantering humour. Surtitles are, after all, a somewhat stilted medium for the hurling of insults.

Ligeti has disclaimed literary merit for the libretto; yet it has

excellent operatic attributes, being pithy, colourful, strongly characterised and genuinely funny. Certainly the drama is in the music, but
the music is inseparably linked to the text, which needs to be directly
understood. For this reason, both in the original version and the 1996
revision, Ligeti changed the French names of Ghelderode's characters
to give them a universality regardless of language. Even when it is
unashamed doggerel, the lines have a certain panache, even elo-
quence, and contain references recognisable to a well-informed
audience. Nekrotzar's account in Scene 3 of the destruction he has
wrought is sung to quite ravishing music; but our pleasure is
enhanced when we perceive the text as a lugubrious, inebriated equivalent of Leporello's catalogue of his master's conquests in *Don
Giovanni*. Leporello's list spans the full social spectrum: 'Some, you
see, are country damsels, / Waiting-maids, and city ma'amselles.'
Nekrotzar, however, is the Grim Reaper (perhaps – Ligeti leaves the
question open) and so his list stretches still further, from Adam and
Eve to recent 'cruel dictators':

> Demolished great kings and queens in scores,
> no one could escape my claws!
> Socrates a poisoned chalice!
> Nero, a knife in his palace!
> Hangman, cutthroat, pois'ner, sniper,
> to Cle . . . Cleopatra I gave the viper . . .

Only in the manner of these verse couplets and their scansion is a connection evident, since the music of Mozart and Ligeti is substantially
different. Yet the 'Bourrée perpetuelle', to which the words are set, is
partly parodistic, hinting at all sorts of precedents from Rameau to
Berlioz. Stravinsky's Mozartian pastiche, *The Rake's Progress* – its
Hogarthian ironies skilfully drawn out by librettists W. H. Auden and
Chester Kallman – was an important model.

Meschke and Ligeti's libretto may not have the quality of a Da
Ponte, or of Auden and Kallman, but its combination of allusion and
sardonic metaphor allows them to develop personality no less effectively. Its scatological stream of insulting epithets is memorable.
Meschke and Ligeti have ingeniously transferred the crude culture of
strip-cartoons into a sort of operatic bubble-language, redolent of
juvenile comics, fairgrounds, Punch and Judy, pop art – and, of course,
the gross pantomime manner of Alfred Jarry, whose seminal influence

on Surrealist theatre is at the libretto's heart. Even coarse language dates, and small amendments to the libretto have been ongoing, postdating the 1996 revision, sometimes arising as singers themselves have proposed more natural or singable alternatives. Yet the libretto skilfully avoids the awkwardness that has overtaken, for example, some of Tippett's colloquialisms.

Synopsis

The bizarre tone of the opera is set by its 'overture', a prelude for twelve car horns played by the percussionists, a sort of clowning version of the opening toccata in Monteverdi's *Orfeo*. The curtain rises on 'the entirely run-down but nevertheless carefree and thriving principality of Breughelland in an "anytime" century'. We are in the countryside where there is a decaying graveyard. Scene 1 is taken up with the contrast between two pairs of characters. Nekrotzar, the Grand Macabre, 'a sinister, shady, demagogic figure, humourless, pretentious, and with an unshakeable sense of mission',[11] emerges from a grave to engage in argument and enslave Piet the Pot, 'a kind of realistic Sancho Panza, always slightly tipsy (his profession is "wine-taster") and therefore always cheerful'. In Ghelderode, Nekrotzar (Death) is a charlatan. In the opera it must be conceivable that he is real. Meanwhile an idealised pair of lovers are searching for a quiet place to make love. So that their love duets will be the more sensuous, they are played by soprano and mezzo-soprano. In the first version of the opera they were given the risqué appellations of Clitoria and Spermando, but Ligeti was soon persuaded by various continental Intendants to amend them, eventually to Amanda and Amando. The couple enter entwined in each other's arms and looking, says Ligeti, 'as if they could have come straight out of a Botticelli painting'. Throughout the scene, the grotesque melodrama of Piet and Nekrotzar is cross-cut with the counterpoint of the lovers: an almost symphonic dialectic between the burlesque and lyrical which solidifies in a sequence of strong tableaux. With quasi-Verdian rhetoric, Nekrotzar announces the impending apocalypse:

> Here tonight, as midnight strikes,
> you will espy a pale horse,
> and on its back sits Death . . .

This sombre warning is declaimed on a measured and deliberate mono-tone, punctuated by rests, which continues for sixteen bars above a grandly impressive chord progression. It is a conscious or unconscious parody of the passage in Act 4 of Verdi's *Falstaff*, when, in Windsor Forest, Verdi's anti-hero counts out the midnight chimes of a distant clock. Piet is ordered to collect from the grave the 'requisites' of Death (scythe, trumpet etc.), and there is a moment of farce as he crashes into the lovers who have retired there to hide. Suddenly the music breaks into a ferocious gallop as Nekrotzar departs riding piggyback, in lieu of a horse, upon the unfortunate Piet. The scene ends with a duet of melting tenderness as the enraptured voices of the lovers float up from the grave.

Following a second car-horn fanfare, Scene 2 reveals the House of the Court Astrologer, Astradamors – a chaotic mixture of observatory, laboratory and kitchen – and of his dominating, sadistic, sex-starved wife, Mescalina. Ligeti's description of the stage set is Gothic in the extreme, with plentiful spiders' webs as evidence of decay and neglect. Mescalina is dressed in leather, Astradamors (optionally) in assorted lingerie. After some grotesque horseplay, Mescalina orders Astradamors to look through his telescope, then falls drunkenly asleep. She dreams of Venus, who appears naked high above her, and whom she implores to bring a real man, 'bow-legged, a hunchback, if you like, but, please, well hung!' The high tessitura of Venus's music has an aura of detached serenity, whilst Mescalina's plea, for all its vul-garity, also has its pathos: 'Oh, my dreary nights, dark with bitterness.' But it is Nekrotzar who arrives astride Piet, and performs a violent, stylised love scene with the semi-hypnotised Mescalina, whilst Venus looks on 'astonished and longingly' and Astradamors and Piet regard the whole display 'cynically, as if it were a sporting event'. Their vari-ous viewpoints are woven into a first appearance of the 'Bourrée perpetuelle', whose haunting ensemble of separate musical personali-ties here takes its cue from Mozart. In a brutal embrace, Nekrotzar bites Mescalina like a vampire. She falls senseless and is carried to the cellar. Sure of victory, Nekrotzar launches into a portentous catalogue of impending disasters. All leave for the Prince's palace except for Astradamors, triumphant to have become master in his own house.

Scene 3 is preceded by a prelude for electric doorbells. We meet 'the gluttonous, infantile Prince Go-go', a spoilt fourteen-year-old (the part should be sung by a countertenor), and his two rival Chief Ministers, leaders of the mutually inimical but ideologically identical White and Black parties, who insult and vie with each other in tyrannising him. Soon the Chief of the Secret Police (the Gepopo) arrives. Clearly, Ligeti wrote her part with the evident relish of poking fun at the three secret police organisations he had most cause to despise: the Gestapo, the Soviet GPU (later renamed the KGB), and the East German Geheime Politische Polizei, the three first syllables of which make up the acronym 'Gepopo'. Of dazzling virtuosity, the Chief of the Gepopo is one of the great coloratura roles in opera and a hilarious portrayal of sleuthiness. She is no Scarpia, but a canary-voiced high soprano, who enters on roller-skates disguised as a fantastic bird of prey, exchanging scarcely concealed 'pssts' with the offstage chorus. The libretto here is a tirade of spy-book clichés, encoded warnings of imprecise substance but sufficient to work her into paroxysms of excitement and panic. It becomes apparent that, as glimpsed by Astradamors and Nekrotzar in Scene 2, a comet is fast approaching, threatening destruction.

The mob is heard offstage, terrified and imploring, and the two Ministers try ineffectually to calm it. Then Astradamors arrives, still celebrating the apparent demise of his wife, during which Ligeti maintains a sense of frenzied anticipation in which the chorus's mounting hysteria plays a considerable role. Suddenly sirens wail from outside the auditorium; there is a deafening drumroll and menacing blasts from a bass trumpet at the back of the theatre. Entering from the rear of the stalls, Nekrotzar 'appears in dark yet magnificent grandeur, riding on Piet, blowing his trumpet and swinging his scythe. Hellish figures, masked musicians and grotesque monsters, as if out of an apocalyptic painting by Breughel or Bosch, make up his entourage.' The procession is accompanied by an audacious 'Collage' of corrupted dance tunes (ragtime, samba, flamenco, etc.) above an orchestral cha-cha layered in three tempi, the whole assembled over a surreal transformation of the finale motif from Beethoven's 'Eroica' symphony. This Ivesian extravaganza is an extraordinary tour de force, unlike anything else in Ligeti's music, and one of very few instances in which he completely suspends temporal synchronisation between different layers of the score.

Scornful of his threats, Piet and Astradamors drink Nekrotzar into a stupor, conveyed musically by a formidable orchestral hocket. The tutti breaks off abruptly, revealing the limpid phrases of the 'Bourrée perpetuelle' heard earlier, almost as if it had been present the whole time.

Now it is bewitchingly extended as accompaniment to Nekrotzar's Leporello-like catalogue, and labelled by Ligeti 'Galimatias' (gibberish), for Nekrotzar is getting increasingly confused. As the 'Bourrée' proceeds, celesta, harp, electric organ and piano re-enter one by one in independent and accelerating tempi. Suddenly there is a loud explosion and general mayhem; brass fanfares echo around the auditorium. Nekrotzar demands to know the time and calls for his scythe, trumpet and horse; but the only steed available is Prince Go-go's rocking horse. Go-go, Piet and Astradamors carry him to it, and with great effort, help him to mount. Nekrotzar adopts a grandiose pose whilst strange light effects herald the approach of the all-destructive comet, which Ligeti depicts in a series of visionary chords. In the midst of them, and of a momentous announcement of imminent doom, Nekrotzar falls out of the saddle – completely, irredeemably stoned.

No fanfare precedes the last scene, the return of the car horns being reserved for halfway through. Instead, an illusory paradise is evoked by impressionistic transformation music, before the curtain rises mistily on Scene 4, set like the first 'In the lovely country of Breughelland' and with the same dilapidated graveyard. One by one, the characters pick themselves up and observe that life seems much as before. Three ruffians appear with a cartload of loot. For Nekrotzar, the disappointment is too much: 'Have I not just laid to waste the entire goddamned world?' Overcome with failure, to the eerie strains of a 'Mirror Canon', 'he begins to shrink, gradually turning into a sort of sphere, gets smaller and smaller, and finally disappears into the ground without leaving a trace'. The fog lifts and the sun comes up. Finally, the two lovers emerge from their tomb, dishevelled and dazzled by the sunlight, unaware that anything has happened.

The opera ends with a Passacaglia, audibly related to the earlier Collage, but now a dignified ensemble for all the principals, except the Chief of the Gepopo and the now-vanished Nekrotzar. Its tone of philosophical affirmation follows the precedent of the moralising epilogues which conclude *Don Giovanni*, *Falstaff* and *The Rake's Progress*. The detail and specificity of Ligeti's stage directions – which, for all their comedy, also involve moments of romanticised theatrical illusion – continue to the last: 'The whole passacaglia is danced with fitting elegance by all the participants. The sunlight grows paler and paler and turns into supernatural light. Then gradually snow starts falling, covering the people onstage.'

The music

Considering the plurality of Ligeti's musical techniques in *Le Grand Macabre*, it is surprising how few of his best-known stylistic devices of the 1960s and 1970s are employed to any substantial degree in the opera. There is, for instance, virtually no micropolyphony in the manner of *Lontano* and no *meccanico* music as in the String Quartet no. 2 or Chamber Concerto. Some of the apparently fresh approach evident in the opera has much earlier roots in Ligeti's experiments of the early 1940s and 1950s, although now grown immensely more sophisticated. The 'Mirror Canon' in Scene 4, notwithstanding its mystic coloration of muted strings, has an austere rhythmic rigidity quite different from the fluid and cloudy counterpoint in his works of the 1960s, still less like the ametrical style of Ligeti's contemporaries. It is closer, at least in spirit, to the Frescobaldi-inspired eleventh movement of *Musica ricercata* and his very early *Polyphonic Study*. It is as if Ligeti was now ready to serve up the deep-frozen ingredients of his Hungarian years, thawed over the flame of avant-garde radicalism, secretly maturing in the recesses of his mind – with all the aplomb of a master chef, confidently disregarding the culinary practice of his colleagues, determined to invent each dish anew.

Where familiar techniques do appear, they are associated with specific characters or events. A clear example is the lovers' duet in Scene 1, which opens with their voices floating apart in contrary motion from a unison A; although, despite the participation of the orchestra, this contrapuntal divergence is barely filled in. Instead, it is lucidly transparent, the intervals between the voices mostly consonant; tritones and major sevenths much less frequent than major thirds and perfect fifths, so that we are reminded of the horn duets in *Melodien*. The euphonious beauty of the lovers' music in the first few minutes of the opera returns when they re-emerge from the grave in Scene 4, bestowing upon the final Passacaglia its own sequence of entirely consonant chords. Ligeti had dared nothing so harmonious for over twenty years, but the implications of this novel yet polytonal concordance would prove vital for the renewal of his style in the 1980s.

Only at one point does he draw extensively on the clusterous techniques of *Apparitions*, *Atmosphères* and *Clocks and Clouds*. Appropriately, they accompany the mysterious transformation – as sun and moon are eclipsed by the approaching comet – with its spectral lighting and subsequent darkness attendant upon the (supposed) end of the world. However, the a-rhythmic 'fogginess' of the earlier scores is discarded here in favour of the measured, more ominous tread of finite time. Piet, after all, drawing first an hourglass and then a huge kitchen clock from his pocket, has just done some eleventh-hour calculations:

PIET
    The time? . . .
    Two and tuppence to midnight . . .
    Now out with it:
    do we live, or do we die?

NEKROTZAR
    Fill up! Cheers! Bottoms up!
    (*suddenly greatly alarmed*)
    H-how late is it?

PIET
    The time:
    umpteen seconds to midnight . . .
    . . .
    At the tone the time will be . . .

Strangely but with spacious dignity the chords change, each on the first beat of a 4/4 bar, to synchronise with the implacable slow tolling of a deep gong. The timbral manipulation of Ligeti's earlier orchestral style is still present, but the metre is no longer obscured; indeed, it is audibly emphasised. In a quasi-apocalyptic manner, the chord changes accelerate and increase in volume, rotating ever faster between different sections of the orchestra. Despite the precedent of the chord rotation in Stockhausen's *Gruppen* (at fig. 119), such periodicity is more than Ligeti would have cared to employ in the 1960s. But as with his reappraisal of harmony, it opens the door to the new polymetric dimensions he would pursue during the following decades, ideas stimulated externally (as he has often acknowledged) but already latent in the opera.

The subsequent scene change, which reveals through 'unreal, dreamlike light' an unaltered and lovely Breughelland, is matched by colouristic music of great charm and delicacy. If the halo of glissandi string harmonics suggests Debussy, Ravel or Stravinsky, it is tinged with something more bizarre. Whilst Piet and Astradamors are seen 'floating freely above the ground' – their dialogue amusingly ironic –

the addition of three harmonicas lends whimsical naivety to the four horns' chordal euphony.

Such contrasts between the 'strange' and the 'lovely' are amongst the opera's strengths. Tension is diffused by a deftly placed 'cuckoo'; sadness amid grotesque slapstick conveyed by such poignant moments as Mescalina's 'Oh pain!' ('O weh!' – the original German reinforces its Mahlerian flavour). Incongruous instruments (alarm clock, metronome, kitchen pot, crockery) bring touches of Fluxus surrealism to otherwise serious and sophisticated orchestration. The score is littered with quotations and pseudo-quotations from earlier composers, which Ligeti likens to the referential character of pop art. He was particularly drawn to the make-believe collages of the British artist Peter Blake – 'an art', he says, 'which is not naive but which conveys an element of innocence. Think of Blake's tableau, *Self-portrait with Buttons*, very ironic and melancholic; and his tableau *The Balcony*: people in a park, behind whom is a false collage; a balcony where you see the royal family who appear to be in a photograph in a journal, but are in fact painted.'[12] *Le Grand Macabre* advanced Ligeti's ideas of illusion – and allusion – coexisting on different layers. It is 'tragic and light-hearted at the same time'.[13] From Monteverdi to Stravinsky this has proved an ideal recipe for theatrical success. In fact, it is a prerequisite for staging the opera.

Musical characterisation draws liberally from the spring of Ligeti's imagination. Indeed, the whole opera has an astonishing range of incident and imagery, its effectiveness evident as soon as the curtain rises upon a juxtaposition between Piet and Nekrotzar's obscene excesses and the blissful lyricism of the lovers. In the cause of psychological development, Ligeti makes extraordinary vocal demands, for which the gesticulating style employed in *Aventures* and *Nouvelles aventures* and in the 'Dies irae' of the Requiem are but a starting point. The capricious, darting pyrotechnics of the neurotic Chief of the Gepopo involve the most spectacular and difficult vocal writing in the score, although Piet and Nekrotzar have to accomplish nearly similar feats.

The chorus, on the other hand, have a relatively formal role, singing entirely offstage (according to Ligeti's directions) until, unexpectedly, a crowd of the people of Breughelland is found to be occupying the stalls, springing up in supplication at the entrance of Nekrotzar and his train through the auditorium. All the choral writing is homophonic, syllabic and rhythmically direct. The pastiche 'Passion Chorale', with

Ex. 18 Piet's cadenza in Scene 1 of *Le Grande Macabre* (1974–77)

which the Chorus of Spirits makes its entry in Scene 1, defines their function throughout the opera: they are a kind of cross between Greek chorus and Lutheran congregation, but they also extend the onstage action into disembodied regions beyond.

Put to work in the theatre, Ligeti's technical vocabulary of the 1960s and 1970s results in surprising developments. But *Le Grand Macabre* is also a transitional work. The necessity of creating a well-paced musical structure, of balancing *parlando* spontaneity with a more delineated continuity, and of writing a far longer work than hitherto, extended his range of resources, encouraging the revival of aspects abandoned when he left Hungary. By now, Ligeti had distanced himself from the avant-garde. His personal vision beckoned; so did the richness of a wider culture, including new ways of treating the past. The Passacaglia with which the opera ends is a case in point. In subtle ways it is related to the Collage accompanying Nekrotzar's processional entrance in Scene 3, whose first bars are taken from Beethoven: the opening of the last movement of the 'Eroica' but now fantastically transformed. Not only does Ligeti's chromatic inflection of Beethoven's simple formula turn it into a twelve-note row; it also links it to a lineage of passacaglias both old and new, since the sequence of semitones and tritones in Ligeti's variant can be associated with precedents in Purcell and Bach, as readily as with Lutosławski (*Musique Funèbre* and the last movement of the *Concerto for Orchestra*) or Boulez (*Rituel*), for example.

Ex. 19a and b Beethoven's passacaglia theme in the finale of the 'Eroica' and Ligeti's twelve-note parody in Scene 3 of the opera.

Ligeti's alteration of the 'Eroica' bass line turns it into a 'modulatory' passacaglia, which he uses to underpin the polymetric layers of the Collage, whereas Beethoven treats his theme in the manner of symphonic variations. Ligeti's pitch variants produce a twelve-note row (repeated ad infinitum without inversion, retrograde or transposition). Rhythmically, however, the theme contains thirteen notes, as in Beethoven. This means that each rhythmic statement begins on a new pitch, one further forward in the row, and that successive statements have a subtly different pitch configuration ensuring that the repeating 'ground' does not get stale.

The conclusion to the opera – the only section actually called

'Passacaglia' – is audibly associated with the earlier Collage, because both it and the 'Eroica' variant have a similar kind of chromaticism and phrase structure. This final Passacaglia is also quasi-serial, in that it consists of a twenty-four-note row in which each pitch appears twice, once combined with a minor sixth interval above, once with the major sixth.

Ex. 19c Ligeti's Passacaglia at the end of the opera

Not only are these twenty-four intervals entirely consonant; they remain consonant even when added pitches turn them into triads, exuding a strange tonal ambivalence arising from the frequent false relations. Ligeti would return to juxtaposed consonant triads in *Fanfares*, the fourth of the piano Études. But the origin of the idea belongs to the period of *Musica ricercata*, whilst a sketch for his unfinished *Istar pokoljárása* of 1955, when he was experimenting with serialism, has a similar twenty-four-note row distributed segmentally, whose rhythmic and registral shapes foreshadow both the Collage and Passacaglia in the opera. Ligeti has spoken of the 'Stravinsky-like orchestration'[14] of the Passacaglia, but there is another precedent: Webern's orchestration of Bach's dignified six-part 'Ricercare' from the *Musical Offering*. Rhythmically, Ligeti is more austere even than Bach, constructing his music almost entirely out of crotchets and quavers, with just a few semiquavers. But the *Klangfarbenmelodie* timbral distribution applied by both Webern and Ligeti conjoins modernism and the Baroque in a manner that is neither old nor new; more an enigmatic hybrid.

Aspects of Alice

Alice in Breughelland? Although hovering in the wings whilst Ligeti was casting around for a subject, by the time he found one Alice had gone from the scene. Beneath the surface, however, are subliminal shadows of where she is or might have been. For years Ligeti has considered the Alice books as a subject for music theatre; indeed he acknowledged the influence of *Alice in Wonderland*, alongside Kafka, Jarry and Vian, in the opera's first programme book. As we have already noted, in the mid-1980s, Ligeti contemplated setting Shakespeare's *Tempest*. It would be another large opera, but on a story which, like *Alice*, he had known and loved since childhood, and it would fulfil his undertaking to English National Opera and the BBC, its joint commissioners. Other projects, however, stood in the way, and by the early 1990s, he had changed his mind. After composing a viola sonata and a madrigal for the King's Singers he would, he said, 'devote myself to an old dream, a theatrical fantasy: Lewis Carroll's *Alice in Wonderland* and *Through the Looking-Glass*. This work will take two to three years. After that, I have promised the Arditti String Quartet a new quartet.'[15] The Viola Sonata and six *Nonsense Madrigals* have been duly completed, including a setting of 'The Lobster Quadrille' and other verses by Lewis Carroll. Neither *The Tempest*, nor the theatrical fantasy based on *Alice*, nor a third string quartet have yet appeared – but both Alice and the quartet are again much in his mind.

Ligeti's original idea for an opera was to create his own satirical 'wonderland', the imaginary 'Kylwiria' he had invented in childhood. If he was tempted by the *Alice* stories, their drawbacks were no doubt as evident as their attractions. Packed as they are with amusing and bizarre incident, Carroll's books are period pieces, dependent on the niceties of an interplay between polite Victorian etiquette and its antithesis: rudeness, obstinacy, spite. Alice is captivating but prim; nor is she an adult. Emerging from the iconoclastic, audacious 1960s, Ligeti needed something more macho and muscular, more extreme, more shocking, more cartoon-like and more contemporary, a satire upon adult foibles but in the spirit of absurdist theatre.

Yet there are similarities between Carroll's irony and the cruel comedy of Ghelderode. Naivety and beastliness occur in both. Both authors delight in exaggeration and fantasy, punning and pathos. Nekrotzar and the Queen of Hearts similarly threaten catastrophic punishment, which proves to be ineffectual – or so it appears, since in neither case can we be entirely sure. Alice's petulance, and that of her ill-mannered and unpredictable friends, is magnified in the outrageous behaviour of the characters in Ligeti's opera. Both in Alice and Le Grand Macabre, orderly society teeters on the brink of anarchy. The relationship between Prince Go-go and his sadistic Ministers parallels that of the Dormouse and his companions at the Mad Hatter's tea party. Besides, the language of the Meschke-Ligeti libretto, especially in Geoffrey Skelton's inspired English translation, is often reminiscent of Carroll. The Mock-Turtle's 'Reeling, Writhing and the different branches of Arithmetic – Ambition, Distraction, Uglification and Derision' are the stuff of the White Minister's address to the People of Breughelland: 'White-wishers, wellwashers and floating gloaters . . .'[16] – in response to which the crowd bombards him, just like his Black counterpart, with a torrent of missiles, in the spirit of John Tenniel's classic illustration of Alice assaulted by a pack of cards.

Stockholm and afterwards

The successive productions of Le Grand Macabre mounted by European opera houses in the late 1970s and 1980s did as much to damage as to consolidate Ligeti's reputation. Only one of these, at Bologna, Ligeti felt to be in harmony with his own concept of the opera, and none adhered to the score and stage directions as written.

In Stockholm, the Meschke-Meczies staging of Scene 3 was undoubtedly effective, with the Black and White Ministers cast as tall Giacometti-like marionettes towering above a roly-poly Prince Go-go, and the Chief of the Gepopo's gumshoe attendants dressed like an aviary of twitching birds. But the success of the premiere owed most to the high standard of its musical performance under Elgar Howarth (conductor of many subsequent productions, although here making his professional operatic debut), with Britt-Marie Aruhn a devastatingly accomplished Chief of the Gepopo, and singers as distinguished as Elizabeth Söderström and Kerstin Meyer portraying the delectable lovers. Visually, Meschke's production was often too cluttered, losing itself in a wealth of detail, whilst the over-extended dialogue proved tedious. According to Ligeti, Meschke had little understanding of the music, or of opera in general, treating Le Grand Macabre as a largely spoken piece.

For its second production in Hamburg six months later, the director Gilbert Deflo devised elaborate antics in the manner of a circus, with harlequins as Chief Ministers, a sadomasochistic animal trainer, and Death as the celebrant of a black mass attended by a troop of clown-acolytes. But these shenanigans were sadly devoid of humour. Ligeti was not alone in finding the production 'horrible'. Already after Stockholm, the German critics had rebuked him for 'surrendering to the bellowing text . . . rather than giving free rein to the music'.[17] Now they were more censorious, concluding that the scenario was ill-conceived, that the opera would have no further performances, and that Ligeti would do well to rescue the music in a concert suite. 'If one closed one's eyes,' wrote Joachim Kaiser in the *Süddeutsche Zeitung*, 'if one overlooked the circus-like idiocy which reduced the music to bland background, then one heard a very brilliant score, rich in allusions and, in its best moments, wonderfully sad. But who goes to the opera to ignore the staging?'[18] In general, however, the director was held to blame. 'Nothing remains of Ligeti's ambiguities,' wrote Heinz Josef Herbort in *Die Zeit*. 'All allusions are pushed aside (except the obscenities), are lost in cheap noise, and we are spared no embarrassment. Here even the absurdity is artificial.'[19] It was a painfully inauspicious German premiere in Ligeti's home city.

The following spring new productions took place in Saarbrücken and in Italy. The latter, which opened in Bologna on 5 May 1979, had for Ligeti the merit of 'wonderful sets' by the French artist, Roland Topor, whose 'demoniac imagination' he much admired. Although they were neither Bosch nor Breughel, Topor's conception retained the essence of these artists, and to this day it remains Ligeti's favourite staging. Admittedly, some of the audience at Il Teatro Comunale were a little bemused, despite (or perhaps because of) the use of Neapolitan dialect insults in the translation. This was also the most pornographic of the opera's many interpretations. Phallic symbols apart, the citizens of Breughelland were shown living in high-rise bottles, their main square lit by a wine glass three times the size of a man, and decorated with monuments of Parma ham, sausage, and boiled eggs. The secret police were dressed as black-hooded Mafia crows, whilst for Nekrotzar's terrorising entrance, the audience were assailed by trumpets, drums and emblems of death from every side. These visual delights compensated for the fact that production costs absorbed so much of the budget that the theatre could not afford the best singers.

In Paris, Daniel Mesguich's staging at the Opéra Garnier distressed Ligeti acutely:

It was very beautiful, extraordinarily poetic, especially the scenery by (Bernard) Daydé, but it had nothing to do with my opera. It was good musically, but the content . . . it was something else, devised by Mesguich with the idea (after Boulez) of the death of opera, which is absolutely not what I intended. I wanted the destruction of the world, which is quite different . . . It is really about the death that comes to this principality of Breughelland in medieval Flanders. But Mesguich doubled or tripled the characters, causing total confusion. I didn't protest, although there was a ballet that passed across the stage completely regardless of the libretto. It introduced a certain philosophical conception according to which everything was simultaneously past, present and future (which is why the characters were tripled). It was totally intellectual, abstract and alien to me. For me, Le Grand Macabre of Ghelderode is direct, concrete and demonic.[20]

To an English observer, it looked as if Nekrotzar was

the protagonist in a surrealist music-theatre-of-the-absurd in which a constant drift of the ghosts of opera stars haunts the broken shell of the Opéra singing fragments of past roles (through Ligeti's music), in which . . . all the principals . . . are presented simultaneously on the stage by always two or three mirror-selves all doing different things at the same time . . . the 'Marx Brothers' traipse across the stage holding one another's coat tails and smoking cigars. Venus in grave-clothes descends in a chandelier. Six others walk naked. Romeos and Juliets stab themselves by the dozen.[21]

The fashionable Parisian public found these cameo appearances by the Marx Brothers, Spiderman, and interpolated scenes from their favourite operas, greatly amusing. But those who understood the real nature of Ligeti's opera echoed his dismay. One Hungarian critic set the brilliance and greatness of the work itself against the 'incredible incompetence' of Daniel Mesguich's production.[22] Ligeti's demeanour was hardly improved when a loudspeaker malfunctioned just before the opening performance. As he stood up to demand that it be turned off, members of the audience, unaware of his identity, shouted at him to be quiet. It must have seemed as if the ghouls of Dada and Fluxus had returned to play havoc with his meticulously wrought opera, taunting him with having himself once been their disciple.

To produce the British premiere of Le Grand Macabre in November 1982, English National Opera had approached Jonathan Miller. Ligeti had not met him, but much later saw and admired Miller's *Mikado* as well as his television production of *Alice in Wonderland*. Disappointingly, only two months before the premiere, Miller withdrew. His replacement, Elijah Moshinsky, adopted as his model Joe Orton's Genet-inspired plays, in which mischief and farce give rise to menace and violence. The production and the stage design – showing a slip road onto the M4 motorway and featuring a hearse (the grave and hideaway of the lovers) stopped beside a No. 27 London bus – were intended to create a Brechtian sense of alienation. Instead of being a spoilt juvenile, Prince Go-go was cast as a naval officer. This production, too, was as much reviled as praised, and Ligeti – always a demanding taskmaster – accused it, in an interview for the *Independent* given in London five years later, of 'an absolute misunderstanding, a reduction to pocket size of what was meant to be threatening. Fear was reduced to petty bourgeois comedy.'[23]

After the opera's eighth production in Freiburg in 1984, no further staging of *Le Grand Macabre* took place for seven years, until another spate of German, Swiss and Austrian productions occurred in the early 1990s. Of these, Ligeti thought that the Berne production came closest to his own ideas. There was little money for the stage sets, but the singers were good, and Eike Gramss seems to have been the only director to understand, to Ligeti's satisfaction, how horror and comedy can coexist. Increasingly, however, Ligeti felt that the opera needed revision, realising that when he composed it, he had been theatrically naive, and had too readily accepted the dramaturgical views of Michael Meschke. In particular, he wanted to reduce the spoken dialogue – he had already slightly pruned it – make musical changes, correct mistakes in the score, and have it typeset. He spent from December 1995 to August 1996 on these tasks. Disaster nearly overtook the opera and Ligeti himself when, by careless inattention to his naked-flame tea heater, he set fire to the first floor of his house in the Vienna Woods. Had it not been for Vera's speedy rescue, he might have lost his life. Had it not been for the equally prompt arrival of the Vienna fire brigade, the outcome would have been much more serious. Several of his manuscripts were destroyed. Virtually everything on the first floor was incinerated – the bathroom, for instance, quickly reduced to a mound of molten plastic – all of which took a year to restore. But miraculously, his Steinway piano was spared, and lying on its lid, some money, his passport and the revised score of *Le Grand*

Macabre. The first performance of this new version took place at the Salzburg Festival on 28 July 1997. Directed by Peter Sellars, it aroused the same eager anticipation that had preceded the opera's world premiere nearly twenty years before.

Meanwhile, a further production of the original version (its fourteenth) was presented by the Münster State Theatre in February 1997, and immediately afterwards toured to Ferrara. In Ligeti's view, this was one of the best: 'musically wonderful – on a level with Salzburg – and a very brilliant production in which Breughelland became the Bundesrepublik'. Inevitably, however, it was overshadowed by the forthcoming premiere of the revised score a few months later, in the hands of one of the world's most charismatic stage directors. Peter Sellars's theatrical style was fêted almost to the point of adulation. He had not been Ligeti's choice; indeed, the composer had scarcely been consulted. But he was optimistic. If he had qualms, he decided to put them aside.

The 1996 revision

The overall duration of Ligeti's revised version remains much as before. But now, instead of being divided into two acts separated by an interval, the opera is in four scenes performed without a break. Without doubt, the 1996 score is stronger both theatrically and musically. The final Passacaglia has been extended. Most of the spoken text has been deleted, albeit with the loss of some witty couplets, but leaving the music much tauter and more dynamic. One of the most significant changes is that Ligeti has now written music for the opposing White and Black Ministers to sing. The earthiness of their original spoken roles sat uneasily beside Prince Go-go's music, and too easily grew tedious. Composed lines allow subtleties of nuance to be conveyed more effectively; for example, by being sung, the irony of the Ministers' synthetic servility and their apparent reconciliation is better conveyed. Similarly, the Prince's 'I beg your pardon' acquires greater poignancy now that its pensive harmony, a tiny oasis of wistfulness in an otherwise madcap scene, is better integrated into the musical structure of the whole.

The revised, typeset score and new CD recording establish *Le Grand Macabre* as one of the most original and important of twentieth-century operas, as well as one whose stage conception is exceptionally well crafted. The basis of Ligeti's fantasy is the distortion and exaggeration of an archaic yet universally understood iconography. As the British critic Peter Heyworth observed in a perceptive review of the original premiere, 'in its mixture of menace and ribald farce *Le Grand Macabre* throws a bridge between a medieval morality play, in which the precepts are stood on their head, and the theatre of the absurd.'[24] Its balance between cartoon-like caricature and genuine humanity, between grotesque excess and profound experience, are shrewdly calculated. A stage director subverts these interlocking layers of meaning at the opera's peril – not his own, of course, for in the modern opera house directors hold sway.

Peter Sellars's staging

The choice of Peter Sellars to stage the revised *Le Grand Macabre* for Salzburg (1997) and Paris (1998) virtually guaranteed that these audiences would not see the opera as Ligeti conceived it. Sellars's production contains the theatrical images one has come to expect of him, but of Breughelland and its inhabitants there is scarcely a trace. Certainly a modern production applied to an eighteenth- or nineteenth-century masterpiece can illuminate a well-worn text. But to treat with similar licence a complex contemporary work, with which the majority of operagoers are completely unfamiliar, is only likely to confuse them. When its composer is not only alive, but has deeply considered views about how his opera should look, to reject these intentions out-of-hand is presumptuous. When that opera is itself constructed upon an elaborate conceit, and is to be sung in a language (English) of which many in the audience may have but a partial grasp, the imposition of a totally different scenario which discards virtually all of the composer's stage directions seems at best wilfully bewildering, at worst egotistically arrogant – as the bemused and subdued reaction of the public at the Châtelet Theatre in Paris in February 1999 made evident.

In Sellars's post-nuclear setting, the impression created by George Tsypin's stage design is of a sci-fi, lunar landscape dominated by huge, impersonal daleks or defunct reactors, amongst which appear incongruously, from time to time, a small explorer's tent, a hospital bed, blindfolded prisoners, etc. The cast appear in nondescript contemporary dress whose unflattering similarity extends, unfortunately, to Amanda and Amando, clad in dungarees and peaked caps –

canoodling in a body-bag. So much for Botticelli! As for Nekrotzar, nothing that he wears or wields conveys that this is Father Time, the Great Reaper, the Angel of Death, or even an impostor. Drained of horror, humour and pomposity, Sellars presents a Nekrotzar who is neither preposterous nor funny, ordinary indeed from his very first entrance – already demeaned. The lack of any significant scene change contributes to a general absence of tension, in which the teasing ambivalence of Ligeti's vision is sadly neutered. This static and bland treatment affects all of the characterisation, including the chorus. To involve them in the stage action is sensible, except that in keeping with Sellars's routine obsessions, they look like Palestinian terrorists newly demobbed from his 1991 production of John Adams's *The Death of Klinghoffer*, still clutching their Kalashnikovs and gas masks.

What had attracted Ligeti to Bosch and Breughel was not only their blend of the tragic and the comic, but their attention to individual incident within the variegated whole of an extraordinarily complex picture. The self-contained detail within these crowded canvases is an essential characteristic also of Ligeti's music. Sellars, however, is celebrated for work in which the broader picture is more important than the nuances. His assuredly brilliant production of John Adams's first opera, *Nixon in China*, treated a topical event known to virtually everybody. For this, Sellars devised a sequence of comparatively static tableaux, energised by the music, each extended across a spacious time-frame – like Adams's score. Designer Adrienne Lobel's 'cardboard cut-out' profile of Air Force 1 and gaudy flat backdrops tellingly conveyed the thin veneer of diplomatic display. Furthermore, Sellars and Adams worked together on their Homeric odyssey from the start.

In Ligeti's opera, by contrast, both scenario and music are volatile and ambivalent. There is no sense of the epic; instead a plethora of detail. Ligeti's opera is both his music and his visualisation of its manner and setting. To perform the music and reject the rest is to present only part of the conception. Ligeti would still prefer to see it set in the 'old Flemish' of Bosch and Breughel: 'neither in modern dress, nor, simplified, nor geometric', pointing out that his stage-picture can easily be recreated from the paintings.[25] It is not unusual for composers to be marginalised in matters of stage design and production on the grounds that they lack professional expertise – unless, like Sylvano Bussotti (b.1931) or Heiner Goebbels (b.1952), they are also accomplished stage directors. Yet it is surely a serious failure of contemporary operatic fashion that, of twenty-three different productions during the first twenty-three years of *Le Grand Macabre*'s existence, not one has attempted to reproduce Ligeti's own iconographic vision. Only Roland Topor's designs for Bologna approached to some degree that Garden of Earthly Delights haunted by a (not so) triumphant Death.

Staging *Le Grand Macabre* is not unproblematic. Even in its revised form, the opera's musical continuity remains a hyperactive mix veering between luminous sensuality and avant-garde mannerism. During the 1960s and 1970s, Ligeti made himself master of the ten- to fifteen-minute piece, exemplified in the seamless flow of *Lontano* and *Melodien*. To compose a full-length opera, he had to involve other approaches: comedy bordering on slapstick, *parlando* verging on speech, parodistic and gestural excesses like those in *Aventures* and *Nouvelles aventures*. The potential incompatibility of these ingredients is exacerbated by unsympathetic production. Stage *Così fan tutte* how you like and its universal themes of love and infidelity can scarcely be obscured. *Le Grand Macabre* has nothing so everyday; rather it is fantasy, caricature, exaggeration and ambivalence. Its artifice and symbolism need to be clarified and enhanced.

Sellars's reinterpretation of Ligeti's opera raises acute questions concerning the imposition of so much personal baggage on pre-existing artworks by fashionable directors. The most damning indictment of his production is that it fails to be funny. In Salzburg, Sellars supplied his own synopsis, contradicting the composer's own, as an insert to the programme. Ligeti complained to the magazine *Der Spiegel* that he had been deceived and his opera 'falsified'. Two days before it was due to open he demanded that Gerard Mortier, Artistic Director of the Salzburg Festival, cancel the production. Alarmed, Mortier asked Christoph von Dohnányi – conductor of many Ligeti performances including the premiere of the Double Concerto – to mediate. Dohnányi pointed out that Ligeti had known and accepted what was planned, and Mortier would be justified in taking action to recover his losses. Bitterly distressed, the composer vehemently dissociated himself from the production, and withdrew from the scheduled public discussion. Should he sue for defamation? Had the opera been a living person (and, in a sense, it is) he might have made a case. But how can a work of art defend itself?

The musical performance was, however, an unqualified triumph, thanks to excellent soloists and the conductor Esa-Pekka Salonen. Agonised by the production's banality and by its betrayal of his vision, Ligeti spent the Paris performances in the recording van. He had already antagonised the pro-Sellars French press by disowning it in a television interview, saying that it was 'not my piece, and totally false'. From its London premiere, scheduled for the glamorous first week of the reopened Royal Opera House at Covent Garden in December 1999, he decided to stay away. As it happened, so did everybody else. Struggling to master its new computerised stage mechanisms, and to introduce eight opera and dance productions as the builders and renovators left the building, Covent Garden's new management found themselves with an impossible schedule. Desperate to release stage time for their other productions, just three weeks before curtain-up, all six London performances of *Le Grand Macabre* were cancelled – leaving the way open, one hopes, for something better, a production worthy of the Breughellian pageant of Ligeti's cornucopian score.

In the midst of life . . .

Alas, where shall I find – when
winter comes – the flowers, and where
the sunshine?
And the shadows of the earth?
The walls stand
speechless and cold, in the wind
the weather-vanes rattle.
Friedrich Hölderlin[1]

Before the premiere of *Le Grand Macabre*, Ligeti had already decided
what he would compose afterwards. There would be a piano concerto,
followed by a horn piece for the British player Barry Tuckwell. But
the huge effort of completing the opera, culminating in the tension
surrounding its premiere, turned the event into something of a watershed. Uncharacteristically, in the months that followed, he experienced
what befalls many composers, a creative block. He was far from
certain in what direction his style should now proceed.

One decision he had firmly made: that the pastiche, verging on quotation, which underpins so much of the opera's characterisation, he would
not use again. To revisit this 'flea market', as he wittily derided it, would
compromise stylistic integrity. It was a passing weakness, not to be
repeated. Other aspects of his technique also appeared to have run their
course, whether the canonically saturated microtexture of *Lontano* or
the gestural profusion of *San Francisco Polyphony*. As for the vocal
pyrotechnics of the opera, here too was an extreme he could hardly
repeat, let alone surpass. By contrast, its melodic and harmonic qualities
pointed back to the musical thinking which dominated the early years of
Ligeti's career; but to draw on the past had other dangers. How might
one create a contemporary concept of tonality? The encroaching tide of
neo-Romanticism was anathema. Although many of his composition
students (notably the Germans) had adopted an anti-modernist 'retro'

stance, Ligeti wanted nothing to do with it. His reworking of consonant harmony was implicitly 'postmodern': although in fact, no adequate technical term exists to describe the tonal character of the opera's final Passacaglia, with its succession of disassociated triadic harmonies. Polytonality, pan-diatonicism? Such words carry too many connotations. They might do for a Milhaud or a Martinů earlier in the century, but Ligeti was using techniques he regarded as quite different, associated in his mind with strange temperaments – a condition which, he thought, might even be simulated in equal temperament by abnormal harmonic juxtapositions, or by deploying intervallic structures in such a way as to reinforce their natural overtones.

The dilemma sprang from a widespread uncertainty affecting composers in the late 1970s, following the decline in the authority of Darmstadt and of serialist dogma. His own confusion was compounded by periods of ill health. Nevertheless he worked assiduously, writing hundreds of sketches for the projected piano concerto, only to abandon them. Two short works for harpsichord emerged during 1978, but otherwise there were no further premieres of any significance until the Trio for Violin, Horn and Piano had its first performance on 7 August 1982. In fact, the Trio was written quickly in the first half of 1982, a sudden release from three frustrating years of trial and error. During this time, Ligeti had come across an intriguing book: *Gödel, Escher, Bach: an Eternal Golden Braid (a Metaphorical Fugue on Minds and Machines in the Spirit of Lewis Carroll)* by a previously unknown author, Douglas Hofstadter.[2] Published in 1979, this ingenious interweaving of the music of Bach, the graphic art of Escher and the mathematical theorems of Gödel – a tripartite *ricercar* intended to illuminate the mysterious processes of human thought – found a receptive reader in Ligeti. Amongst its many chapters, Hofstadter reprints an amusing dialogue by Lewis Carroll – an ironic variant of Zeno's elegant conundrum of Achilles and the tortoise – which might have been included especially for Ligeti. Bach's music is a refrain throughout the book. Hofstadter repeatedly relates his discussion of such mathematical models as self-replicating systems, nested structures, frames, strange loops and other hierarchical mechanisms to the technical ingenuity of Bach's inventions and fugues, or to the puzzle canons of the *Musical Offering*, in which Bach layers a single melody upon itself sometimes at different speeds. Whether in an intellectual, visual or musical domain, Hofstadter views these enigmatic phenomena

as determinants of mathematics and also of art. They are both paradox and poetry.

Ligeti was fascinated by Hofstadter's book and its sequel,
Metamagical Themas,[3] especially the second volume's chapter on
'Pattern, Poetry, and Power in the Music of Frédéric Chopin'. Both
books contributed to the climate of ideas from which he was attempting to forge a new style. But in December 1981, he was still trying to
find ways of applying such concepts to the Piano Concerto. Eighteen
months after he had started it, a convincing compositional formula
completely eluded him. He reported to Pierre Michel that

I still must finish it. I have to begin several movements at once but I haven't
found what I want. At present I've come to a stop and begun to write a trio
for horn, violin and piano (I'll finish the concerto afterwards). These two
works mark a change in my melodic thinking in which the ideas of Escher and
Hofstadter play an important role.[4]

He had, indeed, written numerous beginnings; but as for finishing the
concerto, none of them had gone further than two or three pages.
Turning instead to the Horn Trio, its composition went surprisingly
quickly. But this was largely because its stylistic premise belonged to a
different area of reference. A year after the first performance of the
Horn Trio, the *Drei Phantasien nach Friedrich Hölderlin* and *Magyar
Etüdök* (both for sixteen voices, a cappella) made their appearance.
During the next two years Ligeti completed nothing more, until the first
book of piano Études in 1985. The studies demonstrated a vigorous
renewal of Ligeti's creative confidence. But his vague preliminary ideas
for a second opera would not gel, whilst the piano concerto continued
to cause him endless difficulty. By the date of its scheduled premiere in
1986, he had completed only three movements, and had put further
work aside until he could see the way ahead. Only in 1988, a decade
after its conception, was the concerto heard complete, its five movements providing hard-won proof not only of the rigorous self-criticism
Ligeti has consistently imposed upon himself, but of a triumphant ability to reinvent his music's deepest technical and aesthetic foundations.

Macabre moments

During this apparently fallow period, whilst *Le Grand Macabre* was
going the round of European opera houses, Ligeti made a shortened

concert version of the opera for four solo voices and orchestra plus *ad libitum* chorus. The suggestion came from his publishers, following the dismissive comments about the opera's viability made by the German critics. Ligeti warmed to the task, and arranged several of its highlights in two movements around the orchestral Collage, to last nearly fifty minutes in performance. *Scenes and Interludes from Le Grand Macabre* was first heard in Berlin in December 1978, in Copenhagen a month later, and was introduced to London in 1981 and Munich in 1983. The following year in Graz, when the Styrian Autumn Festival mounted the most extensive review to date of Ligeti's output, the *Scenes and Interludes* made a powerful impression. The response was more muted when the concert suite was performed at the opening of New York's 'Horizons' festival on 21 May 1986 (the complete opera is still to be staged in America). Apart from this performance by the New York Philharmonic, all these performances were given under the auspices of broadcasting and by radio symphony orchestras. They were temporary substitutes, in effect, for full theatrical production, and Ligeti now regards the *Scenes and Interludes* as outdated.[5]

Later, whilst Elgar Howarth was preparing a concert performance of the whole opera in Vienna in 1987, a crisis led to the appearance of another 'off cut'. Eirian Davies, who was due to sing the Chief of the Gepopo, fell ill, and no replacement could be found. Howarth proposed that her spectacular coloratura music be played by the Swedish trumpeter Håkan Hardenberger. The incident was unfortunate in that the performance was being recorded for a CD, whose issue was accordingly delayed. Musically, however, Ligeti so liked this emergency solution that he allowed Howarth to arrange her music for trumpet and piano under the title *Mysteries of the Macabre*, and then authorised further versions for trumpet or soprano with instrumental ensemble (both make entertaining display pieces) as well as for soprano and piano.

Another step was to detach for concert use the orchestral nuggets which could be performed without voices or soloists: the car-horn prelude, the Collage, 'Bourrée perpetuelle' in its second appearance ('Galimatias'), the transformation music with which Ligeti portrays the non-event of the end of the world, and the final Passacaglia. These sections were assembled by Howarth under the title *Macabre Collage*, published by Schott, and first performed at Maggio Musicale in Florence on 16 May 1992 as a surprise birthday present for the composer. They, too, make an effective sequence – not unlike Berlioz's *Three Pieces from The*

Damnation of Faust. Ligeti was appreciative, but feels that the music does not live without the singers. Howarth is allowed to perform the arrangement, but it has been deleted from the Schott catalogue.

Hungarian rehabilitation

Ligeti's only completed compositions in 1978 were the two pieces for harpsichord, whose character, as well as their titles, suggest that he was taking a renewed interest in his Hungarian roots. Although neither lasts above five minutes, they are engaging additions to the instrument's repertoire, if also indicative of his wider stylistic dilemma. Both are pastiche, intended as 'ironical remarks' to Ligeti's students 'who always wanted this kind of retro-music'. Several of his students 'accepted tonal music completely'. One took pop music as his point of departure: 'Their idols were no longer Beethoven, Webern or Stockhausen, but Bob Dylan for example.'[6] But the harpsichord pieces also relate to precedents in the opera, particularly its final Passacaglia, since each is based on an ostinato. *Hungarian Rock* is built on a one-bar pattern that repeats continuously in the bass without transposition, like a seventeenth-century chaconne. *Passacaglia ungherese* has a four-bar ostinato that starts in high register and recycles across four octaves; its repetitions overlap to form a consistently repetitive harmonic formula, to which Ligeti adds additional counterpoints above or below.

Hungarian Rock was written in May 1978, immediately after the premiere of the opera. Its dedicatee is Elisabeth Chojnacka, a theatrically extrovert and virtuoso harpsichordist who had moved from her native Poland to Paris, inspiring Xenakis to write some extremely difficult music for her. Ligeti's short composition is less demanding, despite its progressively detached 'boogie-woogie' relationship between improvisatory right hand and repetitive left. This ostinato consists of the same one-bar pattern played 176 times. But Ligeti harmonises it in four ways. By writing a different chord sequence in each of the first four bars,

Ex. 20a Ostinato in *Hungarian Rock*

he ensures enough harmonic variety for the larger four-bar cycle to appear forty-four times. A 'Bulgarian' time signature of 2 + 2 + 3 + 2 quavers to the bar (sometimes sounding 2 + 3 + 2 + 2) allows the variations to convey, if not exactly 'rock' (since 'everything is fake'), at least its spirit, as well as that of Balkan folk music. Both its rhythm and chords remind one of the first of Bartók's *Six Dances in Bulgarian Rhythm*. More interesting, however, is the role of *Hungarian Rock* as a prototype for the second movement of the Horn Trio and, after that, the fourth of Ligeti's piano Études, *Fanfares*. All three are built on repeating one-bar ostinati (the Trio and the Étude using exactly the same phrase), and a comparison between their quite different but equally inventive working out provides a fascinating insight into the composer's craft.

Passacaglia ungherese was written in December 1978 for Eva Nordwall, wife of the musicologist Ove Nordwall, whose monograph on Ligeti had been published in Sweden in 1968 and in Germany in 1971, and to whom he felt indebted. Seventeenth-century models also lie behind this piece, whose developing variations around a repeating ostinato follow the manner of 'divisions upon a ground', a favourite of English and Italian harpsichord composers. Indeed, Ligeti's chromatic ground is not unlike the theme of the Frescobaldi homage that concludes *Musica ricercata*. In the *Passacaglia ungherese* it is sixteen minims long, and similarly contains all twelve pitch-classes (four of them used twice). But here he is haunted by the quasi-tonal, consonant finale of *Le Grand Macabre*. As soon as the ostinato re-enters half-way through the first statement, the combination of both produces consonant dyads.

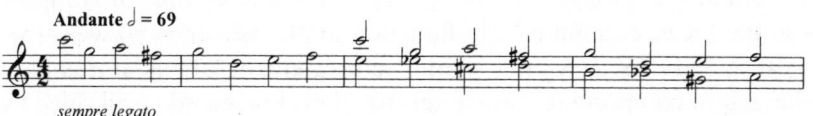

Ex. 20b Ostinato in *Passacaglia ungherese*

Thereafter, two statements of the ostinato always overlap in complementary phase, and the whole composition consists of consonant dyads in one hand – all either major thirds or (their inversion) minor sixths – and melodic variations in the other, the combination of both creating an astringent multi-tonality. Ligeti directs that the piece should preferably be played on an instrument tuned in mean-tone temperament, in which case all these thirds and sixths will be 'pure' or nearly so – i.e. untainted by the 'beating' produced by equal temperament – whilst the melodic arabesques sound tortuously chromatic. On the Sony collected edition, Elisabeth Chojnacka plays both pieces on a modern harpsichord tuned to equal temperament; but she points up the anachronistic character of *Passacaglia ungherese* by treating it to *notes inégales* and a degree of rhythmic licence more usually associated with Baroque music.

Whilst he was composing *Passacaglia ungherese*, Ligeti was aware that a portrait concert of his music was being planned in Budapest itself. As early as 1967, a more liberal Hungarian government had declared an amnesty for political refugees. That year, Ligeti's mother obtained a visa to visit him; she fell ill whilst in Vienna and Ligeti persuaded her to stay. Two years later he was invited to join a jury judging a competition being held in Budapest. He agreed on condition that the organisers arranged with the police to allow him access to his mother's locked flat ('With the Communist authorities you could bargain'). Thus in 1970, Ligeti found himself back in Hungary for the first time in fourteen years. The visit, which took place two years after the Soviet 'invasion' of Czechoslovakia, confirmed his view that he had been right to leave the Eastern bloc.

By the late 1970s, festivals in Western Europe featuring Ligeti's music had become both frequent and substantial. Typical of these were the Ligeti days at Aix-en-Provence during July–August 1979, which included six concerts of his music and lectures by the composer. Since 1965, many of his works had also been performed behind the Iron Curtain at the annual Warsaw Autumn. But almost none in Hungary – so the Ligeti evening held in Budapest in November 1979 was especially gratifying. It was a public reinstatement of his status as a Hungarian composer in the capital city of his homeland – still ruled by Communism. Felicitously, the festival featured the music of both Ligeti and Kurtág. The Ligeti concert included three of his most important large-scale works: *San Francisco Polyphony*, the Double Concerto and the Requiem. By now, Budapest had recovered some of its glamour, though we should note Ligeti's comment that 'If you come from Paris to Budapest you think you are in Moscow. But if you go from Moscow to Budapest, you think you are in Paris.'[7] This homecoming both strengthened Ligeti's relationship with other Hungarian musicians and marked a further distancing from the Franco-German avant-garde. Hungarian, after all, is still his mother tongue, the language in which he thinks and dreams, and which embodies the 'indestructible culture' of his childhood.[8]

Homage to Brahms . . . and Beethoven

When, after four years of almost unbroken creative silence, the Trio for Violin, Horn and Piano appeared in 1982, it raised critical eyebrows, not for any folk or Hungarian references, nor unsettling modernity, but on account of its acknowledged classical-Romantic parentage. The new work bore an incriminating subtitle, 'Hommage à Brahms'. Had Ligeti, the arch-iconoclast, deserted the cause of modernism?

To the post-Nono, post-Cagean radicals dismayed by the advance of neo-Romanticism, this looked like betrayal. Ligeti had already offended the left wing in Darmstadt, ten years before, by his rejection of musico-political fashion. In their eyes, the Horn Trio confirmed the suspicion that he had become an enemy of progressive ideals. At the Styrian Autumn Festival in Graz in 1984, during the four days of concerts and seminars on Ligeti, his stance was aggressively criticised. At one of the symposia, Ligeti was even taunted with being an agent of the CIA, on the grounds that he had deserted Hungary and outspokenly condemned the Communists. In Hamburg, Helmut Lachenmann openly attacked him; Ligeti was not present, but he read the speech. The progressives felt they had been provoked, for Ligeti had scarcely disguised his irritation with the avant-garde, which he now regarded as moribund and 'very boring'. But it was no personal antagonism. He was as tired with his own cluster-textural techniques as with post-Adorno posturing, with the dying convulsions of Fluxus, with the neo-tonal insouciance of his students. The Horn Trio was a calculated counterblast against all these conditions, issued in the belief that every radical stance eventually ossifies, and that true originality proceeds not forwards, but sideways, or zigzag, or even in reverse.

More than anything else, the character of the Horn Trio arose from inner necessity, and from Ligeti's desire to refresh his style from an impeccable, if unfashionable, source. During the late 1970s, he had developed the habit of playing classical and romantic chamber music with students from the Hochschule. Ligeti himself played the piano, making the most of his competent if far from professional ability. Their repertoire consisted of trios, quartets and quintets by Haydn, Mozart, Beethoven, Schubert, Schumann and Brahms (he cites especially the Brahms Piano Trio no. 1, op. 8). The players met at his apartment, never learnt anything up to performance, merely sightreading – but 'it was a joy and a must'. Similarly, for perhaps an hour every day, Ligeti played himself the piano music of Bach, Schumann, Liszt, Rachmaninov, Scriabin, Debussy, Prokofiev and above all Chopin – but also Beethoven, for the late Beethoven string quartets and sonatas were 'my bible . . . well, one of my bibles'. The absence from this repertoire of anything by living composers is revealing. So much time spent working through the eighteenth- and nineteenth-century masters – who were also the subject matter of his lectures – had even delayed his completion of *Le Grand Macabre*. Increasingly, it influenced his creative bent.

In reality, the description 'Hommage à Brahms' was not Ligeti's choice, but a requirement of the Trio's commission. Although Ligeti had agreed to compose something for Barry Tuckwell, and the American pianist Anthony de Bonaventura was eager to commission both the Trio and the Piano Concerto, the request to which Ligeti acceded came from a colleague at the Hamburg Hochschule, Eckart Besch. It was Besch who suggested composing a companion piece to the Brahms Horn Trio, and promised to engage the horn player Hermann Baumann and violinist Saschko Gawriloff (already a friend of Ligeti and subsequent dedicatee of the Violin Concerto) to join him in performing it. Besch also undertook to approach the ZEIT-Foundation in Hamburg to commission the work in honour of the 150th anniversary of the birth of Brahms, who had been born in the city in 1833. Thus it was that the chairman of the foundation asked Ligeti to incorporate themes and melodies from Brahms's own music. Dismayed, Ligeti insisted that he could not accept such terms. But, as a compromise, he would inscribe the score 'Hommage à Brahms'; although it would have been musically more appropriate – and he would have preferred – to write 'Hommage à Beethoven'.

These circumstances might have weighed heavily on the composition. Instead, time has vindicated the Horn Trio, which has proved itself to be a work of distinctive and unique personality – indeed greatness. For all its classical phrase-patterns and symmetries, its sound is utterly unlike Brahms. Ligeti's use throughout of the deflected pitches of 'natural horn' harmonics gives the whole work a rarefied sonority, and turns out to be a step on the road towards their more exotic use in the Violin and *Hamburg* Concertos. All four movements explore technical and expressive areas which would become highly characteristic of late Ligeti: the lean, purgative counterpoint of the first sweeping aside the Augean density of his earlier scores; the second movement's ostinato, rotating like a spindle whilst other melodies hurtle around it; the asymmetrical homophony of the third; the ice-chilled, desolate *lamentoso* music of the last – from these fresh fields springs much of Ligeti's subsequent work. Yet the allusions and semi-quotations, which he had resolved to discard after the opera, still haunt the Trio. Most significantly, given its reinstatement of motivic causality, the Trio is an unashamed inheritor of classical tradition.

Structurally it is an astonishing volte-face. One need take only the first movement with its linear logic, its classically ordered thematic discourse and A–B–A formal symmetry, to find attributes far removed from Ligeti's last completed chamber composition, the String Quartet no. 2. The micropolyphonic mist of earlier works has cleared away; every detail is now audible. Ideas once hovering on the margins of Ligeti's style come centre stage, executing their less familiar routines with dazzling accomplishment. For, despite its change of direction, the Trio is a work of absolute maturity that ushers in an important new era in Ligeti's music. No wonder those who had neatly pigeonholed the composer were taken aback.

Yet in another sense, the Trio resonates with everything else in Ligeti's creative life, since it makes clear for the first time an expressive thread which had been lurking under the surface for many years, and which would increasingly haunt his music during the next two decades. Not until the Trio had this *idée fixe* revealed itself so unmistakably. We have already alluded to its essence: a distinctive three-phrase sequence dis-tilled from a range of lamentations, *adieux* motifs, folk keening, grounds and passacaglias, all of them involving a degree of regret, sorrow, even tragedy – ritualised perhaps – which surfaces occasionally even in his earliest compositions, and is now accepted as their central core.

Personal circumstances

Perhaps it was inevitable that the exuberance of his earlier music, which had marked Ligeti as one of the most playful and flamboyant amongst the avant-garde, should give quarter to a vein of melancholy. By now the avant-garde fraternity had lost its cohesion, bereft by the death of Maderna in 1973 whom Ligeti had so loved and admired. For Ligeti, nevertheless, the 1970s had been a time of contentment. He had entered into a long-term romantic relationship with Aliute Meczies, the German stage designer who created the decor for the world premiere of *Le Grand Macabre* and whom he had met in Darmstadt in 1970 where she was assisting in a production of *Aventures* and *Nouvelles aventures* conducted by Maderna. Vera was inevitably hurt, but had to accept the situation. For a decade Ligeti and Aliute lived together, first in Berlin, then in the apartment where she had her atelier, ten minutes' walk from Ligeti's modest Hamburg flat where he maintained his composing studio and in which he taught his students. Both continued their professional work, Aliute with distinction in many major theatres, including Covent Garden. But in the early 1980s difficulties developed, and Ligeti's decision to detach himself was burdened with guilt. For a while he enjoyed another relationship with a French singer – 'a beautiful time' – but there were pressures from her family that they should marry. Such a commitment, once again, he could not make. In any case he was still married to Vera. Beneath this 'very balanced life' was the reticence he had learnt as a child.

My life's problem, if I go deeper, was perhaps the character of my mother. She was extremely correct. She could be very nice in a formal way, but she had no warm heart – and other ladies had . . . Maybe, therefore, I'm alone now and could not establish a continuous family.[9]

Just as Ligeti was completing the first movement of the Horn Trio, his mother died at the age of eighty-nine. Brahms's mother also died a few months before he began his Horn Trio, and its third movement – perhaps the whole work – is a lament for her. Ligeti and his mother had never been close; but despite her 'coldness', she had been wonderfully helpful at times of difficulty. He was glad she had been able to live her later years in comparative comfort in Vienna. Ligeti himself was nearly sixty, and the tragic legacy of his early life, far from receding now that he was again free to visit Hungary, only increased his bitterness about the lost years under Nazi and Communist oppression, the inhumanity, above all the murder of his brother. Every artist is isolated by destiny and experience. For Ligeti, the *lamento* motif would be the companion of that inner seclusion. Moreover, in its ancestry were the laments performed by paid mourners in the houses of those who had died, which he had heard as a small child in Transylvania.

In 1982 another dilemma presented itself. Ligeti was offered the prestigious position of succeeding Messiaen at the Paris Conservatoire. Mindful of the honour, he took time to think about it. But he feared the bureaucracy, sitting on committees, and French cultural politics. Not wishing to be trapped by responsibilities which would limit his freedom, he refused. Staying in Hamburg had its advantages, although here, too, he had grown somewhat disaffected. The Hochschule had been a good choice in the 1970s. Now, under a new director, he sensed an increased interest in commercial music and less support for his composition classes.

The retrospective style of the Horn Trio

If the Horn Trio is more reflective than earlier Ligeti, we should recognise that – as in Mozart and Beethoven – the emotional quality of a specific composition and the relative contentment or pessimism of its composer do not necessarily coincide. Backward glances were implicit in the Trio's commission. It has a certain empathy with the melancholic nostalgia of Brahms, although in terms of structure its allegiance is more to Beethoven. The music opens with a 'germinal motive', a motto, whose presence is felt in every movement (like Schumann's 'sphinxes' in *Carnaval*), and which consists of an 'altered' version of the 'horn call' motif at the beginning of Beethoven's 'Les Adieux' Piano Sonata op. 81a (see Ex. 21, p. 256). Its significance to Beethoven – an expression of regret at the parting of friends – should not be overlooked, although in neither composer is the treatment programmatic. Why Ligeti felt drawn to it he does not know. His adaption retains Beethoven's first and third intervals, but compresses the second into a tritone, a favourite interval. Beethoven, in his way, 'deflects' the diatonic innocence of the E flat major motif, not by chromaticising it, as Ligeti does, but by cadencing first with a chord of C minor, and a few bars later, with an astonishingly remote C flat major. Already, in Beethoven, this simple 'horn call' is emotively charged. But it is not, of course, actually played on the horn – and nor is Ligeti's motto. To achieve timbral parity between its upper and lower notes, he scores it either for keyboard or for violin in double stops. This two-part counterpoint is reminiscent of the cadential duets in *Melodien*, which *are* played by two horns. Here, in the Trio, the single horn is free to contribute the arching counter-melodies that complement the violin and piano lines.

Ex. 21 Beethoven's 'Les Adieux' motto and Ligeti's adaption of it in the Horn Trio (1982)

The formality of the Trio's first movement is the last thing anybody could have predicted of the composer of *San Francisco Polyphony*, let alone of *Aventures* and *Nouvelles aventures*; but it is not unprecedented. After all, the huge quasi-fugal 'Kyrie' in the Requiem is rigorously structured, as is, more simply, *Musica ricercata*. But, in the Trio, the symmetries are many and far-reaching. Phrases follow each other in the classical manner of 'antecedent and consequent'; a clear example is the very first entry of the horn, but it is a characteristic of the whole movement. Indeed all of the first (and last) third of this movement is classically ordered. It consists of three similar paragraphs, each containing four segments, each segment containing an antecedent and consequent. The segments are all essentially composed in three-part counterpoint, shared between the double-stopped dyads of the violin and the complementary melody of the horn. The fourth segment, however, concludes with the addition of a cadential refrain from the piano – its only contribution – based on the *'adieux'* motto, and which gains one extra chord at each playing. This last segment sounds icily mysterious and is marked *quasi eco*: it requires 'hand-stopped' notes from the horn, and the violin is directed to play *sul tasto* (on the fingerboard), *flautando* (making a flute-like sound).

The structural framework of the Trio's first movement, or at least its two outer parts, therefore has a strikingly precise and disciplined architecture. Within this frame, however, Ligeti's habitual artistry and love of rhythmic fluidity ensures that it never sounds mechanical. In the first paragraph, segments one and two are led by the violin, the third is led by the horn, and in the fourth both enter together. Although this formula similarly underpins paragraphs two and three, the music evolves organically, as one would find in Beethoven. There are exchanges in leadership, and every phrase is purposefully reshaped. Each is unique and has its own contour, sometimes elongated, sometimes compressed.

The final piano refrain, at the end of the third segment, signals the beginning of a more fulsome codetta in which all three instruments play together. This is the end of the first part of the A–B–A ternary structure. There follows a faster 'B' section, homophonic and dance-like, using hemiola rhythms. Its material also derives from the germinal motto and has similar refrains (at the original tempo), based on the horn's 'antecedent–consequent' melody – but now frozen, aphoristic and eerily Webernesque, with luminous high violin harmonics followed by scurrying tremolos played *sul ponticello* (near the bridge). The final 'A' section is an exact reprise of the first – something one would search hard to find anywhere else in Ligeti's music – except that violin and horn are now muted. Throughout this movement the piano plays its two-part counterpoint duplicated in octaves between the hands. This might indicate a rather stark austerity, but in fact Ligeti has chosen every pitch and harmony with the greatest sensitivity, so that the music has a rare and special beauty, in which judiciously placed consonant triads gleam like tiny jewels.

The second movement revisits the repetitive ostinato used in *Hungarian Rock*, which Ligeti would again rework in the fourth of the piano Études (see Ex. 26k, p. 297). Here it is a one-bar unit made from a repeating eight-note scale, comprising two tetrachords a tritone apart. Around this moto perpetuo the instruments develop an astonishing fecundity of ideas, the pace and intricacy of their interplay a constant delight. The idea is simple, the working out inventive. The metre is 3 + 3 + 2 = 8 quavers throughout, an *aksak* ('limping') rhythm as defined by Constantin Brăiloiu and used by Bartók. But the cross-accentuation and non-synchronisation of phrases has players and listeners teasingly on their toes; indeed, the speed of these shifting rhythmic relationships and the sheer athleticism required of the performers presents a formidable challenge to both technical and ensemble precision. The profusion of melodies above the repetitive ostinato derives from Ligeti's new-found interest in Latin American music (stimulated by his Puerto Rican student Roberto Sierra), as well as in Balkan folk musics – traditions quite unlike each other except for their asymmetrical rhythmic formulae. Ostinato apart, there is little symmetry. The form is vaguely ternary, encompassing a middle section in which the ostinato is transposed, and the piano plays a quasi-Bartókian 'chorale'. This chorale (at bar 145) is really a variant of the four-segment sequence in the first movement, similar in harmony, and in that each segment (except the fourth) ends on a first-inversion major triad. It is interesting that each contains a different number of chords, and has its own distinctive shape, features which also connect it to the *lamento* archetype. As in classical style, changes of register have structural import, although they are also used for colouristic atmosphere. A fine instance of the latter occurs at bar 75 where the piano left hand and violin harmonics play together, an elegant yet strange melody, doubled six octaves apart.

The third movement, a March, is also ternary. The contrast between its assertively rhythmic outer sections and the legato, *espressivo con delicatezza* 'trio' is distinctly classical. In form and material, this movement was directly inspired by the second movement, 'Vivace alla Marcia', of another Beethoven piano sonata, op. 101. The first section of Ligeti's movement involves only the violin and piano, and begins like a dislocated parody of the Beethoven. Both play together the same jerky rhythm, as if yoked together in an awkward three-legged race. The violinist plays double stops and the pianist chords; but these are only dyads doubled at the octave (with a few exceptions). The dyads are all either tritones or major thirds and their inversions, the intervals of the original motto. Ligeti's theme has a three-bar rhythmic cycle, but to this he applies a process of phase-shifting – closer to the technique of Steve Reich than anything else in Ligeti – which results in a jagged, swaggering hocket, as violin and piano move out of synchronisation. The 'trio' section reintroduces the horn, and is composed entirely in even, fluid crotchets. Its contrapuntal style and legato phrase structure are classical. But, throughout the movement – as elsewhere – the effect is quirkily original. As in the first movement, the reprise is an exact restatement, except that the horn is added, bell raised, playing highly dramatised variants of its first movement melodies, flamboyantly out of step with the other instruments and using natural untempered overtones.

The emergence of the 'lamento' motif

After such bravura playing, the soft, lean economy of the final 'Lamento' is achingly poignant. Here the Beethovenian motto finds its melancholic heart: the opening dyad is a minor (not a major) third, and the continuation of the melody descends mainly in semitones. In extending the motto, it has become something else. As the violin re-enters at bar 14, we find that Ligeti's lamento archetype, hovering embryonically for years in his music's darker shadows, has at last found its identity: three descending stepwise phrases, the second one note longer than the first, the third longer again, starting a semitone higher and ending lower. Everything else is stripped away in this numbed, icy descent. The opening four bars, containing concords of E minor and then of A flat minor, suggest a mysterious, Renaissance purity, until the harmonies intensify and thicken, and the pace increases. Ligeti's later versions of the lamento motif add a strict durational formula to this characteristic contour (see Ex. 26, pp. 296–97). In this movement, the descending phrases occur in free rhythm at varying speeds, and the music grows surprisingly agitated, passionate and dramatic. The declamatory keening, the asymmetrical counterpoint reaching out to registral extremes and punctuated by clusterous cascades in the piano, coloured by the natural harmonics of the horn – these ingredients unmistakably establish a new musical persona.

The aura of tragic grandeur has the stamp of Beethoven, but its pessimism is Ligeti's – no facile postmodernist breast-beating, but a deepening and darkening of his art which he could not escape.

A Hölderlin fantasy

Despite the months of uncertainty that preceded it, once started, Ligeti composed the Trio at speed. Within days of finishing, he was at work on another composition which he also completed in 1982. This was the *Drei Fantasien nach Friedrich Hölderlin*, three pieces for unaccompanied sixteen-part choir: commissioned from a familiar quarter, Swedish Radio, and first performed on 23 September 1983 by the Swedish Radio Choir under its distinguished conductor Eric Ericson. Interestingly, however, although they have aspects in common, the Horn Trio, the Hölderlin fantasies and *Magyar Etüdök* of the following year pursue essentially different technical processes. As in the 1960s, adjacent compositions take alternative routes through the vortex of ideas coexisting in Ligeti's mind at any one time. A novelty of the Trio had been its replacement of colouristic and textural composition by a linear and motivic causality. Up to a point, Ligeti felt that this had been 'a detour' – if a necessary one – and that the polymetric explorations in *Monument–Selbstportrait–Bewegung* of 1976 and the piano Études of 1985 belonged to the 'main road'. Certainly there is no classical dialectic in the Hölderlin fantasies, which are impulsive, onomatopoeic, expressionist compositions, much closer to the style of *Atmosphères* and the String Quartet no. 2. By contrast again, in *Magyar Etüdök* Ligeti adopts a 'constructivist' approach to match the light-hearted experimental inventiveness of Sándor Weöres's epigrammatic poems.

The Hölderlin fantasies were Ligeti's first settings of pre-existing poetry since before he left Hungary. The choice of texts by the unhappy and isolated Friedrich Hölderlin (1770–1843), an exact contemporary of Beethoven and spiritual counterpart of Schumann (who, like Hölderlin, was afflicted with insanity), seems to reinforce the emotional aesthetic of the Horn Trio, providing confirmation of that work's introspection. From Hölderlin, Ligeti chose and skilfully abridged three unconnected poems, as if they belonged to a cycle. A stanza from the first poem heads this chapter. All of them explore that painful discrepancy between the ideal and the real, between a treasured past and a bleak present. They tell of growing old, of separation, of the cold winter, but also of a golden spring in which the pantheist poet hopes to find 'roses without number, purple clouds, light and air in which love and sorrow vanish' – a longing for serenity and peace.

Placing to one side the quasi-classical constructs he had adopted in the Horn Trio, for *Drei Phantasien* Ligeti writes music that is vivid and intuitive, not merely reflecting, but amplifying the nuances in the text. Micropolyphonic canons weave dense chromatic clouds through all its three movements, solidifying in powerful rhythmic unisons declaimed by the majority of the voices, all in their highest ranges. Extreme contrasts of dynamic and register contribute to an intensely dramatic emotional climate, whose sixteen-part texture and highly charged chromaticism have their roots in early twentieth-century Expressionism. Truth strikes home through the chilling impact of stark open fifths sung *tutta la forza*. Elsewhere, the drifting harmonies, reminiscent of *Lontano*, are tinged with regret. But they embody also a pictorial and metaphysical vision. In discussing the Hölderlin fantasies, as with *Lontano* Ligeti cited the influence of a 'favourite' painting: Altdorfer's *The Battle of Alexander*, which he had first seen in his father's art books – a vast landscape of immense turbulence and grandeur, its golden sunbeams breaking through blue-grey storm clouds.

Syntactical experiments

The playful side of Ligeti's nature, never long absent, reappears in *Magyar Etüdök (Hungarian Studies)*, composed immediately after *Drei Phantasien* for Clytus Gottwald and his Schola Cantorum of Stuttgart. Gottwald had devised a celebratory concert held on 18 May 1983, just before Ligeti's sixtieth birthday. Pierre Boulez was engaged to conduct the Stuttgart Radio Symphony Orchestra in *Ramifications* and the Chamber Concerto. Saschko Gawriloff, Hermann Baumann and Eckart Besch performed the Horn Trio; Elisabeth Chojnacka played *Passacaglia ungherese* and *Hungarian Rock*; and Mauricio Kagel composed a three-minute special birthday tribute, an *Intermezzo* for soprano, chorus and instruments. The *Magyar Etüdök* were intended to grace this occasion; but Ligeti had completed only two of them, and the third was premiered later that year at the Rencontres Internationales de Musique Contemporaine in Metz.

For these texts, Ligeti returned to the work of his old friend, Sándor Weöres, which he had last set in *Éjszaka* and *Reggel*, the two short choral pieces he completed a year before leaving Hungary. Weöres's collection of more than a hundred poems is also called *Magyar Etüdök*. Many of them describe commonplace events, but use idiosyncrasies of rhythm, rhyming and connotation, dependent more upon linguistic artifice than semantic meaning. Much as Ligeti dresses the harpsichord pieces in synthetic styles, Weöres had created 'fake' poetry and cultures, as if in some bogus Indonesian or Pacific tongue. He had invented an erotic eighteenth-century lady poet complete with biography, writing a fictitious book of her poems in the language of her time. Ligeti wanted to convey the 'humouristic, sometimes crazy, experimental stance' of this fundamentally abstract art in his musical construction. As a result, the *Magyar Etüdök* are more exploratory than either *Drei Phantasien* or the Trio, although in all three works there is a vein of nostalgia. Ligeti had just travelled again to Hungary where, on 20 March 1983, during the Budapest Spring Festival, *Clocks and Clouds*, the Cello Concerto and the Requiem were performed. It was fitting that Clytus Gottwald should add to his birthday programme for Stuttgart the first performance in the West of *Magány*, Ligeti's earliest setting of Weöres, which he had composed whilst a student at the Franz Liszt Academy in 1946. Ligeti himself had sung in the original performance, and this was his first chance properly to hear the piece. Also that year (1983), he heard the Cello Sonata for the first time, played in Paris by Manfred Stilz. By now the String Quartet no. 1 was being performed with some regularity. A dismissive view of his early works was neither necessary nor justified. He had found a new affection for them and their stylistic roots. As he began another Weöres composition, he relished the prospect of setting Hungarian again. He had found little chance to use the language for over a quarter of a century, but it still held for him a uniquely musical *animus*.

Folk tradition is clearly audible in the second of the *Magyar Etüdök*, and even more in the third, with its street-vendor cries. The first is more abstract. Here Ligeti combines his canonic aptitude and interest in polymetre. The text in this movement (Étude 9) describes an icicle thawing, dripping intermittently, then more rapidly until it becomes a puddle 'knocking at the door'. Ligeti writes a mensural mirror canon, its theme replicated exactly, in pitch and rhythm, for each of the twelve voices. The starting pitches of their entries cover all twelve notes of the chromatic scale. But the music is colouristic as well as rigorous. The first notes of the theme are just tiny droplets of sound, separated by long rests, to depict the words 'csipp' and 'csepp' ('drip' and 'drop'). Choir I articulates the canon in 6/4 (six crotchets to the bar), Choir II in 2/2 (four slower crotchets to the bar), the uneven interaction of these duple and compound metres a technique reminiscent of the opening of *Monument*. The entries are arranged so that each new statement of the canon begins on the next step of a rising whole-tone scale beginning on D flat; whilst entries of the inversion, the 'mirror', occur on successive steps of the complementary descending whole-tone scale starting on D. Thus the contrary-motion expansion grows from a narrow pitch band, in the opening bars, to chromatic 'saturation'. It is a commonplace Ligeti process, but in this instance, an apt representation of the text.

The virtually 'automatic', mechanistic technique of this first piece is relaxed in the second, a more madrigalesque composition in sixteen parts using echo effects and a variety of impressionistic textures. Ligeti combines two short poems (Études 40 and 49), both alluding to frogs, whose croaking 'Brekekex, brekekex, brekekex', maintains an amusing counterpoint against the 'bim-bam' chiming of a village bell. From a technical standpoint, the third composition (setting Étude 90) is the most experimental, although its simultaneous counterpoint of five muscle-flexing melodies, each in its own tempo and metre, and several times repeated, recalls the *Polyphonic Study* from as far back as 1943. These encircling entities (sung by five groups placed around the audience), each repeated without transposition, development or variation, recycle in a similar manner to the modules of Ligeti's student piece. But now he takes the logical step of discarding metrical synchronisation – up to a point. The parts still must end together; their individual tempi all relate to the alto part, and must not deviate so far as to jeopardise harmonic coherence. Nevertheless, this somewhat anarchic and Ivesian picture of a noisy fairground delightfully conveys the market bustle described by the poet. For these texts Ligeti extracts five stanzas from a longer poem, each with a different structure and metre. His choice of texts in *Magyar Etüdök* as a whole is highly selective, and the result too succinct and laconic to convey Weöres's real breadth and stature. Ligeti would do him better justice seventeen years later.

Beginning the piano Études

After the first performance of the completed *Magyar Etüdök* on 8 November 1984, Ligeti released nothing else for another two years.

Ex. 22 First sketch for the piano Études (November 1984)

But he was not idle. Three days later he began to sketch the piano Études. A single sheet, dated 11 November, is headed Étude 1 and contains three projected titles: *Hemiolák*, *Noir et Blanc*, and *Pulsation*. None of these titles survived (neither for this nor any of the studies), his eventual choice for the first being *Désordre*. But the idea of using white notes in the right hand and black in the left, with metrically opposed melodies enclosing a central core of polytonal quavers, is clearly established in this first sketch, as it is fundamental to the finished study. Soon afterwards he wrote a slightly different draft, this time headed 'Étude de Septimes (en blanc et noir)' in pencil, and 'Trois Études polymétriques' in red. On 31 December he sketched a third version, now labelled 'PULSATION 7/5 (BLANC/NOIR), Étude polyrithmique I pour Pierre Boulez', jotting beside the title the digits 15, 5, 10, 10, 5. More sketches followed, as Ligeti tried to refine the relationship between their polymetric layers, and before he thought up the disintegrative formal process that led to the final title *Désordre*. By the end of 1985 he had completed not three, but six studies. Ideas were coming so fast that he began to plan a second set. Fifteen years later, the initial three polymetric studies had grown into three books of studies, by now a huge and comprehensive exploration of pianistic and compositional ideas uniting the preoccupations of a lifetime.

12

The Dynamics of Disorder

The making of almost any art involves looting. People often
say this is just plagiarism. Well, it's only plagiarism if, in fact,
you loot very large configurations and claim them to be your
own. It becomes art when you take components and then
recompose them into new configurations; and I think a great
deal of the history of art is the history of looting and reconstruction from the debris of the past.
 Jonathan Miller[1]

One often arrives at something qualitively new by uniting
two already known but separate domains.
 György Ligeti[2]

Although to the outside world, during much of the early 1980s, Ligeti
must have seemed tantalisingly unproductive, in the workshop of his
mind he was gathering the materials for a series of compositions based
substantially upon new premises. Old enthusiasms and recent discoveries combined to unleash a flood of composition, of which the first
result was music for piano: not yet the Piano Concerto – still a stum-
bling block – but in the infinitely pliable and variable genre of the
piano étude. The great series of piano études of the nineteenth and
early twentieth century had not been much replicated – except in the
mid-century by Messiaen and Stockhausen. Yet the solo study was an
ideal medium in which to carry forward the polymetric explorations
which Ligeti had made in *Monument–Selbstportrait–Bewegung*. He
considered the opera with its stylistic caricature, and the Horn Trio
with its classical references, to have been something of a diversion. It
is the first book of piano Études, completed in 1985, followed by his
hard-won completion of the Piano Concerto in 1988, that renews his
polyrhythmic, polytonal and ethnic explorations, the fruits of which
he has harvested right through to the *Hamburg Concerto* and Weöres
song cycle composed near the end of the century.

The most productive of these fresh stimuli was Ligeti's discovery of the player piano studies by Conlon Nancarrow. Hardly less influential was his encounter with the music of Central Africa – symptomatic of a lifelong interest in ethnic musical cultures – and with the computer-generated fractal images created by Heinz-Otto Peitgen and Peter Richter in Bremen. Amongst old enthusiasms, lines of continuity run through all of Ligeti's career; or they disappear and then resurface. One about to gain new impetus was his love of non-Western temperaments. Another was a deep interest in the music of the fourteenth century, especially the work of composers like Machaut and Ciconia, and the rhythmically complex *ars subtilior*.

In the years since Ligeti had studied medieval and Renaissance polyphony as a student, much more had been published. Willi Apel's editions of fourteenth-century French secular music were pored over by Ligeti as by others. Metrically barred, with clear if alien modern time signatures, they highlighted the way in which simultaneously conflicting, and frequently changing, metres appeared soon after the very invention of mensuration signs in the fourteenth century; and how, combined with extensive syncopation and virtuoso canonic writing, they led to the 'crazy subdivisions' – as Ligeti describes them – of such late *ars subtilior* composers as Senleches and Rodericus. The extreme rhythmic intricacy of this highly mannered music virtually disappeared until the twentieth century. If it had little immediate influence, for composers half a millennium later it became a revelation and a licence. It was as crucial for Ligeti's new metrical thinking as his discovery of Nancarrow and Central African music. Meanwhile, the work of Hofstadter, of writers like Kafka, Borges and Vian, of the art historian Ernst Gombrich, of the molecular biologist Jacques Monod, physical chemist Manfred Eigen and other prominent scientists, continued to absorb him. All in all, Ligeti's many obsessions of the 1980s, both musical and extra-musical, had the effect of revitalising his whole technical, aesthetic and intellectual resource-base.

Nancarrow

Conlon Nancarrow (1912–97) is now revered amongst twentieth-century originals. But for many years his work was known only to a few North American composers, and promoted by scarcely anyone other than John Cage, who in 1960 persuaded Merce Cunningham to choreograph some of Nancarrow's early studies. Even in the 1970s reference books on contemporary composers made no mention of Nancarrow. Only in the mid-1980s did awareness of this reclusive composer spread, assisted by the gradual publication of selected studies in Peter Garland's journal *Soundings*,[3] by the emergence of recordings, by apologists like the American composer-analyst James Tenney – and by Ligeti's enthusiastic advocacy.

Nancarrow had been a wayward radical since his youth. Removing himself from school, although he submitted to some formal conservatoire education, he inclined more to jazz (he played the trumpet) and left-wing politics. In 1937 he joined the Republicans in the Spanish Civil War, was wounded, contracted hepatitis and eventually made a hazardous escape hidden in a ship's cargo and then over the mountains to France. Back in New York he contributed to the influential journal *Modern Music*, and was friendly with Aaron Copland and Elliott Carter. Disillusioned with his own musical prospects, by a hardening of anti-Communist intolerance and by the FBI's refusal to allow him a passport, he decided to emigrate to Mexico City. There he made a short-lived second marriage and, through his artist wife, engaged the muralist Juan O'Gorman to design a modernist villa, complete with soundproof studio-cum-laboratory in which he composed.

Already in the 1930s he had experimented with mechanical means in the pursuit of speed. In 1947 he spent a modest legacy on the purchase of a player piano, adapting it to his purpose by making the key mechanism more dynamic and adding steel tacks. In composing for it, Nancarrow wrote initially on manuscript paper, then punched holes himself in the long piano rolls, a hugely laborious task since even a single mistake meant that one had to start all over again. To produce seven minutes of music could take eighteen months. But the results were astonishing. Mechanical reproduction allowed Nancarrow to achieve feats of polyrhythmic velocity which no human performer could attempt – certainly not at that time. In an extraordinary series of futuristic studies, composed mainly between 1950 and 1968, he combines the canonic contrapuntal style of Bach, ragtime and boogie-woogie, Latin American rhythms and complex abstract mathematical relationships (one study is based on the square root of 47!), in music so fast that it could deliver as many as one hundred and seventy notes per second. Nancarrow never learnt to play the piano himself. Early commentators thought the zany impetuousness of these studies too mechanistic and inhuman – like the soundtrack of *Tom and Jerry* cartoons. For Ligeti, this only increased their attraction. Above all, he was astonished by the polyrhythmic counterpoint of the later studies with their syncopated, asymmetrical lines which simultaneously accelerate and slow down.

Ligeti learnt of Nancarrow's existence only in 1980, through a catalogue of mechanical instruments written by the Berlin art curator and Fluxus advocate René Block, who had met Nancarrow in Mexico City two years earlier.[4] A page of Nancarrow's notation, reproduced in Block's article, caught Ligeti's attention and he immediately realised that he had found 'something wonderful'. Half a year later he came across two LP recordings in a Paris store, purchased them and was fascinated. In January 1981 he wrote to the American composer and radio producer Charles Amirkhanian: 'this music is the greatest discovery since Webern and Ives . . . something great and important for all music history. His music is so utterly original, enjoyable, perfectly constructed, but at the same time emotional . . . for me it's the best music of any composer living today.'[5] The following year Ligeti persuaded Musikprotokoll in Graz, host of that year's ISCM festival, to honour Nancarrow's seventieth birthday by inviting the composer. There was no player piano available, but Nancarrow arrived with tapes and a slide/recording show compiled by Eva Soltes, a performing arts producer who had secured Nancarrow his visa. In Graz, for the first time, Nancarrow and Ligeti met, after which Ligeti accompanied Soltes, Nancarrow and his family on further visits to Innsbruck, to IRCAM (at the invitation of Boulez) and to Cologne.

Here they met Jürgen Hocker, a German chemist and player piano enthusiast. Hocker promised to hunt down an instrument capable of performing Nancarrow's work, eventually locating an Ampico-Bösendorfer grand player piano in Belgium which, after two years of restoration, made its debut in Amsterdam in 1987, in performances of Nancarrow's original piano rolls given with the composer's assistance. A year later, West German Radio mounted a Nancarrow–Ligeti presentation in Cologne called 'Music and Machine'. Meanwhile, Ligeti had been active in persuading the MacArthur Foundation to award Nancarrow its prestigious 'genius' award, a five-year stipend amounting to $300,000, and by now Nancarrow's music had begun to generate interest amongst many other composers and critics.

Other cultures, other musics – Ligeti and his students

Ligeti's admiration for the Nancarrow studies encouraged him to consider ways in which a living interpreter might handle such complex rhythms. It was a question shared with his Hamburg students, amongst whom were young composers from around the world – their knowledge and enthusiasms a refreshing stimulus, even if the neo-Romantic tendencies of some were a cause for dismay. During the 1970s, German composers had formed the majority, like Hans-Christian von Dadelsen, Detlev Müller-Siemens (both neo-tonalists) and Wolfgang von Schweinitz; but later the mix grew more international including Kiyoshi Furukawa from Japan and Unsuk Chin from Korea. In Ligeti's estimation, the most interesting were the English composer Benedict Mason, a French-Canadian, Denys Bouliane, a 'crazy but gifted' Argentinian, Silvia Fómina, and two whose knowledge of non-Western music – as we have seen – greatly assisted him: Roberto Sierra from Puerto Rico, and the German composer Manfred Stahnke. Others, like Hans Abrahamsen from Denmark, were not officially enrolled, but regularly attended the gatherings at Ligeti's apartment.

In Stockholm, where Ligeti had taken over the existing syllabus from Karl-Birger Blomdahl whilst the latter was on a sabbatical, he had adopted the teaching manuals by Jeppesen and Hindemith already in use. Once established in Hamburg, however, his attitude gradually changed. To deliver the counterpoint course he was entitled to an assistant; but he never got one, so in his early years at the Musikhochschule, Ligeti himself ran a class in rigorous Bachian counterpoint. Later, he handed this over to an ex-student, Wolfgang-Andras Schultz, whom he had 'tortured with inventions and fugues for two years', so that Ligeti could devote his time to free-composition seminars.

Concluding that creativity cannot be taught, and not wishing to interfere in his students' stylistic choices, he set no exercises and gave no individual lessons, instead presiding over what were effectively masterclasses in which he and his students met together to play through and discuss their work. Ligeti would focus especially on orchestration, but discussion was uninhibited and wide-ranging. The seminars often expanded into whole days, after which all would repair to a café. At first Ligeti taught at the Hochschule, but after it moved into a building with less satisfactory soundproofing, he held the classes in his apartment. For seventeen years during term times in Hamburg, unless he was away, he delivered a four-hour analysis lecture every week. Only in the year before he retired did Ligeti focus extensively on his own music. Nor did he dwell on twentieth-century music any later than Webern and Stravinsky. Berlioz, Wagner, Bruckner, Debussy and Strauss were explored for their mastery of tex-tural colour, and a whole year was devoted to the late sonatas and quartets of Beethoven. He spent half a year on *The Rite of Spring* and a further semester on the '*lamento*-bass', drawing on examples from Purcell and the Baroque. This was in the late 1970s and undoubtedly bred ideas for the Horn Trio.

He had an insatiable appetite for such investigation and took his teaching responsibilities seriously. Each semester he chose another theme. Later, standards at the Musikhochschule appeared to him to have declined and his classes were combined with those at the University. In the final decade, he gave his lectures in tandem with con-tributors from other faculties so that they were, in his words, 'quite interesting . . . full not only with musicians'. They had become a veri-table Hamburg institution and had to be held in large lecture halls.

In the early days, Ligeti's scepticism about the 'retro' tendencies of his German students led to heated discussions, symptomatic of wider divisions between the arid legacy (as he saw it) of the avant-garde, the growth of 'pure' minimalism into a more general quasi-tonal post-modernism, and a developing interaction between global musical cultures. Roberto Sierra inundated the class with recordings of music from the Caribbean, Africa and elsewhere. Ligeti had become interested in ethnic music even before he studied Romanian folklore as a student. In the 1970s he started collecting records of South-East Asian music – a special hobby. He also listened to many examples of the Brazilian samba and was reasonably familiar with Caribbean music. But Sierra possessed recordings not easily obtainable in Europe, so that the weekly meetings became a virtual world music exchange. There was salsa, for instance, forged in New York out of the encounter of Puerto Rican and Cuban music with big-band jazz; whilst Sierra's records of the Banda-Linda tribe from the Central African Republic were not only completely new to Ligeti: from a compositional standpoint they were astonishing. Here was a complex polyrhythmic music produced by a pipe 'orchestra' of around eighteen instrumentalists, to which each player contributed just one or, at the most, two pitches, skilfully dovetailing his own unique rhythmic pattern into the totality of the whole. Ligeti was struck by the similarity of the process to late Medieval European 'hocket', Machaut's *Hoquetus David* being an eponymous (if simpler) example.

The little-known and relatively inaccessible music from Central Africa had been investigated by an Israeli ethnomusicologist, Simha Arom. To notate its repertoire, Arom had the ingenious idea of recording the full ensemble, then playing the tape on headphones to each instrumentalist in turn. Each would perform (and Arom record) his part in reference to the whole, for only in this way could he play his part in isolation. It was Simha Arom's recording of Banda polyphony that Sierra played to Ligeti in Hamburg.[6] Two years later, on a visit to Jerusalem in the spring of 1984, Ligeti happened to meet Arom, who showed him his written transcriptions in score, whilst Ligeti undertook to write a preface for the English-language edition of the book on African polyphony and polyrhythm that Arom was preparing for publication.[7] In his introduction Ligeti describes the 'paradoxical nature' of the Banda-Linda music, and how, through repeated listening, he had been struck by the way

. . . patterns performed by the individual musicians are quite different from those which result from their combination. In fact, the ensemble's super-pattern is in itself not played and exists only as an illusory outline. I also began to sense a strong inner tension between the relentlessness of the constant, never-changing pulse coupled with the absolute symmetry of the formal architecture on the one hand and the asymmetrical internal divisions of the patterns on the other. What we can witness in this music is a wonderful combination of order and disorder which in turn merges together producing a sense of order on a higher level.[8]

Fractal mathematics

Order and disorder had acquired a new topicality in the early 1980s. Ligeti had long deemed disorder to be an inevitable attribute of life, and therefore of art. But its serious scientific investigation had begun quite recently. Ligeti has always valued the work of experts in other fields: in the non-musical arts, and especially in the natural sciences in which he had once intended to pursue his own career. In 1984 – the year that he met Simha Arom – his friend Manfred Eigen, who twenty years before had shared the Nobel Prize for his study of high-speed chemical reactions, showed Ligeti some of the computer-generated fractal pictures created by Heinz-Otto Peitgen and his colleagues at the University of Bremen. The illustrations were contained in catalogues of their exhibitions, since Peitgen and Richter's elegant book *The Beauty of Fractals* was yet to be published.[9] Fractals, however, were already evoking widespread interest, in part, because they appeared to reinstate a poetic and visionary dimension to science, which had been largely absent from the objective rationalism of Newtonian physics. Ligeti was one amongst many creative artists to be inspired by the intricacy of these strange images, and intrigued by the mathematical principles behind them. Typically, however, he entered keenly into the detail of their physical properties and potential relevance to music. As a result, chaos theory, as the new science of non-linear dynamical systems is popularly called, provides a procedural model for the first of the piano Études – *Désordre* – and underpins several of the others.

The study of non-linear dynamics took off in America and elsewhere in the 1970s and quickly spread into many areas of scientific theory. Put simply, Newtonian physics dealt with things which could be precisely measured and predicted (e.g. mechanical forces, the behaviour of the solar system), but viewed as aberrant and marginal those which could not. Modern mathematics has sought to explain these volatile, non-deterministic systems. Impelled by the urgency of understanding apparently random phenomena – like the weather, turbulence, population growth, money markets, the behaviour of gases and fluids – scientists have sought to find coherence within confusion, recognising that the precarious balance between order and disorder in an evolving organism is hugely affected by minute discrepancies in the initial conditions. Through the 'amplification of error', hidden variables give rise to dramatically different results; simple systems quickly become complex. Tiny imperfections within a linear process destabilise it, cause it to oscillate, bifurcate, branch out through successive 'period doublings' into an accelerating state of chaos. Water flowing past an obstacle, or a plume of cigarette smoke rising from an ashtray, show visibly how turbulence develops – although the outcome is neither easy to define nor precisely predictable. As the British mathematician Ian Stewart maintains,

Chaotic behaviour obeys deterministic laws, but it is so irregular to an untrained eye that it looks pretty much random . . . Chaos is apparently complicated, apparently patternless behaviour that actually has a simple, deterministic explanation . . . Chaos is a cryptic form of order.[10]

Similar principles of branching gives rise to fractals, first so named by the Polish-born mathematician Benoit Mandelbrot, whose book *The Fractal Geometry of Nature*[11] elegantly demonstrates their essential attributes of iteration and scaling – and their aesthetic appeal. Fractal patterns repeat themselves at ever-decreasing sizes, like nesting Russian dolls, or as the overall form of a cauliflower is replicated in its smallest florets. Such self-similarity, says Mandelbrot, is as appealing in art as it is a perennial concept in nature.

Ligeti read Mandelbrot's seminal book in 1985 and the following year they met in Bremen. Around the same time, Peter Richter telephoned Ligeti suggesting that they should be in touch, having been recommended to do so by John Chowning in Stanford, to whom Ligeti had reported his interest. Ligeti invited Richter to lecture to his composition class at the Musikhochschule, where he demonstrated non-linear systems using physical experiments. After Ligeti also met Heinz-Otto Peitgen, there followed several collaborative presentations between Ligeti and the Bremen mathematicians – usually with Peitgen. At a mathematical congress in Bad Neuenahr, Ligeti and Mandelbrot both lectured. Ligeti analysed *Désordre* – 'for mathematicians' – plus the 'Kyrie' of the Requiem: 'my pre-fractal, unconscious kind of fractal (in voice-leading, structure and texture) in which everything is not quite the same, but it is similar.' A decade later, in 1996, the issues were still alive. In March that year, the Festival Archipel in Geneva and Grame/Musiques en Scène of Lyons organised a two-stage conference in both cities, called 'Fractals and Music' and 'Music and Mathematics'. Amongst a number of mainly French speakers, Ligeti and Mandelbrot were cast as principals, took centre stage in round-table discussions, and between them gave four lectures. The special synergy of these encounters is recorded in an affectionate sketch written by Peitgen for the composer's seventy-fifth birthday:

At our first meeting in Bremen it is raining cats and dogs. He opens a beautiful Old English umbrella, which doesn't fit at all with his decidedly casual clothes. I steal an admiring glance and comment on the precious object, and it immediately becomes mine. The obvious joy he derives from this gesture sets the tone for two unforgettable days which culminate in a wonderful concert for the television channel 3sat.

His letters have anticipated the new email style: postcards or simple white sheets of paper without heading, often every square centimetre used. No introduction, no formal ending, just a few highly condensed thoughts, extremely efficient and focused. No waste of time and energy on unimportant ornaments or accessories: pure communication.

Our discussions are debates, which flow unrestricted, becoming journeys of discovery that demand the highest level of concentration. No mental leap is too daring – and questions, questions, questions . . . Infinite curiosity, supported by the most rigorous intellectual yet unconventional observation. A Lichtenbergian[12] whose breathtaking fantasy allows us researchers to quench his thirst for knowledge.[13]

Only in the fourth movement of the Piano Concerto has Ligeti attempted to structure music directly in imitation of fractal iteration on a diminishing scale. But the processes of deformation and divergence which occur in many of the piano Études are clearly influenced by the broader domain of chaos theory. The new science gave currency to attributes which already existed in his music. Ligeti himself has cited the Requiem. *Ramifications* deals in bifurcation and branching. 'Phasing' – as it occurs in *Monument–Selbstportrait–Bewegung*, or the third movement of the Horn Trio – is bifurcation of a sort. In a completely different manner (since they are certainly not fractal) the dislocated anti-logic of *Aventures* and *Nouvelles aventures* teeters on the verge of anarchy.

Music is a transient art, unfolding as a process in which order and instability are ever-present opposites. Contemporary science provides apposite models for contemporary musical structure, whereas earlier composers looked to landscape, and to real and fictional heroes for inspiration. Ligeti's fascination with such things as the 'plasticine geometry' of topology continues a metaphorical view of music evident throughout his working life and deeply embedded in the art form. Analogy is also a tool of science. In the words of Jonathan Miller, continuing the quotation at the head of this chapter, 'Creative scientific thinking, indeed creative thought in the arts as well, has been dictated by metaphors. Metaphorical devices set you thinking about what you ought to be looking for.'

Aspects of ambiguity: a labyrinth of improbabilities

Metaphor, conceived in terms of the most elaborate and extravagant fantasy, provided the Argentinian writer Jorge Luis Borges (1899–1986) with the basis of his short stories. Ligeti was predictably attracted to this remarkable author, whom he began to read in the late 1950s. For Borges, every story was a conceit, an illusion: his narratives appear, in their first paragraphs, to be so precise and logical, that they seem entirely probable, until pushed to an extreme where reasonable propositions become patently absurd. His satirical wit and philosophical playfulness find a sympathetic spirit in Ligeti. Scornful of filling five hundred pages with what can be said in a few, Borges never wrote a novel. Ligeti, too, has preferred short forms. In concision, dexterity, ingenuity, and in their paradoxical vision, Borges, Ligeti and Escher are curiously alike. Borges's *Collected Fictions*, Ligeti's piano studies and Escher's metamorphoses all explore aspects of ambiguity, but in different art forms. In each of the stories, as in each piano study and each engraving, author/composer/artist execute some technical sleight-of-hand: whether depicting a library so vast that it contains all the books which have not been written as well as those which have ('The Library of Babel'), or by creating an illusion of untempered harmony on the tempered keyboard (*Galamb borong*), or of water ascending a watercourse that is simultaneously flowing down (*Waterfall*). Borges's 'The Lottery in Babylon'[14] describes a utopia in which chance becomes the only organising principle, with incalculable consequences: 'fortunate' play may result in elevation to high office, 'unfortunate' in imprisonment or death. In 'The Lottery in Babylon' Borges refers to the parable of Achilles and the tortoise, which teaches us that time is infinitely subdivisible. Ligeti was as aware of its link with Lewis Carroll's imaginary dialogue 'What the Tortoise Said to Achilles' – published in 1895,[15] giving Zeno's paradox an extra twist – as of the contemporary conundrums posed by computer science and set theory. All of these in different ways confront the limits of logic and intuition. How far can one pursue a paradoxical proposition, a contradictory inference, a recursive musical formula?

Ligeti had touched upon such questions as far back as *Musica ricercata*. Now he would address them again – drawing on a vast reservoir of acquired knowledge – and on a grand scale.

13

The Piano Études

It's no wonder that chaos theory appeals to musicians.
The interplay between pattern and disorder is one of music's
central and sublime mysteries.
  Jon Pareles[1]

In my music one finds neither that which one might call
'scientific' nor the 'mathematical', but rather a unification of
construction with poetic, emotional imagination.
  György Ligeti[2]

The piano Études now number eighteen compositions spanning seventeen years. Into them Ligeti has poured forty years of experience, and his new technical ideas and conceptual vision. At the time Book 1 was published in 1985 he planned to complete two books, each containing six pieces, perhaps following the example of Debussy's two books of twelve Préludes and two books of three *Images*. But inventing them grew addictive. To the second volume he added two extra pieces, and then began a third set on which he is still working. Performed together in one concert the Études make a splendidly varied sequence: breathtakingly virtuoso, tender, playful, sorrowful, ingenious, monumental in turn – or all at once.

A wide range of intellectual stimuli went into their composition. But they equally owe their character to something more mundane: Ligeti's fingers. During the previous decade he had habitually played piano music, either classical chamber music with students from the Hochschule, or solo repertoire to himself. This almost daily contact with the keyboard triggered his own creative ideas, just as J. S. Bach used to play other composers' music as a prelude to writing his own. Why, then, had he written nothing for solo piano in the preceding thirty years? At first, of course, because he had no piano. Subsequently, because he had other commissions – which as it happens did embrace the piano, both in *Monument–Selbstportrait–Bewegung* and the Horn

Trio. Perhaps it needed the wider stylistic changes of the 1980s, his more determined independence from the avant-garde and personal reconnection with tradition, to make it possible. Thereafter, the muscular impetus of actually playing became a catalyst:

I lay my ten fingers on the keyboard and imagine music. My fingers copy this mental image as I press the keys, but this copy is very inexact: a feedback emerges between ideas and tactile/motor execution. This feedback loop repeats itself many times, enriched by provisional sketches: a mill wheel turns between my inner ear, my fingers and the marks on the paper. The result sounds completely different from my initial conceptions: the anatomical reality of my hands and the configuration of the piano keyboard have transformed my imaginary constructs . . . The criteria are only partly determined in my imagination; to some extent they also lie in the nature of the piano – I have to feel them out with my hand . . . A well-formed piano work produces physical pleasure.[3]

Apart from the influences of Nancarrow, Central African polyphony, the new mathematics and the old *ars subtilior*, the Études reflect Ligeti's fascination with puzzles, paradoxes and illusion, with turning the ancient art of *trompe l'œil* into *trompe l'oreille*. Polymetre and cross-accentuation are combined to produce secondary-level accents – 'supersignals' he calls them – like holographic images projected three-dimensionally above a two-dimensional plane. Rhythmic and metrical exploration is at the heart of all the studies. Many of them feature the *aksak* juxtaposition of two and three that occurs from early dance to present-day folk music. In Ligeti these relationships are generally more complex – three to five, to seven, to eleven or more – and use prime numbers for the sake of asymmetry. Bar lines almost never imply accents.

To this rhythmic vitality is allied the development of Ligeti's harmonic language. Some of the Études – *Automne à Varsovie* and *Vertige* for example – are more chromatically saturated than anything else in his music. A quite different effect is produced by the simultaneous use of complementary scales in *Désordre*, *Galamb borong*, *En Suspens* and *Entrelacs*. Elsewhere, following the precedent of the Passacaglia in *Le Grand Macabre*, he writes bar after bar of consonant triads and strophic melody (e.g. *Fanfares*), but in contexts so tonally ambiguous that the music sounds novel and exotic. Illusions of temperaments and temporality occur together. Although some of Ligeti's initial ideas appear disarmingly simple, the impression is soon dispelled. His simultaneous working out of different mechanisms and sheer plurality of vision take innocent and unsuspecting material into astonishingly remote areas. The result is music of Lisztian dimensions: volcanic, expansive, dazzling – and obsessive.

Sketches and titles

Amongst the large quantity of Ligeti's manuscripts, preliminary working notes, documents and memorabilia transferred to the Paul Sacher Foundation in Basle at the end of 2000 are three folders of sketches for the Études, plus piles of verbal notes, lists of titles and ideas, written on anything that was to hand, from the smallest slip of paper to large sheets. It is immediately evident that titles and musical ideas associated and reassociated themselves so freely in Ligeti's mind – changing partners, changing order – that the published sequence was only one possible way in which this profusion could be connected. Some concepts are relatively resilient; the 'Warsaw' study is one. Begun on 11 June 1985, and soon to be named *Automne à Varsovie*, Ligeti knew that it would reflect the political plight of Poland and that it would have a Chopinesque character. He did not yet know how it would begin, nor that it would be a vehicle for an outpouring of the *lamento* motif, nor that it would become the final Étude in Book 1. After a few false starts, however, all these attributes came quickly. Other titles, like *Clair-Obscur* and *Noir et Blanc* (a provisional title for the very first Étude), dally with various partners in successive sketches, never effecting marriage, never sufficiently groomed for performance, before being honourably retired into the vaults in Basle.

Often Ligeti decides on the title only after writing the music. On other occasions titles occur to him before he has written a note. The list of titles that have not yet been used for finished pieces is extensive and multi-lingual. It includes, in French: *Irisation, Luminosité, Éclairage, Densité, Quintes, Obstiné, Vexation, Nocturne mécanique, Caméléon, Changeant, Gymel, Métamorphose, Melancolia, L'Orient imaginaire, Signales dans la brume, L'âge d'or, Le paradis, Bartoque, Faux pas?, Demi-dormant, Joie et Lamentobass*; in English: *Obstacle Course, White Mechanism, Inherent Patterns, Jungle, Twilight, Sea Change* and *The isle is full of noises, sounds and sweet airs*; and in Hungarian and other real or invented languages: *Harmoniak, Lassú,*

Magyarázat, Kondor Tombol, Gran Cànone, Konvex-Konkav, Salsa-Bolgár, Folyékony (Hungarian for 'flowing'). His preliminary jottings include specially constructed scales and numerous polymetric and durational grids. For instance, on 2 February 1985, he mapped out the following rhythmic matrix for Étude 1 – similar to, but not the same as that which exists in the finished study.

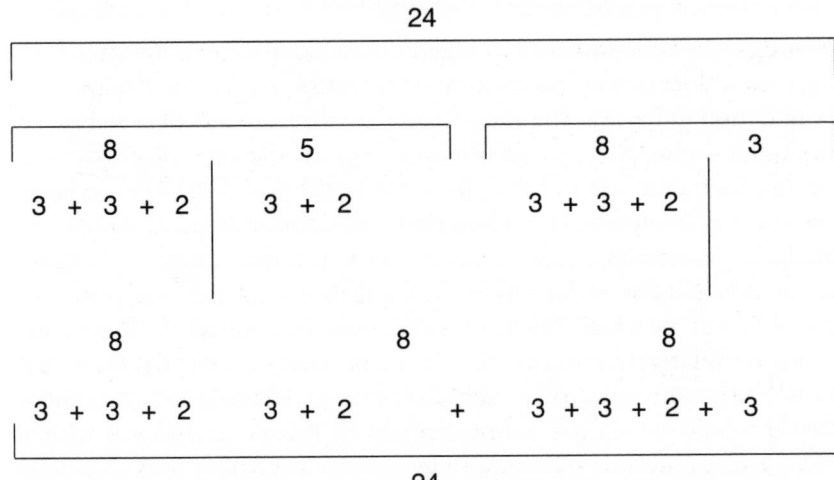

The completed Études were first published in facsimiles of Ligeti's handwritten fair copies, inimitable in character but of excellent clarity. Now that Books 1 and 2 have been issued in typeset editions their musical procedures are even easier to follow.[4] Because the Études are a compendium of the composer's techniques during the last two decades of the twentieth century, the remainder of this chapter is devoted to a relatively detailed commentary upon each Étude in turn. It is easy to be carried away by the minutiae of their craft. Nevertheless, I have tried to make my observations as concise and lucid as possible, intelligible without reference to the scores, and leavened with references to a wider world.

PREMIER LIVRE

Étude 1: *Désordre (Disorder)*, 1985

Désordre was first conceived as a 'pulsation' study and an exercise in segregating the black keys from the white, but as Ligeti worked on it, it also became an ingenious representation of chaos theory. In this first Étude he

Ex. 23 The opening of *Désordre* (1985) in Ligeti's autograph

© B. Schott's Söhne, Mainz, 1986

establishes techniques common to many, namely the simultaneous unfolding of independent but related processes in each of the pianist's two hands. The allocation to each hand of complementary scales creates what might be called 'combinatorial tonality' (i.e. the illusion of a third or resultant tonality produced by the interaction of different modes). Meanwhile, their divergent rhythmic patterns generate evolving polymetric counterpoints. Ligeti then plants the seeds of further disturbance into these already unstable textures. The process of dissolution is systemic: it is as if he had injected his metrical patterns with toxins, calculated to deform them insidiously from within – inexorably, but at different rates.

281

However aware of these processes, the listener can scarcely register their inner detail, given the metronome mark of semibreve = 76 (608 quavers per minute), any more than one can 'see' degenerative disorders of the nervous system except in the pathology lab and under a microscope. *Désordre* celebrates the excitement of living dangerously. Its sense of reckless acceleration is like the heady exhilaration of riding a roller coaster. On the surface the music is wonderfully homogeneous. Underneath are hazardous currents where orderly phrase structures grow wayward, and complex systems race towards destruction.

Throughout *Désordre* the right hand plays only white notes, the left hand only black. The right-hand music is therefore heptatonic, the left-hand pentatonic. The study contains an unbroken continuum of quavers grouped asymmetrically, mostly in *aksak* patterns of three and five. The main notes of each group are accented, doubled at the octave and prolonged, in order to project more spacious melodic lines in both hands – a technique whose ancestry stretches back to Schumann and Chopin. Ligeti's melodies are not legato but detached and jagged, and are of different lengths in each hand. The right-hand melody consists of three phrases repeated fourteen times, but with gradually compressed metre, and with each successive statement transposed up one step of the hypophrygian mode. The first cycle starts on B^4 and the fourteenth on B^6 two octaves higher, after which the étude stops. The left-hand melody is of similar character but has four phrases instead of three (lasting four, four, six and four bars per cycle, as opposed to the right hand's four, four and six bars). This cycle is also repeated successively, each time transposed down a fourth, except where missing steps in the pentatonic scale necessitate an adjustment. The register of *Désordre* is at its most extended towards the centre, as the two hands move outwards in contrary motion. In the final section the left hand supports the gradual ascent of the right, until both seem to disappear off the top of the keyboard.

The pitches of these cyclic repetitions are entirely predictable once the intervals of transposition have been chosen. More interesting are the deconstructive metrical processes which corrupt their durations. For the first three bars both hands sound rhythmically together. Although notated in eight quavers to the bar, their accentual patterns are 3 5, 3 5, 5 3. This rhythmic unity is soon subverted. From bar 4, by deleting one quaver from the right hand to make a 7/8 bar, and thereafter reducing every fourth bar to 7/8, the right hand moves progressively ahead of the left.

In fact the two hands move apart more rapidly, since the phrase structure of the left-hand cycle lasts four bars longer. The net effect of these
differences is that the number of quavers in the first full statement of the
right-hand melody totals thirty-one, thirty-one and forty-seven (three
phrases lasting 109 quavers), and those in the uncorrupted left-hand
total thirty-two, thirty-two, forty-eight and thirty-two (four phrases
lasting 144 quavers). In no time the metrical patterns have diverged dramatically, not through a process of Reichian phase shifting, but through
inbuilt inequality and progressive compression.

Two other deconstructive mechanisms operate in the right hand to
turn orderly *aksak* patterns into a headlong stampede of incessant
accents. Their effect can be seen in my diagrammatic representation of
the right-hand phrase structure (Ex. 24, pp. 284–85). This shows the
number of quaver beats in each bar and their *aksak* imbalance. For
instance, in bar 1 the melodic durations of three and five quavers are
represented by black and white rectangles, and the concluding seven-
quaver note in bar 4 by grey. The first of the deconstructive
mechanisms is the way in which the truncated 7/8 bar, by occurring
every fourth bar, changes its position in the repeating phrase structure,
so modifying the *aksak* rhythms in different places. The diagram
shows, for example, how in the second statement of the melody (starting on C⁵), the 7/8 bar becomes the second bar in each phrase instead
of the fourth. The other mechanism is more far-reaching. Starting with
the fourth cycle, by a further deletion of quaver beats, cycles are progressively squeezed until we reach the third phrase of the tenth cycle.
Here every note of the melody is reduced to its shortest possible duration (i.e. a quaver), the prevailing *aksak* character is eliminated and
the sense of acceleration is at its most frenetic.

The restoration of the original 3 + 5 (and 5 + 3) rhythm occurs
close to the golden section, and is stabilised for eighteen bars in both
hands, before divergence begins again. Now it is the right hand that
remains constant, and the left which draws back by extending every
third bar to nine quavers. Thus the 9/8 bar shifts within the left-hand
cycle, its further abduction of extra quavers leading to longer and
longer bars of eleven, twelve, thirteen, fourteen and finally twenty-
four quavers.

The result of these cumulative discrepancies in the first two thirds of
Désordre is metrical mayhem. The study replicates a fundamental idea
of chaos theory, that tiny differences in initial conditions lead rapidly

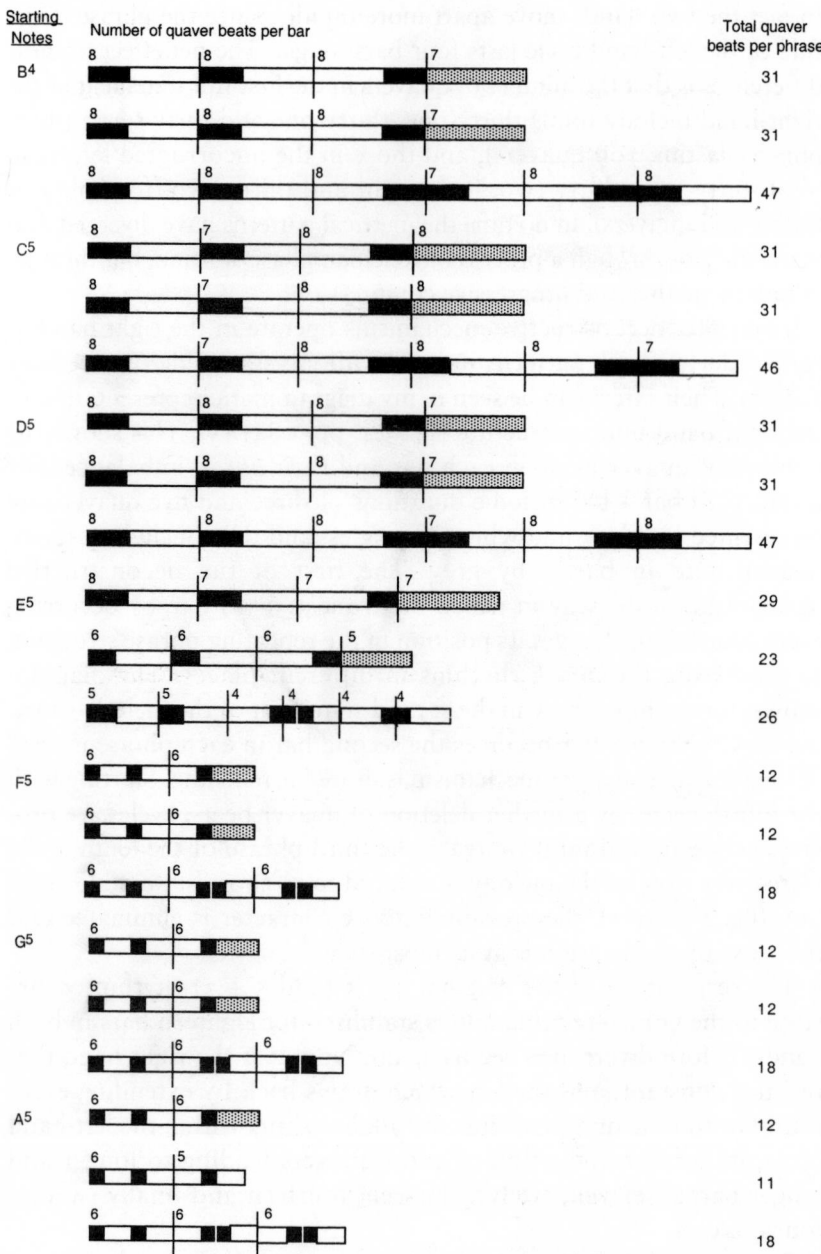

Ex. 24 *Désordre*, phrase and rhythmic structure of the right hand

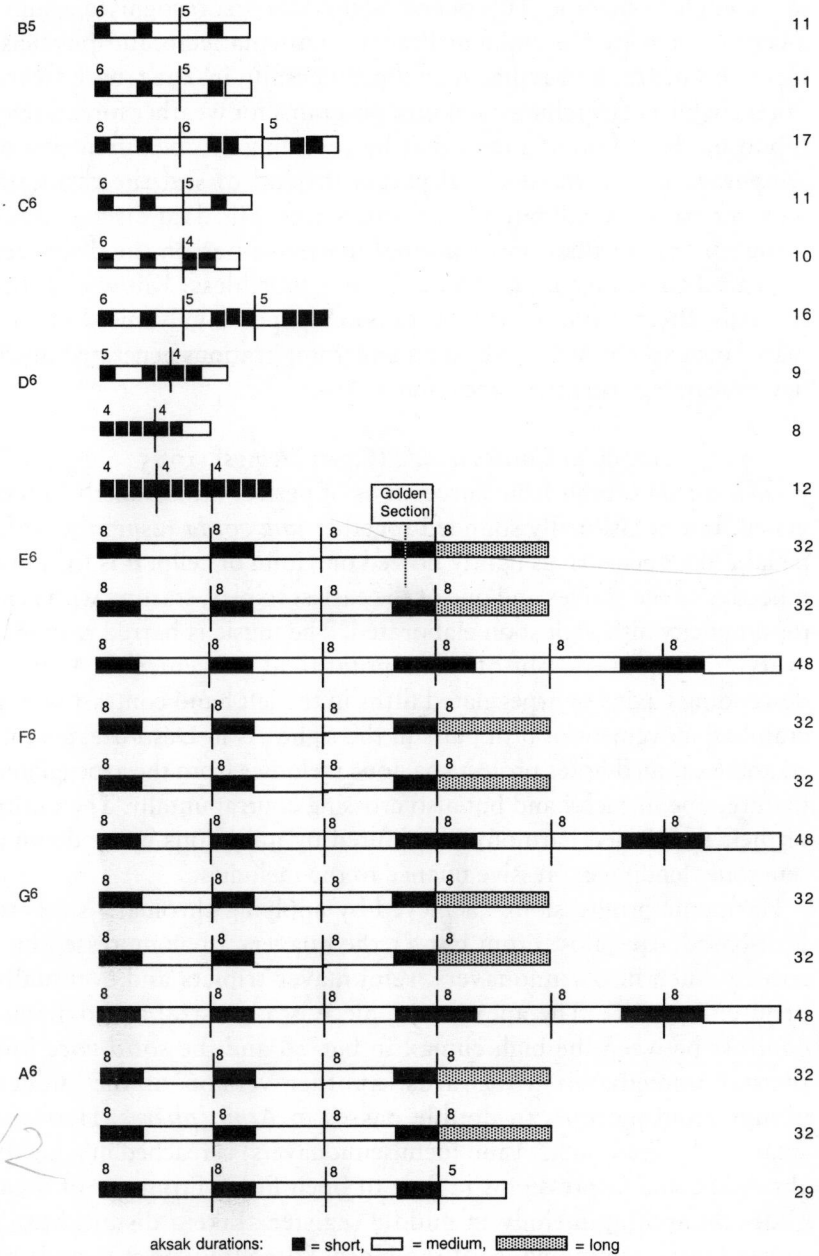

aksak durations: ■ = short, ☐ = medium, ▨ = long

285

to a complex outcome. This phenomenon was first recognised around a century ago by the eminent French mathematician and physicist Henri Poincaré, and rediscovered accidentally in 1961 by Edward Lorenz whilst researching computer programs for weather forecasting. Inputting data, Lorenz found that by rounding off measurements of temperature to three decimal places instead of six, the resultant weather patterns exhibited huge differences. His data discrepancies being no greater than observational margins of error, the discovery appeared to render long-term forecasts worthless. Known as 'the butterfly effect' from the title of Lorenz's paper, it galvanised mathematicians and physicists, whilst its wider implications generated much new research during the 1970s and 1980s.

Étude 2: Cordes à vide (Open Strings), 1985

Cordes à vide is built from successions of perfect fifths, mostly arpeggiated, but occasionally sounded together una corda (using the 'soft' pedal), like open strings lightly bowed on violin or cello. It is the most reflective of the studies and one of the easiest to play, starting with gentle simplicity although soon elaborated. The music is barred regularly every eight quavers, but only for notational convenience. At first, descending chains of arpeggiated fifths in the left hand contrast with a crab-like movement of fifth pairs in the right. As in Désordre, accented and sustained notes project spacious melodies from the arpeggiated texture, one in each hand but also crossing contrapuntally. The purity of their fifth-based harmony is coloured by inflections up or down a semitone, lending expressive nuance to the melodies.

Harmonic progression is achieved by applying chromatic shifts to fifth-based arpeggios. From bar 21 the quavers are compressed into triplets, then into semiquavers, semiquaver triplets and eventually demisemiquavers. The apex of the piece is a registral and dynamic contrast between the high climax in bar 26 and the sotto voce low register immediately afterwards: another version of the sudden plunge from piccolos to double basses in Atmosphères. Here the smallest rhythmic subdivision (demisemiquavers) is reached in a highly chromatic and impressionistic flow of open fifths. From out of them glides an arching melody in middle register. 'Like a distant horn', writes Ligeti, reminding us of the Horn Trio; although it is perhaps Liszt who comes most readily to mind – Liszt and the fountains of the Villa d'Este.

Étude 3: *Touches bloquées (Blocked keys)*, 1985

In *Touches bloquées* we have a specific throwback to an earlier work, the second movement of *Monument–Selbstportrait–Bewegung,* whose blocked-key technique cried out for further exploration. In the study, the effect of silently depressing with one hand keys selected from melodic patterns played by the other is clearer, through being articulated by one pianist, not two. Both hands play on the same group of keys, selectively sustained by one hand, reiterated by the other in ascending and descending chromatic scales. Silently sustained pitches are indicated by diamond-shaped notes, non-sounding notes in the scales by smaller note-heads, following the notation used in *Selbstportrait.*

Like many of the studies, *Touches bloquées* is built on an incessant quaver continuum, except that in this instance some keys do not sound. Thus an impression of bumpy irregularity is achieved just by playing moto perpetuo, a comparatively easy task physically, although the audible result is peppered with holes like a pianola role, holes which increase in frequency as the music proceeds. The unevenness is enhanced by irregular bar-lengths coinciding with the peaks and troughs of the running quavers, and which are therefore in this study of accentual significance. At first 7/8 and 8/8 bars alternate (there are no written time signatures), but soon the music grows more elastic. Overall, the study contains bars of almost every length between two and twenty-two quavers.

There are four strands of development and one tongue-in-cheek episode: for the pianist's apparent inability to maintain regular quavers is compounded by some hilariously unsuccessful attempts at playing octaves – or so it seems during an increasingly frantic central episode (bars 72–91) in which an impetuous flight of quadruple octaves repeatedly misses its aim. Ligeti's image is of circus clowns 'who pretend to be unable to execute some feat they can really perform wonderfully'. Perhaps the whole study is a joke, although it is as precisely organised as we would expect of Ligeti. Its fourfold organic growth is achieved firstly through harmonic expansion, secondly through the development of legato groups amongst the 'stuttering' quavers, thirdly through a greater preponderance of blocked keys causing ever longer silences, and finally, by means of an emerging hocket of fragmented quavers. The hocket develops through single quavers or pairs of them being dropped into the 'holes' left by the other hand, then used to reinforce (or contradict) the growing prominence of the legato groups.

From a semitonal cluster in mid-register, pitch development proceeds characteristically. The opening cluster spans a perfect fifth, but within it three notes are blocked and so always silent. As this cluster expands more keys are sustained until, from bar 20, the fingers of the left hand hold down six adjacent keys, leaving the thumb to play two others staccato. New harmonic centres are defined along the way: first A flat (bar 24), then a chord of E flat minor in low register (bar 52). As these notes decay and become silent blocking agents, their tonal significance also fades and adjacent pitches take over.

In the first seventeen bars, the silent 'holes' last one quaver each. Then more notes are blocked. Gaps come in pairs, then threes, and finally in chains of inaudible ostinati, filled only with the ghostly patter of fingers tapping the ivory. Towards the end of the study the texture grows increasingly threadbare like a moth-eaten cloth, rather like the skeletal fabric of Lachenmann's music.

Étude 4: *Fanfares*, 1985

Fanfares has a more conspicuous *aksak* character than any of the other studies and owes much to Bartók. Indeed, in what appears to be a first sketch dated only two months before the premiere, Ligeti gives it the title *Bartoque*. Yet it brilliantly demonstrates the difference between plagiarism and originality. A casual listener could be forgiven if he failed to notice that the whole study is built on an incessant ostinato, repeated, with only octave transpositions, no less than 208 times. Using relatively routine material, Ligeti's resourcefulness in marrying invention with elegance and virtuosity is striking. His melodies are euphonious, his phrase structures neatly proportioned, the harmonies audaciously consonant. Is this a postmodernist Ligeti, a turncoat radical, the once big bad iconoclast cavorting in the fleecy triads of diatonicism?

'Yes!' he proclaims[5] – but the answer is not so simple. Ligeti has never followed the flock and firmly rejects superficial labelling. His roots have always remained closer to Bartók than to the Second Viennese School and its legacy. In the context of his whole output, *Fanfares* merely resumes a line of thought characteristic of his Hungarian period – and transforms it spectacularly. It is about obsession, equally an attribute of *Lontano* or the *Poème symphonique*. Obsession is risk-taking, the pursuit of a singular vision, driven to the point where it forges something new and unique. It is certainly not the comfortable and easy path of reinstating the familiar. Nor is euphony an aesthetic position for Ligeti, as it is for others; it is rather the consequence of a particular inspiration, appropriate to one set of premises, not to another. Ligeti manages to use consonant harmony and yet remain radical through the speed and rhythmic intricacy with which unrelated triads hurtle past. Triads are but part of a wider palette of pitch usage, shortly to include, in the Piano and Violin Concertos, microtonal and timbral inventions – as strangely formed as one might hear from any spectralist.[6] His awareness of tradition is deeply assimilated. Like Bach, he uses existing norms as the starting point for music whose technical, expressive and structural dimensions are magisterially his own.

The study's ostinato also occurs in the second movement of the Horn Trio, and Ligeti's return to the same one-bar formula – an archetypical moto perpetuo – is intriguing. The later sections of the Horn Trio movement are almost bacchanalian, but in *Fanfares* the 'working out' is elegant and urbane. Above or below the ostinato's 208 repetitions gallops a bright, sonorous melody – or rather a homophonic duo (see Ex. 25, p. 290), for this is another horn-type fanfare of mostly dyads and triads, occasionally unlaced in whirling figurations. At each appearance it is melodically and rhythmically varied, generally alternating between right hand and left. The duo melody consists of four phrases whose symmetry admits to folk and classical precedents; its harmony and phrase structure are not unlike those in the first of Bartók's *Six Dances in Bulgarian Rhythm*. The ostinato comprises two identical ascending tetrachords an augmented fourth apart, whose tritonal axis is matched throughout the study by a balance of diatonic and chromatic ingredients, here favouring the diatonic and consonant. Astonishingly, considering Ligeti's avant-garde reputation, not only are the first thirty-four chords all consonant; virtually the whole piece is built on concords, interspersed with a sprinkling of diminished triads and seventh chords. Moreover, the norm is for major triads to characterise the motif when it is in the right hand, minor triads when it is in the left. Only towards the end does a more dissonant bitonality prevail.

The first full statement of the duo melody is in the right hand. Combined with the ostinato, each of its phrases contains four chords, all of them major. The four phrases between them embrace all the major triads plus inversions which it is possible to construct on the first, fourth and sixth notes of the ostinato, in step with its 3 + 2 + 3 *aksak* character.

Ex. 25 Opening of *Fanfares* (1985)

Successive variants of this four-phrase motif change hands, and consequently also exchange major and minor modes:

RH, bars 2–8: sixteen chords containing nine different inversions of six major triads

LH, bars 10–17: eighteen chords containing thirteen different inversions of seven minor triads

RH, bars 18–26: twenty chords consisting of major triads and inversions, plus seventh chords

LH, bars 28–36: twenty-three chords consisting of minor triads and inversions, plus diminished chords

RH, bars 37–45: twenty-three chords consisting of major triads and inversions, plus seventh chords

Despite the prevailing consonance, Ligeti's rapid juxtaposition of unrelated triads sounds bright and piquant. For psychoacoustic reasons, the perceived tonality is more complex than a systematic use of concords might suggest. Due to a 'persistence of hearing', comparable to the 'persistence of vision', our brains continue to register sounds momentarily after they have ceased. In *Désordre* 'combinatorial' tonality arose from the vertical superimposition of different scales. In *Fanfares* it results from the speed of the horizontal sequence, which concertinas successive harmonies, as if we were hearing them together. To this multi-diatonic mixture is added the tritonally related hexachords of the ostinato, and a divergent counterpoint based on conflicting diatonic scales. The whirl of these different tonal ingredients around the rotating spindle of the ostinato sets up centrifugal forces, as harmonies are spun outwards above and below the centre, on one occasion flying off to the extremities of the keyboard (bar 137).

An approximate count reveals around 600 chords in *Fanfares*. The study lasts just over three and a half minutes, so we hear an average of 175 chords per minute. Most of these chords are consonant. But at speed, they generate a less definable 'supertonality' (Ligeti has called it 'consonant atonality'), due to the dance of upper partials above so many triadic roots. To Ligeti it seemed like an illusion of unequal temperament, prompting him to explore the idea of simulating alternative tuning systems on a conventionally tuned piano, as he attempts in *Galamb borong*.

But the main thrust of the study is rhythmic. At its heart is shifting accentuation. Its starting point is the 3 + 3 + 2 *aksak* rhythm of the

ostinato, but between the two hands the variety of cross-metrical relationships is legion. There are combinations of 7/8 right-hand groups
with the 8/8 ostinato (bar 116); there are left-hand groups of 9/8, 6/8,
6/4 and dotted crotchet units, all against 8/8 in the right hand (bars
167–176). Typical of Ligeti is the notated rallentando (a technique used
by Charles Ives). During the last two and a half pages, successive phrases
move from quaver units to crotchets, to dotted crotchets. As the left
hand descends, the chords get longer and louder, virtually obliterating
the now distant ostinato, their successive durations of three, three, four,
four, four, five, five, six, seven, eight, nine and ten quavers leading to the
lowest and loudest chord of all, held for twenty-three quavers.

Despite its commonplace material, *Fanfares* is never banal.
Theoretically, a number of earlier twentieth-century composers might
have written the piece, since it contains nothing intrinsically alien to
their common technical vocabulary. Yet none did. Perhaps only Ligeti,
with his Hungarian upbringing and obsession with polymetrics, could
treat the ever-shifting relationship between immutable ostinato and
melodic caprice to such a dazzling acrobatic display.

Étude 5: *Arc-en-ciel (Rainbow)*, 1985

Arc-en-ciel was a title unsure of its destiny. One sketch links it to a
polymetric 'Allegro molto vivace', another to a more relaxed pattern
of legato semiquavers in both hands. As published, it is a graceful
intermezzo, less intense than most of the other Études, more improvisatory and thoughtful. Ligeti only attached the title, in fact, after
completing the music. But it seems to have been tailored for its position as a gentler interlude in Book 1, whose contents, until he wrote
the second book, he imagined would be performed in order. The textural character of the study was inspired by a specific kind of jazz
pianism: Thelonious Monk and the elegance of Bill Evans. Harmonically
it suggests the rich hues of Skryabin, at least at times. Rhythmically it
combines different irrational values and desynchronised accents, but
without the rigorous structure of some other Études.

Étude 6: *Automne à Varsovie (Autumn in Warsaw)*, 1985

The Warsaw Autumn is one of the longest established festivals of new
music: it has taken place annually since 1956, with the exception of
1957, and again 1982, when the tense political situation in Poland caused
its suspension. Ligeti felt a strong bond with the organisers who, over the

years, had programmed nearly all his music. This had not been without a struggle. Admittedly his short electronic piece *Artikulation* had crept unnoticed into a concert of taped music as early as 1958. But when, in the early 1960s, Karl-Erik Welin proposed the more flamboyant *Volumina*, the Hungarian delegation protested, saying they would not attend if *Volumina* was performed. Lutosławski did his best to argue for it but failed. Even to this day – but surely through oversight – *Volumina* has never been played at the festival. However, by 1965 Lutosławski and his colleagues had won their case. That year *Apparitions* was performed, to be followed by the Requiem in 1968, when the Warsaw Autumn also hosted the World Music Days of the ISCM.

In 1985 tension flared up between Solidarity and the right-wing Communist government. That year a number of Ligeti's works were scheduled for the festival, including *Atmosphères*, *Ramifications*, *Drei Phantasien*, both string quartets and the Horn Trio. Ligeti had been asked also to write a new piece and was invited to attend, but he had no time to go. Saddened by the difficulties weighing upon his Polish friends, he conceived and dedicated to them this melancholic Chopinesque study, whose French title has an evident poetic and emotional connotation. Obliquely it also refers to 'L'Automne à Pékin', a story by the tragicomic writer Boris Vian (1920–59), disciple of Jarry and co-founder with him of the 'College of Pataphysics' – devoted to 'the science of imaginary solutions', an idea that must have found in Ligeti a natural ally.

Automne à Varsovie is much more than a Chopinesque tribute, being the longest of the first book of Études and the most far-reaching. Structurally it is a combination of African thinking and the augmentation and diminution principles in the fugues of J. S. Bach, filtered through the music of Nancarrow and the graphic ideas of Escher. Another link is with the fourteenth- and fifteenth-century practice of prolation typified in Ockeghem's *Missa Prolationum*. All these references are distilled in Ligeti's treatment of the *lamento* motif, which is heard insistently like an ostinato, superimposed at different speeds against a background of continuous pulses. For the first time in Ligeti's music the *lamento* motif occurs profusely, indeed over eighty times.

It is amazing that Ligeti can write a piece based almost entirely on descending chromatic scales, one of the most routine nineteenth-century clichés, yet produce music so personal and profound. Certainly, the mass of subsiding phrases treading their weary descent through this study – like tired labourers returning home, united in resignation and only distinguishable by the speed of their gait – imparts an enduring bleakness to the music. So many melodies, always descending yet never seeming to get lower, suggest the infinite melancholy of Escher's faceless figures in *Ascending and Descending*, toiling for the umpteenth time around an endless staircase that gets neither higher nor lower.

The metrical relationship between these melodies – which variously employ units of 3, 4, 5 or 7 semiquavers but are otherwise fundamentally alike – creates the illusion of different speeds. The phrases glide through every register, above and below as well as weaving their way across or inside the semiquaver continuum. Initially the accompanying patterns cross four open octaves, but elsewhere they become more lyrical, hovering in the background except for three instances where everything erupts in accelerating crescendi. These patterns are mostly in groups of four semiquavers, but groups of three and five are also used. At the climax of the second and final crescendo, groups of three reduce to two and then to semiquaver scales. By contrast, the first crescendo expands, fives growing into sixes, sevens, then eights and so on, until suddenly arrested by the frozen stillness of the central section, from which all semiquavers have been numbingly expunged.

Lineage of the lament

It is in *Automne à Varsovie* that Ligeti fully establishes the distinguishing features of the *lamento* motif, used so obsessively throughout the study. But far from it exorcising this melancholic formula from his mind, it remained to haunt him throughout the late 1980s and 1990s. We have seen it prefigured in his music of twenty, even thirty years before, and noted its presence (without any *talea*) in the final movement of the Horn Trio. Considering how pervasive this *idée fixe* had now become, it is timely to examine it more closely.

In its complete form, the *lamento* motif exhibits three or four of the following attributes:

1. It is a three-phrase melody, the third phrase of longer duration.
2. Each phrase descends stepwise in semitones and whole tones, interspersed with upward leaps.
3. Notes of greater expressive significance (e.g. immediately after the upward leaps) are intensified harmonically.
4. Different versions of the formula similarly adopt strict rhythmic *taleae*.

Most appearances of the motif in *Automne à Varsovie* exhibit all these features. Exx. 26 a and b (pp. 296–97) show the formula as heard in bars 18–24 and 62–72, but re-notated to clarify the metrical units of their *taleae*. Note that prominent notes, generally the last of each phrase, are assigned double duration. In both of these examples the melody is enhanced by chords, the first flavoured with tritones, the second more varied. In each case the three-phrase pattern is evident, as is the greater length and expressive weight of the third phrase. Each descends in tones and semitones, except where tension is increased by an upward lift. Each of these 'lifts' (marked * in the examples), as well as the starting note of each phrase, are further intensified by the occurrence of a major seventh interval between the melody and its 'shadow', i.e. the line which replicates it, usually at the octave or sixth below. Note also how the piquant major seventh pervades the third phrase of Ex. 26a. The rhythmic formula is applied similarly in each example, except that one uses units of five semiquavers, the other units of seven.

These are the characteristics of the *lamento* motif as it appears in various guises throughout *Automne à Varsovie*. These are its characteristics as it appears in movements of the Horn Trio (Ex. 21), the Piano Concerto (Ex. 26c), the Violin Concerto (Ex. 26d) and the Viola Sonata (Exx. 26g, h and i). The *Hamburg Concerto* (1999) contains a short appearance in untempered tuning. The second and third movements of the Piano Concerto are saturated with the *lamento* motif. Even in the 1960s, when Ligeti seemed to abandon melodic and rhythmic definition, its embryonic presence can be sensed. It is implicit in a quite different archetype, the fan-shaped twelve-note countersubject for the 'Christe' section in the Requiem (Ex. 26e). Some of its attributes are evident in the 'mesto' melody for solo bass flute near the end of the first movement of the Double Concerto (Ex. 26f) – no durational *talea* here, nor in the Requiem for that matter, but the division into three phrases, the chromatic descent, and the 'lifts' already exist. Ligeti's later passacaglia treatments of the *lamento* connect it with music further back, his own 'Omaggio a Girolamo Frescobaldi', the first movement of Bartók's *Music for Strings, Percussion and Celesta*, and more distantly with Baroque archetypes: the 'Crucifixus' of Bach's B Minor Mass, Purcell's 'Lament' in *Dido and Aeneas* (Ex. 26j), and examples from Buxtehude and others. Deeper still it has an ancestor in the funeral laments of traditional folklore, including the Romanian *bocet* which Ligeti heard as a child.

Ex. 26a: Étude 6: 'Automne à Varsovie', b.18

Ex. 26b: Étude 6: 'Automne à Varsovie', b.62

Ex. 26c: Piano Concerto, second movement, b.12

Ex. 26d: Violin Concerto, fifth movement (opening)

Ex. 26e: Requiem: second movement

Exx. 26 a–l The *lamento* motif.
Numbers below the staves show durations of the *taleae*.

Ex. 26f: Double Concerto, first movement, b.81

Ex. 26g: Sonata for viola solo, fifth movement, 'Lamento' (showing *lamento* formula in larger noteheads)

Ex. 26h: Sonata for viola solo, sixth movement 'Chaconne chromatique'

Ex. 26i: *lamento* formula of Ex. 26h (3 phrases x 2)

Ex. 26j: Ground bass from Purcell: *Dido and Aeneas*

Ex. 26k: Horn Trio   Étude 4: Fanfares

Ex. 26 l: Piano Concerto, first movement

In *Automne à Varsovie* each of the eighty-odd appearances of the *lamento* motif sticks rigidly to a durational unit of either three, four, five or seven semiquavers. Its first appearance in bar 2, for example, contains three phrases measured in five-semiquaver units (except that to improve articulation, some durations consist of a note followed by a rest). Each phrase has a similar lachrymose melodic style. The first two share the same starting pitches; but the second is a note longer and ends lower. The third starts higher but is double the length of the others, twisting as it falls to end lower still. As the piece continues, melodies are frequently overlaid. The sense of aspiring ever higher yet falling lower, as if unable to gain either height or depth, becomes more urgent and desolate.

The first superimposition of melodies at different tempi begins in bar 18, where an alto part hurries by in dotted quavers, overtaking the slower pace of the right hand as it maintains its units of five and ten. Soon three or four melodies are heard together at different speeds, as in bars 77–79 and again in bars 85–87. Both instances feature mensural canons of four descending chromatic lines in durational units of three, four, five and seven, the first against a semiquaver background grouped in fours, the second against a background grouped in threes. Two of the canonic melodies between bars 85 and 87 are heard not as single notes but doubled in fifths. Indeed, the varied harmonic coloration of these plaintive lines – through octave doubling, added intervals and chords – is a feature of the study.

But how to halt, how silence these doleful personages endlessly trudging up and down? Ligeti's solution is to compound confusion through an increasing anarchy of pitch and rhythm, until everything collapses in a thunderous descent into the bottom octave. The strangest moment, however, is not the end but that chilling emptiness in the middle (bar 55), where the semiquavers unexpectedly stop and we are left with the melody alone, governed by a five-semiquaver *talea*, each of its three phrases doubled at the tritone but at the extremities of the keyboard, five and a half octaves apart. It is one of those mysterious voids, like the vacant space in *Lontano* where everyone falls silent leaving only the disembodied whistle of the orchestra's very highest and lowest pitches.

The *lamento* motif in *Automne à Varsovie* gives the piece a wider resonance. Whereas in the study, Ligeti can indulge his multitemporal lines only in so far as one pianist can perform them, the orchestral resources of the Piano Concerto remove any such restriction. The study, for all its elegance and intricacy, turns out to be a black-and-white line drawing, later to be expanded on a richer canvas where instrumental coloration and subtleties of perspective increase its strangeness and piquancy. If Étude 6 is Autumn in Warsaw, then the second and third movements of the Piano Concerto (see Chapter Fourteen) are its Winter: surreal, deserted, touched with a raw hallucinatory light.

DEUXIÈME LIVRE

In early sketches *Fanfares* is shown as the third study of Book 1, *Automne à Varsovie* as the fourth, and *Vertige* as the sixth. But *Vertige* Ligeti decided to defer for a second book. Clearly, once he had made his final choice of studies for Book 1 – all composed relatively quickly in 1985 – he had ample ideas left over. Soon he drafted schemes for its sequel. An early one lists:

7. *Galamb borong*
8. *Quintes*
9. *Clair-Obscur* (for Mauricio Kagel)
10. *Staccato*
11. *Lassú* (gamelan)
12. *L'âge d'or*

In the event all but *Galamb borong* were replaced by stronger titles or musical ideas – so many in fact that the published Book 2 contains not six but eight studies, the last in two versions.

Étude 7: *Galamb borong*, 1988–89

The music of Book 2 often seems to be influenced by Debussy. A primary model for *Galamb borong* was the gamelan-inspired *Cloches à travers les feuilles* from Debussy's second book of *Images*. But whereas Debussy uses a single whole-tone scale, Ligeti uses two simultaneously. As in *Désordre*, right and left hands have complementary scales, in this case whole-tone scales a semitone apart. But it is Ligeti's precise choice of pitch relationships that produces an ambivalent tonality. Generally avoiding semitonal clashes, he emphasises consonant combinations of a major sixth and major third. Experimenting at the keyboard, he decided that whole-tone scales played a major sixth apart could mimic gamelan tuning due to the fact that any three adjacent steps in the paired scales contain contradictory accidentals ('false relations').

The result is an 'imaginary gamelan music, indigenous to a strange island which is not to be found on any map . . . neither chromatic nor diatonic, nor based on whole tones, hidden away in the normal tempered tuning of the piano but, until *Galamb borong*, not properly heard before.'[7] It was a step on the road leading to the hybrid tunings and exotic sonorities of the Violin Concerto.

The music has a lovely transparency which Paul Griffiths has likened to 'a sort of rotating glass sculpture'.[8] Neither intervallic nor rhythmic usage is rigid. An additive pulsation structure is applied loosely, sounding more fluid and intuitive than one would find in original gamelan music or, for that matter, in the faithful transcriptions for two pianos made by Colin McPhee. Being 'fake gamelan music' the study has a fake title, a juxtaposition of two Hungarian words which together sound like 'imaginary Javanese' – at least to non-Hungarian speakers. In Hungarian, says Ligeti, they happen to mean 'melancholic pigeon'.

Étude 8: *Fém* (*Metal*), 1989

This study was at first to be called *Quintes*. Its present title occurred to Ligeti whilst he was improvising fifth-based ideas at the piano. 'Fém' in Hungarian means 'metal'. Its sound resembles 'fény' meaning 'light' – so a metal that is bright and gleaming. The music is also hard-edged, brilliant and metallic, and is to be played with vigorous and resolute precision – although also with 'swing' – so that the polyrhythmic relationships emerge clearly. Like *Fanfares*, the chords in *Fém* are quasi-diatonic. They are mainly based on perfect fifths, and coincide or alternate between the hands to produce multiple-fifth aggregates fluctuating between the black and white keys. For the first three pages, the music proceeds in tautly organised cycles, each of twelve bars. The second cycle is a transposition of the first down an octave and a fifth; the third a harmonic variant, transposed down an octave.

As in *Désordre*, each hand has a different rhythmic structure. But *Fém* seems more influenced by Banda-Linda polyphony than the other studies, not only through its use of hemiola and hocket, but in the way the opening right-hand motif alternates between two adjacent pitches. The hocketing rhythm derives from the continuous repetition of two simultaneous *taleae*, one in the right hand totalling eighteen quavers, the other in the left totalling sixteen. The study is notated (although not beamed) in 12/8, and each twelve-bar cycle contains a total of 144 quavers. As 144 is the lowest common multiple of sixteen and eighteen, this enables nine complete right-hand *taleae* to terminate on the same quaver beat as eight *taleae* in the left. Each *talea* can be subdivided into 3/8 and 4/8 components, both patterns sharing (in my redrawn notation) their second and their last two bars.

Ex. 27 Rhythmic *taleae* in *Fém*

Their different overall durations push the two cycles gradually out of phase and back again, so avoiding any impression of regular metre. Only the coincidence of quaver rests (rests being the prerequisite of a hocket) provide regular as well as seemingly random punctuation: regular at the end of every third bar where the changing phase relationship of the two cycles produces, as if by magic, a synchronous rest; irregular in all the other bars.

There is another brief synchronicity where two adjacent quaver rests coincide between the hands at the end of each twelve-bar cycle. Like *Désordre*, *Fém* is a teasing mixture of the regular and the irregular, and of shifting phase relationships. But the more times the twelve-bar cycle is repeated, the greater the risk of ossification. To avoid this, before the completion of the third cycle (in bar 34), a rhythmic degeneration of each *talea* begins.

Like most of the studies, *Fém* is single-minded yet organic. Ligeti soon subjects both rhythmic and pitch patterns to new variants. The perfect fifths, which characterise the harmony, multiply and are further brightened by the addition of whole tones, whilst the clean bitonality of the opening grows more chromatic. As the rhythmic patterns expand into continuous quavers, rests are replaced by notes. Meanwhile, the contrast between forte (*tre corde*) and piano (*una corda*) dynamics, which at the start coincided exactly with the twelve-bar cycles, begins to take its own course, becoming less regular and more extreme. For a full bar at the climax (bars 56–57), both hands are synchronised, the final chord at the apex of the crescendo being the only eight-note chord in the whole study, and the only chord preceded as well as followed by double quaver rests. It is a moment of truth, the point at which both hands hammer out the same rhythm. Instantly the focus shifts. All energy is dispelled in a poised and graceful epilogue. We hear a slow-motion and distant version of the material, its metallic edge softened by legato articulation and limpid harmony.

Étude 9: *Vertige (Dizziness)*, 1990

The ninth study was commissioned by the town of Gütersloh for a concert in honour of Mauricio Kagel. Ligeti again thought to use his concept of 'Clair-Obscur', but replaced it with another perennial image, the multiple superimposition of descending micropolyphonic lines, here a plethora of chromatic canons. Volker Banfield, who had premiered all the previous Études except *Désordre*, had been injured in an accident, leaving him insufficient time to learn the new study's irregular chromatic combinations at the extremely fast tempo of between six and seven chords a second. Ligeti sought the help of the player piano expert Jürgen Hocker, who had assisted in the first authentic European performances of Nancarrow's studies. Hocker quickly made a transcription, and the study was performed mechanically in Cologne in time for Kagel's birthday. He stepped in again when Pierre-Laurent Aimard insisted that Étude 14 was too difficult for a human pianist, after which Ligeti allowed Hocker to make player piano versions of several other Études, as well as of *Continuum*.

Études 9, 13 and 14 form a related subgroup of studies, since each explores the same technical problem in its own way: how to create musical equivalents of the spirals observable in nature (in fluids, plants, shells, galaxies etc.), in man-made objects (drills, spindles), as well as in a teasing auditory paradox devised by the Stanford computer scientist Roger Shepard[9] and adapted by Jean-Claude Risset. Having met Risset at the Abbaye de Sénangue in the summer of 1973, at the meeting convened by Boulez to discuss his plans for IRCAM, a friendship developed, fuelled by Ligeti's interest in new areas of research. Risset played tapes of his computer-created acoustical illusions, one being a spiral of pitches that appear to ascend for ever yet always remain the same. All three of Ligeti's studies are directly linked to this phenomenon. All contain overlapping and recursive scales. In Étude 9 we hear wave upon wave of falling chromatic scales. Étude 13 is built on repetitions of an ascending chromatic motif in vigorous *aksak* rhythm. Étude 14 has crab-like patterns in two parts developed as an ascending and overlapping series of expanding and contracting intervals. All these musical spirals suggest an infinity of motion, their rotating systems apparently capable of endless repetition. Each sets up a giddy vortex, as if the ground itself were turning and the listener spinning on a revolving plane.

The feeling of physical instability is present in other Études. But so it is in Ligeti's earlier music. The title *Vertige* acknowledges that the metaphor has never been far away. Like *Automne à Varsovie*, Étude 9 is saturated with falling semitonal scales, only here they are much faster and minutely microscopic. There is also an incisive melody. This, however, drops dizzily in ever larger leaps until, at the climax, it becomes a series of cross-cutting rhythms, bright intervals and ringing concords.

Ligeti begins with material that could hardly be less distinctive: a descending chromatic scale in even quavers. The character of the music rests entirely on what happens to it. Firstly, there is repetition; for this is an infinitely repeating spiral, flooded with new entries in overlapping waves, as their predecessors sink from view. Then there is change. The time distance between entries is constantly varied; so is the number of descending semitonal steps in each scale. At first all of the scales have sixteen notes, with intervals of eight, seven or five quavers between each entry. Soon the gap between entries shortens to only two or three quavers (and occasionally four or five), disorientating the listener by the apparent acceleration, although the tempo of the quaver pulse itself never alters. Meanwhile the scales themselves either expand or contract, reducing in length where a mass of overlapping entries inhibits movement, but also extending down to seventeen, nineteen, twenty, twenty-one, twenty-two, twenty-seven, and even thirty-seven descending semitones, as the clusterous pitch band of the opening fans outwards. The first seventeen scales all contain sixteen semitones falling from B^4 (sometimes notated as C flat) to A flat^3. Thereafter the first notes start progressively higher and final notes drop lower: C^5 commencing the twenty-third scale, D flat^5 the twenty-sixth, D^5 the thirty-second, and so on, rising in semitones. This (quasi-*lamento*) process is less systematic than it seems. Composing at the piano, whenever Ligeti found his fingers unoccupied, he inserted another melody – 'that simple: musical imagination triggered by anatomy!'

Although the semitonal material – the musical liquid – is consistent, the waves disturbing its surface are never the same. Their swaying is hypnotic, yet the piece is not without stability. The

melodies heard from bar 25 mostly end on chords, usually a consonant triad in first or second inversion, distributed rather like the
'interval signals' in *Lux aeterna*. Also prominent is an F sharp pedal
underpinning the first fortissimo climax (bars 54–57). Spaced out
through the music, like pillars supporting the chromatic canopy, the
tonal import of these harmonies is confirmed by a bright B major
triad in bar 131. We already noted that the opening scales reiterate B
(their starting note) no fewer than twenty-two times before moving
upwards. Atonal and tonal elements amidst these chromatic quick-
sands are intricately balanced: this is no facile neo-tonality. Yet by the
end it seems that threaded through the vertiginous scales, there has
been a tonal lifeline. The subconscious affirmation of B major, perhaps? Or was B the dominant of a non-existent tonic, a melancholy
E minor? Without the composer even noticing, his harmonic instinct
was secretly at work.

Étude 10: *Der Zauberlehrling* (*The Apprentice Magician*), 1994
After *Vertige* it was three years before Ligeti completed any further
Études. In 1993 he wrote *L'escalier du diable*, but decided that its
immense dramatic energy required that it be played last. To complete
Book 2 he had to compose the intervening Études 10 and 11. *Entrelacs*
came next and was numbered 11 (it is now 12). But as he wrote the
study to precede it, *Coloana infinită*, he realised that this even more
merited the final position, immediately after *L'escalier du diable*. Book
2 still awaited its gentler episode.

For the moment, at performances of the twelve existing studies in
Münster and Huddersfield in November 1993, the Études were numbered 1 to 13, with number 10 missing. At these concerts they were
played by Pierre-Laurent Aimard, pianist of the Ensemble
InterContemporain since its creation by Boulez in 1977. Aimard had
given the French premiere of the first three Études in 1986 and was so
impressed by them that he decided to devote serious study to all of
Ligeti's piano music. He had also premiered *Coloana infinită*, but
found it so difficult that he asked Ligeti to simplify it. Nevertheless the
precision, energy and strong characterisation of Aimard's interpretations set them in a class of their own. He has become Ligeti's preferred
pianist, a close friend whose inspirational playing combines exceptional musicianship and technique with an intimate knowledge of the
composer's personality.

A year later Ligeti composed not one but two more Études, numbering them 10 and 11, and renumbering the others 12, 13 and 14. The two new studies had been commissioned by the 'Musica' Festival in Strasbourg where they were played by Aimard in October 1994. One of them, however, Ligeti felt ashamed of and immediately discarded. The surviving study, *Der Zauberlehrling*, takes its cue from *Continuum*, whose tempo Ligeti cites as a yardstick. Like *Continuum* it begins with reiterated patterns in a narrow pitch band. Unusually, and unlike *Continuum*, these patterns are grouped regularly in 12/8. In their euphonious diatonicism we again hear Debussy – the Debussy of *Les tierces alternées* perhaps. Only towards the end of the second page do other rhythmic groupings occur, resulting in an ebb and flow of secondary accents; and only well into the third page do chromaticisms colour the harmony. A starting point for the composition was the *balafon* (xylophone) music of Malawi, as recorded by Gerhard Kubik, an Austrian ethnomusicologist for whom Ligeti has high regard.

The title has no connection with this and came afterwards, being taken from a poem by Goethe. But it is not inappropriate. The apprentice magician appears to be practising his sleight-of-hand. The notes ruffle up and down, disappear from sight and reappear seven octaves higher, fan outwards and as rapidly collapse, suddenly to emerge exactly where we first heard them. In a final flurry, the Debussyan harmony of thirds and tritones blossoms into an upward sweep of consonant dyads – preceded by a whole-tone scale rising in octaves through rippling ostinati – then as rapidly descends, and all is done.

Étude 11: *En Suspens (In Suspense)*, 1994

Ligeti called his first attempt at Étude 11 *L'Arrache-coeur* (*Heartsnatcher*) after another story by Boris Vian. Dedicated to Kurtág, it was premiered at 'Musica' in Strasbourg in 1994. The piece began with a stark melody in slow crotchets and dotted crotchets, using only two pitch classes (E and F) to create distorted octaves, i.e. through major seventh and minor ninth dissonances. Its austerity recalls the second of *Musica ricercata*. But it was an oversimplification. Having discarded it, Ligeti wrote *En Suspens* as a substitute.

En Suspens is also relatively modest, being in a linear-melodic style unusually devoid of elaboration. But as in *Désordre* and *Galamb borong*, there are crucial differences between the hands. This time Ligeti employs two hexachordal scales a tritone apart: D flat, E flat,

F, G flat, A flat, B flat in the right hand; G, A, B, C, D, E in the left – later exchanged. Metrically, the two hands also contrast: a crotchet-based 6/4 right-hand metre against a dotted crotchet 12/8 left-hand metre. Both have gently swaying modal melodies. The right hand leads; marked *grazioso*, it has the graceful simplicity of a cradle song. Its rhythm consists of two-to-three *aksak* patterns grouped in three phrases totalling twenty-five beats, whose regular repetition means that each complete statement begins one beat later in the bar.

A similar process occurs in the first movement of the Piano Concerto. But in the study there are only two layers, one in each hand, and the uncharacteristic absence of quavers until near the end of the piece ensures its chaste lucidity. Swapping modes between the hands makes do for modulation. There is no other chromaticism until the last two bars. Otherwise, the only decorative features are restrained: a couple of brief, high glockenspiel-like interjections and two hushed glissandi.

Étude 12: *Entrelacs* (*Interlacing*), 1993

Originally Étude 11, *Entrelacs* was moved to position 12, displacing other contenders (see p. 304). Amongst these were ideas for a study called *Sea Change* or *The isle is full of noises, sounds and sweet airs*, begun (as we shall find) in California. One sketch for it shows rising arpeggios in fifths, which Ligeti must soon have decided was too naive. It seems to have progressed no better than his planned opera on *The Tempest*, by now already abandoned. Many of the discontinued ideas are either too gestural and impulsive, or have metrical systems barely worked out. Unless he could create his 'technical gadgets', they lacked a necessary tension between system and intuition. *Entrelacs* achieves this by superimposing a more complex combination of polymetric layers than in any other study.

The word 'entrelacs' comes from art and architecture and means interlaced design or interwoven ornament. The study concentrates solely on pattern. Against a background of continuous semiquavers, seven layers are constructed from durational units of three, four, five, seven, eleven, thirteen and seventeen semiquavers – all prime numbers. The component notes in each layer often have to be shared with the semiquaver background; but they also project into the foreground, through louder dynamics and through being sustained. In the score, the different layers are distinguished by having additional stems and being written as either minims, crotchets, quavers or semiquavers; although in practice, each is sustained for as long as the fingering allows. The first voices to enter have the longest durations (thirteen and seventeen semi-quavers) and are highlighted in minims. The next pair use units of seven and eleven semiquavers and are written in crotchets; the following entries use units of four and five and have quaver stems; whilst the last (in units of three) has semiquaver stems. Three times during the study these rhythmically differentiated voices enter in this manner, like a mensural canon. There are hints of pitch imitation too. Three times their accumulation results in a climax of interlocking pulses. The listener cannot pick out individual layers, hearing only a composite organism. The overall effect, therefore, is neither contrapuntal nor linear but of rhythmic patterning, as in *Galamb borong*.

Entrelacs is another study built on different hexachordal modes in each hand, one the inversion of the other. Around two thirds of the way through, the two hands exchange modes.[10] On two occasions – once each side of this exchange, and so using each hexachord in turn – an asymmetrical cantabile melody, growing into a melody of chords, is heard in relief above the semiquaver background. These episodes apart, *Entrelacs* is a well-regulated relative of the disorderly ticking clocks in the third movement of the Chamber Concerto.

Étude 13: *L'escalier du diable* (*The Devil's Staircase*), 1993
L'escalier du diable was composed in the spring of 1993 in Santa Monica, California, where Ligeti was staying as a guest artist of the Paul Getty Foundation and when he also attended the American premiere of the Violin Concerto in Los Angeles. He had been invited for a whole year, and did, in fact, spend longer in America, but was in California for only six weeks. During this time he lived alone and enjoyed cycling every day beside the Pacific. At the piano in his apartment he experimented with 'tactile figurations, sonorities, shapes and technical propositions'. He had in mind the airborne, sun-drenched, dazzling cascades in the piano music of Liszt and in Debussy's *L'Isle joyeuse*, and had begun a study based on such ideas. This was Ligeti's first attempt at the piece that might have become Étude 12, and which he intended to call *The isle is full of noises, sounds and sweet airs*.

The thirteenth study, as it now exists, took a different course after an El Niño weather system hit the coast with terrifying force, unleashing storms so ferocious that Ligeti could only struggle back to his apartment with the greatest difficulty, as luxury villas on the heights above him slid wholesale downhill, and he feared for the survival of those living rough on the beach. He had gone for breakfast to a coffee house some two miles away. 'I had to cycle back against the wind, which took about three hours. I had no coat and was completely wet. On the seashore, with the storm coming from North to South, I could not ride – all the time thinking about the disappeared homeless people.' Battling his way up the ascent to his apartment, the music and title of *L'escalier du diable* came into his mind: an endless climbing, a wild apocalyptic vortex, a staircase it was almost impossible to ascend.

We have already noted the use of recursive musical spirals in Études 9, 13 and 14 – descending in *Vertige*, ascending in the other two – and their relationship to the acoustic illusions of Roger Shepard and Jean-Claude Risset. *L'escalier du diable* also alludes to the modern mathematics of chaos and dynamical systems in both its title and rhythmic structure. A 'devil's staircase' is the name given to a specific example of self-similarity based on Cantor sets. The Cantor set is a paradoxical abstract construction which, although first propounded by a nineteenth-century mathematician, Georg Cantor, only came into its own when Benoit Mandelbrot noticed its relevance to the geometry that would result in fractals. Cantor sets are formed by a simple, well-known recursive process. To make one, start with a numerical interval, which can conveniently be represented by a straight line. From this remove a central sub-interval, say the middle third. Two segments remain. Reapply the process to both of them. Now four segments remain. Continue the process ad infinitum. The result is Cantor dust, an infinite number of points arranged in clusters, infinitely sparse, whose total length is zero. One is struck by the rapidity with which the Cantor set accelerates towards nothing, or, at least, towards points so small that they quickly defy both printer's ink and human eyesight. A 'devil's staircase' is a secondary phenomenon derived from the Cantor set, a staircase of unequal steps produced by plotting the mathematical relationship between the eliminated and surviving segments. Drawn graphically, it looks something like a rock face. Devil's staircases also appear in probability theory and play a role in 'mode locking', i.e. the synchronisation of frequencies between oscillators, clocks, pendulums etc.

Although Ligeti was aware of the geometry of a 'devil's staircase', he used the idea only metaphorically, making his own numerical framework. The music, however, is certainly reiterative, and its rhythmic relationship of two to three is at the heart of the Cantor equation. But it was the symbolism of the title and the physical experience of the storm that inspired the piece. Indeed, *L'escalier du diable* is the most extravagant and menacing of all the Études, and culminates in a series of immense, portentous chords swinging back and forth demonically.

The piece starts softly but ominously with energetic, additive rhythms based on metrical modules of seven, nine and eleven quavers. After a bar and a half's 'false start', a basic pattern is presented, and then repeated over and over. Each module is subdivided into rhythmic cells of two or three quavers. The three-quaver cell is the last in each module, and makes a small plateau, like the wider steps occuring in the staircase. The sequence of modules repeatedly expands and contracts as follows: 2 + 2 + 3 / 2 + 2 + 2 + 3 / 2 + 2 + 2 + 2 + 3 / 2 + 2 + 2 + 3 / 2 + 2 + 3 etc. There is also a pitch module, but out of phase with the rhythmic modules. The first note of each pitch cell starts progressively higher, following a twelve-note chromatic scale from B to A sharp. The remaining pitches come from two matching intervallic groups, contained within a whole-tone scale commencing on F sharp/G flat. Their combination gives the whole line a more complex tonality than if it were only chromatic or only whole-tone.

Ex. 28 Opening pitch modules in *L'escalier du diable*

This pattern recommences on the note B after every twelve cells. But since the pitch module has twelve cells and the rhythmic modules total sixteen before repeating themselves, rhythmic and melodic patterns combine differently on each occasion. Together they climb into the upper octaves as if mounting an endless staircase, flight upon flight. Meanwhile the patterns restart in low register, as if emerging from dark subterranean dungeons, a resolute ascent recurring ad infinitum like the Shepard–Risset spiral.

But the process is never rigid. Typically, it is tempered by Ligeti's instinctive sense of development and by what the hands can physically play. Entries soon overlap, come more frequently, begin on different pitch classes and are doubled in a variety of parallel thirds, fourths, fifths and sixths. Around halfway through, the upward spiralling quavers are arrested by a deep B flat minor triad. This initiates the fateful slow section of gradually rising chords climbing semitonally, one note at a time, as if laboriously clambering up limb by limb. The awesome harmonies rise majestically and inexorably, increasing in volume until drawn into two superimposed cycles of clangorous ostinati. Pairs of chords toll in uneven ratios of 2:4, 2:3 and simultaneously 3:4. 'Like a wild ringing of bells', 'like bells, gongs, tamtams', Ligeti writes in the score, reminding one of Berlioz's *Symphonie Fantastique* – or even more graphically, of Quasimodo. Here we have Ligeti at his most melodramatic in music which makes an overwhelmingly powerful and thrilling climax to the fourteen studies of Books 1 and 2. *Coloana infinită* follows on machine-like, its own ascending quaver sequences reinforcing those of the previous study, hammering home unrelentingly – brilliant and blinding, like beaten bronze.

Étude 14: *Coloana infinită* (*The Infinite Column*), 1993.
Also published as Étude 14A: *Coloana fara sfârsit* for player piano
(ad lib. live pianist)[11]

Étude 14 exists in two versions, and these alternative solutions to the same technical challenge are as interesting to compare as Ligeti's different treatment of the ostinato motif in Étude 4 (*Fanfares*) and the second movement of the Horn Trio. Both versions of the study are to be performed as fast as possible, the suggested tempo requiring seven chords per second. The original version is 14A. But even Pierre-Laurent Aimard had difficulty playing it and asked Ligeti to simplify the texture by reducing the number of dyads in each hand. This necessitated changing some of the pitches. As a result, the harmonic structure of the second version (actually printed first as Étude 14) is significantly different. The dramatic effect of both is much the same, but the original is to be preferred as a more perfect realisation of the concept. Since Jürgen Hocker transcribed it for mechanical piano, some pianists attempt this version too, including Aimard – although in concert he performs the revised version. On one occasion he ended by hitting not top C, but the wood beyond it. Ligeti liked the effect and Aimard continues to end this way.

The study is named after the thirty-five-metre column created in 1937 by the Romanian sculptor Constantin Brâncuçi in the Romanian town of Târgu-Jiu. Brâncuçi used both titles, the one meaning 'infinite column', the other 'column without end'. It was a subject to which he

repeatedly returned. Several examples can be seen amongst the collected sculptures which he retained in his studio, and which are now
rehoused close to the Pompidou Centre in Paris. But its realisation in
Târgu-Jiu is the most impressive. Cast in iron and coated in bronze, so
that it gleams in the sun, the column is a repetitive series of expanding
and contracting pyramidal shapes (base to base, apex to apex), threaded
vertically, like beads, onto a square internal steel shaft. Abstract and
elegant, its soaring geometry appears capable of infinite extension.

Ligeti had seen only pictures of the column, but was inspired to
choose it as a subject before he had composed any of the music.
Initially he mapped out different contrary-motion symmetrical scales,
but then did not use them. Two aspects of Brâncuçi's design are reflected
in the published first version of the Étude, although the connection
was unconscious. The Târgu-Jiu column has sixteen and a half abutted
pyramidal shapes, or modules, zigzagging skywards: an extended
single pyramid at the base, fifteen full modules, plus a half-module on
top. Each musical module is an ascending column of pitches composed
essentially in two lines, the intervals between the dyads alternately
expanding and contracting, like the pattern of the column. A more
extraordinary coincidence is that the original version of the study also
has sixteen and a half modules, beginning in low register and ascending progressively higher. Played alternately by each hand, they produce
overlapping spirals, requiring the pianist repeatedly to cross hands in
order to start again at the bottom on progressively lower notes. In
each hand the modules start on successive steps of a descending whole-
tone scale from C^2 to C^1. It is only because Ligeti decided to repeat the
first Cs in each hand before commencing the descent, that this totals
sixteen rather than fourteen modules, to which is added a truncated
half-module at the end.

It would be satisfying for the musicologist if the similarity had been
intentional, but it was not. In devising the music, Ligeti was thinking
more of Risset's computer illusion of ascending spirals that stay in the
same place. In any case, his modules are not, like Brâncuçi's, all alike.
Ligeti's get progressively longer, beginning in the left hand with forty-
four quavers and culminating in a last full right-hand module of 129
quavers. The astonishing length of this last is made possible (despite
the apparent limit imposed by the eighty-eight keys of the piano)
because the pitches zigzag, moving alternately up and down, and only
ascending as a general tendency. The final section of this marathon

ascent is reinforced by the truncated 'half' module of forty-five quavers in the left hand, the bravura ending being marked by the composer, with characteristic extravagance, to be played *ffffffff*. In the original version the sixteen full modules end progressively higher, as they also commence progressively lower. One other element contributes to the grandeur of the music: an imposing theme of chords in the *aksak* rhythm 3 + 2 + 2 + 3 + 2 + 2 + 2, heard twice during the last third of the study, once in each hand.

TROISIÈME LIVRE

Étude 15: *White on White*, 1995; Étude 16: *Pour Irina*, 1996–97;
Étude 17: *À bout de souffle* (*Out of Breath*), 1997;
Étude 18: *Canon*, 2001

So far Ligeti has composed four studies in Book 3, and their similarities justify considering them together. They are gentler and less dramatic than their predecessors, in fact more of a consolidation. But although variants of familiar processes, each pursues a slightly different concept. Characteristic of all four are their unbroken rhythmic lines, either in quavers, crotchets or minims. In each except *À bout de souffle* (which is played 'Presto con bravura' throughout), the tempo increases in a series of steps, resembling the 'division' playing of seventeenth-century music, in which lines are progressively split into shorter and shorter notes to create variations. All the Book 3 studies except *Pour Irina* are written in strict canon, either at the octave or double octave, the second part trailing the first by only one or two pulses. Ligeti handles the special demands this close shadowing makes upon contrapuntal and harmonic technique with apparent ease.

White on White was the result of a request for a new Étude by the Royal Conservatory in the Hague. To fulfil the commission Ligeti tried out several ideas, including one entitled *Métamorphose (Hommage à Maurits Escher)* and another called *Presto en blanc (Hommage à Alkan)*. The notion of writing a piece entirely on the white notes was the logical outcome of a gradual retreat from chromaticism dating back to *Lux aeterna*. Indeed, it recalls the selective disciplines of *Musica ricercata*. Poised, chaste and exquisite, *White on White* consists of two sections: a mild-mannered canon at the octave and a bright Vivace. Both employ only the white keys, until lightly dusted with accidentals in the final three lines. Despite its temperate harmony the study contains no concords, maintaining a gently dissonant climate throughout.

The same character appears in *Pour Irina*, dedicated to Pierre-Laurent Aimard's wife, the pianist Irina Kataeva. This time the opening section is written on the diatonic scale of D flat major – but without A flats, so it is really hexatonic; other accidentals are withheld until the last eleven chords. The melodies of each hand are similar but this time not canonic. The second section doubles the tempo and introduces chromatic coloration. The third redoubles it and is more multitonal.

Canon at the octave returns in *À bout de souffle*, which is written in non-stop quavers led by the right hand, with the left following one quaver behind. Again Ligeti uses mainly the white keys plus selective accidentals (frequent E flats and an alternation between A flat and natural) to suggest an Indonesian or Melanesian flavour. But the breathless changes of direction are like a Mack Sennett movie. Irregular accents trip up the chase. There is a sudden reversal where the right hand pursues the left, and just as suddenly reveals a cantabile melody. The tempo is arrested by five stark chords, each double the length of the one before.

Originally to be called *Casse doigt* (*Finger-breaker*) – a title used by Jelly Roll Morton – Étude 18 ended up as just *Canon*. It is composed mostly in dyads trailed by the canon two quavers later, this time at two octaves below. At first the dyads emphasise perfect fifths played on the white notes, but the harmony soon becomes chromatic and multitonal. There are no bar lines and, for the first page, no accents. The onward flow of four-note chords occupies most of the study and is played twice: the first time fast, the second even faster. Finally there is a slow soft coda of mildly dissonant triads, also played in canon to produce piquant six-note discords.

The concentration in Book 3 on white notes and a gently inflected modality is unprecedented in Ligeti's music. Doubtless, he felt that he needed to move away from the tonal and rhythmic complexity of the studies in Book 2, all but one of which are marked 'Vivacissimo', 'Presto' or 'Prestissimo'. This leaves open the question of whether Book 3 can achieve the stature of the other two. Yet the existing eighteen studies, as a totality, already constitute an astonishing document of imagination and intellect. For pianists able to encompass their great technical demands they offer spectacular additions to the repertoire. For composers and musicologists they are a textbook of compositional processes; for ordinary listeners a vivid and arresting introduction to music in the late twentieth century. Performed in concert, the cumulative effect of exploring similar issues from so many viewpoints creates a sequence of encyclopaedic breadth, from which both performer and listener emerge exhilarated and enriched.

The Grawemeyer Award

The year after he composed them, Book 1 of the Études won the 1986 University of Louisville Grawemeyer Award. Endowed in 1984 by a retired Louisville engineer, it is the world's most lucrative prize for composition. After Lutosławski won the first Grawemeyer Award in 1985 for his Third Symphony, he was asked to assist in choosing his successor, a practice which has continued. Ligeti, in turn, joined the American critic Martin Bernheimer and Lawrence Leighton Smith, music director of the Louisville Symphony Orchestra, in choosing Harrison's Birtwistle's opera, *The Mask of Orpheus*, to win the award in 1987. The two composers were but slightly acquainted, and Ligeti got to know Birtwistle personally only in the late 1990s. Warming to his 'very special humour', and deeply interested in his music, he found Birtwistle to be one of the few composers with whom he could still exchange ideas with the frankness and freedom of the Darmstadt years.

Ligeti's ability to attend the Grawemeyer Award ceremony was at first in question. During the early 1980s, he had suffered periods of ill health; struggling to control high blood pressure, he doubted whether he would be able to fly again. In the event, the Grawemeyer distinction encouraged him to return to America for the first time in many years. In November 1986 Vera and Lukas accompanied the composer to New York and thence to Louisville. Now nineteen, Lukas was himself studying composition as well as percussion in Vienna and, with his penchant for jazz, he was particularly eager to experience the city in which he would subsequently choose to live. The day after the presentation the family returned to New York, where the Book 1 Études and the Horn Trio were performed in a celebratory concert at Merkin Hall – both works played twice – and Ligeti's spoken introductions were typically charismatic. Staying on for several days, he made three visits to the Metropolitan Museum of Modern Art, specifically to study again the formality of shape and colour in Cézanne.

14

Curiouser and curiouser

After each completed composition I revise my position; I
avoid stylistic clichés, and know no 'single right way'. I keep
myself open to new influences, as I am excessively intellectually curious. All cultures, indeed the whole wide world is the
material of Art.

György Ligeti[1]

Work in progress

In the Paul Sacher Foundation in Basle, amongst numerous sketches
for the Piano Concerto, is a grey folder containing twenty-one A3
photocopies. Ligeti gave the originals to Mario di Bonaventura along
with the autograph score, in line with their commission agreement.
These photocopies are but the tip of an iceberg, but they tell an astonishing story. All are different attempts to write the first page. Since
many of them are riddled with crossings out and amendments, it is
surprising to find that the second of them is actually a fair copy. Dated
summer 1980, it is an orderly version of ideas mapped out in his first
sketch on 16 July, and was presumably written out in Ligeti's best
hand to send to di Bonaventura as evidence that he had begun (see
Ex. 29a, p. 317). It was a long time before this promissory note would
be redeemed. Ligeti was soon dissatisfied with it and trying other
possibilities. Only at the twenty-first attempt, dated 1985–86, do we
find ourselves looking at the opening of the first movement as we now
know it. The fact is that it took Ligeti the best part of six years finally
to decide how the Concerto should begin.

The sequence is a fascinating testament of trial and uncertainty, of
Ligeti's repeated rejection of ideas that failed to live up to his ideal. It is
easy to see why the Bartókian rhetoric of his first attempt displeased
him. By September 1980 he had disrupted its conventional continuity
by inserting longer rests. The opening three pitches are reinterpreted as

four separate phrases using syncopated semiquavers, triplet quavers, triplet crotchets and quaver-crotchet groups displaced across the beat – four rhythmic treatments of the same intervallic cell like the opening of Webern's Concerto op. 24. Two years later the same idea becomes a jagged hocket for wind against strings; but Ligeti has not worked out their metrical relationship to his satisfaction. Other sketches develop the motif as a mensural canon: quavers in the piano, triplet crotchets in the bass, quintuplet quavers (varied and inverted) in an unspecified treble. The ninth sketch shows a more developed variant of this idea. It is actually the fourth page of an earlier effort, renumbered to become the first page of a new version, and with the quintuplet quavers in the piano (Ex. 29b). Into this material, in a later sketch, Ligeti injects an incisive ascending chordal theme for the soloist. By 4 August 1984 the chordal theme has become more commanding, the hocket reduced to a fragmented accompaniment. But it is a blind alley. All his attempts so far are marked 'Agitato', 'Allegro appassionato', or similar. A page from December 1985 cools their ardour and emphasises rhythm: 'Risoluto, Allegro molto ritmico energico'. But it contains very few notes.

Composition of the first six piano Études in 1985 suggested other ways forward for the Concerto. Now he tries a texture of rippling semiquavers supporting a *lamento*-style melody, as in *Automne à Varsovie*. Transferred into 6/4 and headed 'Appassionato funebre', the rippling becomes more polymetric; but the texture proves to be too dense and is completely crossed out (Ex. 29c). The twentieth sketch is the first to show the swinging triplets, contrasting black and white scales, and asymmetrical melodic style of the final composition. This seems to have gone well, although as yet it is scored only for piano and percussion, lacking the strings. Some overwriting shows that the next, and final, 'first' page originated as page five of another draft, probably its immediate predecessor. This twenty-first attempt is the first to notate different key signatures, and to define the polymetric relationship as it exists in the published score (Ex. 29d).

During all these years, Ligeti also explored ideas for the other movements, but with similar difficulty. Once he found a viable formula for the first, composition appears to have proceeded much more quickly. But there are still many crossings out and corrections of detail. By autumn 1986, six years after he had begun, Ligeti felt obliged to permit performance of the three movements then complete, knowing that the Concerto's internal balance still required him to write more.

Exx. 29a, b, c and d (see following pages)
Four of Ligeti's many attempts at the Piano Concerto's first page, written
between 1980 and what he finally adopts as its opening in 1986

Ex. 29b

Ex. 29c

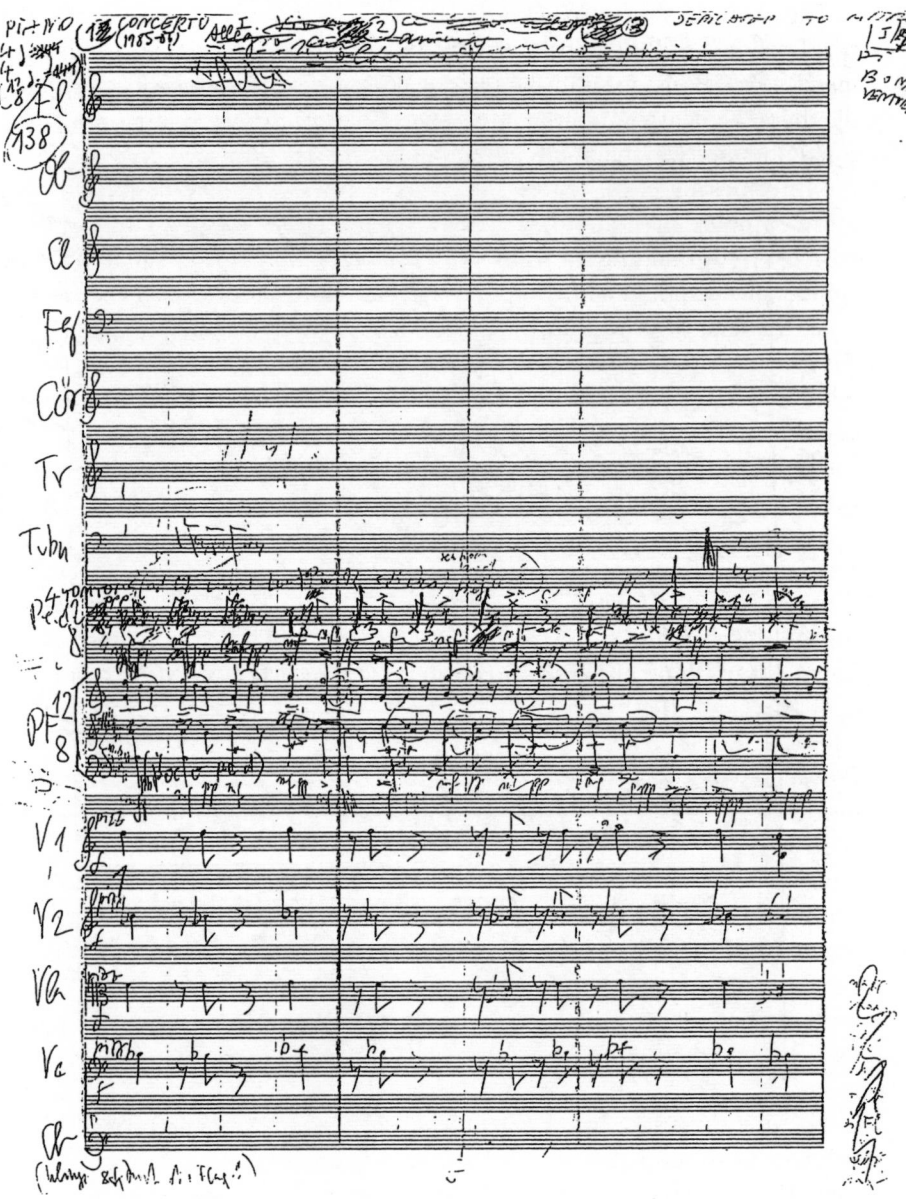

Ex. 29d

The problem was stylistic; not so much a lack of ideas, but of structural models for their integration. The solution lay in finding new metrical relationships and the technical assurance with which to handle them. Nancarrow, mathematics, the *ars subtilior*, the Banda-Linda, tonal and metrical machines: all mingled in Ligeti's mind as he devised the interlocking cogs, whose interaction in the finished Concerto is more complex than anything he had constructed. This was the price paid for reformulating his technique, yet again, from the ground up. A similar problem had confronted him in *Aventures* twenty years earlier – i.e. the lack of procedural precedent. As a result he had broken off *Aventures* at the point where it then seemed long enough, resuming where he left off three years later, and calling its successor *Nouvelles aventures*. The disinclination to repeat himself and relentless search for renewal intensified in the 1980s, causing Ligeti constantly to discard, revise and augment.

The Piano Concerto was neither the first nor the last of Ligeti's compositions to receive its premiere incomplete. The Violin Concerto went through several stages. The *Nonsense Madrigals* grew from an initial four to the current six. The *Hamburg Concerto* is undergoing revision. Ligeti is not alone among contemporary composers in making piecemeal progress: Boulez is a similar case. Significantly, however, Ligeti has written no extended single movement since *San Francisco Polyphony* of 1973–74. His musical thinking has become increasingly modular, with the possibility of adding components and changing their order. New possibilities arise after hearing work in progress. Considering the uncharted terrain into which his polymetric exploration, novel temperaments and microtonality have led him, the value of testing in performance is understandable. And rigour demands time. Ligeti's reluctance to authorise engraved or computer-set editions even of relatively old pieces such as *Melodien* stems from the fact that, by his own meticulous standards, he has not yet had time to perfect them.

The first three movements of the Piano Concerto were performed in Graz in October 1986 by Anthony di Bonaventura and the Vienna Philharmonic, conducted by Mario di Bonaventura to whom the whole work is dedicated. With the addition of the fourth and fifth movements, the complete work was premiered in Vienna in February 1988, also by the Bonaventura brothers but with the Austrian Radio Symphony Orchestra. In its final form it is a ground-breaking achievement that is ingenious, passionate and athletic, yet sounds surprisingly effortless. Presenting a formidable challenge to the pianist, there is, however, very little opposition between orchestra and soloist, the concertante piano part being but the most prominent component of an intricate polymetric counterpoint in which every instrument functions soloistically. Pierre-Laurent Aimard writes of how the composer's

profusion of ideas . . . remains astonishingly controlled, with the wildest musical arguments fully integrated into a language of astounding coherency . . . To perform it requires insane gesticularity and virtuosity and an unbridled imagination, but it also demands a constant concern for a sense of balance, together with great respect for the work's polyphonic textures and an acute sense of rhythmic and formal integration. And all this must be combined with the most relaxed flexibility, the most unbearable dramatic tension and the most caustic conceivable humour.[2]

The Concerto is scored for single winds and brass, plus two percussionists, but with the option of using either a small string ensemble or solo quintet. The horn part is written frequently in natural harmonics, as in the Horn Trio, its deviant intonation not to be 'corrected'. Because Ligeti worked on the Concerto concurrently with the Trio and then with the Études, there are similarities in keyboard style and technical concept. The first movement relates to *Désordre*; the second revisits the 'Lamento' finale of the Trio and the third *Automne à Varsovie* – like them, exploring different treatments of the *lamento* motif. The fourth movement is Ligeti's closest representation of fractals, at least in intent. For to the ear, the second, third, fourth and fifth movements seem also to be variants of each other; indeed, the whole work is remarkably homogeneous.

Exploring the secrets of erratic phenomena, which were regarded as inexplicable according to Newtonian physics and wrongly thought to be exceptional, became an intoxicant for many scientists and the wider intellectual community during the late twentieth century. Fractals, as James Gleick remarks, have kept science in tune with 'a peculiarly modern feeling for untamed, uncivilised, undomesticated nature',[3] and with what we now understand to be a predominantly non-deterministic world. From early on, Ligeti's music inclined towards a volatile discontinuity, and the explorations of contemporary physics influenced the Piano Concerto most of all. It relates to those non-linear phenomena which Gleick likens to 'walking through a maze whose walls arrange themselves with every step you take'.[4] The music is founded on instability. It invents its structural map as it proceeds, although it is also a composite of the fixed relationships eventually defined in the score. As Ligeti wrote before the Graz performance, the Concerto represents 'frozen time, as an object in imaginary space' which unfolds in the reality of passing time, but which we can 'imagine to be present in the simultaneity of every moment'.[5]

The Piano Concerto's five movements

The first movement returns to the polymetric concept of *Désordre*, but with an entirely different outcome. At its heart is the simultaneous use of two time signatures, 4/4 and 12/8. They share the same metronomic speed (crotchet/dotted crotchet = 138) but use different durational formulae, so are audibly distinct. Here there is less pulling apart than in the study, but instead a dazzling collage of simultaneous yet separate routines, like individual dancers in an intricate ensemble of ever-changing allegiances. Into this rhythmic vortex Ligeti throws a continuous variety of ideas, individually scored, each in its own metre, meshing them together in music of breathtaking speed and dexterity.

The 12/8 layer is built on a recurrent sequence grouped assymetrically in 3 3 3 2 3 3 3 4 2 2 2 compound-time quaver beats, totalling two and a half bars per cycle. The 4/4 time signature of the other layer makes it sound more spacious, because the quaver subdivisions move more slowly. This repeats a pattern of 3 3 3 4 2 2 3 2 2 simple-time quaver beats, totalling three bars per cycle. For almost the whole movement both cycles run simultaneously, at one point reduced to only their rhythmic outline (just before the first piano episode at letter F). Far from being fixed, they are variously distributed so that no instrument sticks to one cycle consistently. As the music evolves, Ligeti adds other layers, using units of ♪, ♩♪ and ♩♪, resulting in a mercurial kaleidoscope of contrasting melodic characters and articulation. The new layers race ahead and slow down, always with an *aksak* inequality. No rhythmic cycle dominates, neither in 12/8 nor 4/4. What is remarkable is that in music so dynamic there is no fundamental pulse at all, but rather a compendium of pulses. In this it differs, for instance, from John Adams's polymetric technique in his Chamber Symphony (1992) and *Century Rolls* (1996), whose rhythmic intricacies are hierarchically related to a predominant crotchet beat.

Amid such instability, it is of little consequence that the initial 4/4 and 12/8 cycles coincide every fifteen bars. After only thirty bars, time signatures are exchanged and the pianist introduces a new cycle of fifteen dotted quaver pulses in the right hand against the 3 3 3 4 2 2 3 2 2 quaver cycle in the left. For the two cycles to coincide again, they would have to run for one hundred and seven bars plus seven quavers. Ligeti retains them for only eleven bars, by which time other rhythmic distractions have occurred: cycles of twelve dotted quavers in the strings (previously heard at letter A), and of 5 5 5 10, 5 5 10, 5 5 semiquavers (i.e. units of ♩♪) in the horn at letter G. This formula comes from the *lamento* motif of *Automne à Varsovie*, and returns in the Concerto's third movement. Meanwhile (from bar 31) the original 12/8 pattern of 3 3 3 2 3 3 3 4 2 2 2 continues. As a result, at letter G, we hear five separate cycles simultaneously, all of different duration and featuring four different metrical units: ♪, ♪., ♪₃ and ♩♪. The dotted quaver unit is used by both piano and strings, but out of phase with each other. As the movement proceeds, these simultaneously whirling mechanisms, with their eccentric instrumentation, trigger more bizarre partnerships, like the gyrations of one of Tinguely's flamboyant sculptures. In Ligeti's own analogy, 'when it is properly played, after a certain amount of time this music will "lift off" like an aeroplane. The rhythmic event transforms into a hovering.'[6]

As in many of the Études, right and left hands of the piano part are written in complementary modes, here a white six-note scale in the right hand and its inversion in the left (see Ex. 26l, p. 297). Together they make a twelve-note row, but it has no serial significance. The same two scales characterise many of the instrumental parts, such as the flute and clarinet duet in bars 33–35, but there are other harmonic components too, including enhanced overtones and untempered natural harmonics – a foretaste of the Violin Concerto. The music is flooded with melody, not only buoyant playful dance tunes (like that for the piccolo at letter O) but others spaciously serene (like the expressive violin melody at bar 43). Melodies trigger others at different speeds, as if through a system of asynchronous gears. But the forces of disorder are never far away. In the middle of the movement, at letter N, both hands in the piano follow the familiar 4/4 cycle of 3 3 3 4 2 2 3 2 2 quavers, but with a discrepancy in the last unit of the left-hand sequence (3 3 3 4 2 2 3 2 3) threatening, as in *Désordre*, to throw orderliness into disarray. Ligeti's control of these disparate strands is a triumph of cohesion, at the climax of which five metrical layers again occur together.

Harmonically the music draws upon familiar ingredients, but sounding at times quite other-worldly. Together, the two six-note scales produce a preponderance of 'open' intervals: perfect fourths and tritones for the flute and clarinet duet; perfect fifths, tritones and major thirds at the beginning. Although rhythmically distinct, the 4/4 and 12/8 cycles have related intervallic content, as if they were simultaneous variants of the same melody: compare, for instance, the pitches of the piano right hand and the first violin from bar 1. With its transparent harmony, this gives the music a curiously Asiatic flavour. Ligeti avoids the twelve-note chromaticism which could arise from aggregating his two scales. As the movement develops, the repertoire of intervals grows more astringent and the chords get thicker. But there still remains a Gauguin-like 'primitivism' and, as in Debussy, a blurring of the distinction between chord structure and timbral coloration. Melodies become melodies of chords – or, rather, of timbral enhancements. One such appears at letter A, where the rhythmic cycle of twelve dotted quavers has a melody doubled at the fifth and tenth in major triads, but differentiated in volume and timbre so that the upper notes colour the fundamental, played by high bassoon. Variants of this chord-melody employ different partials: dominant seventh enhancements at letter G; root, seventh, ninth and eleventh at H; first inversion major triads played in high artificial harmonics at K; minor triads built upon a major seventh above the root at V; the same construction but with fourths added to each minor triad at letter AA. These interlocking micro-mechanisms reveal Ligeti's love of devising 'technical gadgets', a tendency he has disarmingly called 'ridiculous'.[7] But it is not at all ridiculous when playfulness, intelligence and inspirational musicianship work together.

The second movement, *Lento e deserto*, sounds like an arrested, stripped-down, desolate version of the first. But in fact the second and third movements are siblings, inheriting melodic features from the same parents: the last movement of the Horn Trio and *Automne à Varsovie*. There is no prime version of the *lamento* motif in either movement – any more than there is in the study – but rather its essence: a sorrowful, generally chromatic, scalic descent and the characteristic contours and durational *taleae* of its three component phrases (see Ex. 26c, p. 296). In the second movement at letter N, where the *lamento* melody is a stream of soft but piquant chords, the descending steps are mainly tones, not semitones; but the angst of earlier versions is intensified, in that every accompanying chord contains a major-seventh interval. In whatever format the *lamento* formula reappears, its identity is unmistakable. Observe, for instance, how in different contexts these dissonances and melodic lifts (usually on the fifth and ninth notes) divide the third phrase into two or three descending segments.

At the start of the second movement, the motif is transformed into a quasi-canon of isolated fragments, punctuated by long rests, as if frozen in that hollow register where the low notes of the piccolo and the top notes of the bassoon just overlap. (A more flippant encounter between these two instruments concludes the last of the *Ten Pieces for Wind Quintet* of 1968.) Curious orchestration is a feature of the movement, with quasi-canonic entries for slide-whistle and ocarina, a long bleak *lamento* melody from the solo piano in perfect fourths and tritones stretched across a void of six and a half octaves, and many other instances, eerie or strident, straining at the registral extremities. The opening of the movement is written in Messiaen's third mode of limited transposition: tone/semitone/semitone/tone/semitone/semitone, etc. Was this done consciously or unconsciously? With Ligeti, it is hard to tell. Up to bar 30, all the imitative entries use this mode in the same transposition (i.e. C, D, E flat, E, F sharp, G, A flat, B flat, B), hence the consistent emotional atmosphere. The stark piano passage between bars 32 and 40 employs the scale in both hands, transposed a semitone lower. The shrill counterpoint of extremely high lines between letters I and M adopts another transposition. Later these plaintive harmonies open out into brighter fifths and sixths. As in the first movement, melodic lines subdivide, so that the most elaborate texture occurs at the end, where five differently harmonised versions of the *lamento* motif are heard together. The ringing resonances of each strand – notably the fifths and fourths in the piano – endow this climax with an almost heroic passion, the solo pianist 'belabouring the instrument like a man possessed'. Elsewhere are dark nocturnal shadows.

Echoes of *Automne à Varsovie* haunt almost every bar of the third movement. The music is headed by three related time signatures, $\overset{2}{}\!\!\overset{}{}$, and $\overset{8}{}$, but without courting the complexity of the first movement. As in the study, there is a continuous background of incessant semiquavers, first in groups of two, then four, expanding from a cluster of pitches as in earlier Ligeti. Soon, these patterns are joined by other tempi. Variants of the melancholy *lamento* melody from Étude 6 flow above, below, and within the texture, just as they did in the study, but now adhering more dutifully to the durational *taleae*. They employ even more metric units than the study, of which the following are a selection, all measured in multiples of semiquavers:

bar 6, piano RH: 7 7 7 14, 7 7 7 7 14, 7 7 14 7 7 7 7 14, 14 7
bar 15, piano RH and flute: 10 10 10 20, 10 10 10 10 20, 20 . . .
bar 16, piano LH: 6 6 6 12, 6 6 6 6 12, 6 6 12 6 6 6 6 6 6
bar 26, piano RH: 5 5 5 10, 5 5 5 5 10, 5 5 10 5 5 5 5 5 5 10 5 5
bar 25, piano LH: 6 3 3 6, 3 3 3 3 3 6, 3 6 3 3 3 6
bar 52, piano RH: 11 11 10 23, 11 11 11 11 22, 22 11 11 11 11
    11 11 22 22 11 11 . . . (the third and fourth durations are either
    expressive licence or incorrectly calculated)
bar 77, piano, flute and oboe: 9 9 9 18, 9 9 9 9 18, 9 9 18 9 9 9 9
    9 18
bar 79, piano LH: 4 4 4 4 4 4 4 4 4 4 etc . . . .

Simultaneous patterns are differentiated by their dynamics. And, as in the study, the pianist must often play faster accentuation in the left hand, whilst the right glides above in longer notes. In the Concerto movement there is greater contrast between the durational units of the slowest *lamento* melodies and the semiquaver continuum, which trickles through the texture like a Schubertian brook. To accompany the *lamento* motif other tunes emerge, creating a contrapuntal fabric reminiscent of *Melodien*. All of them relate to material in the first movement – the horn melodies, for example, have similar characteristics throughout the whole work. The episode at letter G brings brighter *aksak* rhythms, also reminiscent of the first movement. These, too, are heard in increasingly spirited variants as the texture reaches a frenzied and extravagant climax.

To many of those hearing the intermediate three-movement Concerto, it may have sounded a little short, but musically not incomplete. Ligeti, however, believed that other dimensions were needed, but precisely what it was hard to identify. Why a five-movement piece? Up until now he had composed nothing in five movements; indeed, only his piano and wind music had more than four. One reason was that the disjointed manner of the fractal movement taking shape in his head could not conclude the composition. There would have to be a fifth movement with more continuous energy and momentum. As a result, the Concerto's final structure is an alternation between the flowing and the fragmentary, continuity and discontinuity.

Ligeti wanted to represent fractal processes in sound but was unsure how to do so. He could have applied a precise numerical formula, the Mandelbrot Set perhaps. But despite his own bent for mathematics, he preferred to work intuitively, inspired by the visual images produced by the Bremen team with their interest in computer graphics. Heinz-Otto Peitgen was the first person to realise the Julia Set as a computer graphic (which its inventor, Gaston Julia, did not live to see), and his '29 Arms at Seahorse Valley' – a mathematical study of the Mandelbrot Set – was a direct inspiration for the Concerto. The building blocks in its fourth movement are conventional: again, two six-note hexachords comprising all twelve semitones (although not used serially), from which Ligeti extracts triads like Berg in his Violin Concerto. But the music evolves in the manner of animated computer fractals, from a simple beginning to a complex outcome. A classic fractal experiment is to trace the path of an oscillating iron pendulum over three coloured magnets, every position from which the pendulum is released being marked with the colour of the magnet above which it comes to rest. The traced image is self-reflective, but becomes increasingly exuberant. Progressive elaboration, both intricate and flamboyant, has long been part of Ligeti's music. In this specifically fractal movement, the musical gestures are dislocated by cessations, silences, reversals, antitheses, in ever-decreasing values and ever increasing density.

Its formal process is fractal in time: reiterating the same formula, the same succession always in different shapes, using simultaneous augmentation and diminution of the same models . . . focusing on smaller and smaller details – self-similar in everything, e.g. gestures, intervallic shapes . . .[8]

The final movement is a more seamless mixture of ideas from earlier in the work. Its rhythmic interplay and unfailing pace have a Stravinskyan dexterity. Like the third movement, it sports three related time signatures: really three different ways of dividing twelve quavers to the bar. Characteristically, these subgroups and their accents are frequently displaced both across the bar line and against each other; indeed, in metrical virtuosity, this *Presto luminoso* approaches the complexity of the first movement. It brings to an exhilarating conclusion a work that establishes a formidable new style, independent from both the avant-garde and fashionable post-modernism.

Nonsense Madrigals

In May 1988, Ligeti turned sixty-five. European festivals from Aarhus to Amsterdam featured his music, amongst them the Berliner Festwochen in a package of four concerts given in the small hall of the Philharmonie on 24–25 September. On this occasion the first four of the *Nonsense Madrigals* were premiered by the King's Singers in a concert which also contained first performances of Études 7 and 8.

The commission from Berlin enabled Ligeti to revisit an old addiction, the work of Lewis Carroll, and also led him to other Victorian poets like Edward Lear and the more obscure William Brighty Rands. At an early age, he had discovered *Alice's Adventures in Wonderland* in the Hungarian translation by Frigyes Karinthy. Karinthy was himself a great humorist: dry, sceptical and sarcastic, like Jonathan Swift, whom he also translated. Ligeti came to realise that Hungarian and English literature uniquely share a rich tradition of nonsense. To set Hungarian he need look no further than Sándor Weöres; but for a performance by British singers, he wanted English texts. He was 'aware that people from the Continent like myself can never really capture the nuances of British understatement and humour', but 'could not resist the temptation to try'.⁹ Eventually he chose texts by Rands and Carroll for the first two madrigals, based the third on the alphabet (treated phonetically), and for the fourth used a Victorian translation of 'The Story of Flying Robert' from Heinrich Hoffmann's *Struwwelpeter*. The fifth madrigal was commissioned by London's South Bank Centre for its 'Ligeti by Ligeti' Festival in 1989, and sets Carroll's 'Lobster Quadrille'. The final text, 'A Long, Sad Tale', comes from *Alice's Adventures in Wonderland* mixed with word-patterns from Carroll's *Original Games and Puzzles*. Commissioned by the King's Singers themselves, this was premiered during a first performance of the complete set of *Nonsense Madrigals* at the Huddersfield Contemporary Music Festival in 1993.

The *Nonsense Madrigals* are fast, pithy, and dexterous, their wit conveyed by rapid verbal delivery and mimicry. The humour is never ostentatious; indeed, it is somewhat obscured by Ligeti's rhythmic complexities. As he wryly observes, one can listen to the pieces either as 'technical virtuosic constructions or as emotionally charged messages. Both are nonsense!'[10] The first madrigal is multi-layered. Its polymetric character relates to the Piano Concerto and the first book of Études, although the use of three simultaneous texts recalls the French motets of the thirteenth century. The piece combines two related poems by William Brighty Rands, and a 'cantus firmus' on Carroll's parody of the nursery rhyme 'Twinkle, Twinkle, Little Star' ('Twinkle, Twinkle, Little Bat' in Carroll), from which Ligeti quotes both words and melody – the latter in the key of C flat.[11] Instead of even beats, however, each phrase has a durational pattern of 10 5 10 5 10 5 10. Around the 'cantus firmus', one of the Rands poems is set in divisions of three minims to the bar, the other in divisions of four dotted crotchets. Busy with their metric independence, the separate texts are barely intelligible. We hear brief snatches – 'nine knickerbocker suits . . . little drummer boys' etc.; and the last lines of the two poems, with their contradictory 'bread and cheese', 'bread and jam', are amusingly pitted against each other.

'Cuckoo in the Pear-Tree' also has polymetric passages, but is texturally simpler. Its narrative is easily followed; the distorted nasal tone for the cuckoo's voice and cautious reply, 'perhaps you are not the right cuckoo . . . the proper one', made teasingly ridiculous. For the third madrigal, Ligeti uses the phonetic alphabet as a frame on which to build a slow chordal expansion from a nucleus, a familiar technique, but here lighting momentarily on concords. In the fourth, the prim injunction that, when it rains, 'all good little girls and boys stay at home and mind their toys', is made suitably nauseating; whilst the unhappy demise of Flying Robert – who thought that 'when it pours it's better out of doors', and gets blown aloft clutching his umbrella – is conveyed in windblown, whistling roulades of onomatopoeic ferocity.

The 'Lobster Quadrille' is nicely tailored to the King's Singers' bent for parodistic mimicry. Indications of manner range from 'annoyed' and 'indignant' to 'chattering snobbishly', 'very impatient' and 'hilarious' – almost as extreme as in *Aventures*. The lines of the poem are set against the cyclic repetitions of a terse little march. Just four and a half bars long, it is sung thirteen or so times, always to the same pitches and featuring euphonious dyads and quasi-pentatonic melody. At the words, 'The farther off from England the nearer is to France', there is the barest hint of the British and French national anthems. The final madrigal, 'A Long, Sad Tale', again combines two texts, their music strongly contrasted. A long melisma (mostly in the bass voice) for the Dormouse's 'tale' is accompanied by busy word-patterns in the other parts, in which nouns transmute into their opposite by changing one letter at a time, always via real words: e.g. 'HEAD, heal, teal, tell, tall, TAIL' and 'WITCH, winch, wench, tench, tenth, tents, tints, tilts, tills, fills, falls, fails, fairs, FAIRY!' Predominantly rhythmic and staccato, these mechanistic games make an entertaining, slightly jazzy finale.

Strange attractors – Vivier and the Violin Concerto

As long ago as 1984, Saschko Gawriloff, violinist in the first perform-ance of the Horn Trio, had suggested commissioning a concerto from Ligeti. But it was only towards the end of the decade that Ligeti seri-ously began work on it. Having decided that in this concerto, at least, he would write a highly virtuosic work 'in the tradition of the great violin concertos', he read before beginning composition 'everything about violin technique and, as I always do, studied the instrument's literature. My models were Paganini, the Bach solo sonatas, Ysäye's solo sonatas, Wieniawski and Szymanowski.'[12] During the late 1980s he had discovered another enthusiasm, the music of the French-Canadian composer Claude Vivier (1948–83), who had been murdered tragically young in Paris, and whose distinctly personal style was generating a posthumous cult.

Vivier had studied composition with Stockhausen at the Musikhochschule in Cologne; but it was after he returned from an extended journey through Asia in 1976 – during which he spent months in Iran, Bali and Japan – that his style grew into a singular blend of the Oriental and the ancient. Gregorian chant and an Asiatic homorhythmic harmony meet in music that is ritualistic, exotic, pas-sionate and hypnotically melodic. It dispenses with virtually all counterpoint, but is harmonically and timbrally striking. Like Weöres, 'Vivier imagined a sort of non-existent far Eastern culture'.

Ligeti was attracted to the music for itself, but also to the fact that Vivier was an outsider, forging a path that had little connection with any school or establishment. 'What is so intriguing is he uses a new kind of tuning system for a very subjective, romantic, decadent music.'[13] In 1991 Ligeti gave an interview about Vivier to the

Montreal-based journal *Circuit*.[14] As the music began to receive attention, he made a point of attending performances, and those who knew
of his enthusiasm programmed both composers' music together. For
instance, when the Asko Ensemble with Jonathan Nott and the
Netherlands Chamber Choir toured a mixed concert of Ligeti and
Vivier to five Dutch cities in March 1992, Ligeti was invited to introduce them. His own music he brushed aside; it was the lonely vision of
Vivier he wished to extol.

This new fascination coincided with the direction in which Ligeti's
own muse was leading: towards a hybrid harmony combining 'perfect'
and tempered intervals, Western and non-Western musical elements
and instruments. He had been moving towards it for years. But
although the Violin Concerto uses similar techniques to the Piano
Concerto, it also explores harmonic and timbral combinations in ways
more typical of live electronic treatment. Ethnic musical cultures provide assorted models, particularly the 'amazing harmonics and
overblowing pipes' Ligeti had heard on recordings of music from
Indonesia, New Guinea and the Solomon Islands. At six foot, the
sacred flutes of the Sepik area of Papua New Guinea are the longest in
the world. They are played in groups by around half a dozen men –
women are forbidden even from seeing them – and their extraordinarily ethereal sound comes from the interlocking tonalities produced by
flutes of varying lengths. Many examples of music from the Pacific
islands have been recorded by David Fanshawe; but once more, it was
to Roberto Sierra that Ligeti owed his introduction.

He had no wish to imitate exotic cultures – but how to create his
own 'impure, deviant' harmony posed problems. He could not play it
on an equal-tempered piano. How could he test what he imagined? He
began to experiment on a Yamaha DX7ii synthesiser; in fact, it was
partly due to Ligeti that this instrument existed. The original DX7 had
been marketed in 1983, based on John Chowning's research at
Stanford. Ligeti told Chowning he could not use it; he wanted 'free
tuning' for microtonal music, and together they persuaded Yamaha's
representatives in America to propose this new development to the
company in Japan. Using the DX7ii, Ligeti tried many different tuning
systems, but after two months he became fed up with synthesised
sound. Then he thought of using 'real' instruments that were easy to
tune, like the harpsichord and harp.

I sat down with a harpist for a few days and we tuned the seven strings within the octave so as to divide the octave into seven equal intervals. Next I tried chromatic transpositions, using the pedals. The complexity of the resulting system of harmonies was staggering. It is possible to tune a harp according to any tonal system, which can be trebled by using the pedals. The possibilities latent in the harpsichord are more numerous, yet at the same time fewer: there is no possibility of multiplication by means of pedals, but there are twelve notes to the octave. Finally, I gave up both instruments, realising that I was entering a harmonic labyrinth so complicated that I was getting lost in it.[15]

Whatever ingredients Ligeti put together he would have to rely on his inner ear. Nevertheless, he devised a method, at least to provide a framework for tuning the modestly sized orchestra. Amongst the eleven orchestral string players, one violinist and one viola retune their instruments to the natural harmonics of the double bass (the seventh partial on the G string and fifth partial on the A). This results in the violin being tuned fractionally higher than normal, and the viola lower. The two flutes, oboe, two clarinets and bassoon also inflect notes microtonally whilst the two horns and trombone play natural harmonics as well as tempered passages. Colouring these harmonic spectra are several instruments with imprecise pitch: ocarinas, slide-whistles, a recorder, and a preponderance of metal and tuned percussion. Ligeti's idea was to distribute amongst certain instruments in the orchestra the overtones of the harmonic series, and he imagined 'wonderful new harmonies built of combinations of these overtones . . . It was like solving a three-dimensional crossword puzzle in which the three dimensions, harmony, melodic line and instrumental technique, had to fit together perfectly.'[16] Amid this strange mixture, the solo violinist plays in normal intonation.

Noises, sounds and sweet airs

It took Ligeti four years (between 1989 and 1993) to compose, revise and complete the Violin Concerto. Three movements were premiered by Gawriloff and the Cologne Radio Symphony Orchestra in November 1990, after which Ligeti replaced the first movement and added two others. Between working on the two versions he had to spend some weeks in hospital, and used the time to study Haydn's late string quartets in depth, believing that 'from Haydn you can learn how to achieve the clearest effect with the simplest means:

When having to choose between a more ornate structure and a skeleton, Haydn always chooses the skeleton, never using one note more than he needs. I applied this principle of avoiding unnecessary complexity in the second version of the Violin Concerto and thought that it brought me closer to my ideal.

This five-movement version was heard in Cologne two years later. He then reorchestrated the third and fourth movements, and the definitive Violin Concerto was performed by Gawriloff with the Ensemble InterContemporain conducted by Pierre Boulez on 9 June 1993. In the programme note for the partial premiere in 1990 Ligeti wrote:

I am not in favour of this situation, but I compose very slowly, destroying ten or twenty attempts before attaining the final score. Despite the pressure of scheduled future performances, the creation of art is not an everyday task and I must achieve, without compromise, the end result which is my imagined ideal.

His habitual self-criticism and industry paid off. To the technical methods established in the Piano Concerto Ligeti adds outlandish but alluring harmonic and timbral combinations. His preoccupation with Shakespeare's *Tempest* – both as a long-mooted operatic project and as a potential subject for the piano Études – seems to have been subsumed into the poetic sound-world of the Violin Concerto. Prospero's island becomes the real island music of Melanesia. And this is also a 'real' concerto. Whereas the soloist in the Piano Concerto is something of a polymetric machine, the solo violin is lyrical, pensive, mercurial and demonstrative. There is plentiful opportunity for display and for holding an audience under the spell of soft ethereal melodies. The music's technical, imaginative, expressive and virtuosic qualities are ideally integrated in a work that is as masterful as it is inventive.

The new first movement is a brilliant synthesis. In its temporal plurality it is hardly less ingenious than the first movement of the Piano Concerto, with its cyclic ostinati and additive patterns. But the curious harmonic spectra are soon evident, as the soloist and retuned violin and viola play open string arpeggios simultaneously in three different tuning systems. The use of perfect fifths and consonant diatonicism, within an exotic and hybrid tonality, is striking. Beneath the airy sparkle of glittering upper registers, the underlying chords radiate a benign harmonic purity, almost like that of minimalism.

Ex. 30 Planning the second movement of the Violin Concerto (1989)

The second movement, entitled 'Aria, Hoquetus, Choral', is effectively a set of variations, mostly in high register and conceived even more sectionally, as the sketches reveal (see p.335). It opens with the simplest of legato melodies played by the solo violin in low register. Ligeti adapted this melody from the third of his *Bagatelles for Wind Quintet*, introducing a tritonal flavour by writing augmented as well as perfect fourths above the tonic. Slowed down and nearly two octaves lower, its keening has a grainy allure. For seventy-four bars the melody unfolds on the G string of the violin, eventually joined by the retuned viola and gradually by other instruments. To the post-Nono avant-garde, who had bristled at the Horn Trio, such sensuality must have seemed criminal. Later in the movement, for the 'Hoquetus' section, Ligeti applies the techniques of Machaut's *Hoquetus David*, whilst the brass 'Choral' recalls Stravinsky's *Symphonies of Wind Instruments*. It is a strange mixture, in which the earlier homo-phony of ocarinas and slide whistles risks an over-naive primitivism. When Boulez arrived at this movement whilst recording the Violin Concerto, Ligeti asked whether he could stand it. Boulez merely laughed.

The third movement has an elegant violin melody of a different order accompanied again by the whole orchestra in high register. It is a soaring cantilena above a super-dense canon of descending scales. Here, as in the second movement, natural harmonics are played by the two horns and trombone. The fourth movement is a soft, intense Passacaglia rising to a passionate climax. In the fifth we meet a version of the *lamento* motif that has shed its semitonal attire in favour of complementary whole-tone scales a sixth apart (see Ex. 26d, p. 296), which he had first used in *Galamb borong*. Exceptionally for a modern concerto, Ligeti asks the soloist to devise his or her own cadenza. The suggestion came from Gawriloff, who proposed basing it on material from the discarded first movement, as one can hear in his recording. But there is also a case for drawing on material which the audience have actually heard in the finished work. The bell-like flute and *pizzicato* effect at the end of the movement is 'borrowed' from Shostakovich's Symphony no. 4, says Ligeti, explaining that

Layers upon layers of conscious and unconscious influences are connected together to form an organic, homogeneous whole . . . But for this to result in something new and complex, I always strive to melt these exterior impulses into my own interior images and ideas.[18]

The Viola Sonata

In the summer of 1990 Ligeti was guest of honour at the annual Bartók Seminar and Festival in Szombathely. He had travelled twice to Hungary during the previous year, but this was his first official visit since 1983, despite having a standing invitation to Szombathely since 1985. During a busy fortnight, he taught the composers' masterclass, lectured on the piano Études and other works, and attended rehearsals and concerts. The atmosphere was lively and stimulating, not unlike Darmstadt in the late 1950s. It was an opportunity to meet his Hungarian composer friends again; amongst these was Kurtág, intensively engaged in tutoring chamber music and, like Ligeti, deeply respectful of the classical canon. Performances of Ligeti's Cello and Piano Concertos were given by the Ensemble Modern; the *Six Bagatelles* and *Ten Pieces* were played by the Festival's Wind Quintet; and the Chamber Concerto, *Aventures* and *Nouvelles aventures* were presented at the final concert, conducted by participants in the conductors' course. Whenever there was a spare moment Ligeti was besieged by journalists.

Back in Hamburg he continued working on the Violin Concerto, due for its premiere on 3 November. Around the same time, at a concert in Cologne, he heard the viola playing of Tabea Zimmermann, one of the remarkable young instrumentalists of the 1990s. The distinctive low register of the viola had won his affection many years before through two pieces of classical chamber music: Schubert's last string quartet and the slow movement of the Schumann Piano Quintet. The 'peculiar astringency' of its lowest string, Ligeti notes in a tongue-in-cheek metaphor, is 'solid, a little husky, with an aftertaste of wood, earth and tannic acidity'.[19] Hearing Zimmermann's 'robust and powerful, yet always tender'[20] playing on the C string sparked off the idea of writing a sonata for the instrument. The following year he composed *Loop* (now the Sonata's second movement) as a birthday present for the Director of Universal Edition, Alfred Schlee – a more dignified tribute than his provocative *Fragment* of forty years earlier. *Facsar* (now the third movement) was written in 1993 in memory of Ligeti's composition teacher, Sándor Veress, who had died in Bonn. With four further movements, the complete Viola Sonata was performed by Tabea Zimmermann at the Gütersloh Festival in 1994.

This was Ligeti's first substantial composition for a solo string instrument since the Cello Sonata, written in Hungary in the early 1950s; but there is a world of difference between the youthful accomplishment of the one and the consummate mastery of the other. Both, however, reveal their kinship with Bartók; for by the 1990s Ligeti had lost all concern for whether he might appear 'old-fashioned'. The Viola Sonata shows how far he had moved away from the polemical avant-garde. Its style could not be more different from the solo instrumental pieces of, for instance, Lachenmann or Spahlinger, let alone that of younger composers nurtured at the German new music establishment's annual Donaueschingen festival. Not for him any socio-political, ideological or philosophical creed as legitimiser of the music itself. The six movements of the Viola Sonata are purely musical solutions to intrinsically musical 'problems'. The approach was exactly the same as that of *Musica ricercata*, composed fifty years earlier.

Ligeti began the Viola Sonata whilst still at work on the Violin Concerto. In his usual manner, he immersed himself in the tactile and physical properties of both instruments, noting their differences – the disembodied ethereal top register of the violin, the dark velvety low notes of the viola – as well as their similarities. All six movements of the Sonata treat the low C string as a point of reference or departure. This is for both aesthetic and pragmatic reasons: use of the unstopped bottom string, by freeing the left hand, increases the variety of upper-register stopped chords that can be combined with it. But in any case, throughout the Sonata, Ligeti shows a preference for including open strings in the many stopped chords, added to which the high natural harmonics that sound so well on the C string act as a model for other microtonally inflected pitches.

The idea of 'looping', which gives rise to the title of the second movement, occurs in several movements, including the last, since a chaconne is exactly that – a loop constantly repeated. The chromatic theme and rhythm of this last movement recall one of the most famous of ground basses, 'Dido's Lament' from the end of Purcell's opera, and it follows logically from the fifth movement, which is actually called 'Lamento'. This contains another version, if more rarefied, of the *lamento* motif, in double-stopped artificial harmonics.

Another aspect of the Viola Sonata emphatically removes it from the Germanic avant-garde: its references to folk tradition. Original folk music is never quoted, nor are the folk allusions solely Hungarian, but

they stem from that ethnographic awareness which Kodály, Bartók –
and to an extent Liszt – bequeathed to Hungarian musicians. Growing
up in Hungarian enclaves in Romanian Transylvania, Ligeti was aware
of different cultural traditions from an early age. With advancing years
he has wanted to revive these childhood impressions, now informed by
a wide knowledge of other ethnic musics with which they are histori-
cally linked, as the title of the first movement implies:

'Hora lungă', literally means 'slow dance'; but in the Romanian folk tradition
the phrase is applied not to dances, but to songs – nostalgic and melancholy,
richly ornamented – from the northernmost province of Maranures, in the
Carpathian mountains. *Hora lungă* bears a striking similarity to the *cante
jondo* of Andalusia and the folk music of Rajasthan; it is hard to tell whether
they are related because of the migration of gypsies, or whether they are
derived from a common Indo-European tradition of diatonic melody.[21]

This movement is played entirely on the C string, and with its specific microtonal usage and strophic character, it has a strong, if
unspecific sense of locale. The music is entirely melodic and there are
no double-stoppings. The pitch framework of the first eight bars is
interestingly similar to the fourth movement of the later Weöres
song-cycle, *Síppal, Dobbal, Nádihegedüvel*, with its 'fake' folk
melody evoking 'the grass-lands of North-Central Transylvania'. Both
melodies are based on diatonic scales integrating augmented fourths.
In 'Hora lungă' the diatonic framework is deflected by downward
departures from normal intonation, all of them measured by reference
to natural harmonics (as described in a note printed at the bottom of
the score). The opening phrase occurs six times, each with a different
continuation, eventually much extended. Towards the end of this
movement, the music floats away, ascending to the seventeenth harmonic, four octaves higher than the open string.

Subsequent movements have different characters. The gyrations of
'Loop' become increasingly energetic. The fifth movement, 'Lamento',
with its parallel seconds and sevenths, was says Ligeti 'indirectly influenced by various ethnic cultures: similar examples of two parts
moving in seconds are to be found in the Balkans (Bulgaria,
Macedonia, Istria), on the Ivory Coast (Guére) and in Melanesia (on
the island of Manus).'[22] Intervallic qualities of the other movements
also suggest folk links. But the structure of the Sonata as a whole is
thoroughly sophisticated, and the sequence of the six movements (a

larger number than in any previous instrumental work by Ligeti except the *Bagatelles* and *Ten Pieces*) has a spacious, cumulative dignity – like that of the Bach solo suites.

The last two movements ally the Sonata with a whole genus of laments, but here contrasting ferocity with icy remoteness. Within the formidable double-stopped dyads that open the fifth movement is embedded a three-phrase melody containing nearly all of the *lamento* motif's identifying ingredients, as we have already observed them (see Ex. 26g, p. 297). In the final movement, 'Chaconne chromatique', the distillation of the *lamento* formula – both its intervallic and durational character – into the most basic shape reveals not only that, at heart, it is just a descending chromatic scale, but also that its rhythmic and phrase structure is more firmly rooted in musical precedent than we might have imagined (see Exx. 26h and i). Audibly, this may be less evident, for Ligeti interprets the word 'chaconne' in its original sense to mean a fast, exuberant, passionate dance – although less dissolute than its rival, the 'immoral' *zarabanda*, predecessor of the dignified sarabande, whose encouragement of obscenity caused the Spanish authorities in 1583 to ban it. Ligeti's 'Chaconne' may be impetuous. But it also achieves, via passages of increasingly difficult triple- and quadruple-stopping, a climax of considerable grandeur, before the consonant final section ends with a typical fingerprint: the cool glow of a first-inversion major triad.[23]

15

On (Not) Writing Opera

It matters a great deal to me that my works should be understood. But my prime concern is to put an idea in writing. My
ideal is Cézanne, who didn't care whether his paintings were
exhibited or not. To do it: that's the main thing. Everything
else – putting forward grand theories, gathering followers,
becoming a 'guru' – leaves me cold.

    György Ligeti[1]

The success of the first production of *Le Grand Macabre* in Stockholm
in 1978 encouraged Ligeti to think about new operatic possibilities.
Theatres were eager to commission him. In the early 1980s he agreed
to compose a new work for English National Opera in London, which
he thought for a while would be based on Shakespeare's *The Tempest*.
Few authors can have inspired more composers, but Ligeti's treatment
would surely have been different from any other. In 1983 Boulez and
Nicholas Snowman, Artistic Director of IRCAM, took Ligeti to dine
in Stuttgart, hoping to persuade him to produce an electronic tape for
The Tempest. By the end of the meal they had reassured Ligeti that one
did not need to know everything about the computer in order to work
at IRCAM, and he agreed to come. Due to administrative oversights,
it seems, the visit never took place.[2] But the concept of electronic
sound transformation remained in his mind:

The first sketches . . . begin with a very fast melody, which is not really
monodic but made of a complex mixture-sound. In other words, many parts
run in rhythmic synchrony, and blend into a governing 'part', whose sound
spectrum is made sometimes from harmonic overtones, sometimes from a
composed noise structure, but chiefly from the transition from one sound
state to another. A harmonic spectrum is gradually changed in colour – the
partials are so placed – that bell-like sounds arise, and then pass into coloured
noises . . . What then happens . . . is influenced by the thought-world of interactive calculus and recursive structures. The melodic line becomes, so to

speak, multiplied with itself, like the endless reflections that result when one sees oneself between two parallel mirrors.[3]

Although *The Tempest* never advanced beyond these tentative imaginings, there is something of its sonic vision in the Violin Concerto. The years rolled by without any further progress on the opera. Throughout the 1980s and 1990s Ligeti was preoccupied with many other projects: the Horn Trio, the piano Études, the Viola Sonata, three compositions for vocal and choral groups, three instrumental concertos – two of which took an unconscionable effort to complete. Every one of these works ventured into the territory of new compositional 'hobbies' – ethnic musics, polymetre, temperaments, fractal mathematics, the *lamento* ostinato – or resulted from a rekindled interest in his Hungarian and classical antecedents.

Compositions long promised to outstanding instrumentalists took precedence. Also pressing was Ligeti's wish to revise *Le Grand Macabre*, a task which took nine months. Enthusiasm for writing its sequel must have been diminished by his pained reaction to many of its productions, culminating in the agonising 'catastrophe', as he saw it, of Peter Sellars's staging of the revised version at Salzburg in 1997. We should note again that, of twenty-three different productions the opera has received – both in its original and revised version – not one has represented Ligeti's vision of a grotesque, run-down, but happily thriving Breughelland, using the iconography he himself envisaged, and most have failed to convey its ambivalence.

So many negative encounters must have called into question the wisdom of courting them again. Added to which, with his dislike of manipulative artistic politics, Ligeti has kept his distance from operatic circles and lacks trusted theatrical collaborators. But his long hesitation over the idea of a second opera has less to do with the chequered history of the first than with the difficulty of establishing the parameters in which to compose it, indeed of defining its very nature. For *The Tempest* Ligeti envisaged not a dramatic opera, but 'a big staged poem, calm and deep with human feelings, delicate relationships'.[4] He was still searching for a melodic style that did not rely on the tonal system. The technical explorations which inform all his mature compositions mean that none simply utilise expertise already acquired. A new opera could be a summation. But it also involves considering again the nature of theatrical and musical style, temperament and instrumentation, narrative (or its absence) and continuity. In the last decade Ligeti's music has become significantly more episodic. The *Hamburg Concerto* began life with six compact movements, and Ligeti now intends it to have eight. Each is a sequence of laconic, self-contained 'sound-objects', some lasting no more than eight bars.[5] Can such mosaic chains sustain the discourse of an opera?

Around 1990 Ligeti became less convinced about setting *The Tempest*. After many failed attempts he began to think it might be pretentious to treat so 'delicate' a text, especially the complex character of Prospero, whose 'depths of Britishness' a continental could not fully understand.[6] But he had not dismissed *Alice*, whose surreal adventures had lurked below the surface of his music all his life, influencing its attitudes and mannerisms. That both his chosen subjects are masterpieces of English literature is due to their existence in fine Hungarian translations. Frigyes Karinthy's *Alice's Adventures in Wonderland* and Mihály Babits's inspired Hungarian version of *The Tempest* had been two of Ligeti's favourite books since he was twelve. In the *Nonsense Madrigals*, for the first time, he actually set Carroll's words. A stage scenario for *Alice* began to gel. He decided that it would be not an opera, but 'a theatrical fantasy . . . a musical or a revue with acrobats and stage machinery, singers, dancers, pantomimes and a little orchestra of twenty to twenty-five players, each of whom will be used as a soloist'.[7] Along with passages from the *Alice* books, he would use Carroll's nonsense poems and mathematics. Alice herself would be played 'by an actress, since no singer would be able to be on stage the whole time . . . a young actress who can also sing'. Another role he planned for Richard Suart, whose portrayal of the Lord High Executioner in Jonathan Miller's production of *The Mikado* Ligeti had much enjoyed. Yet still he did not begin. Would it be sacrilege to transpose Carroll's verbal and conceptual fantasy into a wholly different medium? Others have made extensive musical treatments, notably the American composer David del Tredici. But Ligeti remained cautious.

A unique recording project abandoned . . .

Whilst he deliberated, a momentous project began to take shape: the recording of his entire output for a single edition of CDs, to include all the early Hungarian works Ligeti considered worth reviving. This ambitious plan was made possible by the wealthy president of one of

Britain's most enterprising orchestras, the Philharmonia. During the autumn of 1989 London's South Bank Centre mounted a festival of nine Ligeti concerts introduced by the composer. Thirty-five of his compositions were presented in the course of two and a half weeks, including the eight completed piano Études and all of his large-scale works – *Apparitions*, *Atmosphères*, *Clocks and Clouds*, *San Francisco Polyphony* and the Requiem – plus a concert performance of *Le Grand Macabre*. The large pieces and the opera were performed by the Philharmonia Orchestra and Chorus and London Sinfonietta Chorus, the conducting being shared between Elgar Howarth and the orchestra's principal guest conductor Esa-Pekka Salonen. That the four large-scale concerts took place was largely due to the financial support of the orchestra's president, a French banking heir, Vincent Meyer. A mutually respectful bond developed between Ligeti and his patron, Ligeti noting that Meyer was not only charming but genuinely interested in his work.

Three years later Meyer attended a concert in Paris given by the Ensemble InterContemporain, at which Florent Bouffard performed the Piano Concerto with Peter Eötvös conducting. Ligeti was in the audience alongside Boulez, the ensemble's founder. In the four years since he had completed the concerto it had received several performances, but there were no recordings and it was still not well known. There had been unease in the rehearsal, and during the lean and exposed opening of the second movement, the bassoonist failed to enter. Eötvös acted quickly to save the situation but in doing so had to cut twelve bars. The audience scarcely noticed but Ligeti was characteristically upset. Sitting dejectedly in a restaurant with Vincent Meyer, the conversation turned to the way in which busy conductors (although not Eötvös) rely on recordings to learn new pieces when they have too little time to study the score. Ligeti bemoaned the lack of definitive recordings of his music which people could refer to 'when I'm dead'. Immediately Meyer responded. He would make the recordings and underwrite the considerable cost himself.

By September that year his initiative was taking shape. Sony Classical agreed to issue a 'György Ligeti Edition' which would contain Ligeti's complete oeuvre on thirteen CDs. In spring 1993, whilst Ligeti was in California as a guest of the Paul Getty Foundation, he attended the American premiere of the Violin Concerto given by

Saschko Gawriloff and the Los Angeles Philharmonic, part of a Ligeti weekend devised and conducted by Salonen. Impressed, he asked Salonen to conduct the complete recording project. Ligeti hoped that the orchestral works would be recorded in Los Angeles, but the huge cost of so extensive a project with an American orchestra and the inflexibility of its subscription series commitments made this impossible. Meyer enlisted the Philharmonia, a choice which Salonen accepted and Ligeti supported. The decision had an indirect political dimension since it coincided with the Arts Council of Great Britain's consideration of the funding, and consequent fate of the London orchestras, presided over by Lord Justice Hoffmann; and Meyer made clear that his contribution of £650,000 to the project was dependent on the orchestra's survival.[8] The next step was to link recording sessions with public concerts. Salonen's agent, Van Walsum Management, then came on board to coordinate an international Ligeti Festival. Called *Clocks and Clouds*, it would span two years and ten countries: it would be launched in December 1996 to coincide with the release of the first four Sony CDs and culminate in 1998, Ligeti's seventy-fifth birthday year. As Van Walsum proudly proclaimed, it would be one of the most remarkable cultural events of the decade.

But it had become dangerously overstretched. In particular it was vulnerable to the habitual pressure of British orchestral working conditions, especially those of an orchestra touring internationally. Orchestras in the UK – and conductors – are used to achieving outstanding results on the barest minimum of rehearsal. In London most days contain three full sessions; when they do not, players frequently augment their modest income by fitting recording engagements or teaching into a day which already contains a full rehearsal and an evening concert.

All Ligeti's music had been played before; indeed, virtually all of the larger works by the Philharmonia itself. By now, however, the plan was for the Philharmonia to record the chamber orchestral works as well, using solo strings as Ligeti prefers. Afterwards, Salonen realised that this was a serious miscalculation, and that to use an ensemble like the London Sinfonietta or Ensemble Inter-Contemporain would have been wiser and simpler to schedule. But he had the laudable aspiration that all of Ligeti's larger and smaller orchestral works and concertos should become a part of the canon: components of the orchestral repertoire as valid – even familiar – as any Haydn symphony.

345

It was easy to forget that concert performances and definitive recordings require different degrees of perfection. Ligeti's scores are exceptionally detailed and demanding. His handwritten annotations in the Requiem necessitated its publishers providing a twenty-three-page translation of the footnotes alone for English-speaking performers. In composing works like *Atmosphères* and the Requiem he had envisaged a week of rehearsals, the norm for the radio orchestras of the 1960s for whom they were written. Salonen knew both the music and the Philharmonia extremely well. But in approving the schedules, he placed too much trust in its working routines and underestimated the exhausting pressures imposed by British cultural economics.

The beginning was inauspicious. Salonen began with a three-hour string rehearsal on *San Francisco Polyphony* – Ligeti's most intractable score, which few conductors attempt without sectionals, on account of its many layers of soloistic and tutti virtuosity, rhythmic desynchronisation and problems of balance. Ex. 17 (see p. 204) demonstrates the challenge to unanimity confronting the fifteen violins, made acutely more difficult if it is played, as directed, with the wood rather than the hair of the bow. In performance, small discrepancies can be masked by the rest of the texture. But this was the first time Ligeti had attended a rehearsal of the string parts starting from scratch – he had not been invited to the work's premiere in San Francisco – and the degree of imprecision horrified him.

For the orchestra it was a typically busy week. On the morning of Tuesday, 3 December 1996, fourteen of the players gathered with Salonen and Ligeti at the Blackheath Halls in the London suburbs (the Philharmonia lacks its own permanent rehearsal base) to rehearse the Cello Concerto, a work best performed by a small ensemble of soloists. In the afternoon the whole orchestra worked on *San Francisco Polyphony*. On Wednesday afternoon they rehearsed Mahler's Fourth Symphony with Salonen in the Royal Festival Hall, before and after which they prepared and performed a completely different programme with another conductor and in a different venue, St John's Smith Square. On Thursday evening the Cello Concerto, *San Francisco Polyphony* and the Mahler were performed in concert at the Festival Hall, preceded by a general rehearsal.

The next day the orchestra returned to Blackheath for two rehearsals of Russian music conducted by Gennadi Rozhdestvensky, due to be performed on Saturday in a concert at the Corn Exchange in Bedford, fifty miles outside London. Before leaving for the general rehearsal in Bedford however, they convened on Saturday morning at 9.30, now in the inadequately heated Bishopsgate Institute, to rehearse Ligeti's Requiem with Salonen and the soloists – a work which, before its premiere in Stockholm, had been meticulously prepared across weeks rather than days. Apart from being cold the Bishopsgate Institute is badly lit. Most of the orchestra were huddling in their outdoor clothes. Nowhere but in London do major orchestras rehearse in such dreary rented accommodation, and the atmosphere was anything but conducive.

The 'Introitus' of the Requiem rises from the depths. As sounds emerge, colours change and, almost imperceptibly, chords take shape. The work requires six double basses, three of them with five strings, the lowest tuned to B natural a fourth lower than the bottom string of the normal four-string bass. At bar 26 there appears a very soft cluster of infinitesimal stillness, held for nearly a quarter of a minute. It is scored for the six double basses and two cellos, all playing natural harmonics which, for the three five-string basses, can only be produced on the extra low B string. When the rehearsal reached this point Salonen stopped to ask why some of the double-bass harmonics were sounding an octave too high. Because, said the players, they had no five-string basses. Delayed by the London traffic, the Philharmonia's instrument van had arrived outside the hall too late to unload them. Salonen could ill afford to disrupt the rehearsal, so he decided to correct the passage the following day and meanwhile to continue. Ligeti was furious that there was no time even to discuss it. Disappointed that the Los Angeles orchestra had not been chosen, and what he had judged to have been an inadequate performance of *San Francisco Polyphony*, he felt that his music was not being taken seriously and railed at Salonen and the orchestra. The atmosphere was soured, however, more by hurt pride and a failure to reassure the composer than by the incident itself. Ligeti felt that he was not being listened to, that his concerns were being brushed aside. Tension increased: the composer edgy and irritable, the orchestra offended and Salonen tight-lipped.[9]

The Requiem received one more full rehearsal the next morning, now with the addition of the chorus and in the main hall of Goldsmith's College in Lewisham. (This was the fourth rehearsal venue the orchestra had used that week – for on Monday they had worked in the Henry Wood Hall – not including the general rehearsals and concerts which they had already undertaken in three different concert halls.) In the afternoon, and still at Goldsmith's, conductor, orchestra, soloists and chorus turned to Debussy's *Le martyre de Saint Sébastien*, which was to precede the Requiem in the concert the following night. Then, regardless of it being Sunday, the orchestra and its instruments transferred to yet another venue, the Watford Coliseum, to play for a three-hour recording session of operatic arias, not ending until 10.30 p.m.

It is amazing that despite such a lifestyle, despite the acrimony that had marred rehearsals of the Requiem, the performance seemed to be of outstanding quality to the large audience (including this author) that gathered the following evening in the Royal Festival Hall. The huge wail of the 'Kyrie', the volatile drama of the 'Dies irae', the frozen tears of the 'Lacrimosa' – all spoke with the most powerful intensity. Salonen's moulding of the score seemed masterful, both in its subtlety and in its pacing. The precision of the (very expensive) hundred-strong professional chorus trained by Terry Edwards could hardly be matched in any country. Its virtuosity contributed hugely to the music's impact, and the soloists were similarly impressive. But Ligeti, listening intently to his calculated detail, found many aspects of the orchestral playing unsatisfactory.

A few days later the Philharmonia flew to Valencia in Spain, then to Paris, and went on by train to Brussels. During these four days, which included travelling as well as four concerts, they repeated both Ligeti programmes, one of them mixed with different works that had been rehearsed over a week before. At the Châtelet Theatre in Paris they were joined by Ligeti, the soloists and chorus to perform the Requiem again; but on this occasion the hushed opening was ruined by an unsuppressed mobile phone somewhere in the auditorium. At each venue there was an average of one hour's rehearsal. Most of the second day in Paris was free. But it was not within anyone's capacity to use it for remedial rehearsal. The physical strain of such exhausting schedules becomes absolute.

After Christmas Ligeti returned to London to attend recording sessions at the Abbey Road Studios. Despite its excellent technical facilities, Abbey Road is a confined space for the 180 musicians required in the Requiem. Ligeti had proposed a larger (though probably too resonant) venue, All Saints Church in Tooting, but he was overruled. A more serious problem was Salonen's choice of a record-ing producer with whom he had worked for ten years, but in whom Ligeti had little confidence. Relationships, already fractious with the orchestra, were now exacerbated by tensions with the recording team. Ligeti felt marginalised from interpretative decisions and from the cru-cial role of mixing, believing that the textural and aesthetic subtleties of his music were not being understood. Listening at the mixing desk, he reluctantly said he was satisfied, but on rehearing the tapes he con-cluded that the sound was cramped and lacked perspective, and that there were still orchestral inaccuracies. He was deeply dissatisfied with *San Francisco Polyphony* and the *Romanian Concerto* (which with the Cello Concerto was to complete the CD). The recordings, he insisted, must not be released. Back in Hamburg he was sent all the tapes and asked to attempt a remix of the Requiem. He went into a studio with an engineer, but the task proved 'hopeless'.

Ligeti had no authority to veto the disc, but without the composer's approval it could hardly be issued. The public had little inkling of this situation. All the subsequent *Clocks and Clouds* concerts proceeded as planned. Performances and tours of the several remaining large- and medium-scale works took place in February and November 1997 and in May 1998, doing much to enhance Ligeti's reputation. Salonen and the Philharmonia's persuasive performances of Ligeti's major works, through concert series in London, Paris, Brussels, Spain and elsewhere, were extremely well received, and by a largely new audience. Orchestra and conductor remained unshaken in the conviction that they were performing great and important music.

Problems continued, however, and not only behind the scenes. The inadequate rehearsal time before the next Philharmonia concert on 19 February was more unfortunate. Besides the relatively unknown Violin Concerto, with its special tunings and strange sonorities, the concert included Bartók's *Music for Strings, Percussion and Celesta*, not a repertoire piece and embarrassingly starved of rehearsal. Again Ligeti insisted that the Violin Concerto was not fit to record. Vincent Meyer's visionary project had ground to a halt without a single one of the large-scale works being issued.

Tragic though this outcome was, it was not the end. A few months later the Philharmonia and Salonen gathered in Salzburg to rehearse the revised *Le Grand Macabre*, along with the singers and Peter Sellars, the opera's director. At the first piano run-through on set Ligeti seemed to be enthusiastic; but by the pre-dress rehearsal, as he came to realise the extent of Sellars's reinterpretation, he had completely changed his mind, a reversal 'so sudden and drastic' that Salonen was taken aback, and still finds it inexplicable.[9] Ligeti's dismay at the production inevitably compounded his difficult relationship with the orchestra. At times distraught, he could be as peremptory as the Queen of Hearts, the double basses again being subjected to an angry, if happily metaphorical, 'Off with their heads.' As we have already noted, Ligeti tried in vain to have the production cancelled. In the event, Salonen's unflappability and resolution, allied to his undoubted musical gifts and understanding of opera, ensured thorough preparation of the score. The CD, recorded live during five performances at the Châtelet Theatre in February 1998, achieved everything Ligeti could desire. Its success was secured not least by the composer's alert ears in the recording van, but also by his good relationship with the producer and engineer for this recording, the excellent Ulrich Schneider and Marcus Herzog.

The recording of the opera was issued by Sony in 1999 as the eighth and last of its projected thirteen-CD György Ligeti Edition. The previous seven had encompassed all the keyboard, vocal and chamber works, plus an intriguing disc of keyboard music played entirely on mechanical instruments. Lamentably, it looked as if the large orchestral pieces and the Requiem, so long in need of new recordings, would have to wait indefinitely. These works were not short of performances. Salonen himself, with the same chorus but now with the BBC Symphony Orchestra, gave a fine performance of the Requiem during the BBC Proms of 2001. But the work's only commercial recording remained that of 1968, transferred to CD from the original LP. Of *Clocks and Clouds* no recording existed at all.

In retrospect, Salonen believes that he should have built an extra three-hour 'buffer' into the rehearsal schedule for each piece, not least to accommodate Ligeti's wish to vet every detail himself. At the start of the project, nobody involved realised the nature of the composer's expectations in the recording studio. It had been naively assumed that he would take a back seat. But if Salonen had been defeated partly by miscalculation, he had also been dogged by cumulative bad luck. Unforeseen mishaps, orchestral fatigue, inadequate rehearsal and recording conditions and a breakdown of relationships had all played a part. Ligeti himself was deeply depressed. At the turn of the millennium he could see no prospect of the project ever being revived.

The problem had been 'a labyrinth of personal interests, money interests and marketing interests'. Faced with these imperatives he felt that Salonen had been too compliant, to the detriment of quality. But he continued to admire and praise his musicianship. Meanwhile, between rehearsals and recording sessions, he had done something therapeutic. On free Sunday mornings he visited St Paul's Cathedral, not to go inside – although he did – but to stand outside, listening to the change-ringing of its bells.

. . . and reborn

Throughout all of this Vincent Meyer remained steadfast. Perplexed by what had happened and no less saddened than Ligeti, he nonetheless promised his continued financial support. Despite his regard for the Philharmonia, he accepted that if the music had to be recorded by others, then so be it. Due to Meyer's continued patronage, the project was unexpectedly reborn, now in association with Teldec. Teldec's first Newline 'Ligeti Project' CD was issued in 2001, recorded by the Asko and Schoenberg Ensembles with one of Ligeti's most trusted conductors, Reinbert de Leeuw. Besides the Chamber and Piano Concertos and a first recording of *Mysteries of the Macabre*, it includes a wonderfully transparent account of *Melodien*, as luminous and pristine as a newly cleaned oil painting.

The second Teldec CD contains first recordings for many years of *Apparitions*, *Atmosphères*, *Lontano* and *San Francisco Polyphony*, plus, at long last, the *Romanian Concerto* of 1951, all performed by the Berlin Philharmonic Orchestra conducted by the relatively young British conductor, Jonathan Nott. Well respected in Europe, especially by new music ensembles, Nott had rarely been employed in Britain, except at the Huddersfield Festival in 1993, when he directed the Asko Ensemble in an all-Ligeti concert attended by the composer. Nor had he previously conducted the Berlin Philharmonic. But the result is impressive. His treatment of *San Francisco Polyphony* proves to be a revelatory vindication of this difficult score, as we have already noted. And if the performances of *Atmosphères* and *Lontano* are less seamless than those of Rosbaud and Maderna many years before, this is partly because of their precise interpretation of Ligeti's dynamics.

A first ever commercial recording of *Clocks and Clouds* (made thirty years after its composition), occupies the third Teldec CD, along with

Síppal, Dobbal, Nádihegedűvel (see below) and new recordings of the Violin and Cello Concertos. The clarity of detail in the shimmering microtonal mosaic of *Clocks and Clouds* is similarly revealing, and sounds surprisingly prophetic of the Violin Concerto, which – placed next on the recording – seems to flow directly from the strange undulating airs of *Clocks and Clouds*. Evidently, Teldec's promise of 'good communication' between composer, performers and recording team was crucial:

My role is to make sure that what is played and recorded corresponds exactly to the score. But I don't get involved with the deviations of free interpretation, the expressive extras, so to speak, of the interpreter. One must be observant in such recordings because the producer, the sound engineer and the composer are sitting separated from the interpreter. There is a glass window between us and no direct contact. We can only speak to each other by interrupting the recording, which is not usually a very inspiring situation because it is a matter of small details. So that is my role, just to listen to see that what is played is what is written . . .

The interpreters do not get all the information from the score. There is a great deal that can only be communicated orally . . . If on a series of recordings the words 'authentic' or 'under the supervision of the composer' appear, that shows that the composer was present at the production and not only had the possibility of expressing his wishes regarding the interpretation, which always has to do with the precision of the score, but that the composer is also responsible for quality. I cannot rest until this level of quality which I envisage has been reached.

That goes for the interpreters and the sound technician. If a painter paints a picture which is exhibited but not lit, is thus on display in darkness, then people do not see the picture. It's the same with recordings. However good the instrumental and vocal interpretation, the producer, the sound engineer and the technical staff are important in ensuring that the interpretation of the performer on the record sounds exactly as the performer played it . . . When there is good cooperation between these people, when they are professionals – which is not always the case – then it is a very nice situation.[11]

Scarred by innumerable unsatisfactory experiences in the performance of his orchestral works, Ligeti approaches recording sessions in a state of hypertension, a mixture of hope and apprehension. The stressful circumstances of orchestral recording – financial pressures, lack of time, impediments to communication – make him understandably anxious. Having taken indulgent months composing the 'Kyrie' of the Requiem and six years repeatedly discarding and restarting his Piano

Concerto, he refuses to accept pressures on time. It is an attitude based on never having been a performer himself. Yet such are the subtleties of balance and micro-detail in his scores that where adequate recordings don't exist, there can be little point in attempting them without the composer in attendance. But his presence is more than some conductors can accept, fearful of losing face when presented with a list of errors they failed to notice. Both Karajan in the 1960s and Abbado in the 1990s refused to admit him to their rehearsals.

In Berlin there was little more rehearsal and recording time than in London, but there were other significant differences. Orchestral working conditions in Berlin are better and there are fewer distractions. The public concert associated with Nott's recording contained *Apparitions*, *Atmosphères* and *San Francisco Polyphony* but started with an unconducted chamber piece by Purcell and ended with *Also Sprach Zarathustra*, which the orchestra knew so well it had nothing to rehearse. Disciplined and focused, for the duration of the project they had no other engagements. There were plentiful sectional rehearsals, assisted where necessary by a second conductor. Most important was the role of the CD producer Christoph Classen. The recording studio was situated one floor higher than the orchestral hall, preventing Ligeti from speaking directly with Nott or any of the players. In Berlin, too, there were minor crises (the absence of a flautist required some instant rescheduling) – but they were resolved. Whilst listening himself, Classen had to field Ligeti's detailed corrections and constant instructions. Trusted by the composer, his musical acumen, technical ability and skill as both communicator and mediator ensured the recording's success.

The *Hamburg Concerto* and Weöres song cycle

The Teldec project extended the original plan for recording Ligeti's complete works, having two new works to include. The *Hamburg Concerto* for solo horn and chamber orchestra (then containing six movements) was completed in 1999, well ahead of its premiere on 20 January 2001. Commissioned by the ZEIT-Foundation of Hamburg, it is dedicated to the German horn player Marie-Luise Neunecker, whose mastery of the difficult writing in the Horn Trio had already impressed the composer. *Síppal, Dobbal, Nádihegedüvel* (*With pipes, drums, fiddles*) is a song cycle for mezzo-soprano and percussion quartet. Although composed after the *Hamburg Concerto*, it was premiered first – in Metz on 10

November 2000. Written for the Amadinda Percussion Group and the bewitching voice of a young Hungarian opera singer, Katalin Károlyí, it is the most emphatically Hungarian of all Ligeti's works, and also a posthumous tribute to Sándor Weöres, seven of whose texts he sets.

In view of Ligeti's growing preoccupation with non-Western temperaments, one might have expected both new works to pursue these interests further. The Horn Trio had already combined natural harmonics with equal-tempered tonalities, whilst the Amadinda percussionists have collected a huge arsenal of non-Western instruments during years of playing together. Nonetheless, *Síppal, Dobbal, Nádihegedűvel* is composed entirely in conventional tuning, because Ligeti decided to use four marimbaphones (xylophone, two marimbas and bass marimba), all of which are normally built in equal temperament. The *Hamburg Concerto*, on the other hand, daringly extends his simultaneous use of different tuning systems. Here, the soloist alternates between the modern double valve-horn in F and B flat and a natural horn in F, four more natural horns being included in the orchestra. In writing for both the natural and the valve-horn Ligeti has available a wide range of harmonics, whose 'pure' tones differ substantially from equal temperament. The higher harmonics, which deviate most, are extensively employed, right up to the seventeenth partial.

Each work breaks new ground in different ways. But they have a similar approach to structure: each is a chain of contrasting miniatures, abruptly juxtaposed in the Concerto, lyrical yet ironic in the song cycle. They also delve deeply into Ligeti's past. In Chapter 1 we noted Ligeti's childhood encounter with a herdsman playing an alphorn in the Carpathian mountains, the evocative call of its natural harmonics made all the more memorable by the player immersing the instrument's bell in a stream as he began to blow. The horn duets in *Melodien* have a distant mystical quality, whereas in *Nouvelles aventures*, the *Ten Pieces for Wind Quintet* and the Horn Trio the instrument has moments of almost bacchanalian abandon. The rustic ancestry of the orchestral horn continues to haunt Ligeti:

The sound is full of poetic associations. Think of German poetry in the nineteenth century. Eichendorff! The distances! The sound of the horn comes out of the deep wood. There are fairytale associations with the horn. The horn composer of the Romantic past was Carl Maria von Weber. He wrote wonderfully for the natural horn. His Concertino is one of the great horn masterpieces. That is an aspect of my liking for the horn.[12]

But it is Ligeti's interest in new harmonic landscapes that has primacy in the Concerto. Natural horns, he says, are 'ideal instruments for alternative pitch systems'.[13] By changing crooks between movements, one has a rich choice of microharmonic combinations. Ligeti calls them 'non-harmonic' – the point being, however, that they are a fusion of harmony and timbre, in which equally tempered pitches are mixed with precisely selected microtones, automatically produced by playing higher-partial natural harmonics.

Blended with the orchestral horns are two basset horns, but playing in equal temperament, as the rest of the orchestra do for most of the piece. It is an uneasy marriage, whose partners must find their own stability. Even in the first few bars, the discrepancy between two horns playing the same pitch class but using different crooks sets up audible 'beats'. The fifth movement, with its chord sequence combining tempered and untempered pitches, enters uncharted fields, far from the framework to which players normally anchor their intonation. Ligeti's intention, as with all his use of microtones, is to create an empirical

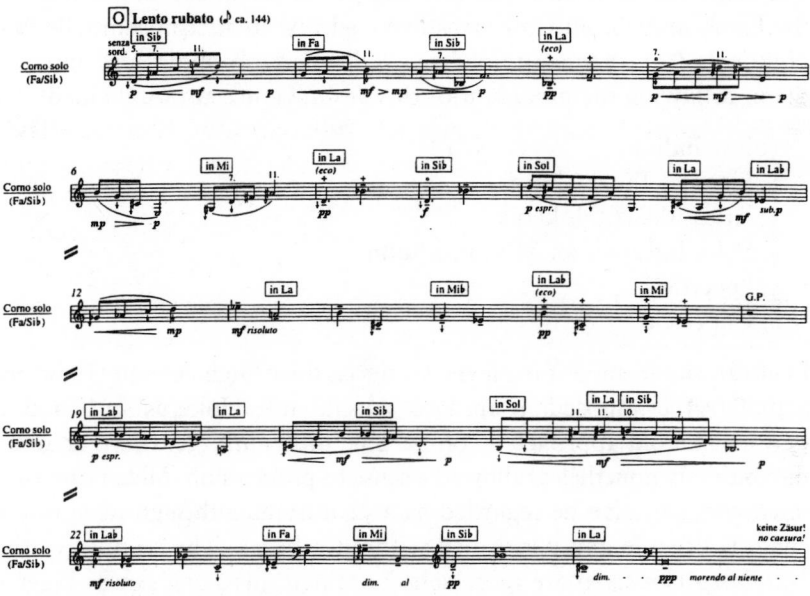

Ex. 31 'Solo' from the *Hamburg Concerto* (1999)

© 2000 Schott Musik International, Mainz

rather than a rigid tonal climate, 'in a spirit of free determination'[14] –
notwithstanding the fact that the numerical positions of notes in the
harmonic series, as well as their percentage deviation from equal temperament, are meticulously notated in the score.

Even by the standards of the Piano and Violin Concertos, the
Hamburg Concerto is a daring venture. The composer-who-had-
meant-to-be-a-scientist reveals his insatiable bent for experimental
enquiry. Would it work? In conversation with the author some months
before the premiere, Ligeti admitted that he wasn't sure.[15] In innovative
works there is a degree of speculation. Rehearsals – even repeat performances – test hypotheses, establish norms, make the strange
familiar and the familiar secure. Despite an impressively convincing
first performance of the *Hamburg Concerto*, ably directed by the composer George Benjamin, Ligeti decided to revise it.

Original structure of the *Hamburg Concerto*

The Cello Concerto has two movements, the Chamber Concerto four,
the Piano and Violin Concertos five each. At its first appearance, the
Hamburg Concerto contained six – all relatively short, and three of
them, following the precedent of the Violin Concerto, subdivided:

1. Praeludium
2. Signale, Tanz, Choral
3. Aria, Aksak, Hoketus
4. Solo, Intermezzo, Mixtur, Kanon
5. Spectra
6. Capriccio

In effect, these amount to eleven sections, since 'Signale' and 'Tanz' are
actually superimposed, as are also 'Aksak' and 'Hoketus'. It is both a
new and an old approach – comparable to *Aventures*, whose episodic
discontinuity nonetheless allowed a sense of progression. *Métamorphoses
nocturnes* can also be regarded as a prototype, although its episodic
chain is organic and performed without a break. The sections of the
Hamburg Concerto are more self-contained: here one senses Ligeti's
kinship with Kurtág, who has elevated fragments, 'microludes', 'messages', even 'doodles', into sustainable art.

The twenty bars of the 'Praeludium' (marked 'Adagio espressivo')
establish the unworldly atmosphere of the whole work, using a

favourite formula, the fan-like pitch expansion that occurs in the first movement of the Cello and Chamber Concertos as well as in *Lontano*. Here it has the added oddity of its microtonality. In both earlier concertos, this mystical expansion alights momentarily on the sunlit openness of multiple octaves. In the *Hamburg Concerto* there is a similar effect, but the octave contains a perfect fifth (B flat to F) – its purity the more startling because the previous step stretched approximately three quarters of a tone up to F from a much flattened E natural, the eleventh harmonic on the B flat section of the double horn. This short movement is full of fifths (elfin echoes of the *cors de chasse*) whose 'perfection' is compromised by their microtonal surroundings.

Throughout all but its last four bars, the second movement is written for the five natural horns alone, and frequently evokes their romantic ancestry. It is a compressed sequence of three ideas, hinting at some unstated scenario. The first, 'Signale', with its solo and echo horns, recalls early hunting calls. They continue in counterpoint beyond the entry of the 'Tanz', which is a brief flowing duet in compound time, ending with the soloist ascending the overtone series from the eighth to sixteenth harmonics. The same series appears in the next movement, but rising a note higher to the seventeenth harmonic. As noted above, the last two components of this movement are also superimposed: the 'Aksak' turns out to be a rocking motif in 4 + 3 + 2 metre, the 'Hoketus' its interlocking accompaniment. The whole movement contains uneven metrical patterns typical of Balkan and Middle Eastern folk music, and by now commonplace in late Ligeti.

'Solo', 'Intermezzo', 'Mixtur', 'Kanon' are four more links in the chain, each clearly differentiated. But the fifth movement is a single entity, pursuing further than any other its 'spectral' progression of microharmonies, with deflected and tempered pitches in new and unsettling combinations. 'Capriccio' is more conventional, striking out energetically in the manner of the 'caprices' of Ligeti's early Hungarian period. It opens with a bravura display from the soloist; but this, too, is short-lived and subsides in another mysterious slow sequence of microharmonic chords. Above them the solo horn enters *dolente*, with a further reincarnation of the *lamento* motif – the only one, however, to use an unequally tempered scale. Even in the Violin Concerto, Ligeti's 'deviant' tunings do not extend to the *lamento* motif which, in that work also, dominates the finale.

With fiddles, pipes and drums

Paradoxically, in the song cycle Ligeti manages to evoke exotic cultures without the aid of special temperaments. This stems from his use of met-allophones – tuned bells, gongs, crotales, glockenspiel and vibraphone (along with xylophone and marimbas) – whose combined overtones contain enough impurities to ensure that even diatonic accompaniments (in 'Keserédes' for example) sound strange. The seven songs are:

1. Fabula (Fable)
2. Táncdal (Dance song)
3. Kínai templom (Chinese temple)
4. Kuli (Coolie)
5. Alma, álma (Dream)
6. Keserédes (Bitter-sweet)
7. Szajkó (Parakeet)

These are make-believe, enchanted pieces. Their collective title is not from Weöres, but a line from a Hungarian children's verse (a kind of counting rhyme). As Ligeti remarked long ago, 'Anyone who has been through horrifying experiences is not likely to create terrifying works of art, in all seriousness. He is more likely to alienate.'[16]

Not only does he use diatonic chordal harmony; he also writes delightful melodies. 'Keserédes', for example, is unashamedly folk-like. The melody (heard four times) is Ligeti's, but has a wider resonance. Katalin Károlyí had sung him a traditional country folk song from Transylvania. Ligeti wanted to hear it repeatedly, enchanted as much by her rendition as by its dewy nostalgia, redolent of spring mornings. His own melody has a simple, timeless beauty, but he also indicates that it 'may be ornamented in the style of the grasslands of North-Central Transylvania'. Entitled 'Bitter-sweet', it matches per-fectly the veiled poignancy of Weöres's poem:

> I ploughed, I ploughed with seven fiery dragons,
> hey, I sowed right through with lily-of-the-valley.
> I ploughed with a lovely diamond blade,
> hey, I sowed right through with my falling tears.
> I dreamt of a hundred roses opening in the forest,
> hey, I didn't sleep longer, I was almost awake;
> I rose at dawn, I heard the cuckoo call,
> hey, they're taking me to my wedding with my sweetheart.[17]

Ex. 32 'Alma, álma' for mezzo-soprano and four harmonicas,
from *Síppal, Dobbal, Nádihegedűval* (2000)

The fifth song, 'Alma, álma' (Dream) is unusual for a different reason. Here Ligeti requires the four percussionists to play harmonicas (mouth organs), instruments which he had already used momentarily in the opera and Piano Concerto – and which are also used by Kurtág. Learning to play the harmonica is relatively easy,[18] but Ligeti's writing is ingenious and intricate (though always practical); and the harmonicas are used, without any other instruments, for the whole piece (see Ex. 32, p. 359). Each harmonica sounds two notes, never less than a tone apart (except for an occasional unison), never more than a perfect fourth. This constraint colours the chordal character of the composition, as dyads sway back and forth, first in pairs, then between the four players. Every dyad is either exhaled or inhaled (shown as + or –). Meanwhile, lever positions are indicated by the encircled pitch indications, whilst the adjacent reeds to be blown or sucked are shown by numbers. For this setting Ligeti extracted fragments from a longer poem entitled *Twelfth Symphony* – 'experimental poetry of supernatural gentleness', as he says in his programme note. Its recurrent images of apples swaying on a leafy branch, of shadows and gentle breezes, of sleep and dreams, are depicted in music sounding somehow familiar, yet sweetly strange. In its premiere performances, Amadinda played 'Alma, álma' from memory, standing in a semicircle around Károlyí, both leading and echoing her phrasing.

Weöres, like William Blake, had a gift for sublimating the naive. Ligeti was attracted to his simultaneous playfulness and profundity, vulgarity and elitism, and to his ability to unite the experimental with the universal. No other poet, he says, so exploited 'the rhythmic-metric and semantic possibilities and impossibilities of the Hungarian language'. Some hints of this occur in the remaining texts, all of which are word-games. The second poem, 'Táncdal' (Dance song), appears to have meaning, but is just a rhythmic interplay of words, real and invented. The vivacious last song, 'Szajkó' (Magpie), employs a patter poem that is at first sight nonsensical, but is onomatopoeically suggestive of a magpie's scolding chatter. 'Kínai templom' (Chinese temple) and 'Kuli' (Coolie) draw on Weöres's love of Oriental culture. The first uses only mono-syllables – all valid Hungarian words but evoking 'imaginary Chinese words' – which Ligeti sets 'like a mystical ceremony'. The accompanying temple bells, deep tuned metal plates, tubular bells and vibraphone lend the slow harmonies a strange inscrutability. 'Kuli', by contrast, is a humorous burlesque in pidgin Hungarian. It is busy, 'to-and-fro' music in alternating 11/8 and 13/8 metre, accompanied by the keyed percussion, and interspersed with cries of 'Rickshaw! Car! Sedan chair!' as the hard-worked Coolie pulls his passengers in an incessant 'roly-poly'. The opening song, 'Fabula' (Fable), with its darker complexion, comes closest to earlier Ligeti – to the composer of *Aventures*, for example; indeed, all the songs draw on technical experience amassed over a lifetime. Yet they sound wonderfully fresh, revealing once more a new sensibility.

'It's my own invention'

Ligeti attended the first performances of both new works, but no others, except of the Weöres cycle in Hamburg, until their recording sessions. Unimpressed by popularity, he scorns those 'who want to be everywhere' and promote themselves to the detriment of integrity. He is sceptical of composers who write too much, too soon, too fast, and can be forthright to a fault. But he is also a person of great charm, warmth and generosity. In conversation he is amusing and informal, devoid of any pomposity, genuinely interested in others, instinctively considerate. After the first set of piano Études had won the Grawemeyer Award in 1986, he was embarrassed to receive so much money and gave most of it away, notably to benefit needy young composers from non-Western countries which lacked a supportive cultural infrastructure. John Chowning relates how, when he was in Europe and at some point was 'in real need', Ligeti 'pulled out of his pocket five hundred marks; he is extraordinarily generous'.[19]

Although reluctant to forgo composing time by attending performances, in October 2000 he went to Helsinki to receive the Sibelius Prize in person. And the previous winter he was in Paris for a unique event: the first ever appearance in Europe of the Banda-Linda pipe orchestra and pygmy singers from the Central African Republic. The concert took place at the Théâtre du Châtelet on 20 December 1999 and also included Ligeti's Piano Concerto played by Aimard with the Ensemble InterContemporain. The live performance by the Banda-Linda orchestra was, Ligeti says, 'a hundred times more beautiful than on record'. Nor were the pygmies as small as he expected – but 'they were cold'!

In November 2001 Ligeti and Vera flew to Japan, where, in the presence of the Japanese Imperial family, he was presented with the Kyoto Prize for Arts and Philosophy, one of the most prestigious of all international honours awarded to individuals for their contributions to science, technology and the arts. The following day, to an audience of twelve hundred, along with the laureates in Basic Sciences and Advanced Technology, Ligeti delivered a commemorative lecture entitled 'Between Sciences, Music and Politics'. A third day was devoted to workshops, including a further lecture by Ligeti on 'Rhythmic Configurations in my Piano Studies', and a symposium rounded off with a concert of his music.

On this occasion, the Kyoto Prize Committee decided to share the events between Kyoto itself and the University of San Diego, where three days of symposia were devoted to the theme of 'Science, Technology, Arts and Peace'. Thus, in February 2002, Ligeti was obliged to set off again for California. The continuity of composing is affected by such interruptions; afterwards he tends to begin again from scratch.

Home from California, Ligeti travelled twice to Amsterdam to attend further Teldec recordings. The second half of 2002 he spent mostly in Vienna. There he wrote a seventh movement ('Hymnus') for the *Hamburg Concerto* and planned an eighth – so far unwritten. As for the 'theatrical fantasy' on *Alice*, Richard Jones had been asked to produce it and Nicholas Payne, General Director of English National Opera, had repeatedly suggested their coming to Hamburg to discuss it. Suddenly, in the summer of 2002 Payne resigned, having lost the confidence of the ENO board as the opera company (already in debt) faced a difficult exile during refurbishment of its theatre.

This was no great cause for concern, since Ligeti had scarcely started. A deeper problem was his reticence about the project as a whole. Could he do justice to Lewis Carroll's unique creations? Although packed with incidents, their humour depends most of all on the semantic playfulness of the text. The endearing vulnerability of the White Knight whom Alice meets in *Through the Looking-Glass,* and who is incapable of staying on his horse, is a case in point. The charm of their conversation lies not so much in the situation, nor even in the White Knight's undignified posture head-down in a ditch (rectified with Alice's assistance), but in its surreal sequence of ideas. One can imagine Ligeti empathising with the Knight's nonsensical logic, with his love of gadgets, with his gloriously eccentric yet resigned philosophy:

'What does it matter where my body happens to be?' he said. 'My mind goes on working all the same. In fact the more head downwards I am, the more I keep inventing new things.'

'Now the cleverest thing that I ever did,' he went on after a pause, 'was inventing a new pudding during the meat-course.'

'In time to have it cooked for the next course?' said Alice. 'Well, that was quick work, certainly.'

'Well, not the next course,' the Knight said in a slow thoughtful tone; 'no, certainly not the next course.'

'Then it would have to be the next day. I suppose you wouldn't have two pudding-courses in one dinner?'

'Well, not the next day,' the Knight repeated as before: 'not the next day. In fact,' he went on, holding his head down, and his voice getting lower and lower, 'I don't believe that pudding ever was cooked! In fact, I don't believe that pudding ever will be cooked! And yet it was a very clever pudding to invent.'

'What did you mean it to be made of?' Alice asked, hoping to cheer him up, for he seemed quite low-spirited about it.

'It began with blotting-paper,' the Knight answered with a groan.

'That wouldn't be very nice, I'm afraid . . .'

'Not very nice alone,' he interrupted, quite eagerly: 'but you've no idea what a difference it makes, mixing it with other things – such as gunpowder and sealing-wax. And here I must leave you.'

Alice could only look puzzled: she was thinking of the pudding.

'You are sad,' the Knight said in an anxious tone: 'let me sing you a song to comfort you.'

'Is it very long?' Alice asked, for she had heard a good deal of poetry that day.

'It's long,' said the Knight, 'but it's very, very beautiful. Everybody that hears me sing it – either it brings tears into their eyes, or else . . .'

'Or else what?' said Alice, for the Knight had made a sudden pause.

'Or else it doesn't, you know. The name of the song is called Haddocks' Eyes.'

In the space of a few lines, the White Knight gives the song three more names, much to Alice's confusion, and, having announced that 'the tune is my own invention', he proceeds to sing. 'But the tune *isn't* his own invention', she realises, recognising a familiar ballad. Her encounter with the White Knight is the most affectionate in the book: an idealised, Victorian, chivalric, nostalgic image. For, despite its many pages of playful dialogue, *Alice* has its deeper currents. Like Shakespeare's comedies it is meaningful on many levels, as Ligeti's music too contains ambivalent and simultaneous layers.

In the two years since he wrote the *Hamburg Concerto* and Weöres song cycle Ligeti has completed virtually nothing. But his most innovatory compositions have always followed periods of thought and experiment. Apparently lean years, like the early 1980s, have exploded in cascades of creativity, the first six piano Études, written in 1985 with the impetus of his new discoveries, being an impressive example.

Ligeti and the Red Queen
(John Minnion after Tenniel)

During 2002, although not for the first time, a medical preoccupation distracted Ligeti from the business of composing, on this occasion
a neurological problem affecting his mobility. As this book went to
press, he was recovering from an operation to cure the condition, and
readers will want to join this writer in wishing him many years of good
health and creative activity. Can Ligeti, like Verdi, compose a deft,
funny, tender, ensemble opera at the age of eighty? Why not! His ear
and discernment are as sharp as ever, his mind no less inventive. He
has a vast technical store from which to draw, yet a cartoonist's
instinct for making a point using just a few strokes. *Síppal, Dobbal,
Nádihegedüvel* reveals astonishingly 'youthful' attributes of simple
charm and melodic lyricism, plus a trenchant vein of caricature; for
there are moments in 'Fabula' and 'Kuli' whose peremptory tone is
already worthy of the Queen of Hearts. Carroll's 'wise and wonderful
nonsense' has lurked beneath the surface of his music ever since
Ligeti read *Alice* in Hungarian at the age of twelve. To realise this
long-considered project would be a culmination: hard to start no
doubt, even harder to complete – but it would surely also be fun!
Could now be the moment to begin?

Notes

Biographical information throughout the book, notably in Chapters One and Two, derives in the first place from a range of published sources, including the many interviews the composer has given over the years. The resulting first draft was checked by Ligeti himself, corrected and extensively augmented, during three days of conversations (recorded on thirteen cassette tapes) which I was privileged to have with him in Hamburg between 25 and 27 February 2000. Most unattributed quotations come from these discussions. Ligeti later reread around a hundred pages of my revised text, and I am grateful for his further clarification of many personal and historical matters.

ONE The Making of the Man

1 Letter to Clara Schumann
2 *Ligeti in Conversation* (London: Eulenberg, 1983), a collection of interviews between Ligeti and Péter Várnai, Josef Häusler and Claude Samuel, and a conversation between Ligeti and himself, p. 21
3 In Hungarian, the name 'Ligeti' is pronounced with equal emphasis on each syllable. English speakers vary between stressing the first syllable (usual in Great Britain) and the second (more common in America).
4 So Ligeti was given to understand. Leopold was born in Veszprém, in the same area of south-west Hungary as György's family; but he has no documentary proof of the relationship.
5 Ligeti's birthplace became Diciosânmârtin. Then in the late 1950s, its name was changed to Tirnâveni, and in the 1980s altered again to the more characteristic Romanian orthography of Târnăveni, its name today.
6 György Ligeti, 'Zustände, Ereignisse, Wandlungen', *Melos* 34 (1967), pp. 165–69; trans. into English in *Ligeti in Conversation*, p. 25
7 *Ligeti in Conversation*, p. 47
8 Ibid., p. 17
9 Ligeti speaking on 'All Clocks are Clouds', *Omnibus* (BBC television, 1991)
10 'Between Sciences, Music and Politics', Ligeti's commemorative lecture on receiving the Kyoto Prize (Inamori Foundation, Japan, 2002)
11 Ibid.

12 Ibid.

13 Ove Nordwall, *György Ligeti: From Sketches and Unpublished Scores 1938–56* (Stockholm: Royal Swedish Academy of Music, 1976), in which the opening of the Sonatina is reproduced.

14 'Between Sciences, Music and Politics'

15 *Unterwiesung im Tonsatz* (Mainz, 1937); English trans. New York, 1941, rev. 1945

16 William Shirer, *The Rise and Fall of the Third Reich* (London: Folio Society, 1995), p. 381

17 Wolfgang Burde, *György Ligeti, Eine Monographie* (Zürich: Atlantis Musikbuch, 1993), p. 29. But note that Ligeti says there are many inaccuracies in Burde's book.

18 György Ligeti, 'Begegnung mit Kurtág im Nachkriegs-Budapest' in *György Kurtág, Musik der Zeit* 5 (Bonn: Boosey and Hawkes, 1989)

19 Ibid.

20 Ibid.

21 Twice in the inter-war years, planned productions of *The Miraculous Mandarin* had been banned in Budapest (in 1931 only after the dress rehearsal), on both occasions because of objections to the prostitution at the centre of the story.

22 See Ligeti's introductory notes to the Sony recording (SK 62306), CD 1 of the György Ligeti Edition (1996)

23 A 'pure-hearted, idealist communist' also later imprisoned.

24 György Ligeti, 'Népzenekutatás romániában' (Folk music research in Romania), in *Új Zenei Szemle* 1:3 (August 1950), pp. 18–22. Ligeti told the author that the 'folk orchestra' was 'fake'.

25 Translated by Friedemann Sallis, *An Introduction to the Early Works of György Ligeti* (Cologne: Studio-Schewe, 1996), p. 239, with minor corrections by Ligeti.

26 György Ligeti, 'Egy aradmegyei román együttes' (A Romanian folk ensemble from the Arad district), in D. Bartha and B. Szabolcsi (ed.), *Kodály Emlékkönyv. Zenetudományi Tanulmányok I* (Budapest: Akadémiai Kiadó, 1953), pp. 399–404

27 Wolfgang Burde, *György Ligeti, Eine Monographie*, p. 49

28 Knud Jeppesen, *Counterpoint: the Polyphonic Style of the Sixteenth Century*, trans. G. Haydon (New York, 1939)

29 This story was told to the author by Ligeti during their conversations recorded in February 2000.

30 Hoffnung's spoof amalgamation of the Darmstadt triumvirate: Bruno Maderna, Karlheinz Stockhausen and Luigi Nono.

31 András Szöllösy in conversation with Endre Olsvay, *Hungarian Music Quarterly* 5 (1994)

TWO Night and Morning: An East European Apprenticeship

1 *Schumann and the Romantic Age* (London: Collins, 1956), pp. 158–60
2 *On Music and Musicians* (London: Dobson, 1956), pp. 39–40
3 Ligeti in conversation with the author in London, 22 February 1997
4 Published by Universal Edition in Vienna, but generally not available in Hungary. Ligeti was familiar with Bartók's settings for female chorus, issued by Editio Musica Budapest.
5 'Between Sciences, Music and Politics'
6 Ligeti's own work-list, written in Hungary on small slips of paper, records only the performance at Hungarian Radio on 21 May 1948, but he thinks it must first have been sung at the Bartók College soon after he composed it in November 1946. See also note 11.
7 On the Sony recording (SK 62311, CD 4 of the György Ligeti Edition, 1996) the order of the Weöres songs is changed from that in the Schott score to a more effective sequence: 2, 3, 1
8 Ligeti in conversation with the author in London, 22 February 1997
9 Ligeti's introduction to the Sony recording (SK 62307, CD 6 of the György Ligeti Edition, 1997)
10 Darius Milhaud, 'Polytonalité et atonalité', *Revue musicale* 4, pp. 29ff
11 These dates are listed in Friedemann Sallis's carefully researched catalogue; but there is uncertainty both as to the dates themselves and how many pieces were performed. Ligeti's memory is that *Magány* was performed in 1946 (see note 3 above) and the piano pieces in 1947 (see his introduction to the Sony recording SK 62307). The date 1948, given on the same recording for the composition *Invention*, is an error. It was 1947.
12 Ligeti in conversation with Paul Griffiths in *György Ligeti* (revised edition, London: Robson, 1983), p. 11
13 Extensively reproduced by Burde, *György Ligeti, Eine Monographie*, pp. 40–41
14 Teldec Ligeti Project II, 8573-88261-2 (2002)
15 Ligeti in conversation with Terry Edwards, related in the programme book for the UK premiere of *Four Early Folksong Settings*, 9 December 1994, Barbican, London.
16 In 'A Tale of Two Movements', a discussion between Ligeti and Steven Paul, printed in the CD notes for the recording of the Cello Sonata by Matt Haimovitz (DG 431 813-2), amended by Ligeti. Ligeti refers to the public premiere taking place in Paris in 1983, unaware at the time of de Saram's earlier performance.
17 György Ligeti, 'Anlässlich *Lontano*', in *Die Begegnung*, the brochure for the Donaueschingen festival, 1967. English translation in LP notes for the Wergo recording, 2549 011 (1967).
18 Warner Home Video SO21158 (2001)
19 See Ligeti's introductory notes to the Sony recording (SK 62305), CD 2 of the György Ligeti Edition (1996)

20 Ibid.
21 From Ligeti's notes to SK 62306, CD 1 of the György Ligeti Edition (1996)
22 Friedemann Sallis, *An Introduction to the Early Works of György Ligeti*, p. 21
23 *Philosophie der Neuen Musik* (Tübingen, 1949); English translation by A. Mitchell and W. Blomster (London, 1973)
24 Several of these preliminary attempts are reproduced in Sallis, *An Introduction to the Early Works of György Ligeti*, pp. 125–27
25 *Ligeti in Conversation*, p. 48
26 György Ligeti, 'Anlässlich *Lontano*'
27 *Anleitung zur Zwölftonkomposition* (Vienna: Universal Edition, 1952)
28 Paul Griffiths, *György Ligeti*, p. 14
29 Reproduced by Ove Nordwall in *György Ligeti. From sketches and unpublished scores 1938–56* (Stockholm: Royal Swedish Academy of Music, 1976)

THREE Catching Up

1 'Megjegyzések a bartóki kromatika kialakulásának egyes feltételeiről', in *Új Zenei Szemle* 6:9 (September 1955), pp. 41–44; translated into English by Z. Finger and F. Sallis in Sallis, *An Introduction to the Early Works of György Ligeti*, p. 259
2 'No easy walk to freedom' speech, 21 September 1953
3 Gertraud Cerha, 'New Music in Austria since 1945', *Tempo* 161–62 (1987), p. 46
4 Ove Nordwall, *Ligeti-dokument* (Stockholm, 1968); German translation, *György Ligeti: Eine Monographie* (Mainz: Schott, 1971), pp. 56–57
5 *Tempo* 47 (1958), pp. 28–29
6 Ligeti in conversation with the author. See, for instance, Jonathan Bernard who remarks that Ligeti arrived 'with scarcely any knowledge of twelve-tone technique'; *Music Analysis* 6:3 (1987), p. 207
7 See Karl Wörner, *Stockhausen* (London: Faber, 1973), p. 237, also quoted by Richard Toop in *György Ligeti* (London: Phaidon, 1999), p. 51
8 *Atonale Musiklehre* (Leipzig, 1924)
9 Pierre Michel, *György Ligeti: Compositeur d'aujourd'hui* (Paris: Minerve, 1985), p. 146
10 Karlheinz Stockhausen, *Texte*, vol. 2 (Cologne, 1964), p. 11, quoted in Michael Kurtz, trans. Richard Toop, *Stockhausen* (London, 1992)
11 An account of Ligeti's technical procedures in *Artikulation*, with reproductions of fourteen of his 110 extant working sketches and a pictorial representation of the music itself, can be found in Rainer Wehinger, *Ligeti Artikulation: An Aural Score* (Mainz, 1970)
12 Nordwall, *György Ligeti: Eine Monographie*, p. 41
13 'Neues aus Budapest: Zwölftonmusik oder "Neue Tonalität"?', in Melos 17 (1950), pp. 45–8
14 Sallis, *An Introduction to the Early Works of György Ligeti*, p. 256–61
15 Ibid., p. 260

16 György Ligeti, 'Pierre Boulez', in Herbert Eimert and Karlheinz Stockhausen (ed.), English translation Leo Black, *Die Reihe 4: Young Composers* (Pennsylvania: Presser, 1958), p. 36. Rereading this during discussion with the author Ligeti questioned its accuracy, saying: 'Because you are not free. At the moment you choose the rules you have to follow them. If I wrote this, I was mistaken.' The *Die Reihe* text presumably reflects Ligeti's more ambivalent view of serialism in the mid-1950s.

17 Ibid., p. 58

18 Ibid., p. 61

19 Jonathan Cott, *Stockhausen: Conversations with the Composer* (New York, 1973), pp. 71–72

20 Hermann Scherchen (ed.), *Gravesaner Blätter* 1 (Ticino, Switzerland, 1955), p. 1

21 György Ligeti, 'Metamorphoses of Musical Form' in Herbert Eimert and Karlheinz Stockhausen (ed.), English translation Cornelius Cardew, *Die Reihe 7: Form – Space* (Pennsylvania: Presser, 1965), p. 10

22 Ibid., p. 17

23 Letter from Ligeti to Xenakis, 2 June 1962, quoted by Nouritza Matossian in *Xenakis* (London: Kahn and Averill, 1986), p. 162

FOUR The Watershed of 1960: International Debut

1 *Seven Types of Ambiguity*, third edition (London: Chatto and Windus, 1953), p. 3

2 Wolfgang Steinecke, 'Das 34. Wetmusikfest der IGNM', *Neue Zeitschrift für Musik* 121 (1960), p. 257

3 Interview with Eckhard Roelcke, recorded on Teldec New Line 2188 (2001)

4 *Zenei Szemle* 5 (1948), pp. 284–85; and *Österreichische Musikzeitschrift* (1948), p. 284

5 *Ligeti in Conversation*, p. 127

6 Ibid., p. 43

7 Ibid., p. 125

8 There is one exception, a missing B natural in the second bar of the seventh Violin II part. That it is an error is made clear by the facsimile evidence of the first edition.

9 *Ligeti in Conversation*, p. 132

10 Helmut Lohnmüller, 'Münchner Musica Viva erinnert an die Pioniere der neuen Musik', in *Melos* 28 (1961), pp. 123–24

11 Jonathan Cott, *Stockhausen: Conversations with the Composer*, p. 73

12 From D^2 to C sharp^5 – although within this huge chromatic spread, one pitch (B^3) is unaccountably missing

13 In György Ligeti, Witold Lutosławski and Ingvar Lidholm, *Three Aspects of New Music* (Stockholm: Nordiska Musikförlaget, 1968)

14 Pierre Boulez, *Penser la Musique Aujourd'hui* (Paris, 1963); English translation Susan Bradshaw and Richard Rodney Bennett (London, 1971)

FIVE Distorting Mirrors: Humour and Antilogic

1 Quoted in Marcel Brion, *Modern Painting*, trans. S. Hood (London: Thames and Hudson, 1958), pp. 35–36
2 John Cage, *Silence* (Wesleyan University Press, 1961)
3 Michel, *György Ligeti: Compositeur d'aujourd'hui*, p. 142
4 Quoted by Louis Christensen in 'Introduction to the Music of György Ligeti', *Numus West* 2:72, p. 12
5 As retold by Louis Christensen, ibid., pp. 12–13
6 La Monte Young and Jackson Mac Low, *An Anthology* (New York: Heiner Friedrich, 1963)
7 Michael Kurtz, *Stockhausen*, trans. Richard Toop (London: Faber, 1992), p. 116
8 From Ligeti's notes to SK 62310, CD 5 of the György Ligeti Edition (1997)
9 Michel, *György Ligeti: Compositeur d'aujourd'hui*, p. 158
10 In 1997, when the London Sinfonietta scheduled *Fragment* in a programme of his music, Ligeti asked the conductor Markus Stenz to omit it.
11 *Partytura na tle wspolczesnej techniki orkiestracvjnej* (The score in the light of contemporary orchestral technique) (Cracow, PWM, 1954)
12 From Ligeti's notes to the first recording on Wergo 60161-50 (1968)
13 From Ligeti's notes to SK 62307, CD 6 of the György Ligeti Edition (1978)
14 Published in *An Anthology*
15 This account (trans. Annelies McVoy and David Feurzeig) accompanies Sony's recording of *Poème symphonique* on SK 62310, CD 5 of the György Ligeti Edition (1997)
16 Ibid.
17 *Ligeti in Conversation*, p. 45
18 György Ligeti, 'Libretto zu *Aventures* et *Nouvelles aventures*', in *Neues Forum* 13 (1966), pp. 774–79; and *Neues Forum* 14 (1977), pp. 88–92
19 The serialists' injunction to avoid octaves, and the consequent overuse of unisons, is one of the criticisms of twelve-note polyphony made by Ligeti in his study of Boulez's *Structures 1a* (see Chapter Three)
20 From a programme note by the composer

SIX Distance and Enchantment

1 Ove Nordwall, 'Sweden', in *Musical Quarterly* 52 (1966), pp. 109–13
2 Runar Mangs, 'Skräkens projektioner på oänlighetens vägg', in *Dagens Nyheter*, 17 March 1965
3 William Mann, 'Ligeti's Requiem: Festival Hall', in *The Times*, 11 November 1971, p. 12
4 *Ligeti in Conversation*, p. 46
5 Ibid., p. 47
6 Sallis, *An Introduction to the Early Works of György Ligeti*, p. 200. Ligeti's letter, now in the archive of the Paul Sacher Foundation, is incorrectly dated 1956.

7 Nordiska Musikförlaget, Stockholm

8 *Ligeti in Conversation*, p. 53

9 *Darmstädter Beiträge zur Neuen Musik* 10 (1966), pp. 23–35

10 Reported by Heinz-Harald Löhlein, 'Musik und Vorlesungen im slowakischen Smolenice', in *Melos* 36 (1969), p. 270

11 *Ligeti in Conversation*, p. 26

12 Broadcast in two parts by Südwestfunk, Baden-Baden, 19 and 26 July 1968; reprinted in English translation by S. Soulsby in *Ligeti in Conversation*, pp. 83-110

13 Ibid., p. 101

14 Robert Cogan, in *New Images of Musical Sound* (Harvard, 1984), pp. 39–43, presents a 'spectrum photograph' of *Lux aeterna*, arguing that its morphology (including overtones generated from the sung clusters) is more complex than the score implies.

15 *Ligeti in Conversation*, p. 29

16 See the preface to George Crumb, *Makrokosmos I, Twelve Fantasy-Pieces after the Zodiac for Amplified Piano* (New York: Peters, 1972)

17 György Ligeti, 'Anlässlich *Lontano*'

18 *Ligeti in Conversation*, pp. 92–93

19 'Anlässlich *Lontano*'

20 *Ligeti in Conversation*, p. 93

21 Michel, *György Ligeti: Compositeur d'aujourd'hui*, p. 170

22 Kubrick documentary, Warner Home Video 3021158 (2001)

23 Ibid.

24 John Baxter, *Stanley Kubrick: A Biography* (London: HarperCollins, 1997)

25 Interviewed by Michael John White, *Independent*, 18 October 1989

26 *Ligeti in Conversation*, p. 22

27 SK 62310, CD 5 of the György Ligeti Edition (1997)

SEVEN A Gestural Kaleidoscope

1 *Ligeti in Conversation*, p. 124

2 Ibid., p. 13

3 Ibid., p. 14

4 Ibid., p. 15

5 Ibid., pp. 18–20

6 See Ligeti's notes to the Sony recording (SK 62306), CD 1 of the György Ligeti Edition (1996)

7 *Ligeti in Conversation*, p. 21

8 Helen Dawkins, 'Pulling on the heart strings', *Sunday Times*, 17 January 1999, section 11, pp. 4–5

9 Wolfram Schwinger, 'Ligetis neues Streichquartett', in *Stuttgarter Zeitung*, 16 December 1969

10 Rolf Gaska, *Neue Zeitschrift für Musik* 133 (1972), pp. 92–93

11 Listed as 6 October 1969 in the Schott catalogue, but it was probably a year earlier. Ligeti recollects that when he arrived in Malmö in January 1969 to rehearse the *Ten Pieces* with the Stockholm Philharmonic Wind Quintet, they told him that they had already played the *Bagatelles*. Ligeti heard them play the *Bagatelles* in Paris in the autumn of 1969.

12 Ove Nordwall, programme note to the LP recording, (E 061–34091, December 1969)

EIGHT Spider's Web: The Labyrinth of Melodies

1 Quoted in Erwin Panofsky, *The Life and Art of Albrecht Dürer* (Princeton, 1955), p. 243

2 Pozzi Escot, '"Charm'd Magic Casements", Mathematical Models in Ligeti', in *Sonus* 9:1 (Cambridge, Mass., 1988), pp. 17–37

3 Conversations with the author, 25–27 February 2000

4 So Ligeti proposes in the instructions published with the score. He now realises that they are 'never imperceptible'.

5 Ligeti's notes to SK 62307, CD 6 of the György Ligeti Edition (1997)

6 Harrison Birtwistle also began his Breughel-inspired orchestral processional, *The Triumph of Time*, in 1971

7 Ligeti has little use for Schenkerian analysis. Its reductive methodology, preoccupied with voice-leading and harmony, is unhelpful in illuminating the multiple structures of his music. Nevertheless, the relationship between motivic surface detail and underlying harmony gives a work like *Melodien* a Schenkerian dimension. Ligeti's frequent use of a deep-seated quasi-tonal architecture (whose clarification for the listener is one of the intentions of this book), means that music like *Lontano*, *Melodien*, *Clocks and Clouds*, and even the apparently non-harmonic *Atmosphères*, might be interestingly subjected to Schenkerian examination.

8 A discussion recorded in 1972 for South German Radio between Ligeti and Clytus Gottwald suggests that Mahler was not far from Ligeti's mind. Published as 'Gustav Mahler und die musikalische Utopie', *Neue Zeitschrift für Musik* 135 (1974), pp. 7–11 and 288–95

9 Ove Nordwall, 'On György Ligeti and his *Melodien* for Orchestra' (Stockholm: Stiftelsen Institutet for Rikskonserter, 1971). Part of this article was reprinted in the programme for the USA premiere of *Melodien* by the Los Angeles Philharmonic on 13 April 1972.

10 Harry Halbreich, *Music and Musicians,* 21 October 1972

11 Walter Schröder, '25. Holland-Festival', in *Musica* 26 (1972), pp. 449–50

12 *Ligeti in Conversation*, pp. 66–67

13 *San Francisco Chronicle*, 15 May 1972, p. 40

14 *Ligeti in Conversation*, p. 54

15 Bruno Bartolozzi, *New Sounds for Woodwind*, trans. R. Smith Brindle, second edition (London: OUP, 1982)

NINE Dis(c)loc(k)ation and Transformation

1 Gyula Krúdy, *Adventures of Sinbad*, trans. G. Szirtes (Budapest: Central European University Press, 1998)
2 Ibid., p. 57
3 Karl Popper, *Objective Knowledge: an Evolutionary Approach*, revised edition (London: OUP, 1979)
4 Ian Stewart, *Nature's Numbers* (London: Weidenfeld and Nicolson, 1995), p. 109
5 Ibid., p. 110
6 Talking with Péter Várnai in 1978, Ligeti said that 'tunes emerge from the fog' (*Ligeti in Conversation*, p. 67); but he now agrees that they do not (conversations with author, 25–27 February 2000). Tunes *do* emerge in *San Francisco Polyphony*.
7 Louis Christensen, 'Conversation with Ligeti at Stanford', in *Numus West* 2 (1972), p. 20
8 Ibid.
9 Ligeti's programme note
10 Conversations with the author, 25–27 February 2000
11 Michel, *György Ligeti: Compositeur d'aujourd'hui*, p. 173
12 It was from one of these performances, in a packed auditorium at Leeds Grammar School in the autumn of 1966, that the author came away convinced for the first time of Stockhausen's 'greatness' as a composer!
13 Henning Siedentopf, 'Neue Wege der Klaviertechnik', in *Melos* 40:3 (1973), pp. 143–46
14 Conversations with the author, 25–27 February 2000

TEN Alice in Breughelland: A Grotesque Carnival of Sex and Death

1 *Ligeti in Conversation*, p. 117
2 Elgar Howarth reports that the music 'took Ligeti, as he himself puts it, "very much by surprise"'. *Opera* 33 (December 1982), p. 1231
3 *Ligeti in Conversation*, p. 114
4 Interview with Dorle Soria in *High Fidelity, Musical America*, MA-2, (December 1973)
5 *Ligeti in Conversation*, p. 111
6 Note that Ghelderode's title of *La Balade* means 'a ramble'; rather than 'Le Ballade', meaning 'a poem'
7 'Entretiens d'Ostende' (Ostend Interviews), trans. G. Hauger, in Michel de Ghelderode, *Seven Plays* (London, 1960), p. 4
8 Ibid., p. 18
9 Programme book for the London production of *Le Grand Macabre*, trans. Geoffrey Skelton
10 Ibid.

11 Quotations in this section are taken either from the revised score, or from the libretto, or from Ligeti's synopsis, trans. Elizabeth Uppenbrink, published with SK 62312, CD 8 of the György Ligeti Edition no. 8 (1999). The revision is dated 1996 on the score, 1997 (the date of the Salzburg production) on the Sony recording.

12 Interview between Ligeti and Hermann Sabbe, significantly titled 'Illusions – allusions', in *Interface* 8:1, p. 29, ed. Swets and Zeitlinger (Lisse, Belgium, 1979)

13 *Ligeti in Conversation*, p. 117

14 Ibid., p. 70

15 'An Art without Ideology', interview with Anders Beyer in *The Voice of Music: Conversations with the Composers of our Time* (Aldershot: Ashgate, 2000), p. 13. Originally 'En ideologifri kunst: Et interview med komponisten György Ligeti', in *Dansk Musik Tidsskrift* 67:8 (1992–93).

16 This line of dialogue occurs only in the first version since (to this author's regret) Ligeti has removed it from his revision. ('Ligeti regrets it too, but circumcision was obligatory!' – conversations with the author, 25–27 February 2000.)

17 Reinhard Beuth in *Abendzeitung*, 14 April 1978, p. 9

18 Reprinted in *Neue Zeitschrift für Musik* 140 (1979), pp. 43–45

19 *Die Zeit*, 20 October 1978, p. 56

20 Michel, *György Ligeti: Compositeur d'aujourd'hui*, p. 177

21 Review by Malcolm Crowthers in *Classical Music*, 2 May 1981, p. 23

22 Márta Grabócz in *Muzsika* 24:8 (August 1981), pp. 12–15

23 As reported by Michael John White in the *Independent*, 18 October 1989

24 The *Observer*, 16 April 1978

25 More recently, Saskia Boddeke and Peter Greenaway's staging of Louis Andriessen's opera *Writing to Vermeer* (1998) suggests that Renaissance iconography is not incompatible with a contemporary production.

ELEVEN In the midst of life . . .

1 'Hälfte des Lebens' (Halfway through life), translated by David Feurzeig

2 Published by Harvester Press (1979), and Penguin (Harmondsworth, 1980)

3 Published by Viking (London, 1985). In 1986 Ligeti sent a cassette recording of the first six Études to Hofstadter, but he replied disdainfully, commenting that 'many composers write fast music – e.g. Alkan', apparently failing to understand their polyrhythmic structures. Ligeti was disappointed.

4 Michel, *György Ligeti: Compositeur d'aujourd'hui*, p. 177

5 Although in view of the unhappy history of its theatrical productions, there is something to be said for performing the whole opera in concert, devoid of ill-conceived stagecraft.

6 Anders Beyer, *The Voice of Music*, p. 8

7 Dorle Soria, 'György Ligeti, Distinguished and Unpredictable', in *Musical America*, September 1987, p. 15
8 Tünde Szitha, 'A Conversation with György Ligeti', in *Hungarian Musical Quarterly* 3:1 (1992), p. 14
9 Conversations with the author, 25–27 February 2000

TWELVE The Dynamics of Disorder

1 Jonathan Miller in conversation with Kevin Jackson in the final programme of *Viewing the Century*, BBC Radio 3, December 1999
2 György Ligeti, 'On my Études for Piano', trans. Sid McLauchlan in *Sonus* 9:1 (Fall 1988), p. 4
3 Between 1977 and 1985 (Berkeley: Soundings Press)
4 René Block, *The Sum of all Sounds is Grey* (Berlin, 1980)
5 Letter to Charles Amirkhanian, 4 January 1981, Vienna; quoted in Kyle Gann, *The Music of Conlon Nancarrow* (Cambridge: CUP, 1995), p. 2. Amirkhanian had published an interview with Nancarrow in *Soundings* 4 (1977), pp. 7–24
6 *Central Africa Republic: Banda Polyphony* (Auvidis–Unesco, 1976/1992), CD D8043
7 Simha Arom, *Polyphonies et polyrythmies instrumentales d'Afrique Centrale* (Paris: SELAF, 1985); Eng. trans., *African Polyphony and Polyrhythm* (Cambridge: CUP, 1991)
8 Ibid., p. xvii
9 Berlin, Springer-Verlag, 1986
10 Ian Stewart, *Nature's Numbers* (London: Weidenfeld and Nicolson, 1995), pp. 113, 123
11 Benoit Mandelbrot, *The Fractal Geometry of Nature* (New York: Freeman, 1982)
12 Georg Christoph Lichtenberg (1742–99), German physicist and philosopher, famous for his aphorisms
13 Schott, *The Journal* 5:6 (1998), pp. 1–2
14 Jorges Luis Borges, *Labyrinths* (Harmondsworth: Penguin, 1970)
15 *Mind* 4 (1895), pp. 278–80. Reprinted in Hofstadter, *Gödel, Escher, Bach* (pp. 43–45)

THIRTEEN The Piano Études

1 Reviewing Michael Gordon's opera *Chaos* in the *New York Times*, 16 October 1998
2 'On My Études for Piano', p. 4
3 From Ligeti's notes to SK 62308, CD 3 of the György Ligeti Edition (1996)
4 Ligeti had insufficient time to proofread the second book, and it is not impeccably accurate.

5 Commenting on the first draft of this chapter

6 A 'school' of French composers, grouped around Gerald Grisey, Michael Levinas and Tristan Murail, concerned with timbral manipulation based on overtone (spectral) analysis.

7 Ligeti's programme note

8 *The Times*, 8 November 1989

9 R. N. Shepard, 'Circularity in pitch judgment', in *Journal of the Acoustic Society of America* 36, pp. 2346–53

10 Although close to the Golden Section, this was not a conscious structural decision.

11 The spelling 'Columna' in the published score is a mistake, a consequence of Ligeti having used this spelling in his sketches.

FOURTEEN Curiouser and curiouser

1 From Ligeti's notes to SK 62311, CD 4 in the György Ligeti Edition (1996)

2 Notes to the Teldec CD 8573-83953-2 (Ligeti Project 1, 2001)

3 James Gleick, *Chaos: Making a New Science* (New York: Viking Penguin, 1987), p. 117

4 Ibid., p. 24

5 Ligeti's programme note for the Graz premiere of movements 1–3, translated by Robert Katz

6 Ibid.

7 Conversations with the author, 25–27 February 2000

8 Ibid.

9 Ligeti's programme note for the *Nonsense Madrigals*

10 Ibid.

11 With its fourth degree raised to F natural – it is not evident why.

12 *Ligeti Letter* 2, ed. Louise Duchesneau (Hamburg, 1992), p. 3

13 Interviewed on *Private Passions* (BBC Radio 3) by Michael Berkeley

14 *Circuit* 2:1–2 (1991), pp. 7–16

15 Tünde Szitha, 'A Conversation with György Ligeti', pp. 13–17

16 *Ligeti Letter* 2, p. 4

17 Ibid., p. 3

18 Ibid., p. 7

19 Ligeti's programme note for the premiere of the Viola Sonata

20 Ibid.

21 Ibid.

22 Ibid.

23 Compare the end of *Fanfares* and the hidden B major tonality in *Vertige*; also bars 12–14 of *Lontano*

FIFTEEN On (Not) Writing Opera

1 Tünde Szitha, 'A Conversation with György Ligeti', p. 13
2 Georgina Born, *Rationalizing Culture: IRCAM, Boulez and the Institutionalization of the Musical Avant-Garde* (Berkeley: University of California Press, 1995), pp. 358–9
3 'Computer und Komposition: Subjektive Betrachtungen', *Tiefenstruktur-Musik Baukunst: Festschrift Fritz Winckel zum 80. Geburtstag*, ed. Carl Dahlhaus (Berlin: Technische Universität, 1987), pp. 22–30; trans. Paul Griffiths, *György Ligeti*, pp. 114–15
4 Interviewed by Michael John White, *Independent*, 18 October 1989
5 For example, the 'Intermezzo' in the fourth movement of the *Hamburg Concerto* lasts only between bars 29 and 36
6 Reservations Ligeti voiced in a public interview in Huddersfield in November 1993
7 Anders Beyer, *The Voice of Music*, p. 13
8 Norman Lebrecht, interview with Ligeti, *Daily Telegraph*, November 1993
9 Tension was perhaps not easily diffused by Salonen's instinctive Finnish reserve. Talking to Richard Morrison about his work with the Los Angeles Philharmonic, he observed: 'In Finland, if you can get by without saying anything at all that is considered the most preferable way of communication. Whereas on the West Coast, if you can use eight words instead of one you do. People you don't know say "Hi, how are you?" on the street. In Finland, that would practically be regarded as a criminal offence.' *The Times*, 23 August 2002, T2, p. 11.
10 Conversation with Salonen, 24 February 2002
11 Ligeti in conversation with Eckhart Rölcke, Teldec Newline Interview CD 2188, trans. Alison Slade
12 Ibid.
13 Ligeti's programme note
14 Ibid.
15 27 February 2000
16 *Ligeti in Conversation*, p. 21
17 Translated by Rachel Beckles Willson
18 Hohner's Chromonica II M270 is specified for all players
19 See Chowning's notes to CD WER 2012–50 (1988), pp. 11–12

APPENDIX

Productions of *Le Grand Macabre*

Theatre	First night	
Swedish Royal Opera, Stockholm	12 February	1978
Hamburg State Opera	15 October	
Saarbrücken State Theatre	3 May	1979
Teatro Comunale di Bologna	5 May	
Musiktheater Nürnberg	2 February	1980
Théâtre National Opéra de Paris	23 March	1981
Grazer Schauspielhaus	17 November	
English National Opera, London	2 December	1982
Freiburg Theatre	1 March	1984
Ulm Theatre	28 September	1991
Leipzig Opera	29 September	
Zürich Opera	22 February	1992
Berne State Theatre	8 March	
Vienna Jugendstiltheater	20 January	1994
Münster State Theatre	23 February	1997
Teatro Comunale di Ferrara	28 March	
Revised version		
Salzburg Festival	28 July	1997
Châtelet Theatre, Paris	5 February	1998
Hanover Opera House	11 March	
Netherlands National Reisopera	16 May	
Tirol Landestheaters, Innsbruck	26 September	
Budapest Opera	29 October	
Teatro Nacional de São Carlos, Lisbon	6 February	1999
(Royal Opera House, London)	10 December	
Theater Krefeld-Mönchengladbach	14 October	2000
Flanders Opera, Antwerp	7 November	
Heidelberg Theatre	3 February	2001
Oldenburg State Theatre	20 September	
Kongelige Teater, Copenhagen	23 September	
Komische Oper, Berlin	22 June	2003

Director	Designer	Conductor
Michael Meschke	Aliute Meczies	Elgar Howarth
Gilbert Deflo	Ekkehard Grübler	Elgar Howarth
Christof Bitter	Walther Jahrreiss	Matthias Kuntzsch
Giorgio Pressburger	Roland Topor	Zoltán Peskó
Götz Fischer	Marco Arturo Marelli	Wolfgang Gayler
Daniel Mesguich	Bernard Daydé	Elgar Howarth
(production from Nuremberg)		Wolfgang Gayler
Elijah Moshinsky	Timothy O'Brien	Elgar Howarth
David Freeman	David Roger	Eberhard Kloke
Ulrich Heising	Guido Fiorato	Alicja Mounk
Joachim Herz	Peter Sykora	Volker Rohde
Marco Arturo Marelli	Marco Arturo Marelli	Zoltán Peskó
Eike Gramss	Eberhard Matthies	Andreas Delfs
Gidon Saks	Gidon Saks	Andreas Mitisek
Dietrich Hilsdorf	Dieter Richter	Will Humburg
(production from Münster)		
Peter Sellars	George Tsypin	Esa-Pekka Salonen
(production from Salzburg)		Esa-Pekka Salonen
Ernst Theo Richter	Hartmut Schörghöfer	Andreas Delfs
Stanislas Nordey	Emanuel Clolus	Reinbert de Leeuw
Michael Sturminger	Renate Martin	Arend Wehrkamp
Balázs Kovalik	Péter Horgas	Jonathan Nott
(production from Hanover)		Karl Prokopetz
(production from Salzburg – cancelled)		
Thomas Krupa	Andrea Jander	Kenneth Duryea
(production from Hanover)		Luca Pfaff
Wolf Widder	Sibylle Schmalbrock	Thomas Kalb
Mascha Pörzgen	Cordelia Matthes	Alexander Rumpf
Kasper Holten	Steffen Aarfing	Michael Schønwandt
Barrie Kosky	Peter Corrigan	Matthias Foremny

Glossary

Absolute pitch Musicians use their sense of 'relative pitch' to identify pitches in relation to another, given pitch. Absolute pitch (also called 'perfect pitch') is the ability possessed by a few individuals to identify a pitch without reference to any other.

A cappella Originally applied only to sacred music, the term now means any unaccompanied choral singing.

Aggregate In musical contexts, used to describe a collection of pitches, groups of pitches or clusters which result in more complex combinations than those of traditional harmony.

Aleatory Derived from the Latin *alea* meaning 'a game with dice', 'aleatory', its etymological corruption 'aleatoric', and 'indeterminate' all refer to music governed to a greater or lesser extent by chance, either in the process of composition or in the act of performance. In the latter, one or more *parameters* normally decided by the composer are determined by the performers, perhaps through the use of less prescriptive notation. Concept and terminology date from the 1950s, in particular the music of Cage and Boulez.

Aksak From the Turkish word for 'limping' or 'hobbled', *aksak* is the pairing of two uneven rhythmic units in the ratio 3:2, and in larger combinations of 3 + 3 + 2 and 2 + 2 + 2 + 3, as found in Balkan folk music. The term was coined by the Romanian ethnomusicologist Constantin Brăiloiu in *Problèmes d'ethnomusicologie,* ed. G. Rouget (Geneva, 1973; English translation, 1984) and has been adopted by Ligeti as the correct terminology for its occurrence in his own music.

Bitonality (alternatively *bimodality*) The simultaneous use of two modes, diatonic keys, or parts thereof.

Canon The continuous imitation of one musical line by others, at regular intervals of time and pitch. Composers since the early development of polyphony have used the technique with varying degrees of sophistication. Canons mostly embrace both pitch and rhythm but can involve just one *parameter*: for example, Messiaen used purely rhythmic canons, and some of Ligeti's *micropolyphonic* canons are imitative only in terms of pitch.

Cantus firmus Literally a 'fixed' or 'firm' melody, i.e. one that remains constant, or is repeated, whilst the surrounding lines change. The term generally applies to the Renaissance technique of using a pre-existing melody, often slowed down in long note values, around which a new *contrapuntal* composition is evolved.

Chromatic Literally meaning 'coloured', this adjective is used to describe music which uses pitches in addition to those found in the *diatonic* major and minor scales.

Cluster The simultaneous sounding of several adjacent pitches (i.e. tones and semitones) extending from three to any number, limited only by practicality. The adjectives 'clustered' and 'clusterous' are both used in this book: 'clustered' simply meaning that notes have been grouped together in this way, 'clusterous' describing the overall effect of composing with clusters.

Counterpoint The art of combining two or more simultaneous musical lines. 'Contrapuntal' is the adjective derived from 'counterpoint'.

Diatonic Music using pitches contained within the major and minor scales, as opposed to *chromatic* music.

Difference tone A physiological phenomenon whereby the inner ear produces the aural sensation of a third (lower) frequency equal to the difference between two frequencies actually sounded. The effect is most apparent when two high instruments such as flutes play together in their upper registers.

Dodecaphony See *Serialism*.

Dyad An intervallic or harmonic entity of two pitches, as opposed to a 'triad' which contains three.

Enharmonic A term which describes the 'respelling' of pitches to change their notation from flats into sharps, or vice versa (e.g. G sharp/A flat), in order to comply with a new harmonic context.

Equal temperament See *Just intonation*.

FM synthesis FM means 'frequency modulation'. In FM synthesis one wave form is used to change the functional characteristics of another, the interaction of wave forms producing a fluid and complex sonic experience. This method of creating music electronically came from research into computer applications carried out by John Chowning at Stanford University between 1967 and 1971, and was embodied in one of the earliest all-digital synthesisers, the Yamaha DX7.

Fugue A *contrapuntal* composition, or section of a composition, in which a melodic phrase (the 'subject') is taken up in turn by every part, each of which continues with one or more secondary melodies ('countersubjects'). After the subject has been presented by each part (exposition), the fugue proceeds through a sequence of episodes and further entries, frequently displaying other contrapuntal techniques like *stretto* (overlapping entries), augmentation, diminution and pedal points.

Hemiola A metrical formula common in the Renaissance and Baroque eras, but also used by composers such as Schumann and Brahms, in which two bars in triple time are stressed as if they were three bars in duple time. For example, two bars of 3/4 may be treated as three of 2/4, or possibly one long bar of 3/2. Although hemiola and *aksak* are different phenomena, there is some overlap between the two terms owing to their common dependence on a 3:2 ratio.

Hexachord In the Middle Ages the hexachord was a scale of six notes ascending through two tones, a semitone and two more tones (eg. C D E F G A, the *ut re mi fa sol la* of medieval music). In *dodecaphony* the division of twelve-note rows into two halves produces hexachords of widely varying character. In recent music, therefore, the term 'hexachord' can refer to any series of six different pitches.

Hocket A rhythmic and textural phenomenon, characteristic of medieval polyphony as well as of some African and Indonesian music, in which melodies are divided between two or more voices or parts, each alternating sound and silence so that notes in one part coincide with rests in another.

Integral (total) serialism The application of serial order to *parameters* other than pitch: e.g. duration, dynamics, density, tempi, tone colour etc. (See also *Serialism*.)

Just intonation A system which maximises the 'purity' of the intervals contained in the principal triads, by tuning them to simple mathematical ratios so that their lower overtones coincide to eliminate 'beating'. As a consequence, more distant chords and intervals are severely out of tune, and *enharmonic* equivalents (e.g. G sharp and A flat) are not the same pitch. In just intonation, therefore, basic tonal relationships are exceptionally harmonious, but *modulation* is limited. In *mean-tone temperament*, by comparison, the pure major third is divided into two equal whole tones, whereas just intonation has two sizes of whole tone. *Equal temperament* further sacrifices the advantages and removes the disadvantages of just intonation, by adjusting *all* 'pure' intervals except the octave, to produce a scale of twelve equal semitones. Purity of intonation is traded for harmonic mobility. 'Tempered' usually means equal temperament, 'untempered' its absence.

Klangfarbenmelodie Literally 'sound-colour melody'. An idea proposed by Schoenberg in his *Harmonielehre* (1911), by which melodic changes of pitch are replaced or enhanced by changes of tone colour.

Mean-tone temperament See *Just intonation*.

Melisma A succession of notes sung to one syllable of text.

Mensuration A medieval technique, defined by Philippe de Vitry, for organising the metrical relationships between note values. Its modern equivalent is the simultaneous or successive use of different related time signatures.

Microharmonic Chord structures involving precisely quantifiable microtones (i.e. intervals smaller than semitones) such as the natural overtones produced by an instrument that lie outside the tempered scale. Although Ligeti's preferred term is 'non-harmonic' (i.e. different from *traditional* harmony), 'microharmonic' has been adopted in this book to avoid the implication that microtonal usage precludes harmony.

Micropolyphony Ligeti's own term to describe the dense *counterpoint* in works like *Atmosphères* and the Requiem, in which many parts contribute slightly different versions of the same sequence. In micropolyphonic passages the listener hears not so much a polyphony of individual lines as the textural totality which is their sum. Micropolyphony does not imply *microtonality*.

Minimalism As applied to music, this term describes pieces in which both the resource base and the degree of variation in melody, harmony and rhythm are deliberately and radically limited, perhaps to focus on slowly evolving processes. Steve Reich, Terry Riley, Philip Glass and Michael Nyman are often cited as archetypal Minimalists.

Modulation Change of key achieved by logical harmonic progression. The most important structural component of most music from the seventeenth to early twentieth century.

New complexity A term coined in the 1980s to describe a school of composition dedicated to extremely detailed, intricate and complex writing, whether for solo or ensemble. Although influenced by Boulez, Stockhausen and central European music, new complexity is a particularly British phenomenon, with composers such as Brian Ferneyhough and Michael Finnissy amongst its leaders.

Notes inégales A well-documented convention of performing notes of even duration unequally: i.e. alternating longer and shorter time values, although the notation makes no such distinction. The practice is commonly applied to stepwise melodies in seventeenth-century French dance music.

Parameter A term misappropriated from mathematics by the protagonists of *serialism* to denote one aspect of the musical whole: i.e. pitch, duration, loudness, timbre etc.

Parlando Singing which emulates the rhythms and stress patterns of speech.

Phasing The displacement of a musical pattern in relation to one or more simultaneous and similar patterns, either by imperceptible tempo change or through the addition or subtraction of rhythmic units. Pattern-phasing requires extensive repetition for its gradual evolution to make an effect. Although phasing also occurs in electroacoustic music, it is a notable feature of early *minimalism*, especially the music of Steve Reich.

Pitch class Pitch class designates a pitch by name but without specifying its octave. This is useful for discussing *serial* music, since rows are expressed as a sequence of pitch classes (not precise pitches), and their component notes can be placed in any octave.

Player piano (pianola) Mechanical piano whose playing mechanism is operated by rolls of perforated paper, so that neither the speed nor complexity of performance are restricted by human anatomy.

Polytonality (alternatively *polymodality*) The simultaneous use of any number of keys, including mixtures of their *diatonic* chords.

Ponticello Correctly *sul ponticello*, an Italian term used in string playing to indicate that the bow is to be drawn across the strings on or close to the bridge. The tone produced lacks lower harmonics and sounds somewhat metallic and disembodied.

Prolation From Latin *prolatio* (prolonging), a fourteenth-century term for the relationship between minim and semibreve, also used for a combination of the four main *mensurations*, the 'quatre prolacions' of Philippe de Vitry. The latter meaning applies to Ockeghem's *Missa Prolationem* in which each of the four voices sings in a different mensuration (in modern notation 2/4, 3/4, 6/8 and 9/8).

Serialism Composition based on a series (or several series) of elements that are repeatedly recycled, but also subjected to variation and/or systematic permutation. Its most common form is the twelve-note serialism invented by Schoenberg in the 1920s – also known as *dodecaphony* – an ordering of the twelve notes of the chromatic scale so that each *pitch class* appears once before any are repeated. The 'series' can be used in prime (original) form, inversion, retrograde, retrograde inversion and in all transpositions. The term serialism is also used for instances in which fewer (or occasionally more) than twelve notes are employed. *Integral serialism* refers to music in which more than one parameter receives serial treatment. *Total serialism* commonly describes the same phenomenon, but strictly means that *all* aspects of a composition are serially related.

Stretto An Italian word meaning 'narrow, tight, confined', applied to the technique common in the later stages of a *fugue* where entries of the subject overlap.

Talea(e) Latin word meaning, amongst other things, a 'set'. In fourteenth-century treatises, *talea* is a rhythmic sequence repeated systematically, usually in different tempi or durational units. The resultant proportional relationships are an essential feature of isorhythmic music.

Tritone The interval of an augmented fourth or diminished fifth (so named because it is the 'sum' of three whole tones); the tritone is exactly half the octave in *equal temperament*. In early theory as well as in traditional harmony, the unstable and ambivalent nature of the tritone led to its classification as a dissonance and the appellation *diabolus in musica* ('devil in music').

Una corda/tre corde Literally 'one string /three strings', the terms instruct a pianist to depress or release the 'soft' (left) pedal. Depressing this pedal has the effect of moving the entire action slightly to one side so that the hammers strike only one string instead of the normal two or three.

Voice-leading The overall linear progression in a piece of music; it governs the relationship between individual melodies in a contrapuntal texture.

Chronological list of works

For works composed between 1938 and 1950 this is a selective list. It includes juvenilia which Ligeti now regards as unworthy of performance, but which chart the development of his ideas. It also lists works of potential interest which have been lost. Lesser lost or incomplete manuscripts and some shorter surviving compositions have been omitted. Fuller lists exist in Ove Nordwall's *György Ligeti: From Sketches and Unpublished Scores 1938–56* (Stockholm, Royal Swedish Academy of Music, 1976) and in Friedeman Sallis's *An Introduction to the Early Works of György Ligeti* (Cologne, Studio-Schewe, 1996). All Ligeti's surviving compositions are published by Schott except those listed as existing only in manuscript (ms) or issued by other publishers. The majority of Ligeti's manuscripts and sketches are now in the Paul Sacher Foundation in Basle, along with originals (and photocopies) of early works published in Budapest. The Paul Sacher Foundation also possesses so far uncatalogued boxes of press cuttings, letters, contracts, programme books, honours and awards, etc.

Music composed in Romania and Hungary

1938–39
Sonatina, for string quartet (incomplete ms)
1939–40
Symphony (incomplete, lost)
1939–41
Kis zongorádarabok (*Little piano pieces*) (ms)
1941
Kineret (*Galilee*), in *Songs of Ararat*, nine songs with piano accompaniment (Budapest, Ararat Kiadó, 1942 – Ligeti's first published composition)
Four Short Piano Pieces (ms)
1941–42
Kis zongoratrió (*Little piano trio*), for violin, cello (or viola) and piano (ms)
1942
Tréfás induló (*Funny march*), for piano four hands

1943
 Kis tréfa (*Little joke*), for piano (ms)
 Polifon gyakorlat (*Polyphonic study*), for piano four hands
1944–45
 Cantata no. 1: *Tenebrae factae sunt*, for mezzo-soprano, double SATB chorus
 and chamber orchestra (ms)
1945
 Dereng már a hajnal (*Dawn is already breaking*), for four-part unaccompanied
 choir (Cluj, Józsá Béla Atheneum, 1945; Budapest, Cserépfalvi, 1946;
 London, The Workers' Music Association, 1947)
 Cantata no. 2: *Venit angelus*, for mezzo-soprano, five-part mixed choir and
 chamber orchestra (ms)
 Három József Attila-kórus (*Three Attila József choruses*), for two- and four-
 part unaccompanied choir (ms)
 Duo, for violin and cello (ms)
 Bicinia Biciae, seven duets for two voices (ms, incomplete, plus drafts in
 sketchbooks)
 Kis szerenád (*Little serenade*), for string orchestra (ms)
1945–46
 Idegen földön (*Far from home*), four pieces for three-voice female choir
1946
 Betlehemi Királyok (*Kings of Bethlehem*), for two-part unaccompanied
 children's choir
 Húsvét (*Easter*), for four-part unaccompanied choir
 Magos Kősziklának (*From the high rocks*), for three-part unaccompanied
 choir
 Magány (*Solitude*), for three-part unaccompanied choir
 Duo, for violin and piano (ms)
 Bujdosó (*The fugitive*), for three-part unaccompanied choir
1946–47
 Három Weöres-dal (*Three Weöres songs*), for soprano and piano
1947
 Ha folyóvíz volnék (*If I could flow like the river*), four-part canon for voices in
 Kánon, ed. Péter József (Budapest, Zeneműkiadó, 1954)
 Capriccio no. 1, for piano
 Capriccio no. 2, for piano
1948
 Invention, for piano
 Tavasz (*Spring*), for unaccompanied four-part choir (lost)
 Mifiso la sodo (*Vidám zene*) (*Mi-fa-sol la sol-do* [*Cheerful music*]), for small
 orchestra (ms)
 Bölcsőtől a sírig (*From cradle to grave*), for soprano, bass, oboe, clarinet
 and string quartet (ms)
1948–49
 Kantáta az ifjúság ünnepére (*Cantata for a youth festival*), for soprano, alto,
 tenor, bass, four-part mixed chorus and orchestra (ms)

1949
Induló (Dance), for orchestra (lost)
Katonatánc (Soldier's dance), for two-part choir and piano, reworked for
orchestra (both versions lost)
Régi magyar társas táncok (Old Hungarian ballroom dances), for string orchestra
with flute and clarinet ad lib. (based on eighteenth-century originals)
Tavaszi virág: kiserözene (Spring flower: incidental music), music for a puppet
theatre on Chinese fairy tales, for seven singers, flute, viola, piano and percus-
sion (ms)
Három tánc cigányzenekarra (Three dances for gypsy orchestra), (lost)
1950
Ballada és tánc (Ballad and dance), for two violins (lost), reworked for school
orchestra
Három Jószef Attila-dal (Three Attila Jószef songs), for soprano and piano (ms)
Two Movements for String Quartet
Chinese Imperial Court Music, for school orchestra (lost)
Petőfi bordala (Petöfi's drinking song), for tenor and piano (Budapest,
Zeneműkiadó, 1950), reworked for tenor and orchestra (lost)
Kállai kettős (Double-dance from Kálló), for unaccompanied four-part
choir
Lakodalmas (Wedding dance), for unaccompanied four-part choir
Négy lakodalmi tánc (Four wedding dances), for three female voices and
piano, reworked as *Három lakodalmi tánc (Three wedding dances)*, for piano
four hands
Sonatina, for piano four hands
1950–51
Rongszőnyeg (Rag carpet), three pieces for piano (nos 1 and 2 in Ligeti's
sketchbooks; no. 3 lost)
1951
Grande Symphonie Militaire op. 69, for orchestra (ms)
Romanian Concerto, for orchestra
Az asszony és a katona (The woman and the soldier), for unaccompanied
four-part choir (Budapest, Zeneműkiadó, 1956)
Haj, ifjúság! (Hey, youth!), for unaccompanied four-part choir
1952
Hortobágy, for unaccompanied four-part choir
Öt Arany-dal (Five Arany songs), for soprano and piano
Pletykázó asszonyok (Gossip), four-part canon for voices in *Kánon*, ed. Péter
József (Budapest, Zeneműkiadó, 1954)
1951–53
Musica ricercata, for piano
1953
Omaggio a G. Frescobaldi: Ricercar for Organ
Six Bagatelles for Wind Quintet
Inaktelki nóták (Tunes from Inaktelke), for unaccompanied two-part choir,
reworked for three female voices and folk orchestra (lost)
Pápainé (Widow Pápai), for unaccompanied four-part choir

1948–53
Sonata, for violoncello solo
1953–54
String Quartet no. 1: *Métamorphoses nocturnes*
1955
Mátraszentimrei Dalok (*Songs from Mátraszentimre*), for unaccompanied two- and three-part children's or female choir
Éjszaka, Reggel (*Night, morning*), for unaccompanied eight-part choir
1956
Chromatische Phantasie, for piano (ms)
Sötet és világos (*Darkness and light*), for orchestra (incomplete ms)
Viziók (*Visions*), for orchestra (lost)

Music composed in the West

1957
Glissandi, mono tape
Apparitions (first version), for twelve strings, harp, celesta, harpsichord and piano (incomplete ms)
1958
Artikulation, four-channel tape
1957–58
Pièce électronique no. 3, completed by Ligeti in score only (realised in 1996 by Kees Tazelaar and Johan van Kreij)
1958–59
Apparitions (final version), for orchestra (Universal Edition; autograph score thought to be lost)
1961
Atmosphères, for large orchestra (Universal Edition; autograph score thought to be lost)
Die Zukunft der Musik (*The future of music*), for lecturer and audience (in *Dé/Collage* no. 3, Cologne, 1962)
Trois Bagatelles, for piano
Fragment, for ten players (Universal Edition)
1961–62
Volumina, for organ (C. F. Peters)
1962
Poème symphonique, for 100 metronomes
Aventures, for three singers and seven instrumentalists (C. F. Peters)
1962–65
Nouvelles aventures, for three singers and seven instrumentalists (C. F. Peters)
1963–65
Requiem, for soprano, mezzo-soprano, twenty-part mixed chorus and orchestra (C. F. Peters)
1966
Lux aeterna, for unaccompanied sixteen-part mixed chorus (C. F. Peters)

Cello Concerto (C. F. Peters)
1967
Lontano, for large orchestra
Harmonies, Étude no. 1 for organ
1968
Continuum, for harpsichord
String Quartet no. 2
Ten Pieces for Wind Quintet
1968–69
Ramifications, for string orchestra or twelve solo strings
1969
Coulée, Étude no. 2 for organ
1969–70
Chamber Concerto
1971
Melodien, for orchestra
1972
Double Concerto, for flute, oboe and orchestra
1972–73
Clocks and Clouds, for twelve-part female choir and orchestra
1973–74
San Francisco Polyphony, for orchestra
1976
Monument–Selbstportrait–Bewegung: Three Pieces for Two Pianos
Rondeau, for actor and tape
1974–77
Le Grand Macabre, opera in two acts
1978
Scenes and Interludes from Le Grand Macabre, for four soloists, chorus ad
lib. and orchestra
Hungarian Rock, for harpsichord
Passacaglia ungherese, for harpsichord
1982
Hommage à Hilding Rosenberg, for violin and cello
Trio, for violin, horn and piano
Drei Phantasien nach Friedrich Hölderlin, for unaccompanied sixteen-part
mixed chorus
1983
Magyar Etüdök (Hungarian studies), for unaccompanied sixteen-part mixed
chorus
1985
Die grosse Schildkröten-Fanfare vom Südchinesischen Meer, for trumpet
Études for piano, Book 1
1980–88
Piano Concerto

1988
  Mysteries of the Macabre, three arias from *Le Grand Macabre* for trumpet
  and piano (arr. Elgar Howarth)
1989
  Der Sommer, for soprano and piano
1992
  Mysteries of the Macabre, version for trumpet or coloratura soprano and
  orchestra, also a version with chamber orchestra (arr. Elgar Howarth)
1988–93
  Nonsense Madrigals, for six male voices
1989–93
  Violin Concerto
1988–94
  Études for piano, Book 2
1991–94
  Sonata for solo viola
1996
  Le Grand Macabre, revised version in four scenes
1999 (rev. 2002)
  Hamburg Concerto, for horn and chamber orchestra
2000
  Síppal, Dobbel, Nádihegedűval, for mezzo-soprano and four percussionists
1995–
  Études for piano, Book 3 (ongoing)

Bibliography

1 Writings by Ligeti: books

Klasszikus összhanzattan [*Classical Harmony*] (Budapest: Zeneműkiadó, 1954)
A klasszikus harmóniarend I–II [*The System of Classical Harmony I–II*]
  (Budapest: Zeneműkiadó, 1956)
Gesammelte Schriften [*Collected Writings*], ed. Monika Lichtenfeld (Basle: Paul
  Sacher Foundation, 2003)

2 Writings by Ligeti: general, analytical and theoretical essays (in order of publication)

'Kóyaismertetések' [Score review], *Zene-pedagógia* 2:3 (March 1948), p. 43
'Kottak' [Scores], *Zenei Szemle* 6 (1948), p. 337
'Bartók: *Medvetánc* (1908) elemzés' [*Bear Dance* analysis], *Zenei Szemle* 5
  (1948), pp. 251–55
'Neue Musik in Ungarn', *Melos* 16:1 (1949), pp. 5–8
'Svervánszky Endre: Vonósnégyes' [Endre Svervánszky: string quartet], *Zenei
  Szemle* (Aug. 1949), pp. 102–3
'Járdányi Pál: Szonáta két zongorára' [Pál Járdányi: sonata for two pianos],
  Zenei Szemle (August 1949), p. 103
'Sugár: Vonóstrió' [Sugár: string trio], *Zenei Szemle* (August 1949), pp. 105–6
'Népzenekutatás romániában' [Folk music research in Romania], *Új Zenei
  Szemle* 1:3 (August 1950), pp. 18–22
'Neues aus Budapest: Zwölftonmusik oder "Neue Tonalität"?', *Melos* 17:2
  (1950), pp. 45–48
'Egy aradmegyei román együttes' [A Romanian folk ensemble from the Arad dis-
  trict], in *Kodály Emlékkönyv: Zenetudományi Tanulmányok I*, ed. D. Bartha
  and B. Szabolcsi (Budapest, Akadémiai Kiadó, 1953), pp. 399–404
'Járdányi Pál és Svervánszky Endre fuvolasonatinái' [Flute sonatinas by Pál
  Járdányi and Endre Svervánszky], *Új Zenei Szemle* 5:12 (Dec. 1954), pp.
  26–28
'Megjegyzések a bartóki kromatika kialakulásának egyes feltételeiröl' [Remarks
  on the development of Bartók's chromaticism], *Új Zenei Szemle* 6:9 (Sept.
  1955), pp. 41–44; part translated into English by Z. Finger and F. Sallis in
  Sallis, *An Introduction to the Early Works of György Ligeti*, p. 259
Preface to Bartók's String Quartet no. 5 in Philharmonia Partituren no. 167
  (Vienna: Universal Edition, 1957)

'Pierre Boulez: Entscheidung und Automatik in der *Structure 1a*', *Die Reihe* 4
(Vienna: Universal, 1958), pp. 38–63; Eng. trans. L. Black, 'Pierre Boulez: decision and automation in *Structure 1a*' (Pennsylvania: Presser, 1960), pp. 36–62

'Zur III Klaviersonate des Boulez', *Die Reihe* 5 (Vienna: Universal, 1959),
pp. 38–40; Eng. trans, 'Some remarks on Boulez's Third Piano Sonata'
(Pennsylvania: Presser, 1961), pp. 56–58

'Wandlungen der Musikalischen Form', *Die Reihe* 7 (Vienna: Universal, 1960),
pp. 5–17; Eng. trans. C. Cardew, 'Metamorphoses of musical form'
(Pennsylvania: Presser, 1965), pp. 5–19

'Die Entdeckung des Raumes in der Musik', *Forum* 76 (1960), pp. 152–54

'Weberns Stil', *Gehört–Gelesen* 3 (Munich: Bayerischer Rundfunk, 1960),
pp. 187–92

'Über die Harmonik in Weberns erster Kantate', *Darmstädter Beiträge zur
Neuen Musik* 4 (1960), pp. 49–64

'Die Komposition mit Reihen und ihre Konsequenzen bei Anton Webern', *Österreichische Musikzeitschrift* 16:6–7 (1961), pp. 297–302

'Musik von anderen Planeten: zur Geschichte und Gegenwart der elektronischen
Musik', *Forum* 91–92 (1961), pp. 292–95

'Neue Notation: Kommunikationsmittel oder Selbstzweck?', *Darmstädter
Beiträge zur Neuen Musik* 9 (1965), pp. 35–50

'Viel Pläne, aber wenig Zeit' [letter to Ove Nordwall of 28 Dec. 1964], *Melos* 32
(1965), pp. 251–52

'Form in der Neuen Musik', *Darmstädter Beiträge zur Neuen Musik* 10 (1966),
pp. 23–35

'Weberns Melodik', *Melos* 33 (1966), pp. 116–18

'Was erwartet der Komponist der Gegenwart von der Orgel?', *Orgel und
Orgelmusik heute* (Stuttgart, 1968), pp. 168–200

'Über neue Wege im Kompositionsunterricht', in *Three Aspects of New Music*
(Stockholm: Nordiska Musikforlaget, 1968), pp. 9–44

'Auswirkungen der elektronische Musik auf mein kompositorisches Schaffen',
Experimentelle Musik in *Schriftenreihe der Akademie der Kunste*, vol. 7
(Berlin: Mann, 1970)

'Music, micropolyphony, technique and humanism', CAPAC–MacMillan Lecture,
abbreviated version in *The Canadian Composer* 83 (Sept. 1973), pp. 16–20

'Apropos Musik und Politik', *Darmstädter Beiträge zur Neuen Musik* 13 (1973),
pp. 42–46; Eng. trans. 'On music and politics', *Perspectives of New Music*
16:2 (1978), pp. 19–24

'György Ligeti', in *Mein Judentum,* ed. H. J. Schultz (Berlin: Kreuz Verlag,
1978), pp. 234–37

'Musik und Technik', *Rückblick in die Zukunft* (Berlin: Severin und Siedler,
1981), pp. 297–324

'Aspekte der Webernschen Kompositionstechnik', *Anton Webern II,*
Musik–Konzepte [special issue] (Munich, 1984), pp. 51–104

'Computer und Komposition: Subjektive Betrachtungen', *Tiefenstruktur–Musik
Baukunst: Festschrift Fritz Winckel zum 80. Geburtstag,* ed. C. Dahlhaus
(Berlin: Technische Universität, 1987), pp. 22–30

'A Viennese exponent of understatement: personal reflections on Friedrich
    Cerha', *Tempo* 161:2 (June/Sept. 1987), pp. 3–5
'Begegnung mit Kurtág im Nachkriegs–Budapest' [Meeting Kurtág in post–war
    Budapest] in F. Spangemacher (ed.), *György Kurtág, Musik der Zeit* 5 (Bonn,
    1986), pp. 14–17
'Zur Anwendung von Computern in der Komposition', *MusikTexte* 28–29
    (1989), pp. 3–4
'Ma position comme compositeur aujourd'hui', *Contrechamps* 12–13 (1990),
    pp. 8–10
'Konvention und Abweichung' [on Mozart's 'Dissonance' Quartet], *Österreich-
    ische Musikzeitschrift* 46 (1991), pp. 34–39
'Rhapsodische, unausgewogene Gedanken über Musik, besonders über meine
    eigenen Kompositionen', *Neue Zeitschrift für Musik* 154 (1993), pp. 20–29
'Between Sciences, Music and Politics', commemorative lecture on receiving the
    Kyoto prize (Inamori Foundation, Japan, 2002)

3 Writings by Ligeti: commentaries on his individual compositions
See also numerous programme notes (listed up to 1970 in Nordwall)

'Züstande, Ereignisse, Wandlungen: Bemerkungen zu meinem Orchesterstück
    Apparitions', *blatter und bilder* 11 (Würzburg and Vienna: Zettner, 1960),
    pp. 50–57; reprinted in *Melos* 34 (1967), pp. 165–69; Eng. trans. J. Bernard,
    'States, events, transformations', *Perspectives of New Music* 31:1 (1993),
    pp. 164–71
'Bemerkungen zu meiner Orgelstück *Volumina*', *Melos* 33 (1966), pp. 311–13
'Nachwort zum Libretto zu *Aventures* und *Nouvelles aventures*', *Neues Forum*
    157 (1967), pp. 91–92
'Spielanweisungen zur Erfassung des zweiten Satzes der *Apparitions*', *Musica*
    22:3 (1968), pp. 177–79
'Requiem', *Wort und Wahreit* 4 (1968), pp. 309–13
'Auf dem Weg zu *Lux aeterna*', *Österreichische Musikzeitschrift* 24:2 (1969),
    pp. 80–88
'Zur Entstehung der Oper *Le Grand Macabre*', *Melos/Neue Zeitschrift für Musik*
    4 (1978), pp. 91–93

4 Interviews with Ligeti

Ligeti in Conversation [interviews between Ligeti and Péter Várnai, Josef
    Häusler, Claude Samuel, and a conversation between Ligeti and himself]
    (London: Eulenberg, 1983)
Häusler, Josef, 'Interview mit György Ligeti', *Melos* 37 (1970), pp. 496–507;
    Eng. trans. in *Ligeti in Conversation*, pp. 83–102
Häusler, Josef, 'Wenn man heute ein Streichquartett schreibt', *Neue Zeitschrift für
    Musik* 131 (1970), pp. 378–81; Eng. trans. in *Ligeti in Conversation*, pp. 102–10
Bachauer, Walter, 'Gespräch mit György Ligeti', *Melos* 38 (1971), pp. 213–14
Ligeti, György, 'Fragen und Antworten von mir selbst', *Melos* 38 (1971),
    pp. 509–16; Eng. trans. in *Ligeti in Conversation*, pp. 124–37

Stürzbecher, Ursula, 'György Ligeti' in *Werkstattgespräche mit Komponisten* (Cologne: Gerig, 1971), pp. 32–45

Lichtenfeld, Monika, 'György Ligeti gibt Auskunft', *Melos* 39 (1972), pp. 48–50

Christensen, Louis, 'Conversation with Ligeti at Stanford', *Numus West* 2 (1972), pp. 17–20

Gottwald, Clytus, 'Gustav Mahler und die musikalische Utopie', *Neue Zeitschrift für Musik* 135 (1974), pp. 7–11, 288–95

Jack, Adrian, 'Ligeti talks to Adrian Jack', *Music and Musicians* 22:22 (July 1974), pp. 24–30

Gottwald, Clytus, 'Tendenzen der Neuen Musik in den USA', *Melos/Neue Zeitschrift für Musik* 1 (1975), pp. 266–72

Berling, Berit, 'Ligeti på svenska då ... nu ... framtiden', *Nutida Musik* 19:4 (1975–76), pp. 25–29

Lesle, Lutz, 'Computer-Musik als Kreativer Dialog zwischen Musiker und Maschine? Gespräch mit dem Komponisten György Ligeti', *Musik und Medizin* 2:5 (1976), pp. 43–45

Sabbe, Herman, 'György Ligeti – illusions et allusions', *Interface* 8 (1979), pp. 11–34

Várnai, Péter, 'Beszélgetések Ligeti Györgyel' (Budapest: Zeneműkiadó, 1979); Eng. trans. in *Ligeti in Conversation*, pp. 13–82

Samuel, Claude, 'Entretien avec György Ligeti' in Topor, Roland, *Le Grand Macabre, dessins des décors et costumes de l'opéra de György Ligeti* (Zürich: Diogenes, 1980), pp. 17–31; Eng. trans. in *Ligeti in Conversation*, pp. 113–23

Von Der Weid, Jean-Noël, 'György Ligeti: mon opéra est un pot au feu que sort de la poubelle', *Monde de la Musique* 32 (March 1981), pp. 71–73

Lichtenfeld, Monika, 'Musik mit schlecht gebundener Krawatte', *Neue Zeitschrift für Musik* 142 (1981), pp. 471–73

Bouliane, Denys, 'Entretien avec György Ligeti', *Sonances* 3:1 (Oct. 1983), pp. 9–27

Hansen, Mathias, 'Musik zwischen Konstruktion und Emotion: Gespräch mit György Ligeti', *Musik und Gesellschaft* 34 (1984), pp. 472–77

Szigeti, István, 'A Budapest interview with Ligeti', *New Hungarian Quarterly* 25 (Summer 1984), pp. 205–10

Lichtenfeld, Monika, 'Gespräch mit György Ligeti', *Neue Zeitschrift für Musik* 145:1 (1984), pp. 8–11

Wiesmann, Sigrid, '"The Island is Full of Noises"', *Österreichische Musikzeitschrift* 39 (1984), pp. 510–14

Klüppelholz, Werner, 'György Ligeti', in *Was ist Musikalische Bildung?*, *Musikalische Zeitfragen* 14 (Kassel: Bärenreiter, 1984), pp. 66–75

Michel, Pierre, 'Entretiens avec György Ligeti', *György Ligeti: Compositeur d'aujourd'hui* (Paris: Minerve, 1985), pp. 127–82

Politi, Edna, 'Entretien avec Ligeti', *Contrechamps* 4 (1985), pp. 123–27

Krützfeldt, Werner, 'György Ligeti über Chancen und Möglichkeiten der Computer-Musik', *Schnittpunkte, Signale, Perspektiven: Festschrift zur Eröffnung des Neubaus der Hochschule für Musik* (Hamburg, 1986), pp. 60–61

Erwe, Hans Joachim, 'Interview mit György Ligeti', *Zeitschrift für Musikpädagogik* 11:37 (Nov. 1986), pp. 3–11

Gottwald, Clytus, 'Entretien avec Ligeti', *InHarmoniques* 2 (Paris: IRCAM, 1987), pp. 217–29

Bouliane, Denys, 'Geronnene Zeit und Narration: György Ligeti in Gespräch', *Neue Zeitschrift für Musik* 149:5 (1988), pp. 19–25

Lesle, Lutz, 'In meiner Musik gibt es keine Weltanschauung: Gespräch mit György Ligeti', *Das Orchester* 36 (1988), pp. 885–90

Bouliane, Denys, 'Stilisierte Emotion', *MusikTexte* 28–29 (1989), pp. 52–62

Dufallo, Richard, 'György Ligeti', *Trackings* (New York: OUP, 1989), pp. 327–37

Oehlschlägel, Reinhard, 'Ja, ich war ein utopischer Sozialist', *MusikTexte* 28–29 (1989), pp. 85–102

Satory, Stephen, 'Colloquy: An Interview with György Ligeti in Hamburg', *Canadian University Music Review* 10:1 (1990), pp. 101–17

Gojowy, Detlef, 'György Ligeti über eigene Werke', 'Für György Ligeti: Die Referate des Ligeti-Kongresses, Hamburg 1988', *Hamburg Jahrbuch für Musikwissenschaft* 11 (Hamburg, 1991), pp. 349–63

Duchesneau, Louis, 'Sur la musique de Claude Vivier', *Circuit* 2:1–2 (1991), pp. 7–16

Szitha, Tünde, 'A Conversation with György Ligeti', *Hungarian Music Quarterly* 3:1 (1992), pp. 13–17

Saalfeld, Lerke von, '"Ich glaube nicht an grosse Ideen, Lehrgebäude, Dogmen . . ."', *Neue Zeitschrift für Musik* 154:1 (1993), pp. 32–36

Mérigaud, Bernard, 'Je compose . . . et je réfléchis après', *Télérama* 2448 (11 Dec. 1996), pp. 66–68

Derrien, Jean Pierre, 'La curiosité comme seule constante', programme for Ligeti concert series (Paris, Châtelet, 15 Dec. 1996 and 27 March 1997), pp. 13–18

Kipphoff, Petra [Fr. trans. L. Kayas], 'Ordre et désordre', programme for Ligeti concert series (Paris, Châtelet, 28 and 29 Sept. 1997 and 8 and 12 Feb. 1998), pp. 13–17

Sabbe, Herman, 'György Ligeti: Entretiens', *Ars Musica* (1997), pp. 22–24

Beyer, Anders, 'An Art Without Ideology', *The Voice of Music: Conversations with Composers of our Time* (Aldershot: Ashgate, 2000), pp. 1–15; originally published as 'En ideologifri kunst: Et interview med komponisten György Ligeti', *Dansk Musik Tidsskrift* 67:8 (1992–93), pp. 254–63

5 Books about Ligeti

Burde, Wolfgang, *György Ligeti, Eine Monographie* (Zürich: Atlantis, 1993)

Dibelius, Ulrich, *Ligeti und Kurtág in Salzburg* [includes contributions by Ligeti], Salzburg Festival programme book (Salzburg, 1993)

– *György Ligeti: Eine Monographie in Essays* (Mainz: Schott, 1994)

Floros, Constantin, *György Ligeti: Jenseits von Avantgarde und Postmoderne* (Vienna: Lafite, 1996)

Griffiths, Paul, *György Ligeti*, second edition (London: Robson, 1997)

Michel, Pierre, *György Ligeti: Compositeur d'aujourd'hui* (Paris: Minerve, 1985)
Nordwall, Ove, *Det omöjligas Konst: anteckningar kring György Ligetis Musik* (Stockholm: Norstedt, 1966)
– *Ligeti-Dokument* (Stockholm: Norstedt, 1968); German trans. Hans Eppstein, *György Ligeti: Eine Monographie* (Mainz: Schott, 1971)
– *György Ligeti. From sketches and unpublished scores 1938–56* (Stockholm: Royal Swedish Academy of Music, 1976)
Restagno, Enzo (ed.), *Ligeti* (Turin: Edizioni di Torino, 1985)
Richart, Robert, *György Ligeti: A Bio-Bibliography* (New York: Greenwood, 1990)
Sabbe, Herman, *György Ligeti: Studien zur kompositorischen Phänomenologie, Musik-Konzepte* 53 (Munich, 1987)
Sallis, Friedemann, *An Introduction to the Early Works of György Ligeti* (Cologne: Studio-Schewe, 1996)
Salmenhaara, Erkki, *Das musikalische Material und seine Behandlung in den Werken 'Apparitions', 'Atmosphères' und 'Requiem' von György Ligeti*, German trans. Helke Sander, *Forschungsbeiträge zur Musikwissenschaft* 19 (Regensburg, 1969)
Toop, Richard, *György Ligeti* (London: Phaidon, 1999)

6 Journal issues, symposium proceedings and other publications devoted to Ligeti, mostly containing articles by several authors

Artes 2:3 (1976)
Burde, Wolfgang (ed.), *Komponistenportrait György Ligeti* (Berlin: Berlin Festwochen, 1988)
'Für György Ligeti: Die Referate des Ligeti-Kongresses, Hamburg 1988', *Hamburg Jahrbuch für Musikwissenschaft* 11 (Hamburg, 1991)
Kollertisch, Otto (ed.), 'György Ligeti: Personalstil – Avant-gardismus – Popularität', *Studien zur Wertungsforschung* 19 (Vienna and Graz: Universal, 1987)
Musik und Bildung 7:10 (Oct. 1975)
Neue Zeitschrift für Musik 144:1 (Jan. 1993)
Numus West 2 (1972)
Nutida Musik 19:2 (1975–76)
Omnibus (BBC television, rev. 1991)
Sonus 9:1 (Fall 1988)

7 Individual articles about Ligeti

Bernard, Jonathan, 'Inaudible structures, audible music: Ligeti's problem and his solution', *Music Analysis* 6 (1987), pp. 207–36
– 'Voice leading as a spatial function in the music of Ligeti', *Music Analysis* 13 (1994), pp. 227–53
Bonnet, Antoine, 'Sur Ligeti', *Entretemps* 1 (1986), pp. 5–15
Bossin, Jeffery, 'György Ligeti's new lyricism and the aesthetic of currentness: the Berlin Festival's retrospective of the composer's career', *Current Musicology* 37:8 (1984), pp. 233–39

Christensen, Louis, 'Introduction to the music of György Ligeti', *Numus West* 2 (1972), pp. 6–15

Dibelius, Ulrich, 'Reflexion und Reaktion. Über Kompositionen György Ligeti', *Melos* 37 (1970), pp. 89–96

– 'Sprachen – Gesten – Bilder. Von György Ligetis *Aventures* zu *Le Grand Macabre*', *MusikTexte* 28–29 (1989), pp. 63–67

Doria, Dorle, 'Artist Life', *High Fidelity/Musical America* 23 (Dec. 1973), pp. 2–6 and 26

– 'György Ligeti: distinguished and unpredictable', *Musical America* 107:4 (Sept. 1987), pp. 12–15 and 27

Fabian, Imre, 'Jenseits von Tonalität und Atonalität', *Österreichische Musikzeitschrift* 28 (1973), pp. 233–38

Florois, Constantin, 'György Ligeti. Prinzipielles über sein Schaffen', *Musik und Bildung* 19 (1978), pp. 484–88

Hicks, Michael, 'Interval and form in Ligeti's *Continuum* and *Coulée*', *Perspectives of New Music* 31:1 (1993), pp. 172–90

Hoopen, Christiane ten, 'Statische Musik: Zu Ligetis Befreiung der Musik von Taktschlag durch präzise Notation', *MusikTexte* 28–29 (1989), pp. 68–72

Keller, Hans, 'The contemporary problem', *Tempo* 89 (1969), pp. 181–86

– 'Music 1975', *The New Review* 2:24 (March 1976), pp. 17–53

Kropfinger, Klaus, 'Ligeti und die Tradition', in *Zwischen Tradition und Fortschritt*, ed. R. Stephan, *Veröffentlichungen des Instituts für neue Musik und Musikerziehung Darmstadt* 13 (Mainz: Schott, 1973), pp. 131–42

Kurtág, György, 'Meine Begegnung mit György Ligeti', in *Ligeti und Kurtág in Salzburg*, ed. U. Dibelius (Zürich: Palladion, 1993)

Lichtenfeld, Monika, 'György Ligeti oder das Ende der seriellen Musik', *Melos* 39 (1972), pp. 74–80

Nordwall, Ove, 'Der Komponist György Ligeti', *Musica* 22 (1968), pp. 173–77

– 'György Ligeti', *Tempo* 88 (1969), pp. 22–25

– 'György Ligeti 1980', *Österreichische Musikzeitschrift* 35 (1980), pp. 67–75

Piper, Clendinning, 'The pattern-meccanico compositions of György Ligeti', *Perspectives of New Music* 30:1 (1993), pp. 192–234

Plaistow, Stephen, 'Ligeti's recent music', *Musical Times* 115 (1974), pp. 379–81

Rourke, Sean, 'Ligeti's early years in the West', *Musical Times* 130:9 (1989), pp. 532–35

Searby, Michael, 'Ligeti the postmodernist?', *Tempo* 199 (Jan. 1997), pp. 9–14

Steinitz, Richard, 'Connections with Alice', *Music and Musicians* 22:4 (Dec. 1973), pp. 42–50

– 'Music, maths and chaos', *Musical Times* 137:3 (1996), pp. 14–20; 'The dynamics of disorder', *Musical Times* 137:5 (1996), pp. 7–14; 'Weeping and Wailing', *Musical Times* 137:8 (1996), pp. 17–22; also published together as *György Ligeti: Studies in Music and Mathematics* (London: Schott, 1996)

– 'György Ligeti', in *Censorship: A World Encyclopedia*, ed. D. Jones (London: Fitzroy Dearborn, 2001), pp. 1432–33

Toop, Richard, 'L'illusion de la surface', *Contrechamps* 12–13 (1990), pp. 61–93

Trillig, Jo, 'György Ligeti und Darmstadt', in *Von Kranichstein zur Gegenwart 50 Jahre Darmstädter Ferienkurse,* ed. C. Fox, L. Knessl, R. Stephan, O. Tomek and K. Trapp (Stuttgart: Daco, 1996), pp. 341–45

Zosi, Giuliano, 'A Preposito di Ligeti', *Nuova Revista Musicale Italiana* 8 (1974), pp. 234–38

8 Commentaries on individual works

ARTIKULATION

Karkoscha, Erhard, 'Eine Hörpartitur Elektronischer Musik', *Melos* 38 (1971), pp. 468–75

Wehinger, Rainer, *Ligeti* Artikulation: *An Aural Score* (Mainz: Schott, 1970)

Miereanu, Costin, 'Une musique électronique et sa "partition"', *Musique en jeu* 15 (1974), pp. 102–9

ATMOSPHÈRES

Kaufmann, Harald, 'Strukturen in Strukturlosen: Über György Ligetis *Atmosphères*', *Melos* 31 (1964), pp. 391–98

AVENTURES AND NOUVELLES AVENTURES

Beuerle, Jürgen, '*Aventures* von György Ligeti', *Analyse: Neue Musik* (Herrenberg: Döring, 1976), pp. 53–56

Kaufmann, Harald, 'Ein Fall absurder Musik: Ligetis *Aventures* und *Nouvelles aventures*', *Spurlinien* (Vienna: Lafite, 1969), pp. 130–58; French trans. in *Musique en jeu* 15 (1974), pp. 75–98

Klüppelholz, Werner, 'Aufhebung der Sprache: Zu György Ligetis *Aventures*', *Melos/Neue Zeitschrift für Musik* 2 (1976), pp. 11–15

CELLO CONCERTO

Schultz, Wolfgang-Andreas, 'Zwei Studien über das Cello-Konzert von Ligeti', *Zeitschrift für Musiktheorie* 6 (1975), pp. 97–104

Stephan, Rudolf, 'György Ligeti: Konzert für Violoncello und Orchester: Anmerkungen zur Cluster-Komposition', *Die Musik der sechziger Jahre,* ed. R Stephan, *Veröffentlichungen des Instituts für neue Musik und Musikerziehung Darmstadt* 12 (Mainz: Schott, 1972), pp. 117–27

CHAMBER CONCERTO

Bernager, Olivier, 'Autour du concerto de chambre de Ligeti', *Musique en jeu* 15 (1974), pp. 99–101

Piencikowski, Robert, 'Le concert de chambre de Ligeti', *InHarmoniques* 2 (1978), pp. 211–6

Searby, Michael, 'Ligeti's Chamber Concerto: summation or turning point?', *Tempo* 168 (1989), pp. 30–34

CONTINUUM

Troxler, Ule, *Antoinette Vischer. Dokumente zu einem Leben für das Cembalo* (Basel: Birkhäuser, 1976), pp. 130–36

Urban, Uwe, 'Serielle Technik und barocker Geist in Ligetis Cembalo-Stück *Continuum*', *Musik und Bildung* 5 (1973), pp. 63–70

DREI PHANTASIEN NACH FRIEDRICH HÖLDERLIN

Floros, Constantin, 'Ligetis Drei Phantasien nach Friedrich Hölderlin', *Neue Zeitschrift für Musik* 2 (1985), pp. 18–20

LE GRAND MACABRE

Le Grand Macabre, L'Avant Scène Opéra 180 (Paris: Éditions Premières Loges, 1997)

Cadieu, Martine, 'D'un space imaginaire', *Musique en jeu* 32 (1978), pp. 123–25

Fanselau, Rainer, 'György Ligeti zum 60. Geburtstag: György Ligeti *Le Grand Macabre* – Gesichtspunkte für eine Behandlung im Musikunterricht', *Musik und Bildung* 15 (1983), pp. 17–24

Howarth, Elgar, Ligeti's *Le Grand Macabre*', *Opera* 33 (Dec. 1982), pp.1229–34

Topor, Roland, *Le Grand Macabre, dessins des décors et costumes de l'opéra de György Ligeti* (Zürich: Diogenes, 1980)

LONTANO

Dadelsen, Hans-Christian von, 'Über die musikalischen Konturen der Entfernung: Entfernung als räumliche, historische und ästhetische Perspektive in Ligetis Orchesterstück *Lontano*', *Melos/Neue Zeitschrift für Musik* 2 (1976), pp. 187–90

Müller, Karl-Josef, 'György Ligeti: *Lontano*', *Perspektiven Neuer Musik* (Mainz, 1974), pp. 215–33

Reiprich, Boris, 'Transformation of coloration and density in György Ligeti's *Lontano*', *Perspectives of New Music* 16:2 (1978), pp. 167–80

Rolin, Robert, 'Ligeti's *Lontano:* traditional canonic technique in a new guise', *Music Review* 41 (1980), pp. 289–96

LUX AETERNA

Bauer, Hans-Joachim, 'Statistik, eine objektive Methode zur Analyse von Kunst? Die Leistungsfähigkeit statistischer Methoden für die Analyse von Kunstwerken am Beispiel von György Ligetis *Lux aeterna*', *International Review of the Aesthetics and Sociology of Music* 7 (1976), pp. 249–63

Beurle, Hans Michael, 'Nochmals Ligetis *Lux aeterna*: eine Entgegnung auf Clytus Gottwalds Analyse', *Musica* 25 (1971), pp. 279–81

Cogan, Robert, 'György Ligeti: *Lux aeterna*', in *New Images of Musical Sounds* (Cambridge: Harvard, 1984), pp. 39–43

Gottwald, Clytus, '*Lux aeterna:* zur Kompositionstechnik György Ligeti', *Musica* 25 (1971), pp. 12–17

Op de Oul, Paul, 'Sprachkomposition bei Ligeti *Lux aeterna:* Nebst einigen Rand Bemerkungen zu den Begriffen Sprach und Lautkomposition', *Über Musik und Sprache,* ed. R. Stephan, *Veröffentlichungen des Instituts für neue Musik und Musikerziehung Darmstadt* 14 (Mainz: Schott, 1974), pp. 59–69

Richter, Christoph, 'Interpretation zu *Lux aeterna* von György Ligeti', *Musik und Bildung* 4 (1972), pp. 237–41

MONUMENT–SELBSTPORTRAIT–BEWEGUNG

Febel, Reinhard, 'György Ligeti: *Monument–Selbstportrait–Bewegung* (3 Stücke für 2 Klaviere)', *Zeitschrift fürMusiktheorie* 9:1 (1978), pp. 35–51; 9:2 (1978), pp. 4–13

Ferguson, Stephen, *György Ligetis Drei Stücke für Zwei Klaviere: Eine Gesamtanalyse* (Tutzing: Hans Schneider, 1994)

PIANO ÉTUDES

Bouliane, Denys, 'Imaginäre Bewegung. György Ligetis *Études pour piano*', *MusikTexte* 28:9 (Cologne, 1989), pp. 73–84

– 'Les six Études pour piano de György Ligeti ou l'art subtil de créer en assumant les référents culturelles', *Canadian University Music Review* 9:2 (1989), pp. 36–83; repr. *Contrechamps* 12–13 (1990), pp. 98–132

Loesch, Heinz von, 'Eine "fraktale Seepferdchen-Etüde". György Ligeti und die Chaosforschung', *positionen* 11 (Berlin, 1992), pp. 7–12

Wilson, Peter Niklas, 'Interkulturelle Fantasien: György Ligetis Klavieretüden Nr. 7 und 8', *Melos* 59 (1992), pp. 63–84

REQUIEM

Kaufmann, Harald, 'Eine moderne Totenmesse: Ligetis Requiem', *Neues Forum* 13 (1966), pp. 59–61

Kaufmann, Harald, 'Betreffrend Ligetis Requiem', *Protokolle* 1 (Vienna, 1971), pp. 158–68

Nordwall, Ove, 'Ligeti's new Requiem', *Musical Quarterly* 52 (1966), pp. 109–13

STRING QUARTET NO. 2

Borio, Gianmario, 'L'Eridità Bartókiana nel Secondo Quartetto de G. Ligeti, Sul Concetto di tradizione nella Musica Contemporanea', *Studi Musicali* 13 (1984), pp. 289–307

Kaufmann, Harald, 'Ligetis Zweites Streichquartett', *Melos* 37 (1970), pp. 181–6

TEN PIECES FOR WIND QUINTET

Lichtenfeld, Monika, 'Zehn Stücke für Bläserquintett von György Ligeti', *Melos* 39 (1972), pp. 326–33

Morrison, Charles, 'Stepwise Continuity as a Structural Determinant in György Ligeti's *Ten Pieces for Wind Quintet*', *Perspectives of New Music* 24:1 (1985), pp. 158–82

TRIO FOR VIOLIN, HORN AND PIANO

Dibelius, Ulrich, 'Ligetis Horntrio', *Melos* 46 (1984), pp. 44–61

VIOLIN CONCERTO

Duchesneau, Louis, 'György Ligeti on his Violin Concerto', *Ligeti Letter* 2
  (Hamburg, 1995), pp. 1–7
Gawriloff, Saschko, 'Ein Meisterwerk von Ligeti', *Neue Zeitschrift für Musik*
  144:1 (1993), pp. 16–18
Nimczik, Ortwin, 'Annäherungen an den 2. Satz aus György Ligetis Konzert für
  Violine und Orchester', *Musik und Bildung* 5 (1995), pp. 33–36

9 Books which have influenced Ligeti and others of general relevance

When publications exist in both an original language and English translation,
only the English edition is listed.

Adorno, Theodor, Eng. trans. Anne Mitchell and Wesley Blomster, *Philosophy of
  Modern Music* (New York: Seabury Press, 1973)
Arom, Simha, *African Polyphony and Polyrhythm* (Cambridge: CUP, 1991), with
  a foreword by Ligeti
Borges, Jorge Luis, *Labyrinths* (New York: New Directions, 1964;
  Harmondsworth: Penguin, 1970)
Carlsen, Philip, *The Player-Piano Music of Conlon Nancarrow* (New York:
  Brooklyn, 1988)
Courant, Richard and Herbert Robbins, *What is Mathematics?*, second
  edition rev. I. Stewart (New York: OUP, 1996)
Eimert, Herbert and Karlheinz Stockhausen (ed.), *Die Reihe* 1–8 (English edition,
  Pennsylvania: Presser, 1958–65)
Gleick, James, *Chaos: Making a New Science* (London: Heinemann, 1988)
Gombrich, E. H., *Art and Illusion* (third edition, London: Phaidon, 1968)
Haraszti, Miklós, *The Velvet Prison: Artists under State Socialism* (New York:
  Basic Books, 1987)
Hindemith, Paul, Eng. trans. Arthur Mendel, *The Craft of Musical Composition*
  (New York: Associated Music Publishers, 1941, rev. 1945)
Hofstadter, Douglas, *Gödel, Escher, Bach: an Eternal Golden Braid (a
  Metaphorical Fugue on Minds and Machines in the Spirit of Lewis Carroll)*
  (Harmondsworth: Penguin, 1980)
– *Metamagical Themas: Questing for the Essence of Mind and Pattern*
  (Harmondsworth: Penguin, 1986)
Jelinek, Hanns, *Anleitung zur Zwölftonkomposition* (Vienna: Universal Edition, 1952)
Jeppesen, Knud, Eng. trans. Glen Haydon, *Counterpoint: the Polyphonic Style of
  the Sixteenth Century* (New York: Prentice-Hall, 1939)
Kubik, Gerhard, *Theory of African Music* (Wilhelmshaven: Florian Noetzel
  Verlag, 1994)
Krúdy, Gyula, Eng. trans. George Szirtes, *The Adventures of Sinbad* (London/
  Budapest: Central European University Press, 1998)

Krúdy, Gyula, Eng. trans. Paul Tabori, *The Crimson Coach* (London: Corvina Press, 1967)

Laszlo, Ervin, *The Communist Ideology in Hungary* (Dordrecht: Riedel, 1966)

Leibowitz, René, *Introduction à la musique des douze sons* (Paris: L'Arche, 1949)

Magee, Bryan, *Popper* (London: Fontana, 1973)

Mandelbrot, Benoit, *The Fractal Geometry of Nature* (New York: Freeman, 1982)

Mann, Thomas, Eng. trans. H. T. Lowe-Porter, *Doctor Faustus* (London: Secker and Warburg, 1949)

Peitgen, Heinz-Otto and Richter, Peter H., *The Beauty of Fractals* (Berlin: Springer Verlag, 1986)

Schroeder, Manfred, *Fractals, Chaos, Power Laws* (New York: W. H. Freeman, 1991)

Shirer, William, *The Rise and Fall of the Third Reich* (New York: Simon and Schuster, 1959)

Vian, Boris, Eng. trans., *'Blues for a Cat' and other stories* (Nebraska University Press, 2001)

Weöres, Sándor, in various Eng. translations, ed. M. Vajda, *Eternal Moments: Selected Poems* (New York: New Rivers Press/Talman, 1988)

Weöres, Sándor, Eng. trans. D. Wevill, *Selected Poems of Sándor Weöres* (Harmondsworth: Penguin, 1970)

Williams, Emmett and Ann Noël (ed.), *Mr. Fluxus: a collective portrait of George Maciunas* (London: Thames and Hudson, 1977)

Discography

The Ligeti discography is dominated by the definitive edition of his complete works, commenced by Sony in 1996 and completed by Teldec in 2003. Despite the exemplary performance and recording quality of the new series, older vinyl recordings are not entirely eclipsed, especially of the orchestral works. Many of them have been remastered by Wergo, whose single disks are also collected in two 3-CD sets. The list below includes other recordings selectively, but excludes vinyl LPs which have not been reissued on CD.

1 Complete works

SONY 'GYÖRGY LIGETI EDITION'

Vol. 1: String Quartets and Duets
String Quartets nos 1 and 2; Hommage à Hilding Rosenberg; Ballada és tánc; Andante and Allegro
Arditti Quartet (1996)
SK 62306

Vol. 2: A Cappella Choral Works
Éjszaka and *Reggel; Idegen földön; Magány; Két kánon; Bethlehemi királyok; Bujdosó; Lux aeterna; Lakodalmas; Inaktelki nóták; Mátraszentimrei dalok; Pápainé; Drei Phantasien nach Friedrich Hölderlin; Magyar Etüdök; Haj, ifjúság!; Húsvét; Hortobágy; Magos kősziklának; Kállai kettős*
London Sinfonietta Voices (1996)
SK 62305

Vol. 3: Works for Piano
Études 1–15; Musica ricercata
Pierre-Laurent Aimard (1996)
SK 62308

Vol. 4: Vocal Works
Nonsense Madrigals; Mysteries of the Macabre; Aventures; Nouvelles aventures; Der Sommer; Three Weöres Songs; Five Arany Songs; Four Wedding Dances
The King's Singers, Christiane Oelze, Phyllis Bryn-Julson, Sibylle Ehlert and Eva Wedin (sopranos), Malena Ernman (mezzo-soprano), Rose Taylor (contralto),

Omar Ebrahim (baritone), Pierre-Laurent Aimard and Irina Kataeva (pianos), members of the Philharmonia Orchestra conducted by Esa-Pekka Salonen (1996) SK 62311

Vol. 5: Mechanical Music
Adaptations for Barrel Organ: *Continuum; Hungarian Rock; Capriccio 1; Invention; Capriccio 2; Musica ricercata.* Adaptations for Player Piano: *Études 7, 9, 10, 11, 13* and *14a* (original version for player piano). Metronomes: *Poème symphonique*
Pierre Charial (barrel organ), Jürgen Hocker (player pianos), Françoise Terrioux (metronomes) (1997)
SK 62310

Vol. 6: Keyboard Works
Piano solo: *Capriccio 1; Invention; Capriccio 2.* Two pianos and piano duet: *Induló; Polyphonic Étude; Three Wedding Dances; Sonatina; Allegro; Monument–Selbstportrait–Bewegung.* Harpsichord: *Passacaglia ungherese; Hungarian Rock; Continuum.* Organ: *Ricercare; Harmonies; Coulée; Volumina.*
Irina Kataeva and Pierre-Laurent Aimard (pianos), Elisabeth Chojnacka (harpsichord), Zsigmond Szathmáry (organ) (1997)
SK 62307

Vol. 7: Chamber Music
Six Bagatelles for Wind Quintet; Ten Pieces for Wind Quintet; Horn Trio; Viola Sonata
London Winds, Saschko Gawriloff (violin), Marie-Luise Neunecker (horn), Pierre-Laurent Aimard (piano), Tabea Zimmermann (viola) (1998)
SK 62309

Vol. 8: *Le Grand Macabre* (revised version)
Laura Claycomb, Charlotte Hellekant, Jard van Nes, Derek Lee Ragin, Graham Clark, Willard White, Frode Olsen, London Sinfonietta Voices and Philharmonia Orchestra conducted by Esa-Pekka Salonen (1998–99)
SK 62312 – 2 CDs

TELDEC 'THE LIGETI PROJECT'

Vol. 1: *Melodien; Chamber Concerto; Piano Concerto; Mysteries of the Macabre*
Pierre-Laurent Aimard (piano), Peter Masseurs (trumpet), Schoenberg Ensemble and Asko Ensemble conducted by Reinbert de Leeuw (2001)
Teldec 8573-83953-2

Vol. 2: *Lontano; Atmosphères; Apparitions; San Francisco Polyphony; Romanian Concerto*
Berlin Philharmonic conducted by Jonathan Nott (2002)
Teldec 8573-88261-2

Vol. 3: *Cello Concerto; Violin Concerto; Clocks and Clouds; Síppal, Dobbal, Nádihegedűvel*

Siegfried Palm, Frank Peter Zimmermann, Asko Ensemble and Schoenberg Ensemble conducted by Reinbert de Leeuw (2002)
Teldec 8573-87631-2

Vol. 4: *Ballad and Dance; Cello Sonata; Artikulation: Aventures; Nouvelles aventures; Musica ricercata* (played by bayan); *Big Turtle Fanfare; Old Hungarian Ballroom Dances*
Sarah Leonard (soprano), Linda Hirst (mezzo-soprano), Omar Ebrahim (baritone), David Geringas (cello), Max Bonnay (bayan), Peter Masseurs (trumpet), Asko Ensemble and Schoenberg Ensemble conducted by Reinbert de Leeuw (2003)
Teldec 8573-88262-2

Vol. 5: *Hamburg Concerto; Double Concerto; Ramifications; Requiem*
Marie-Luise Neunecker (horn), Jacques Zoon (flute), Heinz Holliger (oboe), Asko Ensemble and Schoenberg Ensemble conducted by Reinbert de Leeuw, Berlin Philharmonic and London Voices conducted by Jonathan Nott (2003)
Teldec 8573-88263-2

Interview CD with Ligeti in English and German (2001)
Teldec 2188

2 Wergo CD remasters

The following three CDs are available as 'Special Edition 1' (WER 6901-2), and separately:

Musica ricercata; Capriccio 1 and 2; Invention; Monument–Selbstportrait–Bewegung
Begoña Uriarte and Hermann Mrongovius (pianos)
WER 60131-50

Continuum; Ten Pieces for Wind Quintet; Artikulation; Glissandi; Harmonies; Coulée; Volumina
Antionette Vischer (harpsichord); Zsigmond Szathmáry and Karl-Erik Welin (organs); Wind Quintet of SWF
WER 60161-50

Chamber Concerto; Atmosphères; Ramifications (versions for solo strings and string orchestra); *Lux aeterna*
Ensemble 'die reihe' conducted by Friedrich Cerha; SWF Symphony Orchestra conducted by Ernest Bour; Chamber Orchestra of Saarländ Radio conducted by Antonio Janigro; Schola Cantorum Stuttgart conducted by Clytus Gottwald
WER 60162-50

The following three CDs are available as 'Special Edition 2' (WER 6904-2), and separately:

String Quartets nos. 1 and 2
Arditti Quartet
WER 60079-50

Horn Trio; Passacaglia ungherese; Hungarian Rock; Continuum;
Monument–Selbstportrait–Bewegung
Saschko Gawriloff (violin), Hermann Baumann (horn), Eckart Besch (piano);
Elisabeth Chojnacka (harpsichord); Antonio Ballista and Bruno Canino (two
pianos)
WER 60100-50

Cello Concerto; Lontano; Double Concerto; San Francisco Polyphony
Siegfried Palm (cello), Hessian Radio Symphony Orchestra conducted by
Michael Gielen; SWF Symphony Orchestra conducted by Ernest Bour; Gunilla
von Bahr (flute), Torleif Lännerholm (oboe), Swedish Radio Orchestra conducted
by Elgar Howarth
WER 60163-50

ALSO ON WERGO:

Le Grand Macabre (original version)
Dieter Weller, Penelope Walmsley-Clark, Olive Fredricks, Peter Haage, ORF
Chorus, Arnold Schoenberg Choir, ORF Symphony Orchestra conducted by
Elgar Howarth
WER 6170-2

Requiem; Aventures and *Nouvelles aventures*
Liliana Poli (soprano), Barbro Ericson (mezzo-soprano), Chorus of Bavarian
Radio and Hessian Radio Symphony Orchestra conducted by Michael Gielen;
Gertie Charlent (soprano), Marie-Thérèse Cahn (mezzo-soprano), William
Pearson (baritone), Darmstadt International Chamber Ensemble conducted by
Bruno Maderna
WER 60045-50

Études, Book 1 (with pieces by Messiaen)
Volker Banfield
WER 60134-50

3 Selected other recordings

Atmosphères; Lontano
Vienna Philharmonic conducted by Claudio Abbado
DG 429 260

Atmosphères
New York Philharmonic conducted by Leonard Bernstein
SMK 61845

Chamber Concerto; Ramifications; String Quartet no. 2
Ensemble InterContemporain conducted by Pierre Boulez; LaSalle String Quartet
DG 423 244-2

Cello Concerto; Piano Concerto; Violin Concerto
Jean-Guihen Queyras (cello), Pierre-Laurent Aimard (piano), Saschko Gawriloff

(violin), Ensemble InterContemporain conducted by Pierre Boulez
DG 439 808-2

Cello Concerto; Piano Concerto; Chamber Concerto
Miklós Perényi (cello), Ueli Wiget (piano), Ensemble Modern conducted by Peter Eötvös
SK 58945

Violin Concerto (with Per Nørgård *Helle Nacht: Violin Concerto*)
Christina Åstrand, Danish National Radio Orchestra conducted by Thomas Dausgaard
Chandos 9830

Aventures; Nouvelles aventures; Mysteries of the Macabre; Monument-Selbstportrait-Bewegung; Volumina; Harmonies
Jane Manning, Mary Thomas, William Pearson, Ensemble InterContemporain conducted by Pierre Boulez, Håkan Hardenberger, Roland Pöntinen, Alfons and Aloys Kontarsky, Gerd Zacher
DG 471 608–2

Complete piano music played by Fredrik Ullén
BS-CD783 and BS-CD983

Études 1–17
Toros Can
L'empreinte digitale ED 13125

Études 1–6
Rolf Hind
Factory FACD 256

Works for piano and harpsichord
Erika Haase (piano and harpsichord)
col legno collage 01

Lux aeterna and other vocal works
Groupe Vocal de France conducted by Guy Reibèl
HMV Classics 73466-2

Ligeti/Banda-Linda: *Études Book 1* and Banda-Linda music
Jan Michiels (piano), Ongo Trogodé
Megadisc MDC 7821

Ligeti/Gamelan: *Études Book 2* and gamelan music
Jan Michiels (piano), Gamelan Orchestra Gong Kebyar conducted by I Made Bandem Megadisc MDC 7820

Index

INDEX